Geopolitics of European Enlargement

Under the impact of accelerated globalization, transnational integration and international security concerns, the geopolitics of Europe's borders and border regions has become an area of critical interest. The progressive enlargement of the EU has positioned its borders at the heart of recent discussions on the changing nature of the EU, the meaning of 'Europe' and what constitutional shape a more politically unified Europe might take.

With enlargement, the EU argues that it must elaborate strategies to contend with a fiercely competitive world – and to build fortress-like defences against perceived tensions arising from greater cultural mixing and threats such as terrorism. The authors build up an integral picture of the EU's internal and external borders and borderlands to reveal the processes of re-bordering and social change currently taking place in Europe. They explore issues such as security, immigration, economic development and changing social and political attitudes, as well as the EU's relations with the Islamic world and other world powers. The book embraces an array of disciplinary, ideological and theoretical perspectives. It offers detailed case studies of different border regions and the concerns of the local inhabitants, while engaging in broader discussions of developments across Europe, state policies and the EU's relations with neighbouring states.

Making an important contribution to our understanding of European enlargement, integration and exclusion, and of border studies in general, this book will be of key interest to students and researchers in the fields of European politics, geography, international studies, sociology and anthropology.

Warwick Armstrong is Distinguished Research Associate in the School of Geography, Oxford University Centre for the Environment, University of Oxford, UK.

James Anderson is Professor Emeritus of Political Geography, Queen's University Belfast, UK.

Transnationalism
Series Editor: Steven Vertovec, *University of Oxford*

'Transnationalism' broadly refers to multiple ties and interactions linking people or institutions across the borders of nation-states. Today myriad systems of relationship, exchange and mobility function intensively and in real time while being spread across the world. New technologies, especially involving telecommunications, serve to connect such networks. Despite great distances and notwithstanding the presence of international borders (and all the laws, regulations and national narratives they represent), many forms of association have been globally intensified and now take place paradoxically in a planet-spanning yet common arena of activity. In some instances transnational forms and processes serve to speed-up or exacerbate historical patterns of activity, in others they represent arguably new forms of human interaction. Transnational practices and their consequent configurations of power are shaping the world of the twenty-first century.

This book forms part of a series of volumes concerned with describing and analyzing a range of phenomena surrounding this field. Serving to ground theory and research on 'globalisation', the Routledge book series on 'Transnationalism' offers the latest empirical studies and ground-breaking theoretical works on contemporary socio-economic, political and cultural processes which span international boundaries. Contributions to the series are drawn from Sociology, Economics, Anthropology, Politics, Geography, International Relations, Business Studies and Cultural Studies.

The 'Transnationalism' series grew out of the Transnational Communities Research Programme of the Economic and Social Research Council (see http://www.transcomm.ox.ac.uk). It is currently associated with the Research Council's Centre on Migration, Policy and Society located at the University of Oxford (see http://www.compas.ox.ac.uk).

The series consists of two strands:

Transnationalism aims to address the needs of students and teachers and these titles will be published in hardback and paperback. Titles include:

Culture and Politics in the Information Age
A new politics?
Edited by Frank Webster

Transnational Democracy
Political spaces and border crossings
Edited by James Anderson

Routledge Research in Transnationalism is a forum for innovative new research intended for a high-level specialist readership, and the titles will be available in hardback only. Titles include:

1 New Transnational Social Spaces
International migration and transnational companies in the early 21st century
Edited by Ludger Pries

2 Transnational Muslim Politics*
Reimagining the umma
Peter G Mandaville

3 New Approaches to Migration?
Transnational communities and the transformation of home
Edited by Nadje Al-Ali and Khalid Koser

4 Work and Migration:
Life and livelihoods in a globalizing world
Edited by Ninna Nyberg Sorensen and Karen Fog Olwig

5 Communities across Borders
New immigrants and transnational cultures
Edited by Paul Kennedy and Victor Roudometof

6 Transnational Spaces
Edited by Peter Jackson, Phil Crang and Claire Dwyer

7 The Media of Diaspora
Edited by Karim H. Karim

8 Transnational Politics
Turks and Kurds in Germany
Eva Østergaard-Nielsen

* *Also available in paperback*

9 Culture and Economy in the Indian Diaspora
Edited by Bhikhu Parekh, Gurharpal Singh and Steven Vertovec

10 International Migration and the Globalization of Domestic Politics
Edited by Rey Koslowski

11 Gender in Transnationalism
Home, longing and belonging among Moroccan migrant women
Ruba Salih

12 State/Nation/Transnation
Perspectives on transnationalism in the Asia-Pacific
Edited by Brenda S. A. Yeoh and Katie Willis

13 Transnational Activism in Asia
Problems of power and democracy
Edited by Nicola Piper and Anders Uhlin

14 Diaspora, Identity and Religion
New directions in theory and research
Edited by Waltraud Kokot, Khachig Tölölyan and Carolin Alfonso

15 Cross-Border Governance in the European Union
Edited by Olivier Thomas Kramsch and Barbara Hooper

16 Transnational Connections and the Arab Gulf
Edited by Madawi Al-Rasheed

17 Central Asia and the Caucasus
Transnationalism and diaspora
Edited by Touraj Atabaki and Sanjyot Mehendale

18 International Migration and Security
Opportunities and challenges
Edited by Elspeth Guild and Joanne van Selm

19 Transnational European Union
Towards a common political space
Edited by Wolfram Kaiser with Peter Starie

20 Geopolitics of European Union Enlargement
The fortress empire
Edited by Warwick Armstrong and James Anderson

Geopolitics of European Union Enlargement

The fortress empire

Edited by
Warwick Armstrong and James Anderson

LONDON AND NEW YORK

First published 2007
by Routledge
2 Park Square, Milton Park, Abingdon, Oxon, OX14 4RN

Simultaneously published in the USA and Canada
by Routledge
270 Madison Ave, New York NY 10016

Routledge is an imprint of the Taylor & Francis Group

Transferred to Digital Printing 2008

Typeset in Times New Roman by
Keystroke, 28 High Street, Tettenhall, Wolverhampton

British Library Cataloguing in Publication Data
A catalogue record for this book is available from the British Library

Library of Congress Cataloging in Publication Data
Geopolitics of European Union enlargement : the fortress empire / edited by Warwick Armstrong and James Anderson.
p. cm.
Includes bibliographical references and index.
ISBN 978–0–415–33939–1 (hardback : alk. paper) 1. European federation.
2. Geopolitics—European Union countries. I. Armstrong, Warwick.
II. Anderson, James, 1941–
JN15.G393 2007
341.242′2—dc22 2006033883

ISBN10: 0–415–33939–1 (hbk)
ISBN10: 0–415–47966–5 (pbk)
ISBN10: 0–203–44898–7 (ebk)

ISBN13: 978–0–415–33939–1 (hbk)
ISBN13: 978–0–415–47966–0 (pbk)
ISBN13: 978–0–203–44898–4 (ebk)

Contents

List of illustrations ix
Notes on contributors xi
Acknowledgements xv
Map xvi

Introduction: borders in an unequal world **1**
WARWICK ARMSTRONG

1 **Singular Europe: an empire once again?** **9**
JAMES ANDERSON

2 **From empire to the European Union via the national state: the three ages of the Irish border** **30**
LIAM O'DOWD

3 **Europeanisation, identity and policy in the Northern Ireland borderlands** **49**
THOMAS M. WILSON

4 **Creating border space in Ireland: an EU approach to ethno-national threat and insecurity** **61**
CATHAL MCCALL

5 **Coping with 'Fortress Europe': views from four seaports on the Spanish–Moroccan border** **78**
HENK DRIESSEN

6 **Europe and Islam: Partnership or peripheral dependence?** **90**
GEORGE JOFFÉ

7 Inside/outside the European Union: enlargement, migration policy and the search for Europe's identity **107**
BRIGITTA BUSCH AND MICHAŁ KRZYŻANOWSKI

8 Fixing capitalism and Europe's peripheries: west European imperialism **125**
JAMES ANDERSON AND IAN SHUTTLEWORTH

9 Carving out a 'ring of friends': the impact of the ENP on the shape of Europe **142**
PERTTI JOENNIEMI

10 New borders in a new Europe: eliminating and making borders in Central Europe **160**
MILAN BUFON AND ANTON GOSAR

11 Citizenship beyond the state: on the formation of civil society in the Three-Border Region **177**
ROBERT MINNICH

12 Evolution and perspectives on intercultural coexistence at the Slovene–Italian border **192**
MATEJA SEDMAK, VESNA MIKOLIČ AND MARINA FURLAN

13 Ideologies of 'Fortress Europe' in two Slovenian–Croatian borderlands: case studies from Žumberak and Bela Krajina **206**
DUŠKA KNEŽEVIĆ HOČEVAR

14 Fortress frontiers: global power, global and local justice **223**
WARWICK ARMSTRONG

Index 238

Illustrations

Figures

7.1 Schengen and a Europe of concentric circles 111
13.1 The Slovenian–Croatian border 207
13.2 The contested frontier as presented in the media 209
13.3 The research locales 214

Tables

8.1 Two spatial fixes for crises of overaccumulation in core economies 131
10.1 Slovenia: structure of border crossings per sectors, 1992–2002 168
10.2 Selected characteristics of borders of the Republic of Slovenia, 2002 169
10.3 Selected cross-border mobility patterns, 2000 170

Map

1 Internal and external borders of the European Union (2007) xvi

Contributors

James Anderson is Professor of Geography, Queen's University Belfast. He was previously at the Open University and the University of Newcastle, where he held the Chair of International Development. He is now a Co-Director of CIBR, the Centre for International Borders Research, at Queen's University. His research interests are in political territoriality, nationalism and transnational integration. Publications include edited collections on *The Rise of the Modern State* and (with James Goodman) *Dis/Agreeing Ireland*; and, in 2002, *Transnational Democracy: Political Spaces and Border Crossings* in the Routledge Transnationalism Series.

Warwick Armstrong is Distinguished Research Associate, School of Geography, Oxford Centre for the Environment, University of Oxford. His interest in international border issues has developed essentially since retirement from McGill University, Montréal, where he had specialised in Third World international development and cooperation issues. He has participated in and organised conferences and seminars on borderland studies in Europe, has written papers on the Slovene–Italian international border zone and aims to link his border and Third World research interests.

Milan Bufon is Senior Research Fellow at the Science and Research Centre of the Republic of Slovenia in Koper (ZRC), where he is leading the Research Programme Team for humanity and sociology and a long-term research project (1996–2001) on Slovene Istria and its neighbours within the frame of Slovenian border landscape and cross-border integration processes. He is also the President of the Scientific Board of the Slovene Research Institute (SLORI) in Trieste. He currently leads two international research and exchange projects within the Slovenia–USA and Slovenia–United Kingdom international cooperation programmes.

Brigitta Busch is Head of the Centre for Intercultural Studies at Klagenfurt University (Austria). She has worked for the past ten years as an expert for the Council of Europe (Human Rights, Confidence-building Measures, Transfrontier Cooperation). Her research work on intercultural topics includes empirical studies of the Austrian–Slovenian border region. She participates in the international project 'Border Discourses' (Fifth Framework Programme of the EU).

Henk Driessen is a Cultural anthropologist and Professor of Mediterranean Studies at the University of Nijmegen, the Netherlands. He has carried out fieldwork in Spain and Morocco and specialises in Mediterranean ethnography, and symbolic and political anthropology. His publications include: *On the Spanish–Moroccan Frontier: A Study in Ritual, Power and Ethnicity*, Oxford: Berg, 1992; The 'New Immigration' and the Transformation of the European–African Frontier', in: T.M. Wilson and H. Donnan (eds), *Border Identities. Nation and State at International Frontiers*, Cambridge: Cambridge University Press, 1998.

Marina Furlan is Research Assistant at the Slovenian Science and Research Centre, Koper (SRC Koper). Since completing her Ph.D., she works on themes related to psychological aspects of the border area in which the SRC Koper is situated. From 2002 she has been the editor of 'Glasnik', the bulletin of the SRC.

Anton Gosar is Professor and Dean of the Faculty of Humanities, University of Primorska, Koper/Capodistria. His work includes studies on tourism geography, political geography and population geography in the Balkans, the Alps and the Eastern Mediterranean. He is co-author of *Slovenia – the Tourist Guide*, Vice-President of the Commission on Political Geography of the International Geographical Union and has been awarded Ambassador of Science by the Government of Slovenia.

Duška Knežević Hočevar is Assistant Professor and Research Fellow employed at the Institute of Medical Sciences at the Slovenian Academy of Sciences and Arts. She is working on three projects: social construction of fertility behaviour at the Slovenian–Croat state border; fertility in Slovenia; and suicide in Slovenia. Her 1998 doctoral thesis in historical anthropology was entitled 'Boundaries in the Upper Kolpa valley: identity management within a kin network'. She was a founding member (1992) of the administrative board of the international Centro studi sulle aree di confine – the Centre for Border Area Studies, BAS-SAC.

Pertti Joenniemi is Senior Research Fellow and Programme Director for Nordic–Baltic studies at the Copenhagen Peace Research Institute (COPRI). He is co-editor of the NEBI Yearbook (Yearbook on North European and Baltic Integration), Springer Verlag: Berlin.

George Joffé is an independent consultant and formerly Deputy Director of the Royal Institute of International Affairs (Chatham House) in London. He is now engaged in academic activities and in journalism including print, radio and television work on the Middle East and North Africa. He is a consultant on political, economic and social affairs in the Middle East and North Africa, especially Morocco, Algeria, Libya, Israel–Palestine and Iraq. He has engaged in research and research management in international boundary disputes and economic arbitration. Academic activities include teaching and research. He is founder and co-editor of the *Journal of North African Studies* and is a research fellow at the Royal United Service Institute for Strategic Studies.

Michał Krzyżanowski is Research Associate at Lancaster University's Department of Linguistics and English Language, specialising in critical discourse analysis and its application to the study of: EU institutional change; the European public sphere; social and political transformation in Central and Eastern Europe after 1989; and everyday and institutional racism and discrimination in Europe. He is currently working on an EU Sixth-Framework Research Project 'Media and Ethics of the European Public'. He was earlier at the Department of (Applied) Linguistics of the University of Vienna, with research projects on comparative study of migration and discrimination in the EU and a project on 'The discursive re-construction of European identities' in the institutions of the European Union.

Cathal McCall is Research Fellow, Institute of Governance, Public Policy and Social Research, Queen's University Belfast. Previously in the Institute of European Studies at QUB, he is currently researching contemporary governance, regionalism and identity in Northern Ireland and Scotland. His publications include: 'Postmodern Europe and communal identities in Northern Ireland', *European Journal of Political Research*, vol. 33, no. 3 1998; *Identity in Northern Ireland: Communities, Politics and Change*, Basingstoke: Macmillan 1999 ; and 'The production of space and the realignment of identity in Northern Ireland' in *Regional and Federal Studies*, vol. 11, no. 2 2001.

Vesna Mikolič is Dean of the Faculty of Humanities of the University of Primorska in Koper and Senior Lecturer in Sociolinguistics, Academic Writing and Tourist Discourse. She is a Research Associate at the Science and Research Centre of the University of Primorska in Koper and is engaged in national and international research projects. Her fields of research and professional interest are: sociolinguistics, language policy, language and culture, ethnic identity, communicative competence, languages in contact, bilingualism, intercultural communication, pragmatics and discourse analysis (academic and tourist discourse).

Robert Minnich is Associate Professor of Social Anthropology at the University of Bergen, Norway. Since 1981 he has investigated the 'three border region' (Austria–Italy–Slovenia), publishing on themes relevant to borderland research.

Liam O'Dowd is Professor of Sociology and Director of the Centre for International Borders Research (CIBR) at Queen's University Belfast and a director of the inter-university Centre for Cross Border Studies (Armagh) doing applied policy research in Ireland. His interests are: comparative research on state borders, cross-border cooperation and border regions in Europe and the changing nature of the Irish border and border region. His published work includes: *Borders, Nations and States: Frontiers of Sovereignty in the New*

Europe (1996) and a series of co-edited special issues on borders in *Regional Studies, Administration, Regional and Federal Studies* (forthcoming) and *European Studies* (forthcoming). He has also authored journal articles and book chapters on borders and border regions.

Mateja Sedmak is Head of the Public Opinion Centre at the Faculty of Humanities, and Assistant Dean for Student Affairs and Research Associate in the Slovenian Science and Research Centre, Koper. She is also editor of the sociological and humanistic edition of *Annales* – Annals for Istrian and Mediterranean Studies. She is also a member of the Commission for the Promotion of Women in Science of the Ministry of Education, Science and Sports, Slovenia. Her special research interests on family, gender and ethnic studies, and social policy focus on the Slovene–Italian cross-border area.

Ian Shuttleworth is Senior Lecturer in Geography at Queen's University Belfast, and a member of the Centre for Spatial Territorial Analysis and Research (C-STAR) and the Centre for International Borders Research (CIBR). Research interests lie in census analysis, labour markets, and transnational migration. He has worked on research projects concerning recruitment and redundancy in the labour market, the Northern Ireland Census, and everyday life on the Irish border. He has published in journals such as *Regional Studies*, *Urban Studies*, and *Environment and Planning A*.

Thomas M. Wilson is Professor of Anthropology and Director of Graduate Studies at Binghamton University, State University of New York. Previously at the Institute of European Studies of Queen's University Belfast, he has researched in the Northern Ireland borderlands since 1990. He is the co-author of *Borders: Frontiers of Identity, Nation and State*, Berg Publishers, 1999 and co-editor of *Border Identities*, Cambridge University Press, 1998, among other publications in the comparative study of international borders and border regions.

Acknowledgements

The initial idea for this book arose out of a 'Borders' seminar series, held by the ESRC Transnational Communities Programme and the School of Geography and the Environment, at the University of Oxford. This was followed by a conference, 'Border as barriers and bridges – a comparative look at three borderlands: Slovenia/Italy, Ireland/Northern Ireland, West Mediterranean', hosted by the Science and Research Centre of the Republic of Slovenia at Koper/Capodistria.

We are grateful to the ESRC and the Slovenian Science and Research Centre for funding these meetings, as well as colleagues at Oxford University and the University of Ljubljana for their involvement in the organisation of both events.

We wish to thank the various authors who have come on board – from the conference and others from outside – for their work in creating valuable chapters from papers and for their ready and uncomplaining acceptance of our editorial questions, suggestions and amendments.

Thanks also go to Dr Steven Vertovec, then Director of the ESRC Transnational Communities Research Programme, who made the original suggestion for seminar, conference and book. We are grateful, too, for the organisational help of his staff.

We appreciate the special effort made by Lefkos Kyriacou in producing the map of Europe with minimal notice. And finally, we wish to express our recognition of the long-suffering and extraordinary patience of participants in, and observers of, the prolonged gestation involved in editing this book – the chapter contributors, the publishers, Emma and Maggie for their perfectionist typesetting, and above all, Jane and Róise who have borne the brunt of our labours at close hand.

Warwick Armstrong
James Anderson
February 2007

Map 1 Internal and external borders of the European Union (2007)

Introduction

Borders in an unequal world

Warwick Armstrong

Borders not only exist in the era of globalisation, they continue to flourish and any report of their imminent demise has been greatly exaggerated. Yet, considerable change has taken place in the European Union. As with other regions around the world, the phrase 'a borderless world', when applied to the EU, refers first and foremost to the steady whittling away of those borders between nation-state members *within* the Union. Accompanying this internal consolidation/integration, periodic expansion of the EU's external borders to incorporate European states (usually) contiguous to the EU has occurred over the years. So, much of the border-alteration process has consisted of internal integration and external enlargement – the latest instance of the latter being the absorption of ten new member states into the EU in 2004. The third element in border construction, and an outcome of the process, has been that of exclusion; a strategy of ostracising the unwanted.

Looking first at the process of internal change, we observe that, even here, the pace of border attrition has varied. Some member states continue to hold fast to many of their historic nation-state border controls and rights, while others pursue the process of integration at a faster pace. This has been the pattern in Europe over the past half-century, with certain 'core' states – France, Germany, Italy and the Benelux three especially – prepared to push ahead faster with border dismantling and closer integration, while latecomers to the EEC/EU, notably Britain, have maintained a determined position of reserve and resistance to the sequence of consolidating mergers.

Over the decades, this internal evolution has been gradual, but a significant step forward was taken with the concluding of the Schengen Agreement on 14 June 1985. Five member states of the EU (then, EEC), Belgium, France, Germany, Luxembourg and the Netherlands then created an official demarcation zone that defined and delimited their external borders; by significantly lowering border obstacles between themselves, they created an area of shared movement and exchange of people, commerce and law among their states.

A primary objective of Schengen was to bring an end to the multitude of international border checkpoints and controls within the Schengen area and to harmonise external border controls with/against the world outside 'Schengenland'. Although the members originally acted independently of the EU, the Agreement has since been written into the constitution of the Union. Additional countries have since also signed the convention, bringing the total number of signatories (if not yet members) to twenty-six. Interesting anomalies exist, however; while some member states of the EU have not implemented the agreement, others outside the EU have become Schengen members.

With the Schengen Agreement now extending to fifteen countries (two of them non-EU members), a clear strategy to allow the free internal movement of factors in four areas has become evident: the freedom of movement for goods (excluding agricultural and fisheries products, which the Agreement scarcely takes into account); of people; of services and of capital. To these, the Agreement has added social policy, consumer protection, environmental issues, company law and statistics to complete the extended internal market.

The Agreement has, then, dismantled the inordinate number of border controls which had interfered with the movements of traffic, commerce and people (including tourists). The resulting free market has proven of benefit to many, among others those in previous borderlands where historical regional, neighbourhood, ethnic and familial connections have been resumed or further reinforced. But the greatest beneficiaries of the free market are undoubtedly those in the financial, commercial and industrial capitalist corporate sectors. Provisioning a market of 300 million people and tapping into such a large and growing labour market without let or hindrance from inter-state border barriers has been of enormous advantage/profit to business, both EU and foreign.

Security concerns are supposedly also answered more effectively – although, perhaps, less so than has been authoritatively and officially promised. With the removal of border checks among the participating member states, the logical consequence is that all coordinate their external controls and checkpoints. In turn, this means that they agree, for example, on a common immigration policy so as to create homogeneity in the entry criteria. This further entails the sharing of information about unwanted entrants – the officially 'undesirable'. In policing the Schengen zone, borders should no longer provide a hindrance to the pursuit and apprehension of those considered a threat to EU security. What is known to one member state in such cases becomes common knowledge to all.

The erasing of borders, then, appears to be well under way. It is taking place, first, as part of a commitment by some states in the EU to create an ever more integrated and consolidated Union; secondly, it appears to be happening in accordance with the current neo-liberal philosophy and practice of a global system free from those obstructions typical of earlier phases of nation-state capitalism. Modern capitalist economies and perhaps their most highly visible representatives, transnational corporations with a global reach, require as level and untrammelled a plane as possible for their transactions – a tabula rasa which raises few obstacles to the free flow of goods, services and selective information. The Schengen Agreement seems to slot well within that framework.

The process of integration within the borders of an expanding EU forms an essential element in the chapters that follow. But this is just part of a more encompassing course of action that the Union is engaged upon. In tandem with increasingly concerted internal change, a parallel process is taking place at and beyond the external frontiers of the EU. This development we consider to form the basis for the twin procedures of enlargement and exclusion. The first of these, enlargement, is, to all appearances, a matter of extending the EU's borders. It involves inviting new (usually contiguous) nation-states to join the successful and wealthy fellowship of nations that trade; the inducement offered is that of being able to move freely within the protection of the EU's external borders, to benefit from a large open market and to enjoy the prospect of new working and living opportunities. Again, the conditions for a further step towards the attainment of a borderless world appear to be satisfied as this enlargement takes place.

As certain chapters which follow will make evident, however, the situation is rather more muddied than this straightforward prognosis implies. Even those favoured states who have recently managed accession to the EU will find their aim to function on a par with the core states difficult to sustain. There is already, as contributors to the book explain, a well-established series of concentric circles of inequality within the EU that expand outwards from the inner core of EU member states which fully conform to the Schengen Agreements. This is followed successively by an outer core of pre-2004 member states not fully participating in the Schengen scheme; then the ten newly admitted members of 2004; the two admitted in 2007 and, after that, possible candidates in the future; and finally, those likely to be denied rights to membership well into the distant future.

These last nation-states are those contiguous to the Union's external 'wet' and 'dry' borders which, as officially designated 'neighbours', will form a cordon sanitaire around the EU against an unstable and allegedly threatening world. They are expected to agree to act in common with the EU on filtering and limiting migration and illegal cross-border movements of any kind. What emerges from this is a strategy that aims to establish a clear European identity within the EU by setting up a series of requirements to be adhered to by nation-states beyond the pale of the EU fortress and its external borders. Such demarcations, 'insider' and 'outsider', are echoed unmistakably in the way that the EU's European Convention has gone about establishing its new constitutional structure for an enlarged Europe.

Yet, as a capitalist entity in a world of neo-liberal competition for markets, resources and investment opportunities, the EU is faced with a serious quandary. How can it most effectively reconcile its determination to maintain its strategy of fortress protection against the threats (real and perceived) from unstable and exigent states, hostile movements – including those officially designated 'terrorist' – and persistent migrants coming from outside its borders on the one hand with, on the other, its need to compete freely in a world of already-powerful and emerging competitors? As two authors point out, it is no longer just a matter of choosing the classical global capitalist strategy – or 'fix' – by exporting capital to link up with and exploit the huge reserves of cheap labour in the global peripheries – the traditional solution to capitalism's problem of global competition and declining profit margins. Now, for a series of reasons, capital is also employing an alternative policy – that of attracting labour to sites of major capital formation. Here, the unemployed or under-employed reserves will, at lower rates of pay, be more easily available for work within the EU core and so help to 'absorb' its surplus investible capital.

The function of the EU's external borders, already doubtfully serviceable as solid walls of defence for 'fortress Europe' against illegal migration, is also, in a sense, being further undermined by the actions and attitudes of certain sectors within the EU business community; many businesses are all too happy to soak up the labour available at rates of pay that increase the competitiveness of their operations. The probability that these breaches in an already-permeable external defence system will not only continue but, in fact, increase is heightened by the mounting aversion of EU citizens to engaging in menial, dirty or physically demanding tasks. Nor do the demographic dynamics of an ageing European population help ease the pressures. This is a circle that the supporters of a fortress-like status for the EU have yet to square.

And so there are systemic macro-level contradictions inherent in the EU's expansion as a global – some claim imperial – economic and political power. But the problems arising from the chosen – and possibly irreconcilable – path of enlargement, exclusion and integration do not end at the macro scale. They are further complicated by local borderland difficulties that arise from the same strategy. For centuries, borders have territorially demarcated the effective power of nation-states and, before them, at a lower degree of intensity, the heterogeneous array of sub-state entities – electorates, duchies, principalities and others that have historically comprised Europe's complex diversity. Borderlands have for centuries been prime sites for confrontation and tension between nations and states and those inhabiting them have had to live with the consequences of disputes taking place largely above their heads – and regardless of their particular local interests and well-being.

Decisions taken in remote capitals or at international conferences have landed those who live in the borderlands with the burden of issues that have little to do with their daily reality; communities, families and individuals have been obliged, usually without consultation, to live with the consequences of such decrees and agreements. It is important to recognise that the majority of borders in Europe (and across the world) have been marked out and imposed with little recourse to popular plebiscites or other democratic processes. What has been arranged at high levels of *real politik* by negotiation or *force majeure* – without the involvement of local communities – almost invariably takes no account of the conditions of everyday life in the borderlands themselves or, indeed, the wishes of those residing there.

Borderlines so established are still responsible for the dividing of communities and families and for the fragmentation of local and regional connections and identities. And the practice continues: new locales of tension are still being created – as is shown in the case of the recently established Schengen border demarcating the southern flank of EU territory between Slovenia and Croatia. None of this, of course, amounts to outcomes cast in stone; there have been many examples of borderland regions that have won certain 'privileges' from their respective nation-state authorities, for example, to re-establish limited travel and commercial rights across such border limits. But it has usually been achieved only with the expenditure of time, energy and the unremitting determination by local activists to reverse, or at least minimise, the effects of remote and undemocratic *diktats*. The sad irony is that borders erected in this way over the decades seem more proficient in denying the human needs of divided borderland communities than they are in acting as defensive barriers to keep those the EU considers to be undesirables and 'illegals' away from the fortress.

What emerges from the discussions in this book is that the European Union – in its own terms – has achieved some notable successes over the years. It has assisted in constructing an expanding and functional capitalist common market, integrated certain nation-states (unequally) and effectively ostracised others as it has enlarged its territory over the past half century; and it has managed, on the whole, to push through its policies often with only limited opposition. Many (but not all) votes on critical issues of enlargement and constitutional change have been conducted in an atmosphere equivalent to recognising the authority of an official Brussels fait accompli. As it expands its borders, the EU bureaucracy has imposed its will, above all, on populations at border perimeters whose daily lives and relationships are likely be the most profoundly affected among Europe's peoples by its top-down pronouncements. It has, in bilateral agreements, also deployed its financial and political influence to cajole weaker neighbouring states to the east and south to act as an auxiliary protective buffer zone – its cordon sanitaire – around its stronghold ramparts in its determination to filter out security threats and other influences of world instability.

Union officialdom, both political and administrative, has, then, assiduously promoted the core interests of powerful groups in politics and the private corporate sector over the years. But how far this insistently promoted strategy of self-interest has won the confidence of other states in the wider world may be open to question. Its strict border system reflecting the 'gated community' attitudes of those within, together with commercial barriers protecting domestic sectors against foreign competition while, at the same time, demanding free and open borders from others, do not project the image (or reality) of an entity that is committed to a free and open global capitalist system. The gap between its advocacy and its practice appears as the measure of its self-interest and double standards.

Nor has it carved out a foreign policy that is especially coherent or consistent – or sufficiently distances itself from that of the planet's sole super-power. In its ambivalence towards US global strategy in recent years – reflected in a deep division between wholehearted support and reserve of members states within the Union – especially in an era of growing distrust of the United States in the world, it has demonstrated its essential weakness and internal fragmentation. The recent split over Middle Eastern policies between the 'old' Europe and that other Europe which is more acquiescent to United States policy, for example, indicates the existence of a potentially debilitating divide that runs through the heart of the European Union.

International borders reflect the values, attitudes and beliefs of the societies they encompass. Their effectiveness as barriers and/or bridges is a measure of the society's will to make them work. So, their shortfall in carrying out either strategy effectively replicates a corresponding inadequacy within the Union. Their existence as a (would be) fortress barrier, first and foremost, indicates a lack of real commitment to the goal of global borderlessness and to a worldwide free flow and exchange of people, ideas or commerce. This is true despite the fact that the EU and its member states are, along with the USA, Japan and other wealthy G8 economies – as well as the major world financial and commercial institutions such as the World Bank, the IMF and the WTO – officially ardent proponents of a free, open capitalist global economy.

Yet, the very hesitation that is shown by the EU and its member states about even lowering external political and economic controls speaks volumes about the partial, lopsided and self-referential nature of their global perception and practice. That which is of benefit to the dominant economies, such as the export of capital, services and industrial goods and the importing of low-cost raw materials and non-competitive foodstuffs, is considered to be justly subject to the regulations governing global free trade and exchange. This applies especially to those products produced and traded by their own home-based transnational corporations. That which is less allowable on world markets includes labour migration, scientific and technical knowledge diffusion (subject to patent laws) and 'too competitive' products. Double standards abound in this asymmetrical scenario and the constrictions and controls by the EU's external borders are a reflection of the asymmetrical relationships that exist between Third World societies and the wealthy states of the global capitalist system.

Finally, although this book is, at one level, about borders, borderlines and borderlands, in reality, each author is taking the notion of the border as a *point d'entrée* (even, sometimes as a metaphor) to better understand the nature of the entity – the European Union itself – that the internal and external borders delineate. Ambivalence, division and inconsistency in the charting of future courses of action by EU politicians and administrators – as well as the mindset of the public itself – will be reflected in what happens at the Union's borders. When the public is offered a choice, this ambivalence appears still more visible. A pause for thought has already been demanded of the Brussels establishment in two unequivocal 'anti' votes on their constitutional proposals. What happens at the EU's borders will depend very much on the way in which the Union's leaders respond. Perhaps they should recollect John F. Kennedy's words at his inauguration: 'We stand today on the edge of a new frontier. . . . But the New Frontier of which I speak is not a set of promises – it is a set of challenges'. There will be pressure on the EU to respond more resourcefully to the challenges of new frontiers and with a greater sense of human justice than has its partner across the Atlantic in recent years.

One challenge with which the EU will have to come to grips – and that has direct implications for its external borders – is that of the inequitable state of affairs in world commercial and financial relationships. The introduction of a just international trade system to offset the inequities of the dominant free trade model is essential; and so is the need to reverse the pattern of financial flows between the rich and poor nations globally. If acted upon, both would be worth more than the capital currently provided in all forms of charity. It would help change the employment situation among the planet's poorest nations while shrinking the pressure of migrant labour flows and, almost certainly, reducing threats to the security of the EU. And, in so doing, it might relieve the pressures placed on the EU's system of external borders. Yet, EU leaders, despite their rhetoric, fall well short of accepting that there are deep systemic causes of poverty and global inequality which a change of approach could offset.

The UN Global Policy Forum in 2006 stated:

> Leaders in the developed world profess their commitment to 'poverty eradication,' but none are willing to address the *systemic causes of poverty*. Furthermore, the political and corporate elites at the helm of the world economy have a powerful interest in maintaining the economic status quo.
>
> Multilateral institutions devoted to 'development' overwhelmingly adhere to neoliberal growth-oriented strategies of capital accumulation, privatization, and investment. These institutions, including the World Bank, consistently ignore evidence that growth does not necessarily alleviate poverty and may, in fact, exacerbate it. Many concerned NGOs promote small-scale social development programs in poor countries, but *as long as systemic economic and social policies continue to favor the rich*, global poverty will remain a stark reality for the majority of people in the world.
>
> (http://www.globalpolicy.org/socecon/develop/index.htm; italics added)

A 2006 Oxfam briefing paper makes a similar point rather more starkly. A taste of its message is evident in the following short excerpt:

> Europe's double standards: how the EU should reform its trade policies with the developing world.
> EU double standards on trade policy are a disgrace. The EU forces Third World countries to open their markets at breakneck speed, while maintaining barriers to Third World exports, particularly farm products and textiles. The EU does further damage to livelihoods in the developing world by dumping highly-subsidised agricultural surpluses with which small farmers cannot compete. This paper describes what EU Heads of State must do if they are serious about making trade fair.
>
> (http://www.oxfam.org.uk/what_we_do/issues/trade/bp22_eutrade.htm)

Until the EU addresses these deep and persistent global injustices and begins to chart a course in its social and foreign policies that both recognises and aspires to remedy them, its borders will continue to bear a (growing) pressure that they will find it increasingly difficult to cope with. A careful rethinking of its international association with the United States of America in many of its global strategic initiatives, leading then to a serious modification of its relationships with the rest of the world would be a promising start. Too acquiescent acceptance of US global leadership and participation in, for instance, the internationally illegal practice of 'extraordinary rendition' (or abduction) leading to human rights abuses, insufficiently critical responses to a Washington policy of 'permanent war' against international terrorism and a too-willing adoption of a subordinate role in unilateral global policing will all be likely to invite retaliation. It has already happened and it is more than possible that this will be the destiny of those who play the part of uncritical collaborators – despite fortress-like border barriers.

But, such changes in both economic and political strategy will demand an internal coherence and greater consistency of approach than at present appears possible. Until it comes about, however, the borders of the European Union will continue to be among the first sectors to experience the pressures brought on by the EU leadership failing to come to terms adequately and fairly with the outside world.

1 Singular Europe

An empire once again?

James Anderson

What is the nature of Europe's geopolitics and what is now the European Union? In what directions are they evolving? Since the 'Common Market' was established fifty years ago there have been various answers, some of them heavily conditioned by normative beliefs about what Europe should and should not be. With enlargement there is the additional question 'where is Europe' – how far should the EU extend? What are its relations with neighbouring states and other powers, and the implications for its internal borders? Europe, we are told, is being 'de-territorialised' and 're-territorialised', but what does it all mean?

This chapter considers a range of answers encapsulated in five competing visions of Europe's territorial future: a 'Europe of nations', a 'federal European super-state', or a 'Europe of regions'; ideas about a 'new medieval Europe'; and, more recently, 'Europe an empire'. These options reflect distinct though partly overlapping conceptions of political space and territoriality – *national, medieval* and *imperial*. The territorialities embody different ideas and ideals about the homogeneity/heterogeneity of political, social and cultural space, and the equality/inequality of its constituent elements; about political authority and the relationship between sovereignty and territory; and about borders as lines sharply dichotomising inside/ outside or more fuzzy zones of gradual change or border-crossing interrelationships.

We look at the five options in turn, starting with the first three as variants of the familiar national territoriality and then 'work backwards' through medievalism to the imperial territoriality of empire. While the first three differ markedly – prioritising either national states and national sovereignty, a centralised 'federal Europe' typically modelled on the USA, or decentralised sub-state regions – they all uncritically accept a national or 'modernist' conception of territoriality and sovereignty. As a threesome, they are criticised as a 'Gulliver fallacy' in which the only conceivable alternatives to the existing national state are scale-model replicas.

The more recent fourth and fifth options signal more radical changes in political territoriality and more appreciation of the possible diversity of state forms. They look back to the past (or idealised versions of it) in an attempt to capture something elusively new, a recourse to 'history repeating itself' which of course it never (quite) does. The 'new medieval' metaphor draws analogies from pre-national Europe's fragmented, multi-level and often border-crossing authority systems in order to understand the contemporary EU sharing of sovereignty across national borders and different 'levels' of authority, though it sometimes gives the confusing impression that the EU is now 'post-national'.

The 'empire' metaphor has a wider canvas, harking back to imperialisms such as the Austro-Hungarian Empire, the empire of Charlemagne and even earlier to Rome. It encompasses the EU's external relations as well as its internal territorial form, a potentially decisive advantage over the other four models. It chimes better with enlargement and the EU's standing vis-à-vis other world powers, as well as with its internal empire-like heterogeneity. And crucially, in referring to the Roman Empire and its symbolic recreation by Charlemagne, it refers to periods before medieval 'decentralisation' when Europe's territories were seen to be organised by or around a single imperial core. Considering that Europe has been dominated by a multiplicity of competing political centres for over a thousand years (in fact ever since Charlemagne's brief empire fragmented in the ninth century), and that this multiplicity was arguably a major source of Europe's success (over, for instance, the technologically more advanced but singular and moribund Chinese empire), a return to 'empire' and a single-centred Europe would indeed be both a radical and a paradoxical development.

It would be yet more radical if Europe's 'empire' were to prove real rather than simply metaphorical. Here our fifth option transmutes into a sixth possibility: that rather than present or future territorial forms being merely reminiscent of the past, there could be a real return to a European imperialist polity in the singular. Singularity will only have substantial significance to the extent that the EU literally has imperial features internally and imperialistic relations with other parts of the world, other world powers including the presently hegemonic USA, and of course the rest of Europe. All the options have a tendency to conflate the EU and 'Europe', forgetting that a sizeable proportion of the continent is not in the EU, nor is it envisaged that all of it ever will be. However, EU enlargement means the non-EU proportion is decreasing; and the concept of empire begins to make some limited sense of the still-unjustified conflation to the extent that Europe, including its non-EU part, is indeed beginning to gravitate around an EU core.

There is considerable potential for empire to be more than a metaphor, not least because of interacting with some of the other options.[1] While they are usually seen as mutually exclusive visions of varying (im)plausibility, each of them in fact captures some partial aspects of Europe's evolving reality, and all contribute to an overall sense of Europe's trajectory which is indeed elusive. They can be seen as different tendencies which interact to shape Europe's destiny, and how it progresses or perhaps regresses is an open question. Thus 'Europe as empire' might be derailed if for example the 'Europe of nations' tendency were to strengthen national rivalries or block a legitimising supranational democracy. Alternatively, an empire future could be boosted by tendencies toward a 'federal Europe', sub-state regionalism and/or 'new medievalism'. It could absorb elements of all of these – even elements of nationalism – for empire is perhaps the most trans-historical, flexible and heterogeneous of territorial polities. There are 'formal' and 'informal' variants, and (while we must reject a postmodern parody of empire as singular not to Europe but to the whole world!) empire has taken on new meanings in contemporary capitalism.

But will the EU become an empire, and if so, will it come to dominate Europe to the point of singularity? Cooperative and competitive relations with other hegemonic and would-be hegemonic world powers drive EU enlargement and integration, objectively calling for a single Europe 'speaking with one voice'. On the other hand, Europe could be divided by these external relations acting on its internal fissures of national rivalry (e.g. as in different responses to the US invasion of Iraq). The USA as 'interfering hegemon', and Russia as a partly European rival, threaten singularity. And so, after presenting the case for empire and singularity, we conclude by looking at how these possibilities might be undone.

National territoriality and the 'Gullliver fallacy'

Territoriality at its most general is 'a spatial strategy to affect, influence, or control resources and people, by controlling area'; bordered space or territory is used to control, classify and communicate (Sack 1986, 21–34). But its use varies greatly in different historical contexts, and of our three 'ideal types' of political or state territoriality, the historically most recent *national* type is also the simplest. It reached its apogee in the heyday of the national state after the Second World War – in fact just as the EU was being born; and while it had also overlapped with empires since the eighteenth century, it is very different from earlier territorialities (see Liam O'Dowd's account in Chapter 2). Ernest Gellner made a revealing comparison, likening the pre-modern, pre-nationalism map to a Kokoschka painting: a 'riot' of colours, no clear pattern in the detail, though a clear overall pattern of diversity, plurality and complexity. In contrast his political map of the modern world resembles a Modigliani – very little shading, neat flat surfaces clearly separated from each other, clarity where one begins and another ends, little if any ambiguity or overlap – the familiar representation of national states (Gellner 1983, 139–140).

The claimed characteristics of national space are uniformity or homogeneity within clearly defined state borders; democratic equality for members of the population seen in nationalist doctrine as a cultural community; and independent or absolute sovereignty within its borders. 'Sovereignty' is a slipppery and disputed concept but refers to the claim that final political authority resides *within* the political community and its territory (Hinsley 1986); and here space is usually conceived in unchanging absolute or physical rather than relative, social terms.[2] There is a formal sovereign equality between the different national states; and a sharp 'inside/outside' dichotomy at their borders between 'internal' and 'external' relations (mirrored in the debilitating academic division of labour between 'political science' and 'international relations' – see Walker 1993).

Abstract models in absolute space

It is therefore not surprising to find that our first three options as variants of national territoriality are almost entirely preoccupied with the internal shape of the EU and ignore its external relations. Initially, national space was virtually the only type conceivable or conceived. Even if a federal superstate was not considered a serious possibility, the early, smaller European Community was nevertheless often perceived like a national state. There was for example the official aspiration that its economic space should be rendered homogeneous by regional policies to bring lagging areas and the new and poorer member states such as the Irish Republic and Greece up to the level of existing members. In contrast, such interventionist policies are no longer seen as 'realistic' in the contemporary neo-liberal EU of over twenty-five member states. Its internal space is becoming, and coming to be accepted as, less homogeneous, and in fact more unequal, heterogeneous and empire-like.

Up to the 1980s, debates on the European Community's future were often responses to its so-called 'democratic deficits' (see Newman 1996, 2002). They were about which of the EU's three main territorial 'levels' of elected assemblies was the best for a re-grounding of liberal democracy and sovereignty: a new federal superstate, or a reassertion of existing national states, or the level of sub-state regions. The problem of democracy was abstracted from economic and political realities and reduced to a matter of levels or scale rather than process: to whether national parliaments should cede powers to the European Parliament 'above', or to sub-state regional assemblies 'below'. There was often a spurious zero-sum formulation where more democracy at one level automatically meant less at another, as if there were some fixed total to be shared between levels (Anderson and Goodman 1995, Goodman 1997).

This resonated with contemporary notions that national states were becoming an anachronism, too small for global competition but too big and remote for cultural identification and participatory citizenship. They were apparently losing power simultaneously upwards and downwards, caught in a pincer movement by the EU from above and regions from below. However, the sharing of sovereignty in the EU impinges on state sovereignty very unevenly, strongly in some policy areas (e.g. with repect to economic competitiveness) and more weakly in others (e.g. education, health), and individual states can *gain* power and leverage by sharing sovereignty (otherwise would they all do it?). In reality, national states have continued to be largely in control both of the EU and their own regions. Rumours of the 'death of the national state' were greatly exaggerated – after all, the hegemonic world power, the USA, is are also a national state which belies the nonsense of imminent demise.

However, because most issues had been collapsed by state-centrism to the one level of the national state, it followed that when other alternatives were considered they were almost invariably national state-like bodies at other levels, 'above and below'. Any serious threat or replacement could apparently come only from scale replicas of the existing national state – the state 'writ large', as in a federal 'United States of Europe', or 'writ small' as in 'regional governments'. It was 'business as (nearly) usual', the only changes being ones of geographical scale in absolute space. There was no real recognition that political processes and institutions at different levels are likely to be qualitatively (not just quantitatively) different in character, and not least because of the (ignored) interrelationships *between* levels. This is the

'Gulliver fallacy', named after the societies that Gulliver met on his travels, one a society of giants, the other of midgets, but both exact replicas of human society.

The fallacy follows from *national* territoriality dominating to the exclusion of other conceptions, testimony to the power of the familiar and the ideology of nationalism, and perhaps to the fact that other conceptions – *medieval* or *imperial* – do not have similar ideological backing or popular appeal. It also points to the limits of conventional sovereignty and national democracy when dealing with transnational entities and processes. All three national variants simply accept the standard liberal practice of equating democracy with representative parliamentary democracy, and representation with a fixed territory. But these simple equations hardly exhaust the democratic possibilities, nor are they adequate to a multilevel transnational entity like the EU. National representative democracy, while it has to be defended and indeed strengthened (for it is probably our main democratic arena for the foreseeable future), also needs to be supplemented by participatory forms of democracy which are often better suited to relations between levels and across borders. In reality the EU does not conform to any of the three national variants, nor is it likely, or arguably desirable, that it will in the future (see Anderson 2006a).

'Europe of nations'

The 'Europe of nations' option, which revealingly conflates 'nation' with 'state', assumes that the EU necessarily undermines national sovereignty and democracy. It plays the zero-sum game where more democracy at an EU (or a sub-region) level must mean less at national level. Hence its advocates generally oppose any strengthening of democracy (and legitimacy) in the EU Parliament, any increase in central Commission competencies, and any decrease in national vetoing powers in inter-governmental bargaining. In its milder forms (in practice indulged in opportunistically by opponents as well as by advocates) this nationalistic perspective may delay or weaken the EU's integration and cohesion. In its strong 'Eurosceptic' or 'Europhobic' forms, the restoration of traditional national sovereignty as enjoyed when the Common Market was merely an economic association of independent national states would put the clock back on EU integration, stop the project in its tracks and probably wreck it. The present reality is that the sharing of sovereignty in the EU, and its intricate web of multilevel and transnational links and institutions, already comprises much more than the traditional inter-governmental relations between independent states (the so-called Westphalian system) which is the Europhobe heaven. Already in 1993 John Ruggie was suggesting that the partial 'unbundling' of national territorial sovereignty had gone further in the European Community than anywhere else: it was the world's 'first truly postmodern international political form . . . the first "multiperspectival polity" to emerge since the advent of the modern era' (Ruggie 1993, 140, 171–2).

'Federal Europe'

The 'federal Europe' vision is also blind to such transnational possibilities, again not surprisingly. Its main propagandists have not in fact been enthusiastic European federalists but rather the Europhobes who use it as a bogeyman, a dire warning of supposed outcomes if their own 'Europe of nations' is not accepted and their precious national sovereignties are pooled (and hence 'lost') in a United States of Europe. Unfortunately, public debates about the EU (at least in Britain) are often conducted around these two simplistically misleading poles: they have little to do with genuine European issues and more to do with the elitist manipulation of electorates for national or local ends – perhaps part of the reason for the lack of popular interest in the EU?

With national states remaining powerful players, the EU is not a federal state, nor likely to become one. Nor is a superstate on the model of the USA a desirable possibility. As John Agnew (2002) has shown, the US federal model is inappropriate and inadequate both for Europe and contemporary circumstances generally. It does not address transnationalism; and its archaic division and dispersal of public power was devised in the eighteenth century to ensure that government was decentralised and limited, rather than representative or effective. Its division of powers is enshrined in an inflexible written constitution; it relies on consensus more than oppositional politics; and on a rigid hierarchy of territorial levels (emphasising scale rather than process, like the Gulliver fallacy). In sum, it cannot easily be adapted to changing circumstances and can produce federal sclerosis. But in any case the federal option is implausible – the most to be expected is 'arrested federalisation' (Anderson 1995), a long way short of a fully federal 'US of Europe'.

'Europe of regions'

Prioritising sub-regional representation, this popular if flawed appendage of 1980s integration, is perhaps even further from becoming a reality – more a matter of wishful thinking of the 'small is beautiful' variety to counter the 'large is powerful' centralism of states and the EU.[3] By the same token, a reliance on smaller, weaker regional governments could increase vulnerability to wider global forces, especially in the many, if not most, sub-state regions which lack economic power or political coherence, and often both. There are good reasons for questioning the benign ideology of regionalism and its assumption that 'small' is necessarily 'beautiful'. Regionalisms, like nationalisms, can also be parochial, even xenophobic.

While regionalism in general has been growing in significance ever since the high point of state centralism after the Second World War, the regions remain highly varied and even more problematic than national states as a power base. They come in all shapes and sizes, some little more than figments of a central bureaucrat's imagination without much substance 'on the ground', others clearly demarcated by a long history, a strong regional identity, or a fully fledged sub-state nationalism (see Anderson, 2001b). Indeed, the most likely successes include those exceptions such as Scotland, Wales or Flanders which could plausibly become national states in their own right – the strongest regional threats to national states, far from being opposed to the 'nation state' ideal, have the ultimate (if not immediate or practical) objective of achieving their own state. For these and other powerful regions (e.g., the self-styled 'four motors' of the EU – Catalonia, Lombardy, Baden-Württemberg, and Rhône-Alpes) a 'Europe of regions' might well make sense, but maybe not for Europe's many weak or amorphous administrative units. In short, a 'Europe of regions' overestimates the coherence and potential autonomy of most regions; it underestimates the continuing importance of states; and it concedes too much ground to neo-liberal ideology which would further weaken state intervention and redistribution to poorer regions.

New medieval territoriality and multi-level governance

After the Gulliver fallacy, where the only conceivable territoriality was *national*, the metaphors of new medievalism (Bull 1977) and later empire (Waever 1997) were a breath of fresh air. Recognising that geographic space is becoming more 'relative', they attempted to grasp the elusive new complexities by looking at other types of territoriality.

Like a 'Europe of regions', the medieval metaphor also points to decentralisation, but it focuses on the fragmenting of national territoriality, the dissolving of the sharp 'inside/outside' dichotomy at internal EU borders, and their downgrading and increasing porosity with the partial pooling of sovereignty between states and EU institutions. It was favoured (including by me) when the integration of the Single European Market in the early 1990s challenged the traditional identities and certainties of discrete and self-contained territorial 'levels' in ways reminiscent of medieval Europe.

With the fragmentation of Charlemagne's empire, medieval Europe developed as a highly decentralised though hierarchical order, largely controlled by feudal landowners with their private armies. Authority was shared between a wide variety of secular and religious institutions, between and across different levels, and across the borders of different territories which were often fluid, discontinuous or fuzzy rather than fixed, compact and precise. There was a plethora of territories – lordships, petty kingdoms, principalities, duchies (such as Burgundy), bishoprics, city-states, city leagues (the Hanseatic), proto-national kingdoms (England), dynastic empires (Hapsburg), the Papacy and the Holy Roman Empire. And the latter, larger entities failed to recreate the Europe-wide political dominance or singularity of the Roman Empire (and briefly Charlemagne), partly because of vying with each other.

In Gellner's terms (1983, 139–40) this was the 'pre-modern, pre-nationalism map' as painted by Kokoschka – the 'riot' of colours, no clarity in the detail but an overall pattern of diversity, plurality and complexity. Only now, in the new medieval analogy, it was sometimes dubbed 'postmodern', even 'post-national', though the contrasts with national territoriality were clear enough. *Medieval* territoriality can be characterised by *absences*: no clearly defined borders or at least no sharp 'inside/outside' distinctions, little or no homogeneity, equality or democracy inside borders, no formal equality between different territorial entities, and no claims to absolute sovereignty or total independence. Above all, what we call 'sovereignty' was divided and shared: it overlapped territorial borders and appealed to an *external* God to such an extent that arguably it had ceased to exist.

A new medieval scenario

This was the sort of territoriality which Hedley Bull (1977) speculated might possibly re-emerge in a 'new medievalism'. It was:

> conceivable that sovereign states might . . . be replaced . . . by a modern and secular equivalent of the . . . political organisation that existed in Western Christendom in the Middle Ages . . . a system of overlapping authority and multiple loyalty. . . . If modern states were to come to share their authority over their citizens, and their ability to command their loyalties, on the one hand with regional and world authorities, and on the other hand with sub-state or sub-national authorities, to such an extent that the concept of sovereignty ceased to be applicable, then a neo-mediaeval . . . order might be said to have emerged.
>
> (Bull 1977, 254–5, 273–5)

He pictured a UK government having to share its authority 'on the one hand with authorities in Scotland, Wales . . . and elsewhere, and on the other hand with a European authority in Brussels and world authorities in New York and Geneva'. He imagined the political loyalties of, say, Glaswegians being 'so uncertain as between the authorities in Edinburgh, London, Brussels and New York that the government of the United Kingdom could not be assumed to enjoy any kind of primacy over the others, such as it possesses now'; and with 'protracted uncertainty about the locus of sovereignty' it might be a small step to recognising that the concept was 'irrelevant' (Bull 1977, 254, 275).

Bull thought this might possibly happen when pressures on the state 'from above and below' weakened and diffused rather than clearly relocated sovereignty, as for example in an intermediate stage between the inter-governmentalism of independent states and a federal superstate; or in another intermediate stage where sub-state nationalisms or regionalisms substantially undermined but did not succeed in replicating existing state sovereignty. He drew a clear distinction between these 'intermediate' stages and full success for regional separatisms or the creation of a United States of Europe, which (as in Gulliver) would simply be a quantitative change, increasing or decreasing the number of states, rather than qualitatively changing the nature of states and politics (Bull 1977, 264–7, 273–5).

What Bull thought conceivable in 1977 is even more so today. The EU has been transformed in the last three decades and is arguably now at an 'intermediate stage' somewhere between inter-governmentalism and a federal arrangement; and in at least some EU states (e.g. Spain) sub-state nationalisms or regionalisms have gained significant authority without replicating state sovereignty. And Bull's conception is notable in explicitly *not* requiring anything as implausibly ambitious or decisive as the 'death' of the state or Gulliver replicas.

Already in 1993 John Ruggie was arguing that the EU was 'postmodern' and 'multiperspectival': relations between the (then) twelve member states could no longer be seen as simply involving twelve separate, single viewpoints. The twelve sometimes acted as a collectivity which had its own singularity; the central institutions which were set up by the states, particularly the European Commission and Parliament, were now also to some extent actors in their own right; while in defining their own interests each of the twelve states increasingly had to take into account or internalise at least some of the interests of the other eleven and the views expressed in the central institutions (Ruggie 1993, 168–74).

Likewise ideas of 'multi-level governance' are now fairly commonplace. Contrary to Europhobic notions about 'losing sovereignty' to the level of a 'super-state', practical politics has gone well beyond the counterposing of separate levels, and indeed the very notion of levels is questioned. While formal representative government is based on discrete territories at different levels, social processes operate simultaneously at and between them; and even in the limited sphere of representative democracy, the different scales (wards, constituencies, and local, regional, national and European assemblies) are interdependent and mutually constitutive. Contrary to the zero-sum approach to levels, democratisation more plausibly entails a positive-sum game in which more democracy at one level is likely to encourage and support more at other levels. Postmodernists stress the importance of multiple identities and this can be translated into 'multi-level citizenship' (Painter 2002) which reflects an individual's simultaneous membership of political communities at a variety of spatial scales – local, regional, national, European, and wider. And it can (and should) be extended to various non-territorial communities (such as sexual minorities, trades unionists, other interest groups). In addition to territorial representation, there needs to be participatory democracy and popular involvement which crosses borders and straddles different spatial scales.

There are, however, substantial qualifications and obstacles to this new medieval scenario (Anderson 1996). The 'unbundling' of state sovereignty is highly selective and uneven, as noted, and while the EU may be 'intermediate' it is debateable how far it has actually travelled from its starting points of inter-governmentalism and more centralised states. Postmodernists emphasise multiple identities but often exaggerate the extent and speed with which new ones are adopted or old ones replaced (and too much is perhaps made of subjective identities per se, if for instance individuals may now participate in EU arenas or be strongly influenced by the EU without necessarily registering a significant 'European' identity – see Thomas Wilson on 'Europeanisation' in Chapter 3). While political space seems to be regaining some of its pre-modern and pre-national fluidity and relativity, there are serious limitations in analogies with such a specific time and place as medieval Europe. Some current political forms are entirely alien to it, including nationalism and national states; and despite new territorial arrangements, the present configuration is decidedly *not* post-nationalist. Political space is now a complex mixture of new and old forms, the latter continuing to exist and interact rather than being tidily removed to clear the ground for the former. Furthermore, sovereignty is now supposed to belong to 'the people' or 'the nation', so the unbundling of territorial sovereignty and the growth of multiperspectival politics could mean increasing the 'democratic deficits', unaccountability and lack of transparency, unless there are compensating developments. Here the medieval model is unhelpful, to say the least.

Imperial territoriality: empire metaphor and reality

The empire metaphor has significant advantages over medievalism and avoids some of its blind spots. Far from being tied to a particular place or period, empires stretch from Sargon of Akkad, the first named individual in recorded history and emperor of Sumer in present day Iraq, to the current occupation of Iraq by the US empire and its allies. Imperial territoriality is highly malleable, adaptable and heterogeneous, with a seemingly infinite capacity to absorb. It has incorporated both *medieval* and *national* forms of territoriality in its not so warm but all-encompassing embrace, and yet is distinct from both.

Pragmatically involving power hierarchies and the control of 'external' territories, it is more flexible than doctrinaire nationalism and not constrained by any (even lip-service) commitment to formal equality or democracy, though by the same token it lacks such a strong popular and legitimising ideology. At least in principle, it can subsume elements of our first four options and it is eminently suited to accommodating a heterogeneous mix of relationships, benign and malign, and old, new or hybrid forms. It would be boosted by federalising tendencies (without requiring formal federalisation), and it could happily absorb a diversity of sub-state regionalisms, medieval-like entities and fuzzy borders. Nationalism with its democratic impulse is possibly but not necessarily the exception (see Chapter 2) – it has in fact often coexisted in imperial systems.[4] However, like new medievalism, the empire metaphor is not encouraging for democracy and could indeed become symbolic of democratic deficits – provided of course it is not derailed by them.

Meanwhile, it is the only option which addresses the EU's external as well as internal relations, the breaking down of the 'inside/outside' dichotomy at the edges of the EU, and the possibility of a return to a single-centred Europe. Its twin focus on external expansion and internal differentiation is timely as both have been growing in significance. So much so that it is conceivable Ole Waever's (1997) perceptive metaphor could become reality. He clearly identified key spatial characteristics of imperial territoriality and Europe's trend toward singularity. However his viewpoint needs to be updated and widened, to take account of developments in political economy and the increased importance of territory in the 'new imperialism'.

Imperial territoriality

Summarising imperial territoriality is difficult because of its spatio-temporal scope and diversity, but some general features are common to many empires. All in one way or another have involved gradations of direct or indirect control or domination of 'external' territories. They have expansionist tendencies, often with a self-justifying 'moral superiority' or self-appointed 'civilising mission', and also the danger of imperial 'overreach'. Their spaces tend to be highly differentiated and unequal, their borders varying from precise lines to fuzzy, indistinct zones. Heterogeneity and asymmetries mark the character and interconnections of the various entities making up the empire, with weak (if any) relationships (in the plural) between territory and sovereignty. This is very different from *national* territoriality though now the heterogeneity also encompasses national entities. Despite similarities, it is also quite distinct from *medieval* territoriality in that empires are centred entities with a 'core–periphery' structure (even if the centre moves around as imperial courts sometimes did). There is pattern in the heterogeneity and asymmetry, with spatial gradations of power and authority decreasing outward from the core, and different, increasingly indirect methods of rule which continue beyond the frontiers of empire to include 'external' relations without any sharp inside/outside dichotomy. Thus we can identify a radial, hierarchical pattern of concentric circles – from a central core of *direct rule* through *domination* over subject units with some internal autonomy, to *suzerain* overlordship and indirect rule over variably dependent client states, to a looser, more indirect *hegemony* over formally independent states, to territories which are beyond the empire's sphere of influence and perhaps within the sphere of a rival empire. For Waever (1997, 64–5) with his focus on international security and spatial form, such concentric rings are *the* defining criteria of imperially organised systems. Although understandably not popular in the age of nationalism, Waever notes that 'empires have not always been unpopular or imposed on subject populations', or necessarily unstable: in fact, they have a generally good historical record of creating zones of peace for trade and development (true compared to nationalism whose record of generating conflict is arguably second to none); most imperial centres have seen the value of subsidiarity rather than being over-centralised; and in consequence inclusion has often benefited subordinate political units (Waever 1997, 63–4).

In fact, this looks remarkably like present-day Europe. It fits the increasing differentiation of the EU's constitutive territories and its internal borders, with euro and non-euro, Schengen and non-Schengen member states, and the variable geometry of a 'two-(or more) speed Europe'. And that was before ten poorer countries joined in 2004, and two more in 2007, greatly increasing the economic, political and cultural heterogeneity. Overall, as already noted, the EU is now much further from the homogenising logic of 'national' space than when new members such as the Irish Republic and Greece were to be brought up to the level of existing members: there is no longer such (an even rhetorical) commitment, despite there still being recourse to familiar 'national' forms of rhetoric about cohesion and collective interest (in the absence of more appropriate new forms and perhaps 'empire's' lack of popular appeal).

Empire resonates well with EU expansion – it only emerged after large-scale enlargement came on to the EU's agenda in the early 1990s, and then gained substance a decade later with the ten new members. It fits Ole Waever's defining criteria of concentric rings and graded core–periphery hierarchies: from original or 'core' member states to more recent joiners, while further candidates (of varying immediacy) queue up for membership, echoing the benefits of inclusion in empire. There is additional grading in that pre-2004 members (with exceptions including Ireland and Britain) did not yet automatically admit workers from the new states; and the messyness of empire is further evidenced by the fact (mentioned in the Introduction) that while some member states are not in the Schengen area, some non-members outside the EU signed the agreement.

The inside/outside dichotomy at the EU's edges has been further blurred since 2002 with the addition of a whole new circle to Waever's schema, the EU's wider European Neighbourhood Policy (ENP) formally extending EU influence to neighbouring states which are not candidates for EU membership. This creates a 'ring of friends' (see Pertti Joennieme's analysis in Chapter 8) or a wider border zone of defence to ensure the security and well-being of 'Fortress Europe', though Bohdana Dimitrovova (2006), who sees the EU in empire terms, points to policy contradictions between security and economic cooperation and a possible lessening of EU leverage because the 'friends' are excluded from full membership. Beyond the ENP there are national states (e.g., Ukraine) now in-between the spheres of influence of the EU and Russia which has its own concentric rings, and ones (e.g., Belorussia) within the sphere of the rival empire. The west-to-east gradient resonates with pro-west/anti-east prejudices in popular ideologies across Europe.[5] And the danger of imperial overreach is echoed in the arguments of those who would exclude Turkey from EU membership (supposedly too Muslim, too Asian, and/or too poor).

It is now over two decades since Gellner (1983, 139–40) saw the modern map as a Modigliani image of simple and unambiguous national spaces, not a Kokoschka riot of colours, diversity and complexity. Now a more appropriate image of European territoriality would be a Kokoshka superimposed on a Modigliani.

Informal to formal empire and territorial aggrandisement

To understand how the EU might become an empire – and perhaps constitute a single-centred Europe – consider two related historical processes or movements: (1) from formal to informal and now partly back towards formal empire; and (2) from medieval to modern multiplicity and now towards singularity. The spatial continuum from direct to very indirect control is also a temporal continuum, and the dominant historic tendendency towards indirect, informal control has recently been partially reversed with territory and territoriality again becoming more important.

The dominant tendency since at least the nineteenth century has been for less reliance on formal territorial empire and decreasing use of direct political control to support economic expansion and secure external production. Instead the foreign activities of multinational corporations are secured and protected not by 'their own' state but by the politically (if not economically) independent states in which the activities are located. This historic movement is made possible by capitalism's unique partial separation (or contradictory unity) of 'politics/economics' (Wood 1995). This both facilitates claims to political sovereignty (by separating off economic realities) and enables the cross-border, transnational spread of economic production and influence (separated from more overt politics which would clearly contravene sovereignty and invite nationalistic reactions) (see Anderson 2001a). It has made possible Britain's nineteenth-century informal or non-territorial economic empire in the politically independent countries of South America, Europe's neo-colonialism following the decolonisation of its formal overseas empires after the Second World War, and most of the US empire for most of the twentieth century. And now the EU has a large stake in this informal 'empire of capital' (Wood 2003), dominated by the US but often involving cooperation with other world powers including the EU (e.g. in trade negotiations with Africa and South America). In the empire of capital, hegemonic power is wielded to the benefit of capital in general, not only US capital; and for analysing the global role of the US, John Agnew (2005) has presented an impressive case for preferring a more collective and consensual conception of hegemony *instead of* empire.

However, three important qualifications or counter-tendencies must be added to our incomplete and rather economistic picture – and they are three reasons for preferring to retain the continuum from direct, territorial to very indirect, non-territorial control, and for preferring to use the concept of empire *as well as* hegemony rather than having to choose one or other (see Cooper 2004). First, informal economic empire depends on hegemonic control, political and military, over independent states by leading world powers, most notably the USA, as well as depending on the territoriality of those states themselves. Secondly, the leading powers while often consensual allies in imposing hegemony are also rivals for economic and political advantage, and ultimately for the position of leading hegemon. And thirdly, in this rivalry their territorial home base is very important – as can be seen in the territorial aggrandisement of EU enlargement and its relationship to flows of capital and labour.

The separation of politics/economics is only partial; generally they are mutually dependent and constitute a unity, albeit a contradictory one. And while the political security and support for external economic production is generally left to the respective independent states, they cannot always be relied on to secure the necessary conditions for profitable foreign investment if simply left to themselves. Hence the role of hegemon as 'world policeman'. In the nineteenth century Britain sent the occasional gunboat to threaten South American countries if they prioritised a different agenda of their own. To police today's world-wide empire of capital, the US sends the occasional aircraft carrier, or bombers from its military bases which form a global archipelago of imperial power, a network of points in geographic space rather than continuous territory (cf. nineteenth-century Britain's more modest naval bases). It threatens recalcitrant or 'rogue' states, only enforcing direct rule through military occupation as a (usually) last resort (its costly and counterproductive Iraq occupation suggesting why it generally wants to avoid actually carrying out this threat, and incidentally why traditional territorial empire went out of fashion).

The cooperative element of hegemony in the empire of capital – the fact that it is not only US capital which benefits from US policing – seems to be the small kernel of truth lost in Hardt and Negri's (2001) postmodern farrago, *Empire* with a capital *E*, in the singular and covering the whole world, a leftish variation on the neo-liberal 'borderless world' fantasy and even more misleading. Their 'world empire' is centreless, placeless and cleansed of imperialism,[6] and crucially it tells us that inter-imperialist rivalries have ended when actually they are very much present and probably intensifying: witness the USA's dangerously unilateralist and militaristic exercise of hegemony since 9/11 which was partly intended to upstage or divide rivals for hegemony (see Anderson 2003, 2004); also the rise of China, India, and of the EU as an economic (as distinct from military and political) power. If 'capital in general' benefits from US policing, US capital benefits more than most (e.g. Haliburton in Iraq), but in *Empire* there are no specific imperialisms, nor any recognition that some are 'more equal than others', with the US currently the biggest pig in the pen.

In this highly competitive world, the size of an imperialism's home territory matters; if anything, this base for its transnational activities is becoming more important. While direct control through territorial empire declined historically between the sixteenth and twentieth centuries, Giovanni Arrighi (1996) has pointed out that the territorial home base or core of the world's hegemonic (and would-be hegemonic) powers was becoming ever larger – in his scheme progressing from the city-state of Genoa, through the small United Provinces of the Dutch Netherlands, to the somewhat larger nineteenth-century British state, and on to the continental scale of the USA. With respect to the core–periphery continuum, it is as if the empire's core lost its middle rings of domination and suzerainity (as actually happened to the British and French empires) but greatly expanded its outer ring of looser hegemony, while conversely the possible contenders for leading hegemon needed to have a greatly expanded core (and China, Russia and the EU are also of continental scale, while Japan is not and perhaps is 'dropping out of the race' for that reason?).

It is therefore questionable whether there is now in general a 'declining desire for territory' (Waever 1997, 84–5). Developments since 9/11 suggest the opposite: the so-called 'War on Terror' and related moral panics about international crime, drugs, human trafficking . . . have led to an epidemic of 'Friend–Foe' differentiations and increased desire for territorial control.[7] There are various examples of this in the 'new imperialism', and indeed increased territorialism should be added as one of its defining characteristics, along with the shift to a more proactive neo-conservatism (of e.g. Bush junior) compared to the more neo-liberal 1990s (of e.g. Clinton) (see Harvey 2003, van der Pijl *et al.* 2004). Examples can be found in the defensive territorialism and incipient protectionism of economic blocs such as the EU, NAFTA and Mercosur, with NAFTA also extending control at its edges (see Pellerin 1999); and in the highly territorial matter of controlling the supply and price of oil and other natural resources (and the possible threat of 'resource wars'), with echoes in Iraq and Afghanistan. And of course it was the US invasion of those countries which really put new imperialism and the vogue for empire on the map.

However, Iraq is in many respects a crude throwback to the worst of imperialism, and perhaps a more interesting (as well as more peaceful and effective) example of new imperial territorialism is to be found in and around the core of empires rather than in the peripheries (which overwhelmingly, unlike Iraq, remain subject to loose hegemony). The eastward expansion of the EU is more interesting because it has genuinely new expressions of imperial territoriality. It exemplifies the enlarging of the core of a would-be hegemon (or at least an entity which wants to be able to 'live with' hegemonic contenders); the creation of zonal border defences through a spatio-temporal programme of creating new members, candidates and a 'ring of friends'; and the 'spatial fixes' of cross-border labour and capital flows which themselves are redolent of imperialism and involve territorial incorporation to make high-risk states safe for western investors (see Chapter 8). Eastern Europe was a prime example of independent states which could not be relied on to provide a secure economic environment (partly destabilised by western-encouraged neo-liberalism). But the 'carrot' of formal inclusion in the empire or access to its markets, and implicitly imperialistic, asymmetrical power relationships, have given the EU leverage to effectively impose its norms of liberal democracy and a privatised market on its friends in the east. The objective, in the medium to long term, is to strengthen the EU's global competitiveness, now the main driving force behind enlargement and integration.

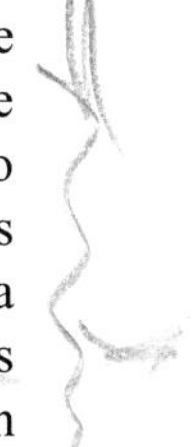

All this gives substance to 'Europe as empire' and shows that behind the spatial forms of empire there are imperialistic relations between Europe's core and periphery and the wider world. Whether it achieves European singularity is perhaps less likely.

European multiplicity to singularity

Far from being organised by or around a single core, Europe has been characterised by multiple centres of power since the fragmentation of Charlemange's 'recreation of Rome' (see Smith J. 2005, 253–92). Medievalism was highly decentralised, despite continued West European imperialism: it pioneered its expansionism on its own Celtic and eastern Slavic fringes before going overseas, and Eastern Europe has a long history of western domination. The post-medieval story of Europe is one of amalgamations and homogenisations, first under absolutism, then under nationalism. But this only resulted in a smaller number of competing centres, and Europe never got remotely close to producing singularity – indeed the fewer but more powerful centres meant in practice it was even further from being a singular polity. Europe was singular only in the sense of 'unique', 'beyond the average', 'extraordinary'. Competing centres, and the absence of a single domineering core (as in China), were seen as a strength, allowing and stimulating Europe to pioneer the transitions from feudalism to merchant capitalism and then to industrial capitalism.

Multiplicity changed from positive to negative, however, when the era of inter-imperialist rivalries led to another European 'Thirty Years War', 1914–1945. Competitive multiplicity had fostered development but it was also having ruinous consequences. And it was this realisation and the wish to forestall another European war which led Jean Monnet, Robert Schumann and others to make the initial moves toward singularity in establishing the Common Market in 1956. Its subsequent history of enlargement and integration can be seen as continuing Europe's territorial story of amalgamations and homogenisations, though now primarily to strengthen Europe's global position.

If the past is 'European' and the present 'American', it seems the future is 'Asian'. This is the external reality to which the EU now has to respond, and as we have seen, it constitutes strong pressures to realise empire and singularity. The EU is increasingly a player in the international system (if not always an effective one), and national politics across Europe are increasingly framed by EU considerations. As Waever (1997, 66, 82) notes, after 1989 European politics unfolded around a single centre rather than reverting back to the traditional 'balance of power' between many centres; and even the advocates of state sovereignty no longer see competition and 'balance' within Europe as a viable security strategy.

Moreover it could be argued that in normative terms, a stronger, politically more unified EU empire could have a benign influence on the looming struggle for world hegemony involving the USA, China and others. Not because of any spurious assumptions about 'superior European values', and not because the EU would be a better hegemon, but, on the contrary, because traditional hegemony is not an effective way to run the world. The US War on Terror, which in fact is largely a war to bolster US hegemony, suggests it is an extremely dangerous way (Anderson 2004); and a militarily weak but economically powerful EU would have strong vested interests in supporting non-militaristic, more collective and (hopefully) more democratic routes to world peace.

Europe's position and 'weight' in the world may now depend on how it develops – or fails to develop – as a singular, coherent polity. Success here would indeed bring singularity in both senses: the EU is already fairly 'extraordinary' as a political entity compared to the world's other economic blocs, but Europe would be even more extraordinary if it were to develop in empire fashion around a single dominant core.

Singularity and empire undone?

External forces, however, are also working against singularity and empire, usually in alliance with internal or self-inflicted counter-tendencies (one of the themes developed by Warwick Armstrong in Chapter 14). The Russian empire blocks singularity on Europe's eastern fringes, but perhaps the more serious obstacle is the non-territorial presence and divisive influence of the 'interfering hegemon'. Relations between the US and the EU are complex and ambivalent because they are simultaneously allies and rivals. Sometimes there is a coincidence of interest and joint action (e.g. as First World empires blocking food imports from the Third

World), but in many instances their interests diverge (e.g. with respect to China and to the EU's near neighbours in the Middle East or Russia). And in the latter circumstances there is always the possibility, often likelihood, of diverging interests between the member states themselves: some (typically with France in the lead) wanting to assert a distinctly European policy, others siding with the USA (e.g., most typically Blair's Britain with its one-sided and self-deluding 'special relationship' with Bush's USA, but also some other right-wing European governments).

The empire metaphor points towards the possibility of empowering Europe to compete globally with other major powers, but it also signals internal differentiation, and if the latter tendency were to predominate it will be no more than a metaphor, and perhaps not a very good one. Whereas the other leading empires – the US, Russia, China – all have a coherent national state and nationalist ideology at their core, the EU, underneath and despite all its significant overlays of transnationalism, is still a collection of separate national states with their own separate ideologies. And this returns us to our starting point, a 'Europe of nations'. While we saw that its advocates are unlikely to succeed in their objective of putting the clock back on the EU project, they could still block any further strengthening of central institutions or the development of a unifying and legitimising supranational democracy (as they have imagined themselves to be blocking a 'federal Europe').

Nationalistic strategies have especial potency when allied to a US hegemon which employs a divide-and-rule strategy (with the UK , for instance, sometimes little more than a pathetic client state). Here the EU's external relations are internalised unevenly and divisively across the different national states (with the result that sometimes the EU as a whole is only slightly less pathetic). Currently there is little sign of progress (e.g., on the problem of US-related divisions on Palestine–Israel), but things could change. While national interest, whether soundly based or misguided, will usually take priority over 'European interest', there are already many instances where national and European interests coincide – after all, and despite their divisions, it is the national states which for fifty years have been empowering integration and enlargement. Furthermore, when US hegemony gets weaker as it almost certainly will (see Mann 2003), perhaps because of its economic vulnerability and the rise of China and other rivals, its ability to divide Europe will also probably weaken, though what new alliances and rivalries might then emerge is impossible to predict.

More immediately, the EU faces the challenge of its own internally generated divisions, lack of democracy and legitimacy. These problems are if anything more serious and deep-rooted – problems of European society and culture, not only of states and politics – but they are also ones which Europeans can immediately do something about. For example Eurocentrism and chauvinism. Several chapters (5 to 8) deal substantially with issues of immigration and migrant labour, and as George Joffé (Chapter 6) and Brigitta Busch and Michal Krzyżanowski (Chapter 7) demonstrate in different ways, there is a strong and potentially very destructive link between external and internal exclusions, for they often apply to the same, or same sorts of, people. Outsiders are already inside. As border regimes seek to exclude immigrants, there are already sizeable communities established by immigrants inside the EU, often spatially segregated or socially excluded. Whether because of 'pure', unthinking racist chauvinism, or because of a temptation to find Europe's elusive identity or unify the 'Self' by excluding and denigrating 'external Others' (e.g. non-Christians, Africans, Asians), the result would be to divide the EU's population against itself, leading to incoherence and worse. It would be more than ironic if an EU empire were hoist on its own petard of Eurocentrisms and chauvinisms, as the US empire has now three times been hoist by its own nationalism (N. Smith 2003, 2005).[8] And the EU's elitism and deficits of democracy and legitimacy could make this more likely.

A 'Europe of nations' is the most serious alternative or challenge to the empire option, but it is quite possible that the future EU/Europe will be stopped short of all the five options, without any clear-cut outcome. The three national options are unlikely in anything like the form envisaged by their proponents, and so too is 'medievalism'. The character of the different territorial levels may continue to change, perhaps in unpredictable ways, and in some policy areas both the EU and the regional levels may continue to gain in relative importance. But the broad outlines of more complex multilevel and border-crossing governance are already visible in present structures and relationships – in that sense the future is already coming into sight and may look quite like the present.

All the options mirror some elements of contemporary reality and reflect ongoing tendencies which will continue to shape Europe. But our malleable empire option is perhaps the most likely, at least in weak form.[9] It covers external as well as internal relations, the contemporary blurring of the inside/outside dichotomy, and the graded heterogeneity from core to periphery. It is capable of absorbing elements of federalism, sub-state regionalism, and a 'medieval' sharing of sovereignty, even elements of nationalism – though that could stretch it to breaking point. If internally the EU is a case of 'arrested federalisation', externally Europe may turn out to be a case of 'arrested singularity'. We could have an empire without achieving (full) singularity, a weak empire but an empire nonetheless. And perhaps better than no empire at all?

But is this what Europe is, or where it's going? Hopefully the rest of the book will help you find your own answers.

Notes

1 I deal more with empire and for the first four options draw on earlier publications and collaborative work with James Goodman, where there are fuller discussions of some of the arguments.

2 'Sovereignty' developed in the Roman Empire and arguably disappeared in medievalism's overlapping authority systems which appealed to external theocratic legitimacy. Then it was revived and later fetishised in national territoriality (see Hinsley 1986, 26–60). It is rooted in a conception of geographic space which sees it as 'absolute and homogeneous' (as in Euclid's geometry and Newton's physics), rather than 'relative and variable' (as in Einstein's universe).

3 It stems from Kohr's (1986) *The Breakdown of Nations* (first published in 1957) where he polemised against 'bigness' and large national states as the cause of modern ills, a thesis popularised by Schumacher's (1973) best-selling *Small is Beautiful*.

4 Imperialism and nationalism have not always been implacable foes, contrary to some (usually nationalist) perceptions. National entities for long co-existed not only with but *within* empires (e.g. nineteenth-century Austria–Hungary was a 'prison-house of nations' but not all wanted independence). Imperial powers have adopted nationalism for their own ends (e.g. British, Prussian and Russian); and some nationalisms have had colonial and imperial pretentions whether stillborn or realised (e.g., Irish and Japanese respectively). Empires, in emphasing political pragmatism over principle and now lacking a strong popular ideology, do not necessarily oppose nationalism at an ideological level. Yet, by appealing to democratic self-determination, nationalisms have been centrally involved in the breaking up of empires (e.g. Austria–Hungary and other empires in Europe after the First World War, European overseas empires after the Second World War) or in resisting their advance (e.g., Latin Americans against US imperialism).

5 Going east from Western Europe, each country tends to present itself ideologically as 'the last bastion of the west', the 'east' starting at its eastern borders. In general 'west' looks down on 'east', and 'east' not unnaturally resents it.

6 A single 'world empire' is probably an impossibility given the geographical uneveness and competitiveness of capitalism (see Anderson 2001a). Hardt and Negri (2001) take the reality of a single world capitalist system and turn it into a grotesque parody by ignoring some basic points: capitalists compete as well as cooperate with each other; competition, unevenness, and the threat or reality of protectionism are a powerful material basis for separate state territories; hence borders are unlikely to wither away before capitalism does – and even more unlikely if resource depletion adds eco-crisis to profitability crisis, and states and capitals adopt a beggar-thy-neighbour approach to survival (Anderson 2006b).

7 For Waever (1997, 84–5), the 'decreasing importance of territory hinges on whether states define the Other as enemy', and most 'Self-Othering' in Europe was not a Schmittian 'Friend–Foe' differentiation. However, because the categorisation of an 'Other' as a 'Foe' is subjective, he very wisely declined to declare 'any definite devaluation of territory'. In fact, Friend–Foeing is rampant since 9/11. He correctly notes that states may find other assets more important than territory; but then suggests that whereas power faded off with distance in classical empires because they lacked control capacity, today it often fades off because of 'the abdication of control (and responsibility) – a lack of interest in territorial aggrandisement'. But the present EU enlargement is a type of territorial aggrandisement, and its ring of friends is a spatial extension of its (indirect) control and responsibility, not a retreat or abdication.

8 Neil Smith (2003, 2005) persuasively argues that US hegemony has been seriously weakened by its own nationalism: after the First World War when Woodrow Wilson's liberal internationalism and the League of Nations were scuppered by American isolationism; after the Second World War when Roosevelt's liberal world vision was undermined by America's aggresive Cold War policies; and similarly now with its globalisation being undermined by its own nationalistic unilateralism.

9 Since this chapter was written, Jan Zielonka has published *Europe as Empire: The Nature of the Enlarged European Union* (Oxford University Press, 2006) which combines our two 'post-national' options in the concept of 'neo-medieval empire'. However, it has not been possible to take his ideas into account.

References

Agnew, J. (2002) 'The limits of federalism in transnational democracy: beyond the hegemony of the US model', in Anderson op. cit., 56–72.

Agnew, J. (2005) *Hegemony: The New Shape of Global Power*, Philadelphia: Temple University Press.

Anderson, J. (1995) '"Arrested federalization"? Europe, Britain, Ireland', in *Federalism: The Multiethnic Challenge*, Smith G. (ed.), London: Longman.

Anderson, J. (1996) 'The shifting stage of politics: new medieval and postmodern territorialities?', *Environment and Planning D: Society and Space* 14, 2, 133–53.

Anderson, J. (2001a) *Theorizing State Borders: 'Politics/Economics' and Democracy in Capitalism*, Electronic Working Paper Series, WP 01, Centre for International Borders Research (CIBR), Queen's University Belfast (*www.qub.ac.uk/cibr*).

Anderson, J. (2001b) 'The rise of regions and regionalism in Western Europe, in Montserrat Guibernau (ed.) *Governing European Diversity*, London: Sage, pp. 35–64.

Anderson, J. (ed) (2002) *Transnational Democracy: Political Spaces and Border Crossings*, London: Routlege.

Anderson, J. (2003) 'American hegemony after 11 September: Allies, rivals and contradictions', *Geopolitics* 8, 3, 35–60.

Anderson, J. (2004) 'Saving the world from American hegemony', *Environment and Planning D: Society and Space* vol. 22, 6, 911–914.

Anderson, J. (2006a) 'Transnational democracy for European diversity', in *Transcultural Diversities*, Council of Europe.

Anderson, J. (2006b) 'Only Sustain . . . The Environment, "anti-globalisation" and the runaway bicycle', in Johnston, J., Gismondi, M. and Goodman, J. (eds) *Nature's Revenge*, Toronto: Broadview.

Anderson, J. and Goodman, J. (1995) 'Regions, states and the European Union: Modernist reaction or postmodernist adaptation?', *Review of International Political Economy*, 2, 4, 600–631.

Arrighi, G. (1996) *The Long Twentieth Century*, London: Verso.

Bull, H. (1977) *The Anarchical Society*, London: Macmillan.

Cooper, F. (2004) 'Empire multiplied: a review essay', *Comparative Studies in Society and History* 46, 2, 247–272.

Dimitrovova, B. (2006) 'Bordering and re-bordering the European neighbourhood: Discourses of security and co-operation', Association of Borderland Studies (ABS) Conference, Centre for International Borders Research (CIBR), Queen's University Belfast, June 2006 – www.qub.ac.uk/cibr.

Gellner, E. (1983) *Nations and Nationalism*, Oxford: Blackwell.

Goodman, J. (1997) 'The EU: reconstituting democracy beyond the nation-state', in *The Transformation of Democracy? Democratic Politics in the New World Order*, Anthony McGrew (ed.) Cambridge: Polity Press.

Hardt, M. and Negri, A. (2001) *Empire*, Cambridge MA: Harvard University Press.

Harvey, D. (2003) *The New Imperialism*, Oxford: Oxford University Press.

Hinsley, F.H. (1986) *Sovereignty* (2nd edn) Cambridge: Cambridge University Press.

Kohr, L. (1986) [1957] *The Breakdown of Nations*, London: Routledge & Kegan Paul.

Mann, M. (2003) *Incoherent Empire*, London: Verso.

Newman, M. (1996) *Democracy, Sovereignty and the European Union*, London: Hurst.

Newman, M. (2002) 'Reconceptualising democracy in the European Union', in Anderson op.cit., 73–92.

Painter, J. (2002) 'Multi-level citizenship, identity and regions in contemporary Europe', in Anderson op.cit., 93–110.

Pellerin, H. (1999) 'The cart before the horse? The coordination of migration policies in the Americas and the neoliberal economic project of integration', *Review of International Political Economy* 6, 4, 468–493.

Ruggie, J. (1993) 'Territoriality and beyond: problematizing modernity in international relations', *International Organisation* 47, 1, 139–174.

Sack, R. (1986) *Human Territoriality: Its Theory and History*, Cambridge: Cambridge University Press.

Schumacher, E.F. (1973) *Small is Beautiful: Economics as if People Really Mattered*, London: Abacus.

Smith, J. (2005) *Europe after Rome: A New Cultural History 500–1000*, Oxford: Oxford University Press.

Smith, N. (2003) *American Empire: Roosevelt's Geographer and the Prelude to Globalisation*, Berkeley: University of California Press.

Smith, N. (2005) *The Endgame of Globalization*, London: Routledge.

van der Pijl, K., Assassi, L. and Wigan, D. (eds) (2004) *Global Regulation: Managing Crises after the Imperial Turn*, Basingstoke: Palgrave.

Waever, O. (1997) Imperial metaphors: Emerging European analogies to pre-nation-state imperial systems, in O. Tunander, P. Baev and V.I. Einagel (eds) *Geopolitics in Post-Wall Europe: Security, Territory and Identity*, London: Sage, 59–93.

Walker, R. (1993) *Inside/Outside: International Relations as Political Theory*, Cambridge: Cambridge University Press.

Wood, E.M. (1995) 'The separation of the "economic" and the "political" in capitalism', in E.M. Wood, *Democracy against Capitalism: Renewing Historical Materialism*, Cambridge: Cambridge University Press.

Wood, E.M. (2003) *Empire of Capital*, London: Verso.

2 From empire to the European Union via the national state

The three ages of the Irish border

Liam O'Dowd

Ireland/Northern Ireland as a historic borderland

Viewed from afar, Ireland as a whole, and Northern Ireland in particular, may be conceived as borderland. Over centuries, a shifting territorial border has marked the waxing and waning of British control of the island. As arguably Britain's first colony, the borders of settler and administrative colonial control in Ireland varied over several centuries. Full assimilation into the British state was never fully realised – in part because of the structure of that state and the nature of British colonialism. The latter functioned indirectly through co-optation of native elites and the limited plantation of settlers in different parts of the country (Brady and Gillespie 1986). The last and most systematic of these plantations was to provide a somewhat imprecise territorial framework for the emergence of Northern Ireland (NI) as a separate political unit. A highly localised and durable Gaelic culture and society also proved stubbornly, if intermittently, resistant to British control. Even when Ireland was fully incorporated into the UK by the Act of Union in 1801, colonial control was narrowly based and exercised largely through elements of the minority Protestant community in the island as a whole. The 1801 settlement ended in 1920/21 with the partition of Ireland and the creation of a new border which has now lasted for over eighty years – one of the oldest in contemporary Europe. It has remained the most violently contested border in Western Europe, however. Thirty years of the NI conflict culminated with the signing of the Belfast Agreement in 1998, marking the latest attempt to reconfigure the Irish border on a more democratic and consensual basis.

Violent contestation, however, reflected other borderland characteristics of Ireland as a whole. Since the Reformation, Ireland has been a place where the 'new' Protestantism of Northern Europe has coexisted and clashed with the 'old' Catholicism of Southern Europe. Much of Britain's concern to control Ireland was strategic – to prevent it being used as backdoor to attack Britain by the Catholic powers of France and Spain. The less than successful attempts at British and Irish nation- and state-building in Ireland in the last three centuries have also created a form of ethnogenesis of which religion was a large part. From 1800 onwards a newly consolidated Irish Catholic Church and the broad nationalist movement became increasingly intertwined. Likewise, adherence to various forms of Protestantism fused with unionist, pro-British and imperialist politics. Religion was also combined in complex and often mutually supporting ways with settler/native mentalities, class differences and differential statuses within the structures of the British Empire and state (McDonagh 1983).

But Ireland as a borderland also forms a bridge between North America and Britain and more recently between North America and the EU. The Irish diaspora stretching from the late eighteenth to the late twentieth century has straddled the Atlantic in ways which have sustained both a romanticised anti-British nationalism and practical structures of support for Irish secessionism. The reactivation of these structures under the Clinton presidency played no small part in the negotiation of the Belfast Agreement of 1998. There is a final and contemporary sense in which Ireland is a new borderland between the EU and North America. The Celtic Tiger economy of the Republic of Ireland has been largely driven by American multinational investment (some of it controlled by Irish-American businessmen) eager to supply the greatly enlarged 'domestic' market of the EU (O'Hearn 1998). This has led to a debate between those who favour the neo-liberal American model of economic organisation versus those who favour the more corporatist models of Rhineland capitalism and European-style social democracy.

Since the 1970s, Irish governments have used both EU membership and Irish-American contacts to reorient the Southern economy away from dependency on the historically slow-growth economy of the UK. The result has been remarkable levels of economic growth since the mid-1990s, the historic transformation of Ireland from a net-emigration to a net-immigration economy and a reversal in the economic fortunes of Northern Ireland and the Republic. For a century prior to the 1970s the Belfast region had been the only industrialised part of Ireland. Over the last thirty years, under the aegis of the new globalised economy, industrial activity has shifted decisively southwards. This, in turn, has altered the meaning of the Irish border and created an economic context for the forms of transnational governance created in the Belfast Agreement. The Irish border now separates a high-growth state economy driven by US investment and committed to membership of the euro from a regional economy of the UK still heavily dependent on public expenditure and retaining characteristics of a war economy arising from thirty years of conflict (Bradley and Hamilton 1998).

The border which partitioned Ireland in 1920 was a poor geographical representation of the historic socio-cultural and historical political divisions which had constituted the island as a borderland. Yet, it did have considerable symbolic resonance. It stood for pro-imperial, British, Protestant Ireland against anti-imperial, Catholic nationalist Ireland. It distinguished an advanced industrial economy which had benefited in relative terms from international free trade and imperial preference from a poor, high-emigration, largely agricultural economy which had been deindustrialised in the course of the nineteenth century under the same umbrella of British capitalism. In the last fifty years of the nineteenth century, in part due to famine and mass emigration, the population of Ireland as a whole halved, and slipped from one-third to one-tenth of the total UK population in the same period. Yet in this same period the area that was to become Northern

Ireland retained its population, due to industrial development and the rapid expansion of Belfast.

Borders in three phases of globalisation

All borders and border regions are a product of specific historical situations and the balance of local and regional forces. However, these forces also interact with, and are shaped by, broader processes of social transformation. In this chapter, I will examine the development of the Irish border since 1925 in the context of economic, political and cultural globalisation. Its point of departure is that the creation, maintenance and transcendence of borders is an integral part of globalisation although these processes can only be examined and compared by attention to the details of specific cases.

Despite its recent discovery in the social sciences, globalisation is not a new phenomenon. It involves processes of homogenisation and differentiation, integration as well as fragmentation, bordering as well as de-bordering. While globalisation simultaneously involves economic, political and cultural dimensions, the relative prominence of each dimension varies over time, as does the way these dimensions relate to each other. For the purposes of framing the Irish case, it is possible to crudely identify three overlapping phases of globalisation.

Early nineteenth to early twentieth century

Here globalisation was driven by the territorial aggrandisement and consolidation of great European empires, the US and Japan and by free trade capitalism under British hegemony.[1] Imperial borders were established by superior military force, sometimes in conjunction with dynastic marriage, purchase or voluntary federation. Borders were relatively permeable, however, to the movement of people and commodities (Hirst and Thompson 1995). The Union of Great Britain and Ireland in 1801 clearly belonged to this phase. The whole of Ireland thus became part of the dominant capitalist state of the period. The effect was to destroy traditional rural industry, concentrate urban industrial production in the Belfast region, shift agriculture from an intensive tillage-based economy to an extensive pastoral one, and transform most of the country into a source of cheap agricultural commodities and labour (via mass emigration) for the industrial cities of Britain and America.

1918–1960s

This period, divided into two sub-periods by the Second World War, was characterised by the globalisation and consolidation of the European state form, a prolonged capitalist crisis in the inter-war period and the growing involvement of states in regulating their economies and societies. In Europe the large empires disintegrated, beginning with those defeated in the First World War. National self-determination was legitimated first by the League of Nations, then by the UN, as the central principle of state policy. This meant the de-legitimating of territorial aggrandisement – further confirmed by the defeat of Nazism and fascism. After 1945, there was a slow, if highly regulated, movement back to free trade while overseas empires continued to fragment. Europe entered a period of relative border stability underpinned by the development of the welfare state in Western Europe and state socialism in the East. Ireland was an early portent of the struggle for national self-determination versus attempts to maintain and consolidate Empire. Once the Irish border was established, however, conditions favoured its consolidation.

1960s–present

In this last period, economic and cultural globalisation under US hegemony dominates. State borders continue to proliferate as empires disintegrate, culminating in the collapse of the Soviet empire. Transnational corporations become the engines of economic and cultural globalisation and transnational governance intensifies, most notably with the emergence of the EU. The EU institutionalises the end of inter-state warfare over territory but inter-state hostilities are replaced by a growth of intra-state or internecine conflicts and divisions. Once again, conflict in Ireland was an early portent of transition in Western Europe, as a combination of internal and external social transformations began to challenge the state borders of the preceding period. The Belfast Agreement signed in 1998 provides one possible image of a new transnational order that might ameliorate conflicts over territorial borders and allow for a more democratic and consensual reconfiguration of state borders.

All political borders may be analysed in terms of their creation, maintenance and transcendence. These processes take place simultaneously although it is also possible to identify historical phases which are primarily devoted to one or other of these processes. James Anderson has dealt with the period 1880 to 1925 during which the border partitioning Ireland was created. In this chapter, I will concentrate on two subsequent phases – 1925–1960s when the emphasis was on the maintenance and consolidation of the border, and the period from the 1960s to the present when the emphasis was on transcending the border, a period which culminated in the Belfast Agreement. In neither of these phases was it possible to practise what Connolly (1991, 1994) terms the 'politics of forgetting', i.e. forgetting the coercive circumstances which led to the creation of the border in the first place.

Establishing the border

The Irish border was established in 1920 at a key point of transition from one phase of globalisation to another, at a time when territorial consolidation and territorial aggrandisement as the centralising strategies of the great powers were giving way to another principle, that of self-determination. At the geopolitical level the Irish border was the result of an internal British arbitration of a clash between a movement for national self-determination and forces committed to consolidation of the UK and the British Empire. At local and regional level, it was a product of the capacity to coerce and the unequal resources available respectively to Irish unionists and nationalists.

Ironically, the principle of partition was established by a form of quasi-coup d'état promoted by Ulster unionists in association with their allies in the British army and Conservative party. In March 1914, British army officers in Ireland mutinied and refused to enforce the Home Rule Bill passed through the British parliament. One month later, the Ulster unionist volunteers were armed by the importation of German rifles.[2] The threat to constitutional government in the UK was averted by the outbreak of the Great War. Thousands of Ulster unionists and Irish nationalists joined the British army with different ends in view, one to maintain the Union, the other to see Home Rule implemented. The republican rising in Dublin 1916 eventually mobilised nationalist Ireland behind the banner of separatism and initiated a guerrilla war against British forces in Ireland between 1918 and 1921.

The eventual partition of Ireland was intimately framed by war and coercion, by the exigencies of the Great War and by the guerrilla struggle. In many respects, the establishment of the Irish border spelled a defeat for the main protagonists in the conflict over Irish independence. For Irish unionists it marked a failure to keep the whole of Ireland within the UK, although it was a victory of sorts for Ulster unionists who, with help from powerful allies in the British military and Conservative party, proved capable of controlling the six counties which comprised the new Northern Ireland. It was also a defeat for UK parliamentary democracy which had voted three times between 1886 and 1912 to grant the whole country Home Rule. Irish nationalists failed to achieve either Home Rule or a thirty-two-county Irish republic (Anderson and Goodman 1998, 9–11). They were left with an impoverished, largely rural, if culturally homogeneous, entity comprising twenty-six of the thirty-two Irish counties. Nationalist Ireland was weakened further by the civil war over the Anglo-Irish treaty of 1921 and a new nationalist minority was created within Northern Ireland comprising one-third of the population. These, in turn, were divided between those in the immediate border region who favoured boycotting the new NI institutions and who felt that the border could not endure, and Belfast nationalists who saw themselves as having little option but to defend their interests within the new system (Phoenix 1994).

Consolidating the border

Once established, however, powerful factors ensured that the new border would be successfully maintained and consolidated. First, the external context favoured the consolidation of the boundary. Post-Versailles Europe privileged the principle of national self-determination which allowed the emergence of several small states as successors to the big empires. The Irish Free State progressively established its formal independence through diplomatic means via the British Commonwealth and the League of Nations, culminating in its neutrality in the Second World War.

This had the effect of transforming the Irish border into a fully fledged international boundary, although this was not the intention of the Irish or British signatories to the Anglo-Irish Treaty of 1921.

Much more important in the consolidation of the Irish border, however, was the form of autonomy accorded to Northern Ireland by the British government. While British governments in the 1920s and 1930s wished to retain the whole of Ireland within their sphere of influence, they were committed to distancing the potentially disruptive 'Irish question' from mainstream British politics. Irish nationalist MPs no longer sat in the Westminster Parliament except for a small number from Northern Ireland. The strategy adopted by British political parties was to claim that all Northern Ireland affairs were purely internal to the UK and therefore not a legitimate concern of the Irish Free State. At the same time, the British parliament itself adopted the self-denying ordinance of not intervening in Northern Ireland's 'local affairs'. In effect, the British parliament devolved sovereignty in areas of policing, the judiciary, education, health, housing and social services to the Unionist party. This party was solely representative of the new Protestant majority created by the border and it was to preside over a one-party monopoly rule in Northern Ireland for fifty years, during which Catholics and Nationalists were excluded from nearly all levels of political power at local and regional level. The Ulster Unionist party which had organised armed resistance to the Westminster parliament now had attained majoritarian legitimacy. In effect, the British parliament had devolved administrative power to one ethnic community to exercise control over another.

The relative insulation of Northern Ireland from British and Irish politics meant that the Irish border quarantined or contained within the new political unit all the most antagonistic elements of historic Irish–British relationships – the long history of 'settler' possession and 'native' dispossession, deep-rooted sectarian animosities expressed in the archaic language of the Reformation and class divisions where a working class divided on ethno-religious grounds had little leverage over a unionist industrial bourgeoisie and land-owning class. These divisions and antagonisms festered and were institutionalised within the new statelet. The insulation of Northern Ireland ironically increased the stability of British and Irish politics and made the stabilisation of the Irish Free State achievable. Its cultural and religious homogeneity helped to overcome the legacy of the civil war but strengthened the border from the southern side despite the fact that all Irish governments saw the ending of partition as one of their primary goals.

While the broad contextual conditions favoured the consolidation of the Irish border, its durability still needs to be explained, given that it was an outcome initially desired by none of the principal protagonists in the national conflict. The border itself did not mark a barrier between unionist and nationalist communities. Along its 280-mile length it frequently divided Catholic from Catholic and Protestant from Protestant. It cross-cut 1,400 agricultural holdings, approximately 180 roads and twenty railway lines, bisecting villages and in some cases private houses. It was in large part an invisible line meandering through the countryside following old county boundaries. By European standards it was relatively open.

No passports have ever been required to cross it. The same language is spoken on either side. Sterling and the Irish pound circulated freely in both Irish jurisdictions on the basis of parity until 1979. It did not designate the ownership of any rich mineral deposits, nor did it have much strategic significance except perhaps for a period during the Second World War.

The key to understanding its successful consolidation lies in the overwhelming imbalance in the resources and coercive power of those supporting the border and the weakness and internal divisions of those opposing it (O'Dowd 1994). But more specifically, it privileged an effective politics of territorial control and a somewhat less effective politics of localised resistance. The Irish border enclosed and re-valorised a complex maze of sectarian borders within Northern Ireland, the lineaments of which could be traced back in many cases to the plantations of the seventeenth century. Rural and urban areas were marked by high degrees of Protestant and Catholic residential segregation. Protestant land abutted Catholic land – historically the plantation had not eliminated the 'natives', merely pushed them on to marginal and often poorer land. The pattern was repeated in the Belfast region where the larger and more advanced industrial sites were largely in Protestant areas.

The conflict over Irish Home Rule had led to a highly effective military mobilisation of Ulster Protestants, many of them with British army experience and with leaders who were officers in that army and whose origins were either in the industrial bourgeoisie or the landed aristocracy. The Belfast government effectively mobilised the bulk of the Protestant community after partition. Once the British government handed over effective policing powers to the unionists a local Protestant militia was established to police their Catholic neighbours – a strategy highly effective in the more religiously balanced border areas. This official paramilitary organisation was supplemented by an overwhelmingly Protestant police force directly answerable to unionist ministers and backed by extraordinary emergency powers to put down any signs of nationalist rebellion.

In addition, a sense of responsibility was created among all levels of the Protestant community for 'protecting the state' against the 'disloyal' and disaffected nationalist minority and the perceived threat from the aspirations of the Irish government for a united Ireland. The key to the system was a remarkably decentralised system of over seventy local authorities, many of whom were responsible for administering public housing, education and health services. Where local nationalist majorities existed, as in the border city of Derry, careful electoral gerrymandering engineered Protestant majorities. Nationalist local authorities in the border region were returned to unionist control. Active discrimination against nationalists was practised in housing allocations and public service jobs while unionist employers in the private sector gave preference to Protestants, with active government support (for overviews, see Farrell 1978, Whyte 1990). What was put in place was not a movement to eliminate or displace minority nationalists on a large scale but detailed and coordinated networks of territorial control designed to keep them in their place and protect the unionist state. The effectiveness of this system managed by the Unionist party and the Orange Order was rendered complete by the tacit and practical support of successive British governments until the late 1960s.

The farcical history of the Boundary Commission (Hand 1969) revealed the rejection of any democratic negotiation or local plebiscite to shape the precise course of the border in line with local identities. Instead, all subsequent Northern Ireland elections were turned into plebiscites on the existence of the Irish border, with predictable outcomes, given the built-in two-to-one unionist majority. No incentive now existed for the dominant ethnic group to negotiate with the large Catholic minority when the latter could be so effectively controlled, while at the same time firmly cementing an all-class unionist alliance committed to the state. Nationalists' participation in NI's form of democracy could be understood as a form of 'democratic' acquiescence in their own subordination with little hope of effecting any change in state policy. Even when the benefits of the new arrangements were not so clearly apparent to the Protestant working class, it was possible to stir up sectarian animosities and to fuel old settler fears of being besieged and threatened by 'enemies within' (for a discussion, see O'Dowd 1990). The impact on Irish nationalism and republicanism was twofold. On the one hand, it continued to assert an intensified, if somewhat utopian claim to a united Ireland. On the other hand, resistance erupted spasmodically along the border and in nationalist areas in Northern Ireland. However, this resistance was highly localised, poorly resourced and easily controlled. It was not until the late 1960s that reformist and paramilitary movements were able to mobilise significant transnational attention and support to challenge fundamentally the terms of the partition settlement (Maney 1999).

The durability of the Irish border, then, did not rest on its military defensibility in any obvious sense, nor even on it being a barrier to cross-border interaction at local level. Rather, it marked the effective geographical extent of a remarkably decentralised, yet highly coordinated network of unionist territorial control. The nature of the areas contiguous to the border lent itself to localised and informal methods of control in dispersed rural settlements of relatively poor land, where for many, unionists and nationalists alike, the existence of the border became a new economic resource as the culture of smuggling became endemic.

The primacy accorded by unionists to institutionalising territorial control made it impossible to create a myth of Northern Ireland as a shared historic homeland – rather it was constructed around a central communal fracture. Unionists' own sense of place was also fragmented (Graham 1998) – a fact underlined by their continuous struggle to ideologically claim territory through overtly triumphalist Orange marches intended by many to remind nationalists of the Britishness of Northern Ireland and of the civil wars which led to the establishment of a Protestant British state and the consolidation of the Ulster plantation. Such over-assertion of ideological control, however, suggested a fear of being sold out by Britain or undermined by nationalists in the rest of Ireland.[3] Moreover, from the inception of Northern Ireland, its industrial base was in decline – with temporary reprieves during war-time – and the employment prospects of Protestants, although better than those of Catholics, were far from secure. Instability was not far below the surface.

Offsetting this inherent instability, there were substantial changes in the economy and the state which served to consolidate the state border. The border did not sever the common Britain–Ireland currency zone or labour market, but the general inter-war raising of tariff barriers and growth of protectionism strengthened the border. North–South trade across the border had initially been reduced by Southern nationalist boycotts of Belfast goods in protest against partition, and cross-border trade was further reduced by an 'economic (tariff) war' between the UK and the Irish Free State in the 1930s. Then the Second World War further enhanced the salience of the border: it temporarily revitalised Northern Ireland's flagging industries, particularly shipbuilding and engineering, thus reaffirming contrasts with the still largely agricultural society south of the border.

The salience of the border was also enhanced by changes in the functions and infrastructural power of the two states, particularly the nation- and state-building of the new Irish state from the 1930s, and the restructuring of the British state during and after the Second World War. The South's priority of securing the independence of the new state from the UK also widened the gulf with Northern Ireland (Kennedy 1988). The South's population was overwhelmingly (*c*.90 per cent) Catholic, effectively 'homogenised' by the border; behind it the state itself became sectarian, its new 1937 Constitution explicitly recognising the 'special position' of the Roman Catholic Church, which in practice legitimated political interference by Catholic bishops. This Constitution's ineffectual *de jure* claim to the whole island of Ireland had little practical leverage within Northern Ireland other than to confirm the suspicions of unionist Protestants and reinforce their rejection of any formalised cross-border links. Partitionist attitudes, North and South, were further reinforced in 1949 when the Irish state unilaterally declared itself a Republic outside the British Commonwealth.

Especially after 1945, the improving health, welfare and educational services introduced by the British state in the North widened the gap in living standards with the South; as Mann (1993) notes, such increases in the infrastructural power of states enhance their territorial boundedness. The South experienced economic stagnation and massive out-migration in the period 1945–60. This marked the zenith of the Irish border as an economic divide. Northern living standards were some 30 per cent higher than the South's (whereas today there are indications that Southern living standards may shortly surpass Northern ones – see Bradley and Hamilton 1998, 73).

The Irish border between 1925 and the late 1960s was consolidated during a historical period that might be called the heroic age of the European national state, i.e. when claims to national sovereignty were more all-embracing than ever before and borders most sociologically salient. Because of the status of the UK as a 'great power' and a victorious state in the two world wars, the 'Irish question' was consigned to a backwater in international relations and scarcely rated a mention on the international agenda. However, new forms of economic and cultural globalisation, the transformation of the Irish border into an internal border of the EU, and the capacity of the NI minority to use global networks to mobilise opposition to the 1920 settlement began to radically transcend the Irish border from the late 1960s onwards.

By the time sustained attempts to reach an inclusive settlement began in the early 1990s, the complex comparative implications of the Irish border were clear. On the one hand, it represented an internal border of the EU and as such had begun to be affected by EU-sponsored transfrontier regionalism. On the other hand, its provenance in the post-Versailles period, and its deep ethno-national roots, pointed to its similarities with post-Soviet borders in Eastern Europe where the US and the EU were seeking to mediate and moderate the re-emergence of territorial conflicts which had been suppressed under state socialism.

Challenging and transcending the border

The outbreak of violent conflict in Northern Ireland in the late 1960s was a reminder that the apparent end of inter-state conflict in Western Europe did not necessarily mean the cessation of intra-state conflicts (see Tilly 1990 on the general point). By the 1960s and early 1970s, new forms of globalisation were beginning to 'unsettle' and re-problematise both the state border with the Irish Republic and Northern Ireland's internal ethno-national borders. Some globalising tendencies seemed to promise a new dawn of cross-border cooperation across both borders, but others facilitated conflict and a major challenge to the partition settlement of 1920. Economic and cultural globalisation began to subvert the status quo while political globalisation in the shape of transnational governance was to eventually suggest a possible alternative to the territorial conflict.

Somewhat schematically, it is possible to identify five processes which in different ways challenged existing Irish borders:

1 The post-war extension to Northern Ireland of the centralised British welfare state.
2 The restructuring of the global industrial economy in the 1960s and 1970s and its impact on North–South relationships in Ireland and on NI's internal borders.
3 The impact of cultural globalisation and the global mass media.
4 The trajectory and direct impact of the Northern Ireland conflict.
5 Membership of the EU.

The British welfare state: threatening internal borders

One of the consequences of the Second World War was a considerable development of the British welfare state with an expansion in public expenditure on education, health, social services and housing. The immediate effect of the new welfare system was to strengthen the border between Northern Ireland and an Irish Republic unable to afford this level of social provision. What was challenged first was the quasi-apartheid system of territorial control within Northern Ireland. As a regional government of the UK, the NI administration now had to implement measures it had opposed in the Westminster parliament on ideological grounds. This began to expose a fundamental contradiction between the universalistic basis of the new welfare state and the exclusivist and discriminatory practices geared to maintaining the control of one community over another. In education, for example, there was now pressure to provide free education at primary and secondary level for all pupils, regardless of religion. There was pressure to allocate housing on the basis of individual need rather than according to the exigencies of local political control.

Nationalists were now brought into contact with a much greater range of state administrative sectors. By the 1960s, a more articulate and better educated Catholic middle class had benefited from the new system but were increasingly impatient with the dominant discriminatory politics of territorial control, e.g. electoral gerrymandering at local level, discrimination in housing and jobs, and the activities of the largely unaccountable Protestant paramilitary police. The stage was set for the outbreak of the civil rights protests from the mid-1960s onwards.

Global economic restructuring

New forms of economic globalisation confirmed the long-term relative decline of the British economy, a decline that had been visible in Northern Ireland since its creation (O'Dowd 1995). By the early 1960s a deindustrialising North and a stagnant, predominantly agricultural South were both looking to foreign (especially US) direct investment for economic recovery. The shared prospect of joining the EEC made them more attractive for US corporations, and both states became more active in regional planning and 'growth centre' policies to attract multinational capital (though membership of the EEC was delayed for over a decade). The new geography of incoming foreign direct investment caused major disruption to the long-established sectarian borders, especially in the Belfast Region. It stimulated the dispersal of Catholic and Protestant working-class communities to new housing centres and towns in the Belfast region.[4] The role of the Stormont government in reshaping infrastructure and influencing industrial location provoked renewed nationalist charges of discrimination (O'Dowd *et al.* 1980).

But the new political economy also raised the prospect of cross-border links with the South. Cross-border cooperation was in fact a low priority for both the Belfast and Dublin governments, but, *inter alia*, the problems of modernising both Irish economies created an opening in 1965 for the first meeting of the two Irish Prime Ministers for forty years. A series of meetings ensued involving other politicians, civil servants, and business interests keen to promote North–South trade (Tannam 1999, 49–57).

The Prime Ministerial meetings were Ireland's version of *Ostpolitik*. While they had limited material effects they had enormous symbolic importance. They raised the prospect of 'normalising' the North–South border by establishing formal cross-border links. However, just as transnational investment was challenged the entrenched sectarian boundaries within Northern Ireland, new North–South contacts highlighted the permanent exclusion of nationalists from all levels of political power in the Northern administration. Neither North–South contacts nor hesitant attempts at reducing anti-Catholic discrimination in the North were able to satisfy nationalist demands. At the same time a unionist backlash developed which saw cooperation with the South as undermining the existence of the border. These unionists opposed any concessions to 'disloyal' Catholics, seeing them as a reduction in their own privileges – a typical calculation in the zero-sum language of territorial conflict.

Cultural globalisation and the impact of the mass media

The 1960s student and civil rights protests in the US and Europe provided models for the early NI Civil Rights Movement allowing them access to a political vocabulary of protest and rights that were comprehensible internationally. The pictures of street confrontations spread around the world, ensuring the international publicising of the case being advanced by the minority nationalist community. The latter was now no longer apparently confined to a regional backwater or preoccupied with particularistic grievances. Although Northern Ireland had little strategic significance globally, the Irish diaspora especially in the English-speaking world, the region's accessibility to the outside media and its location in the UK, meant that the conflict became global news. This form of media globalisation was more about images than cognition (Urry 1999).

It was not the specific details, or history, of the Northern Ireland conflict that were newsworthy so much as images which raised the question as to why such violence was occurring in the UK, the world's oldest parliamentary democracy and in a European Community dedicated to ending such conflicts. Unionists interpreted the civil rights campaign as the latest attempt to undermine NI and local security forces, and loyalist mobs reacted violently to peaceful civil rights protests. The violence was captured on television and broadcast around the world. As the crisis deepened, internment without trial was introduced and targeted only at the Catholic community. The Belfast government lost control of the situation and was suspended as the British government imposed direct rule in 1972.

The implications for borders were twofold. First, the global mass media were now encamped in Northern Ireland. The state border no longer served to insulate NI from British and Irish politics or from the rest of the world. The minutiae of 'domestic' politics were illuminated. Secondly, the internal sectarian borders within Northern Ireland were captured nightly on television with pictures of rioting, intercommunal confrontation and police and army responses.

Whereas Northern Ireland scarcely registered on the global agenda for the previous fifty years, from the late 1960s onwards it became a major factory of globalised images. The new mass media relayed highly selective and frequently decontextualised images which nevertheless fused into an overriding sense of deep-rooted, violent conflict. A virtual Northern Ireland was created, on the television screens, and in the printed media, comprising marching, riots, explosions, police brutality, armed and hooded paramilitaries, atrocities, victims, funerals, militant fundamentalist clergy, church burnings, prisons, hunger-strikers and more recently the 'peace process'. These images were not merely projected to 'external' audiences. They were consumed in particular structured ways, and used as mobilising resources, by the protagonists of the conflict in Northern Ireland. They were central to a propaganda struggle which found its most intense form in the struggle between British governments and the republican movement. In the battle of the images, republicans and nationalists generally were able to partially compensate for their lack of power resources relative to the British government and the unionists and proved far more proficient in engaging sympathetic support in Europe and the US (McGarry and O'Leary 1995).

The conflict

British direct rule policy had dual dimensions. First, it implemented a range of reforms in elections, housing and employment practices and made a number of attempts to reconstruct a regional administration based on cross-communal consensus and participation. Reforms were consistently opposed by unionists and frequently rejected by nationalists as inadequate. The second dimension of policy was to contain and suppress the violence. The IRA re-emerged as defenders of Catholic communities against sectarian attack from local security forces and loyalist mobs and gradually shifted to an offensive strategy against the British army and the police. Republicans adopted a dual strategy of enhancing local borders as barriers against attack while seeking to transcend the Northern Ireland border by internationalising the conflict and mobilising support from a range of constituencies in the US, Europe, and the rest of Ireland. The security response from the British government and from unionists was to use the established networks of sectarian borders to police and contain the conflict while asserting that there was an internal British and Northern Ireland solution to the violence. Thus both the inter-state and the internal sectarian boundaries were used as instruments of policing and military control – but they were also used as means of resistance and even attack by republican and loyalist paramilitaries. The result was intensified violence and territorial division, combined with political stalemate.

With the death by hunger strike of ten republican prisoners in 1980–81, political support for Sinn Féin grew, notably in areas contiguous to the Northern Ireland border with the Irish Republic (as well as in Belfast). This was also the scene of regular engagements between the IRA and the NI security forces. The British army accelerated a programme of road closures and military installations along the border which gave it a new material significance. In the late 1980s and early 1990s, there was an ongoing struggle between borderland residents and the British army, with the former regularly reopening roads and the latter closing them (O'Dowd and Corrigan 1996). This struggle coincided with the introduction of the European Single Market and the abolition of border customs posts. The two governments and a growing number of local groups and councils were involved in cross-border cooperation under programmes such as INTERREG. For a time, British policy was caught between a military policy of inhibiting cross-border movement and an economic policy of promoting it. The EU Commission was becoming an important actor on the ground, alongside the US government, in promoting cross-border cooperation.

The impact of the EU and other forms of transnational governance

As the conflict developed, the policy of treating Northern Ireland as an internal British problem became even more unsupportable. Over time, the range of the actors involved in the political arena widened dramatically to include not just the global media but also the Irish government, the European Commission, the European Court of Human Rights, Committees of the UN and the European Parliament, non-governmental organisations concerned with human rights and other governments, notably the US in its support for the Anglo-Irish Agreement of 1985 and its mediation of the peace negotiations in the 1990s.

Joint membership of the EU greatly increased formal inter-governmental contact between the Irish Republic and the UK and this facilitated closer cooperation over Northern Ireland over time. The negotiation of the Belfast Agreement demonstrated the new importance of the transnational dimension to the conflict as the British, Irish and US governments became directly involved. The actual framework of the Agreement owed much, however, to the structure and institutions of the European Union. What emerged was a novel form of transnational governance which recognised, yet transcended, all the territorial borders involved.

The core institutions established in the Agreement (1998) include the following:

- A 108-member Assembly and a ten-person Executive elected proportionately from the Assembly, with Departmental Committees 'with scrutiny, policy development and consultation role' with respect to each Department.
- A North–South Ministerial Council (including Ministers from the NI Executive and the Irish Parliament) which must define six implementation bodies to oversee cooperation on matters of mutual interest as well as six areas of cooperation between existing institutions.
- A British–Irish Council drawing membership from devolved institutions in NI, Scotland, Wales, elsewhere in the United Kingdom if appropriate, the Isle of Man and the Channel Islands. This Council is to operate on the basis of consensus to 'exchange information, discuss, consult and use best endeavours to reach agreement on cooperation of matters of mutual interest within the competence of the relevant Administrations' (1998, 14).
- A British–Irish Intergovernmental Conference, 'with no derogation from the sovereignty of either government' to 'promote bilateral cooperation' and deal with 'all-island and cross-border cooperation on non-devolved issues' such as security.

Apart from these complex and overlapping institutions, the Agreement establishes a Human Rights Commission in Northern Ireland with the Irish government pledging to set up a similar body. A joint committee of both Commissions in envisaged in the Agreement. The British government undertook to complete the incorporation of the European Commission for Human Rights into Northern Ireland law.

Further sites of deliberation and consultation proposed in the Agreement include the NI Civic Forum, with representation from business, trade unions and the voluntary sector. The Agreement also suggests consideration of a North–South parliamentary forum and an independent consultative forum appointed by Northern and Southern administrations drawn from civil society.

What the Agreement proposes, therefore, is a complex, multilevel architecture of overlapping institutions heavily biased towards deliberation, consultation and consensus while preserving British sovereignty in the critical areas of taxation, the budget and policing. However, the clear thrust of the Agreement is that the British government would be willing to devolve more policing powers to the Assembly, if agreement could be found. Similarly, the Irish government and the Northern Ireland administration would extend the areas covered by North–South bodies if similar agreement could be reached.

The new institutions proposed in the Belfast Agreement are premised on the analysis that majoritarianism has largely failed within the territorial boundaries of Northern Ireland. Governing via the majority principle presupposes widespread agreement on political boundaries, on the legitimacy of these boundaries and on the jurisdictional competency of these units – forms of agreement which have been notably absent in NI since its inception.

What the Belfast Agreement proposes is a multiplication of the arenas for deliberative democracy – Northern Ireland representatives would have access to an Assembly, Executive and Associated Committees, to the North–South Ministerial Councils and implementation bodies, to the British–Irish Council, to the British–Irish Governmental Conference, to the Westminster and European parliaments. To these might be added local councils, civic forums, the British–Irish Parliamentary Body and a possible North–South parliamentary forum. This is a formidable multiplicity of forums for 1.5 million people, and it is a manifestation of internationalisation and globalisation as it transcends a variety of territorial borders, state and non-state.

The institutions proposed explicitly recognise the dominance of the communal divide but also allow for the recognition of a variety of groups and parties within each community. They are predicated on a logic of deliberation and argumentation rather than on the logic of instrumental bargaining. As such, they are meant to be a process of opinion-formation which will facilitate or improve decision taking and change or moderate opinions through argument. These institutions are backed up by a panoply of law and administrative procedures, such as the Human Rights and Equality Commissions and the proposed police reforms aimed at ensuring widespread democratic participation. The new Northern Ireland institutions are predicated on 'communicative rationality' (in Habermas's sense of the word). They are not predicated on a single community of memory, communication or experience. Nor are they predicated on a 'final' agreement on territorial state borders (the state border remains a matter for a majority within NI voting in a plebiscite). Dual British and Irish citizenship is to be available to all Northern

Ireland residents regardless of its state boundaries. The proposed institutions recognise that they may change through majority consent and in the meantime they generate a number of deliberative arenas which cross the disputed territorial boundaries and which thereby sideline the zero-sum struggles associated with the violent conflict in NI.

In many ways, the deliberative democracy proposed in the NI Agreement bears the stamp of the deliberative supranationalism which is enshrined in much of the practice of the EU. Through the latter's comitology a premium is put on negotiation, argument and persuasion. As in the case of the NI Agreement, the EU is backed up by a formidable set of legal, administrative and procedural rules. Unanimous decision making is also encouraged in the former with provision for vetoes and qualified majorities in the NI Assembly while the North–South administrative bodies are to operate on the principle of unanimity in the ministerial council.

However, the deliberative democracy of the consociational institutions proposed for Northern Ireland remain enshrined within a British state committed to liberal majoritarianism. As we have seen, this state has reaffirmed its sovereignty over NI in two critical areas – taxation and security. The tradition of parity between Northern Ireland and the rest of UK in universalistic welfare state provisions effectively removes this area also from the Assembly's remit. The decision-taking capacity of the devolved Assembly, therefore, is highly constrained although the prospect of further powers being devolved to it in relation to policing and North–South cooperation is contingent on a high level of cross-communal consensus in Northern Ireland.

Conclusions

The Agreement, therefore, offers no immediate resolution to the conflict over national sovereignty, although it does seek to replace violent conflict by deliberative mechanisms of consensus and consultation that transcend the disputed borders. It also registers that the meaning of national sovereignty is being redefined in the context of negotiation and consultation within the EU and other transnational arenas.

Ideological support for the settlement is more easily justified negatively: all other initiatives have failed. It marks a recognition that the struggle had reached stalemate. More positively, it holds out the prospect of replacing violent conflict with 'peaceful' politics, and provides a framework for encouraging an alternative politics of prioritising cross-border and cross-communal cooperation and socio-economic construction in the context of continued European integration and new devolved administrations in Scotland and Wales (Anderson and Goodman 1998).

The networks established at local authority level in the border region under the aegis of the EU INTERREG initiatives, the EU Peace and Reconciliation fund, and the International Fund for Ireland provide a 'grass-roots' basis for the broader cross-border strategy of the Belfast Agreement. Local cross-border cooperation is also driven by business interests in both parts of Ireland keen to promote the whole of Ireland as a single island economy capable of competing within the Single European Market. Shared all-Ireland interests in areas such as agriculture, tourism, infrastructural development, export promotion and small and medium-sized enterprises provide much of the impetus for cross-border economic cooperation. Largely in spite of the conflict, and sometimes because of it, the depth and range of cross-border networks has greatly increased over the last twenty years. The Irish border is more permeable but it has not disappeared. Indeed, competition for foreign investment and the fact that the border marks a sterling/euro fault line serves to confirm the territorial border rather than transcend it.

The Belfast Agreement has been stalled over critical issues such as policing and weapons' decommissioning. A popular Protestant reaction has resulted in an attempt to reassert territorial control and local sectarian borders in the face of perceived nationalist advance (both political and demographic) and the decline of unionist power. Protests over the loyalists' right to march through a nationalist area in Portadown (Drumcree) now creates an annual flashpoint. There have been sustained street protests against Catholics going to a church in a Protestant area and protests against Catholic schoolchildren attending a school in North Belfast. Similarly, a low-intensity bombing campaign has been directed at Catholics in overwhelmingly Protestant areas. While considerable progress has been made in creating a political framework for a long-term settlement, it still remains threatened by deep communal divisions and by the threat of territorial conflict and fragmentation. Yet, by 2007, despite enhanced support for the more militant parties on either side of the communal divide, the prospects for the restoration of the power-sharing NI Assembly, suspended since 2002, had improved.

The Northern Ireland case has many unique features not replicable in other ethnic or nationalist conflicts. It demonstrates, however, the complex impact of globalisation on such conflicts and the increased difficulty of insulating intra-state conflicts from inter-state and inter-societal relationships. It suggests that national states retain a key role in new and emerging forms of transnational governance and that national sovereignty is being reconstituted in new ways in response to globalisation. More significantly, perhaps, Northern Ireland demonstrates that nationalist and ethnic conflicts over territorial borders are unlikely to go away and that they are now interacting in complex ways with economic, political and cultural globalisation. The Belfast Agreement does signal some new forms of supranational deliberative governance with the potential to marginalise zero-sum territorial conflicts and turn security, identity and economic development into positive-sum issues.

The Irish border now provides a useful test case of whether new forms of democracy can be developed that can provide legitimate rules for renegotiating the meaning of national sovereignty and for the operation of new forms of transnational governance. If successful, perhaps border change can be more peaceful and 'democratic' than it has been in the past.

Notes

1 In this period, the domestic territories of Russia, Germany, Italy and the US expanded considerably, as did the overseas territories of Britain, France, Germany, Italy, Belgium and Japan. These powers assumed territorial control of all of Africa, Australia, most of Asia and much of North America. Just over 300 European sovereigns were represented at the Congress of Vienna in 1814. At the Hague Peace Conference in 1899, only twenty-six states appeared – six of them non-European (Caplow 1998).

2 In the words of Carson, leader of the Ulster unionists, 'before these two events the British government was armed and the Loyalists of Ulster disarmed, and after them, the British government was disarmed and Ulster Loyalists armed' (cited in Gallagher 1957, 100).

3 A settler 'myth of siege' continued to be part of popular Protestant consciousness which was not diminished by the creation of Northern Ireland. This form of consciousness stressed the existence of 'enemies without', i.e. Irish nationalists and potential traitors within the Protestant community as well as entertaining the possibility of being 'sold out' at some stage in the future by the British government (O'Dowd 1990).

4 When violence erupted in the early 1970s, Catholics poured back into west Belfast leaving the new suburban estates and growth centres around the city to Protestants (Darby 1974).

References

Agreement, The: *It's your Decision: Agreement Reached in Multi-Party Negotiations (1998)* Belfast: Northern Ireland Office.

Anderson, J. and Goodman, J. (1998) 'Nationalisms and transnationalism: failures and emancipation', in J. Anderson and J. Goodman. (eds) *Dis/Agreeing Ireland*, London: Pluto Press.

Brady, C. and Gillespie, R. (eds) (1986) *Natives and Newcomers: Essays in the Making of Irish Colonial Society 1534–1641*, Shannon: Irish Academic Press.

Bradley, J. and Hamilton, D. (1998) *Accelerating Growth and Development: Border Effects in Ireland, North and South*, Report prepared for Border Crossings project supported under Measure 3.1 of the EU Special Support Programme for Peace and Reconciliation, administered by Cooperation Ireland, Belfast and Dublin.

Caplow, T. (1998) 'A model for the consolidation and partition of national states', *International Journal of Sociology* 8 (2): 173–181.

Connolly, W. (1991) 'Democracy and territoriality', *Millennium*, Winter: 463–83.

Connolly, W. (1994), 'Tocqueville, territory and violence', *Theory, Culture and Society* 11: 19–40.

Darby, J. (1974) 'Intimidation in housing', Northern Ireland Community Relations Commission, Belfast.

Farrell, M. (1978) *Northern Ireland: The Orange State*, London: Pluto.

Galbraith, J.S. (1960) 'The "turbulent frontier" as a factor in British expansion', *Comp. Stud. Soc. Hist.* 2, 2: 150–168.

Gallagher, F. (1957) *The Indivisible Island: The History of the Partition of Ireland*, London: Victor Gollancz.

Goodman, J. (1998) 'The Republic of Ireland: towards a cosmopolitan nationalism?' in J. Anderson and J. Goodman (eds) *Dis/Agreeing Ireland.*

Graham, B. (1998) 'Contested images of place among Protestants', *Political Geography* 17 (2).

Guelke, A. (1998) 'Northern Ireland: international and North–South Issues', in Crotty, W. and Schmitt, D.E. (eds) (1998) *Ireland and the Politics of Change*, London: Longman.

Hand, G.J. (ed.) (1969) *The Report of the Irish Boundary Commission, 1925*, Shannon: Irish University Press.

Hirst, P. and Thompson, G. (1995) *Globalisation in Question: The International Economy and the Possibilities of Governance*, Oxford: Polity Press.

Jarman, N. (1997) *Material Conflicts: Parades and Visual Displays in Northern Ireland*, Oxford: Berg.

Kennedy, D. (1988) *The Widening Gulf*, Belfast: Blackstaff Press.

McGarry, J. and O'Leary, B. (1995) *Explaining Northern Ireland*, Oxford: Blackwell.

McDonagh, O. (1983) *States of Mind: A Study of Anglo-Irish Conflict*, London: Allen and Unwin.

Maney, G. (2000) 'Transnational mobilization and civil rights in Northern Ireland', *Social Problems*, 47 (2): 153–179.

Mann, M. (1993) 'Nation-States in Europe and other continents: diversifying, developing, not dying', *Daedalus* 122: 115–140.

O'Dowd, L. (1990) 'New Introduction' to A. Memmi, *The Coloniser and the Colonised*, London: Earthscan.

O'Dowd, L. (1994) *Whither the Irish Border? Sovereignty, Democracy and Economic Integration in Ireland*, Belfast: Centre for Research and Documentation.

O'Dowd, L. (1994a) *Negotiating the British/Irish Border: Transfrontier Cooperation on the European Periphery, Final Report to the Economic and Social Research Council* (Grant No. R000 23 3053), ESRC, Swindon.

O'Dowd, L. (1995) 'Development or dependency?: state, economy and society in Northern Ireland', in Clancy, P., Drudy, S., Lynch, K. and O'Dowd, L. (eds) *Irish Society: Sociological Perspectives*. Dublin: Institute of Public Administration, 132–177.

O'Dowd, L. and Corrigan, J. (1996) 'Securing the Irish border in a Europe without frontiers', in O'Dowd, L. and Wilson, T.M. (eds) *Borders, Nations and States: Frontiers of Sovereignty in the New Europe*, Aldershot: Avebury, 117–33.

O'Dowd, L., Corrigan, J. and Moore, T. (1995) 'Borders, national sovereignty and European integration', in *J. Urban Reg. Res*. 19: 272–85.

O'Dowd, L., Rolston, B. and Tomlinson, M. (1980) *Northern Ireland: Between Civil Rights and Civil War*, London: CSE Books.

O'Hearn, D. (1998) *Inside the Celtic Tiger*, London: Pluto.

Phoenix, E. (1994) *Northern Nationalism 1890–1940*, Belfast: Blackstaff Press.

Tannam, E. (1999) *Cross-border Cooperation in the Republic of Ireland and Northern Ireland*, London: Macmillan.

Tilly, C. (1990) *Coercion, Capital and European States*, London: Blackwell.

Urry, J. (1999) 'Globalisation and Citizenship', *Journal of World Systems Research* 5 (2), 311–324 (accessible at: http://jwsr.ucr.edu).

Whyte, J.H. (1990) *Interpreting Northern Ireland*, Clarendon Press: Oxford.

3 Europeanisation, identity and policy in the Northern Ireland borderlands

Thomas M. Wilson

Europeanisation is a term which is increasingly being used in the scholarship of the European Union (EU), and perhaps even among policy-makers within the institutions of the EU, but there has been a distinct lack of coherence among the methods, hypotheses and theories which have been brought to bear in the name of Europeanisation within EU studies. In fact the concept itself has a variety of meanings across academic disciplines. Sociologists and anthropologists have been at the forefront of attempts to examine Europeanisation and identification with 'Europe' as processes, which are much broader than political and economic adaptations to EU institutions and policies (see, for example, Abélès 1993, Giordano 1987, Hedetoft 1994, Kohl 2000, Tarrow 1994, Ray 2001, Weiss and Wodak 2000).

This chapter focuses on the social anthropology of Europeanisation and EU integration, but this review is suggestive of changes in the scholarship of Europeanisation in other social science disciplines. As a result of the growth in studies of European culture and identity, there is a small but growing anthropological attention to ways in which Europeanisation interacts with the processes of regionalism, deterritorialisation, transnationalism and globalisation. Some of this anthropological interest has been directed at social and political ideas and movements which either strengthen or weaken state power, and sometimes do so simultaneously, both within the EU and among peoples beyond its borders. However, there have been few ethnographic studies to date which relate Europeanisation to the forces of internationalisation and globalisation as they are realised in the everyday lives of local communities in the EU's twenty-five member states. And, as pointed out in the provocative overview on European identity presented by Martin Kohl at the ESA meetings in Amsterdam in 1999, analyses of European identity have relied on nation-state models of national territorial identification, with little attention paid to alternative identities or identifications, whether they be complementary or contradictory. In the discourse on European identity, there is for instance no reference to the distinction between levels of structural complexity of identification and of the conditions under which these are likely to prevail, or to the possibility of ambivalent and hybrid identity patterns (Kohl 2000, 117).

This chapter, based on a longstanding field project, seeks to set out, in rough terms, how these processes might be viewed in a small village on the Republic of Ireland–Northern Ireland (UK) border, and by implication to begin a discussion of some of the methodological difficulties involved in studying Europeanisation as something more than just 'top-down' European policy-making, and/or national and regional institutional adaptation to this EU-led policy process. In so doing, I hope to initiate an examination of Europeanisation as a form of internationalisation of culture, a European version of national and regional acculturation, if you will, which might very well throw into stark relief this process as a European variant of globalisation at work.

Almost by definition, this project must also focus on the methodological problems inherent in attempting to both 'study up' and 'study down', i.e. by tracing EU-related policy and practice both within and beyond the limits of the village. The paper's conclusions suggest that, at least in this one small corner of Europe, Europeanisation is perceived more as a process of economic and political internationalisation and statecraft than as an element of wider cultural globalisation and supranational integration.

What is 'Europeanisation'?

The most useful treatment of Europeanisation outside of the disciplines of political science and international relations is at present that of Borneman and Fowler (1997), who while evading a concrete definition of the process, instead provide a virtual definition by discussing ways in which the process is a force for the transformation of European society and culture, and one which has various historical and contemporary dimensions. They describe Europeanisation as 'an accelerated process and a set of effects that are redefining forms of identification with territory and people' (1997, 489), which they seek to disentangle from more essentialising notions of modernisation, development, and European integration within the EU. In fact, in their conclusion they suggest that it would be more fruitful to consider Europeanisation as 'a spirit, a vision, and a process', and the EU as 'a continental political unit of a novel order' (1997,511).

In this chapter, I in no way wish to dispute these notions. Europeanisation is certainly a process of making things and people 'more European', not least in those aspects of everyday life and culture which Borneman and Fowler identify: language, tourism, sex, sport, and money. All of these things are important in quotidian life at the Northern Ireland border, but at that border, as at others, it is often difficult to pinpoint what, if anything, is 'European', and how do we measure the ways border people become 'more European', if we can at all.

This essay seeks to delineate, in some small ways which are based on my research in one modest corner of Europe, difficulties which I and other ethnographers elsewhere face in our attempts to articulate this process of Europeanisation, without an almost complete reliance on the discourse of European integration. Borneman and Fowler were also clear on this point: it is all but impossible to unpack Europeanisation from European integration. But if this is so, how can we understand European integration and its role or impact in localities of Europe? One way is to study European policy effects, i.e. those of direct EU subvention, as well as the effects of national and regional policy adaptations to the EU as a new and super-ordinate level of political and economic integration in Europe. This, of course, also means that there will be a new level of social and cultural integration, a development that clearly invites sociological and anthropological attention, but this is a perspective on European integration, which is not universally shared by scholars in our cognate disciplines.

To return to Borneman and Fowler's notions of Europeanisation for a moment, and their usefulness to social scientists who are interested in the intersections of nation, state, identity and sovereignty aside, this approach to Europeanisation is one of the least utilised and understood in both European integration studies (largely dominated by political scientists) and in the jargon and other discourses of internationalisation, globalisation and European integration in the everyday lives of Europe. At least, this is how it looks to me from the perspective of local society in Ireland, and how it looked to my colleague Robert Harmsen and I when we attempted to identify and compare the various definitions of Europeanisation which inform the wider social science of the EU, and the EU's impact on Europe as a continental if not global system. In an essay recently published in the *Yearbook of European Studies*, Harmsen and I (2000) identified eight definitions of Europeanisation, only two of which are based on the intellectual interests and methods of anthropology and sociology. These definitions seem to fall into four roughly drawn categories.

Europeanisation as the emergence of new forms of European governance

Europeanisation in this sense is very much focused on the European Union. The emphasis here is placed on the ways in which European integration has led to redefinitions of the conceptions, relations and structures of power at both the national and the supranational levels. This usage of the term emphasises the socialisation potential of institutions – highlighting the extent to which participation in permanent institutional structures leads to longer-term redefinitions of actor interests and self-perceptions. Europeanisation of this type draws attention to the EU's efforts at 'polity-building', and the extent to which the EU has been able to move beyond the formulation of joint and common policies to the creation of a genuine 'public space'. This, in turn, focuses attention on the emergence and development of an EU citizenship.

Europeanisation as national adaptation

Europeanisation here refers to the adaptation of national institutional structures and policy-making processes in response to the development of European integration. Ladrech (1994, 70) has provided a widely cited definition of Europeanisation in this vein as 'an incremental process reorienting the direction and shape of politics to the degree that EC political and economic dynamics become part of the organisational logic of national politics and policy-making'. The central questions of such studies wonder whether the domestic institutions of the member states are becoming more alike one another, and whether a common European model of governance is emerging.

Europeanisation as modernisation

Europeanisation here is applied in the context of the more geographically peripheral and less economically developed member states of the European Union. It is taken to imply a series of structural transformations intended to bring these countries back into the European mainstream, defined with reference to the economic and political models which prevail in the more prosperous and influential 'core' countries. As seen from the periphery, this type of Europeanisation becomes a process of assimilation with the European Union core, in which the extent of political choice and discourse is progressively limited. This approach to Europeanisation concerns the processes of EU enlargement, and it applies to the adoption by the Central and East European member states of a West European state model.

Europeanisation as the reconstruction of identities

The fourth type of Europeanisation brings us back to the more familiar anthropological interest in the reconstruction of identities. This is the broadest usage of the term and refers to the reshaping of identities in contemporary Europe in a manner which relativises (without necessarily supplanting) national identities. Borneman and Fowler (1997, 487) have put forward an influential definition of Europeanisation in this sense, seeing it as 'a strategy of self-representation and a device of power', which is 'fundamentally reorganising territoriality and peoplehood, the two principles of group identification that have shaped the modern European order'. Europeanisation from this perspective must focus on the issues of culture and identity, both in terms of culture as a European Union project (Shore 1993), and in terms of the ways in which EU policy has an impact on, and interacts with, local forms of political and cultural identification throughout the member states (Wilson 2000). The studies of this type of Europeanisation, which perhaps have had the widest impact across disciplinary boundaries, have been of the redefinition and negotiation of identities within EU institutions, among the architects of the integration project itself (see, for example, Abélès 1993; Bellier 1997; McDonald 1996; Shore 1997; for an overview of the social anthropology of the EU, see Bellier and Wilson 2000).

Europeanisation in the Northern Ireland borderlands

This chapter is based on ongoing research at the eastern end of the Republic of Ireland–United Kingdom land border, in Northern Ireland. This project seeks to examine the role which European Union policy plays in the wider processes of Europeanisation at this contested border. Its specific focus is on the ways in which local nationalism and national identity interact with two key processes of EU-inspired Europeanisation, namely increased transnational and cross-border communication and commerce in the everyday lives of EU citizens, and EU Regional and Cohesion Policies, which are intended to further the EU's goals of economic integration and political union among its twenty-seven member states through regional economic development. The project derives in large part from previous work I have done there, whose conclusions suggest that EU initiatives to remove the barriers to the free flow of people, goods, capital and services across its internal borders, in a so-called 'Europe Without Frontiers', have not properly addressed the potential obstacles of local and national culture and identity. My research concerns the impact of three EU development programmes in a small border community, which has been particularly successful in attracting European funding, in order to explore how nationalism and British state centralisation in Northern Ireland converge, and sometimes conspire, to resist the institutions and processes of European integration.

Anthropology, which has long concentrated on the violence and sectarianism of urban Northern Ireland, has been slow to chronicle the changes that the New Europe of the EU has been effecting there (Wilson 1998a). The need to keep pace with the new Northern Ireland of today has been made all the more urgent since the Good Friday Agreement of 1998, in which for the first time in a generation the politicians of both sides in their ethno-national struggle have agreed a plan for the return to peaceful politics. The tensions which inscribe everyday life in the province, as well as the potential for EU-supported economic and political development, are part of the cultural topography of South Armagh, along the border with the Irish Republic.

The Irish border, which partitioned Ireland in 1920, is 360 kilometres long and separates the twenty-six counties of the Republic of Ireland from the six counties of Northern Ireland. County Armagh, south-west of Belfast, Northern Ireland's capital, is ethnically divided between its Protestant population, who inhabit much of the county's northern half, and its Catholic population, who are the majority in the southern reaches of the county, which extend from the urban centres of Armagh and Newry to the border. This small region is known as South Armagh, and it is renowned throughout Ireland as one of the principal bastions of Irish republicanism, the political movement which seeks the reunification of the Irish nation and state, and which through the organisation of the Provisional Irish Republican Army (IRA) has waged a war since 1969 to achieve this goal. (This war is on hold today, although the armed struggle is being carried on by the growing movements of splinter republican groups, the Real IRA and the Continuity IRA.)

South Armagh is almost entirely Catholic (over 90 per cent of the population) and Irish nationalist, and comprises small villages, a few market towns, and many outlying farms. It is one of the most peripheral areas of Northern Ireland, both economically and socially. South Armagh is also infamous in British media and government circles as 'bandit country' because of the strong support there for the

IRA, and because of British perceptions that 'frontier' conditions of lawlessness and violence survive there.

I have done research intermittently in South Armagh since 1991. This fieldwork has concentrated on the effects in the region of the completion of the EU Single European Market on cross-border economic cooperation (Wilson 1995). One of the conclusions reached in this research was that the EU programme to establish a common market (as symbolised by the date '1992', when the single European market was to have been realised) created many new cross-border economic relations. Nevertheless, it had a negligible effect on local attitudes towards closer political, social and cultural integration, both between the two communities of the province, and between Northern Ireland and its neighbours. The resistance in South Armagh to EU attempts to do anything beyond the strictly economic is significant in terms of EU efforts to foster an affective dimension to its Europe-building. Moreover, it may have much to tell us of the role which nationalism and strong national identities may play within the wider processes of Europeanisation in a EU which may approach a membership of thirty countries within the decade.

Recent transformations in the political and economic climate of the region may yet change this picture. The warring sides have held to a ceasefire for over six years. The British government has approved plans for regional devolution, which in Northern Ireland has resulted in the creation of an Assembly, the first self-government in almost twenty years. As part of this new institutional arrangement, there are now North–South consultative government bodies, in six areas of policy, whose members are nominated by the NI Assembly or the Irish government. The Irish economy has grown so fast that it is now known as the 'Celtic Tiger', and its success has made many recalcitrant unionist businessmen reconsider their opposition to cross-border economic development. And the EU has created new funding initiatives for its poorest regions, in a renewed effort to use its policy frameworks to remove regional disparities as one way to create a sense of its legitimacy in the lives of its citizens (Armstrong 1995). Three of these initiatives, INTERREG (cross-border cooperation), LEADER (rural development), and the Northern Ireland Support Programme for Peace and Reconciliation (a cross-community initiative designed solely for Northern Ireland), have been targeted at South Armagh, among other areas in Northern Ireland. These initiatives have now completed two full rounds of funding, and while the full effects of these inputs of capital are not yet clear, it is apparent that major political and economic investments have been made in the region which will influence the strategies that local and regional actors employ to acquire funding in future EU funding cycles.

The community in which I investigate the intersection of European and national policies, and wider notions of Europeanisation, is 'Whitehill' (a pseudonym), situated midway between the towns of Newry and Crossmaglen, about six kilometres from the Irish border. It has a population of 3000 (850 households) within its parish limits, which covers both the village and outlying farms. All but a few people identify themselves as Catholic and Irish. Support for Irish nationalism, including republicanism, is high. The community is also known locally for its success in attracting European funding. Three projects in particular represent the confluence of culture and nationalism that mark local economic development projects, particularly in regard to tourism, sport and education. The Whitehill Trekking Centre, the Ring of Cooley Culture Centre, and the Whitehill Folk Museum (these names are also pseudonyms) have used combinations of international funding and state support to both attract international tourists and to establish cultural links across the Irish border; all represent attempts to create forms of cultural integration that have not existed in this border region for generations. There is considerable overlap of personnel and leadership among these three centres, yet my preliminary research in this area indicates that the leadership of each cultural centre demonstrates divergent views of European integration and policy, as influenced by such factors as kinship, language, education, class, and national identity.

EU funding programmes

Fieldwork in Whitehill commenced in May 2001. Previous research on European funding in the wider region of South Armagh allows me to suggest some tentative conclusions regarding the overall effectiveness of the policies and processes of Europeanisation and European integration in this peripheral area of Northern Ireland.

A detailed review of the origin, structures, aims and objectives of the three European policies which have had a direct impact on local Irish border communities are beyond the scope of this chapter, but their overall dimensions need to be sketched. INTERREG, the main EU fund specifically geared to cross-border and border region economic development, has had a rather unsuccessful time in this region (as outlined in Wilson 2000), due in large part to the centralisation and bureaucratisation of the programme in both Dublin and Belfast (which are 90 and 50 miles away respectively, but more socially and administratively distant than this geography implies). Suffice to say that while communities like Whitehill have received substantial subvention from INTERREG, funds received must always be matched to other sources of capital, and are for large-scale, high-profile enterprises (like the 'Ring of Cooley' Irish heritage and culture centre in Whitehill).

LEADER, the rural development initiative, has fifteen local intermediary agencies in Northern Ireland, termed 'local action groups' (LAGs). These groups are a partnership of public and private bodies, which jointly devise and implement a strategy and a series of innovative measures for the development of a coherent rural area. This is in aid of avoiding some of the problems which beset INTERREG; as a result, LEADER II (funding round 1994–1999) was intended to be an area-based approach (rather than national or regional), and a bottom-up approach (rather than a governmental or administrative top-down one), which entailed cooperation among local organisations in the public and private sectors in order to develop a coherent rural development plan with local, regional, national and transnational networking. The LAG in South Armagh is the South Down South Armagh Local Action Group, which had an operational budget of £1 million in the last cycle. Fully 75% of this money had been spent by the end of 1999, in a wide range of seed grants, capital investments, and locally based rural development schemes, particularly in aid of farm pluri-activity, tourism, cross-border networking and sharing of resources, and international marketing. The farmers of South Armagh clearly see the impact of LEADER on their lives, or if not themselves than on their neighbours.

The Northern Ireland Programme for Peace and Reconciliation, known locally as the 'Peace Programme' or 'Peace Money', was designed specifically by the European Commission for Northern Ireland, but its relative success there has led the EU to consider it as a blueprint for other such special funding initiatives. It was conceived as a truly bottom-up approach to addressing, if not solving, the problems of cross-community (i.e. Catholic–Protestant, or Irish–British) relations, in a way which makes concrete the aims of the EU principle of 'subsidiarity'. Yet it has such a complex system of interlocking local and intermediate funding providers, including each of the local district councils, that again the local and national politics of Northern Ireland act as severe buffers to the realisation of the programme, either from the perspective of the EU or from the standpoint of local actors. Nevertheless, the programme has injected almost a million pounds of capital into the South Armagh region, and has been the most publicised and most warmly received of all the programmes, precisely because it has been projected as a Northern Ireland-only scheme, targeted at local community social and economic welfare.

It is premature at this stage of my research to say much about the strengths and weaknesses of each of these programmes as they have been implemented in the Armagh borderlands, but it can be concluded that they have all supported in varying ways local initiatives in tourism, agricultural efficiency and marketing, local community cultural programmes, and local, regional and transnational networking. Yet they have done little either to foster an awareness of political identification beyond the nation and state, or to engender or enhance 'Europeanisation', whether defined as a process of adapting to the EU in ways more than economic, or as a process of transnational cultural integration allied to parallel processes of deterritorialisation, globalisation and regionalisation. In South Armagh, 'European identity' is all but non-existent, and political agendas are mainly about supporting or subverting the nation and state. This relative absence of identification with Europe has even been the case among farmers (long held in Ireland to be among the most pro-European groups), and is absent even as an important alternative or complement to national identity, in what might be termed elsewhere as a 'creolised' or 'hybrid' identity formation (as proposed for border peoples by Kohl (2000)). While many farmers and a number of local professionals are certainly aware of a wider political and economic world beyond Ireland, of which they are part and which might usefully be regarded as 'Europe', many of whom support European integration, they do not own up to being or feeling European.

While processes of internationalisation are taking root, in that more tourists come to Northern Ireland from over the border, and the new Northern Ireland Assembly has new statutory bodies in common with the Irish Republic's parliament, these are not perceived in local terms to be aspects of either Europeanisation or European integration. While they may very well fit our models of processes beyond the limits recognised by the actors themselves, processes such as Europeanisation and transnationalism, one of the concerns I raise here – and it is a concern expressed to me by many people I have interviewed in Armagh – is that we researchers must be wary of enticements to impose theoretical order on a cultural reality which will have no truck with what we academics wish to see in evidence. Simply put, locals certainly perceive aspects of Europeanisation and European integration in their border areas and in the wider domain of Northern Ireland and Ireland, but to them these are negligible forces in everyday life when they are compared to the dominating orders of nationalism and state and local practice.

As one Automobile Association representative said to me at the side of the road after getting my car started, 'Sure, all the cars have to be up to spec according to the rules of the Common Market, or whatever you call it, but that will never stop people around here buying, selling and driving in the Northern Ireland way'.

Conclusion

Martin Kohl, in his presidential address to the European Sociological Association meetings in Amsterdam in 1999, presented an overview of European identity, which was published as 'Battlegrounds of European Identity' (2000). This essay considers a number of interesting hypotheses, but two are particularly relevant to my discussion here. As mentioned above, Kohl suggests that for European identity to succeed it would have to be based on alternative identities to national ones, i.e. those of nation-state, and that European borderlands might provide excellent venues for the study of multiple, hybrid, creolised, alternative identity formations – experimental sites, perhaps, for the formation of new forms of Europeanness.

He does not say that borderlands are the only sites of such hybrid identity formation. There are of course such developments among migrants in a host of locations, and in transnational institutions like corporations, NGOs, and the UN, for example. However, Kohl also seems to put forward the rather simple notion that borderland people have more occasion and need to adapt to other peoples and identities, an assertion that the sizeable literatures on globalisation, deterritorialisation and post-national identities dispute. Two provocative hypotheses might be distilled from this approach:

1. European identity must be based on something other than the national.
2. Borderlands are one of the few principal arenas within which a European identity might take root.

If these are in any way interesting hypotheses, and I of course suggest that they are, then how do they relate to the related process of Europeanisation, and the overall impetus of European integration? Borneman and Fowler (1997) theorise that Europeanisation is a process and a spirit, which must be kept analytically distinct from EU integration, although many of the forces that drive it emanate from EU institutions and policies. In their view Europeanisation is a strategy of self-representation and power, which is fundamentally reorganising territoriality and identity. They go on to suggest that there are five practices of Europeanisation in everyday life, which ethnographers might fruitfully study: language, money, tourism, sex and sport.

This perspective provides a valuable complement to the growing social anthropology of the EU, which has focused on two related themes (Wilson 1998b): the analysis of EU institutions and policy in the centres of EU decision-making (see, for example, Abélès 1993, Bellier 1997, Shore 1993), and the investigation of local community adaptation to the EU as a new level of governance and a new source of culture (see, for example, Herzfeld 1992, Jaffe 1993, Shutes 1991). Less prominent in these studies has been the EU's role in the deterritorialisation of its member states (Borneman 1998), the supranational assault on state and national sovereignty (Hedetoft 1994), and the weakening of the ties between citizen and state (Wilson 1996). Although these forms of international disorder are often obscure, in part because the state continues to be the strongest structure of power in Europe, scholars have increasingly sought their clarification at international borders (Wilson and Donnan 1998), where transnational relations often elide with state policies in stark ways. The confluence of local attempts to either champion or oppose the state as the arbiter of national order, on the one hand, and supranational forces which upset what many Europeans might consider to be the traditional balance between nation and state on the other, is apparent on the Northern Ireland side of the land border between Ireland and the UK.

The research I have conducted in this border region is an attempt to explore the impact of EU policy and Europeanisation on local national identity, nationalism, and sectarianism, as one way to test local responses to EU attempts to foster identification with the EU, especially in the forms of a common European identity and citizenship. In the Whitehill component of this wider study, I seek to examine the origins and evolution of successful local strategies in the acquisition of state and European development funds. The overall goal is simple in conception but (as might be inferred from this chapter) difficult in operation, namely, to identify the EU's role in Europeanisation in this borderland, in terms of two related dimensions: the removal of barriers to cross-border economic development and cooperation, and the intended increase in cross-border cultural integration, in such areas as tourism, sport, education and consumerism.

At this stage, two things are clear. European funding mechanisms have helped to create a 'culture of European funding', in which the EU is seen principally, and in some cases solely, as a financial resource, with little role to play in national and regional politics and social relations. And while EU initiatives, both economic and otherwise, support the international flow of goods, capital, services and people, thus having some direct effects on structures and relationships which bear on notions of money, sex, language, sport and tourism, the transnational or post-national aspects of such processes remain superficial. At least in this one small corner of Europe, territorialisation, sovereignty, citizenship and identity still reside firmly on the level of the national.

References

Abélès, Marc (1993) 'Political anthropology of a transnational institution: the European Parliament. *French Politics and Society* 11 (1): 1–19.

Abélès, Marc (2000) 'Virtual Europe', in *An Anthropology of the European Union: Building, Imagining and Experiencing the New Europe*, Irène Bellier and Thomas M. Wilson (eds) Oxford: Berg.

Armstrong, Harvey W. (1995) 'The role and evolution of European Community regional policy', in *The European Union and the Regions*, Barry Jones and Michael Keating (eds) Oxford: Clarendon Press.

Bellier, Irène (1997) 'The Commission as an actor: an anthropologist's view', in *Participation and Policy-making in the European Union*, Helen Wallace and Alasdair R. Young (eds) Oxford: Clarendon Press.

Bellier, Irène and Thomas M. Wilson (eds) (2000) *An Anthropology of the European Union: Building, Imagining and Experiencing the New Europe*, Oxford: Berg.

Borneman, J. (1992) *Belonging in the Two Berlins*, Cambridge: Cambridge University Press.

Borneman, J. (1998) *Subversions of International Order*, Albany: State University of New York Press.

Borneman, John and Nick Fowler (1997) 'Europeanisation Annual', *Review of Anthropology* 26: 487–514.

Curtin, Chris, Hastings Donnan and Thomas M. Wilson (1993) 'Anthropology and Irish urban settings', in *Irish Urban Cultures*, Chris Curtin, Hastings Donnan and Thomas M. Wilson, (eds) Belfast: Queen's University Institute of Irish Studies Press.

Donnan, Hastings, and Thomas M. Wilson (1999) *Borders: Frontiers of Identity, Nation and State*, Oxford: Berg.

Giordano, Christian (1987) 'The "Wine War" between France and Italy: ethno-anthropological aspects of the European Community', *Sociologia Ruralis* 27: 56–66.

Grillo, R.D. (1980) '"Introduction', in *'Nation' and 'State' in Europe: Anthropological Perspectives*, R.D. Grillo (ed.) London: Academic Press.

Harmsen, Robert and Thomas M. Wilson (2000) 'Introduction: approaches to Europeanisation', in *Europeanisation: Institutions, Identities and Citizenship*, Robert Harmsen and Thomas M. Wilson (eds) *Yearbook of European Studies Volume 14*, Amsterdam: Rodopi.

Hedetoft, Ulf (1994) 'National identities and European integration "from below": bringing people back in', *Journal of European Integration* 17 (1): 1–28.

Herzfeld, Michael (1992) *The Social Production of Indifference: Exploring the Symbolic Roots of Western Bureaucracy*, Oxford: Berg.

Jaffe, Alexandra (1993) 'Corsican identity and a Europe of peoples and regions', in *Cultural Change and the New Europe*, Thomas M. Wilson and M. Estellie Smith (eds) Boulder and Oxford: Westview Press.

Kohl, Martin (2000) 'The battlegrounds of European identity', *European Societies*, 2 (2): 113–137.

Ladrech, Robert (1994) 'Europeanisation of domestic politics: the case of France', *Journal of Common Market Studies* 32 (1): 69–88.

McDonald, Maryon (1996) 'Unity in diversity: some tensions in the construction of Europe', *Social Anthropology* 4: 47–60.

Ray, Christopher (2001) 'Transnational cooperation between rural areas: elements of a political economy of EU rural development', *Sociologia Ruralis* 41 (3): 279–95.

Shore, Cris (1993) 'Inventing the "people's Europe": critical approaches to European Community "cultural policy"', *Man* 28: 779–800.

Shore, Cris (1997) 'Governing Europe: European Union audio-visual policy and the politics of identity', in *Anthropology of Policy: Critical Perspectives on Governance and Power*, Cris Shore and Susan Wright (eds) London: Routledge.

Shutes, Mark (1991) 'Kerry farmers and the European Community: capital transitions in a rural Irish parish', *Irish Journal of Sociology* 1: 1–17.

Tarrow, Sidney (1994) *Rebirth or Stagnation? European Studies after 1989*, New York: Social Science Research Council.

Verdery, Katherine (1995) *National Ideology under Socialism*, Berkeley: University of California Press.

Weiss, Gilbert and Ruth Wodak (2000) 'Debating Europe: globalisation rhetoric and European Union unemployment policies', in *An Anthropology of the European Union: Building, Imagining and Experiencing the New Europe*, Irène Bellier and Thomas M. Wilson (eds) Oxford: Berg.

Wilson, Thomas M. (1995) 'Blurred borders: local and global consumer culture in Northern Ireland', in *Marketing in a Multicultural World*, J.A. Costa and G.J. Bamossy (eds) London: Sage.

Wilson, Thomas M. (1996) 'Sovereignty, identity and borders: political anthropology and European integration', in *Borders, Nations and States: Frontiers of Sovereignty in the New Europe*, L. O'Dowd and T.M. Wilson (eds) Aldershot: Avebury.

Wilson, Thomas M. (1998a) 'Themes in the anthropology of Ireland', in *Europe in the Anthropological Imagination*, Susan Parman (ed.) Upper Saddle River, NJ: Prentice-Hall.

Wilson, Thomas M. (1998b) 'An anthropology of the European Union, from above and below', in *Europe in the Anthropological Imagination*, Susan Parman (ed.) Upper Saddle River, NJ: Prentice-Hall.

Wilson, Thomas M. (2000) 'The obstacles to European Union regional policy in the Northern Ireland borderlands', *Human Organization* 59 (1): 1–10.

Wilson, Thomas M. and Hastings Donnan (eds) (1998) *Border Identities: Nation and State at International Frontiers*, Cambridge: Cambridge University Press.

4 Creating border space in Ireland

An EU approach to ethno-national threat and insecurity

Cathal McCall

All border towns bring out the worst in a country.

Orson Welles, *Touch of Evil* (1958)

Introduction

In the European Union (EU), contemporary global narratives of threat and insecurity are compounded by the interrelated fears of post-Enlargement mass migration and economic downturn, as well as ethno-national conflicts that percolate through the process of European integration. In dealing with ethno-national threat and insecurity the EU has employed a number of options. One option has been to wield 'soft power', such as establishing conditions for accession to the EU, including those concerned with the protection of minorities, in the 1993 Copenhagen European Council.[1] Another option has been to engage with 'the idea of peacebuilding from below' (Ramsbotham *et al.* 2005, 217–21). The EU Peace programmes for Ireland – Peace 1 (1994–1999) and Peace II (2000–2006) – represented a sophisticated and sustained approach to ameliorating ethno-national conflict from below.[2] As such, they serve as a precedent for a local-level approach to ameliorating other real and potential European ethno-national border conflicts. The promotion of cross-border cooperation and the creation of a transnational border space for addressing the threats and insecurity intrinsic to such conflict are important elements in this approach.

In this chapter, it is argued that the transformation of a border from barrier to bridge via cross-border cooperation can help to create a useful transnational border space in which pivotal perceptions of threat emanating from 'the other side' may be tackled. In doing so, this transformation of a border provides an important element in the EU approach to ethno-national conflict regulation and resolution. Border towns and communities are considered as potential transnational spaces for addressing perceptions and narratives of threat and insecurity rather than primary sites for the perpetuation of conflict and for 'bringing out the worst in a country'. However, if the border as barrier is perceived to be crucial for security in the face of multifarious threats, and the border as bridge perceived to be potentially dangerous, then the transformation of the border and the creation of a transnational border space may be resisted. Resistance to such a transformation is especially likely to come from an ethno-national group for whom the narratives of threat and insecurity are fundamental to its political culture and are intimately associated with the border. The chapter attempts to examine cross-border cooperation and the creation of a transnational border space in relation to such an ethno-national group – the Ulster Protestant unionist community in Northern Ireland.

Borders and (in)security

The post-2001 narratives of threat and insecurity have given rise to a political and media fix on the notion of borders as security barriers. Paradoxically, the 1960s heralded the process of contemporary globalisation with major implications for the protectionist quality of modern state territorial borders. Globalisation is the catchword typically used to encapsulate the breaking down of the inhibiting effects of time, space and borders in the contexts of the movement of goods, services, capital (including labour), and knowledge (Stiglitz 2002, 9). Globalisation also describes a concomitant deterritorialisation of social relations and their restructuring in developing political and economic spaces (Giddens 1990, 21). Consequently, the process of contemporary globalisation has important implications for secure territorial borders and a monopoly of violence invested in the modern state (Tilly 1990). Global information flows, the global movement of capital, global media and culture, the global proliferation of terrorism under the spurious umbrella of Islamic jihad, as well as the military adventures of neo-imperial powers are the dominant global phenomena that appear to traverse modern state territorial borders with relative ease.

One response of nation-state governments to globalisation has been to reorder international political and economic space in an effort to wrest back some control (Brunn 1999). The EU is perhaps the most advanced product of this reordering. The creation of the Single European Market and the adoption of the single currency by twelve of the then fifteen EU member states at the beginning of 2002 were important staging posts in the replacement of independent European trading nations with an EU corporate economic space (Rumford 2002, 19). Member states have also relinquished a substantial measure of legal sovereignty to the 'supranational' EU level but the extent to which political sovereignty has been transferred from member states to the EU is hotly disputed.

However, what is not in dispute is that the EU represents an extension of economic and political space beyond the territorial borders of the member states (Rosamond 1999, 666–7; Shaw 1999, 583–7; Wallace 1999, 503–6 and 511–12). Interdependence, inclusion, accommodation and consent have been the political principles of the EU as it strives to develop an advanced transnational economic and political space designed to meet the contemporary challenges that are presented by global economics and the threat of political instability.[3] Member states have either embraced or acquiesced in the process of European integration in order to: prevent a repeat of interstate war in Europe; improve European competitiveness in the global economy; and, for some member state governments at least, build on EU social provisions.

Despite these transnational developments, territorial state borders remain synonymous with the exercise of social and political power. As such, they represent the physical parameters of possession, protection and exclusion that can provoke emotions of love, hate and violence (Berezin 2003, 4). The deterritorialisation and reterritorialisation intrinsic to the processes of globalisation and Europeanisation inspire perceptions and narratives of threat and insecurity because they undermine state territorial borders as physical parameters of possession, protection and power. Communities where the promise of increasing opportunities in transnational spaces is broken by the reality of confinement in disempowered territorial places are particularly receptive to narratives of threat and insecurity. Consequently, migrant workers, who avail of variable transnational opportunities and breach the physical parameter of the state, can find themselves subjected to racial hatred and violence (Bauman 1998, 2).[4]

The EU has claimed much of the credit for maintaining the peace between hitherto volatile European states and has subsequently turned its attention to ways in which border conflicts involving ethno-national groups may be pre-empted, managed and ameliorated (Diez *et al.* 2004). With the fear of post-Enlargement migration reinforcing narratives of threat and insecurity,[5] the development of an EU approach to real and potential ethno-national conflict and its territorial and cultural borders takes on an added dimension. Cross-border cooperation is a intrinsic element in this approach. However, even in ‘post-conflict’ situations, where the use of politically motivated violence between ethno-national communities has largely ceased but political and cultural manifestations of conflict persist, the hard kernel of distrust and alienation cannot be dissolved easily, undermining the usefulness of cross-border cooperation for the purpose of conflict resolution.

Retelling the conflict, further border incidents with even a hint of an ethno-national sub-plot, continuing ‘border banditry’ including diesel, cattle, alcohol, cigarette and people smuggling, as well as an influx of legitimate migrant labour in economically dynamic border regions help to maintain the climate of threat and insecurity. An economic dynamism, encouraged by European integration, EU Structural Funds and associated Community initiatives like INTERREG may provide some anaesthetic to that climate but it does not address directly the underlying issues of conflict. These underlying issues of nationality, assimilation, identity and fear of cultural hegemony continue to cause fundamental tensions. However, transnational ‘third party’ facilitators like the EU may have a pivotal role to play in diffusing such tensions.

Third party facilitation has been recognised as an important contingent in conflict regulation and resolution (Cockell 2000). Financial support is an integral element of this facilitation. Yet, as the head of the EU mission in the Former Yugoslav Republic of Macedonia, Erwan Fouéré, has commented, ‘You can pour money into countries but if you don’t focus on reconciliation then it is not possible to create conditions for long-term stability’ (in Smyth 2005). Jean-Paul Lederach has highlighted the need for ‘the development of new ways of thinking about categories, responsibilities, strategic commitment to peacebuilding, and a new understanding of socio-cultural resources present in a conflict setting' (1997, 151). The development of a strategic approach that mobilises public, private and third-sector organisations in the collective pursuit of conflict resolution is one that is favoured by the European Commission. Lederach has also prioritised the everyday understandings of local people as key resources in peacebuilding (1995, 26).

Furthermore, he has emphasised the potential of 'middle-range' or intermediary actors to influence political élites and grass-roots organisations in building the 'infrastructure of peace' (1997, 151). In the context of the EU Peace programmes for Ireland, the EU's approach has involved the engagement of intermediary agents and local grass-roots community organisations on either side of the border, and their participation in cross-border partnerships (Pace 2005, 12). As a means to cross-border, cross-community engagement on issues of ethno-national conflict, assimilation, identity and cultural hegemony, this approach will be considered subsequently. First, it is necessary to chart changes in the nature of the Irish border, driven at the political élite level, since the partition of the island in 1921.

The border as barrier

The border between the two parts of Ireland has been of primary significance for the security and identity of the Ulster Protestant unionist community in Northern Ireland. This ethno-national community has prioritised differentiation and separation from its Irish nationalist 'Significant Other' over identification with its contemporary British 'Self' in Britain.[6] The border has served as the primary marker of differentiation and separation and as a symbolic security barrier from the threatening Irish nationalist 'Other'. Therefore, the unionist position has been that the Irish border as a barrier is 'good' and that the border as a bridge is insecure, perilous, potentially treacherous and, therefore, 'bad'.

However, the creation and gradual embedding of the Irish border as a barrier between Northern Ireland and the Irish Free State after partition in 1921 also sharpened the unionist perception of threat emanating from the Irish nationalist 'Other'. The Boundary Commission (1925), which was proposed in the Anglo-Irish Treaty (1921), presented Ulster unionists with the immediate threat of losing territory to the Irish Free State, a threat that failed to materialise (Kennedy 1988, 73). Other threats proved to be more durable. The Irish state's constitutional claim to the six counties of Northern Ireland persisted until the 1998 Belfast Agreement was signed. The violent campaign of the Irish Republican Army (IRA) presented a recrudescent physical threat that was intimately associated with the border in ideological and practical terms. The approach of the British government to the Irish border compounded unionist insecurity. For example, in 1940, the British Prime Minister Winston Churchill offered Irish Taoiseach Éamon de Valera Irish unity as an incentive for granting Allied troops permission to use Southern Irish ports. The combined effect of these constitutional, perfidious and physical threats emanating from Dublin, Westminster and the IRA respectively, reinforced an Ulster unionist political culture characterised by threat and insecurity, and focused on the border.

Despite the paralysis induced by this political culture, some covert North/South contact did take place. For example, in 1949 Sean MacBride (then the Republic's Minister for External Affairs) met Northern Ireland's Sir Basil Brooke twice (Arthur 2000, 8). More concrete practical, low-level cooperation was achieved during the 1950s with: North/South cooperation on the Erne Hydro-Electric Scheme (1950) (Kennedy 2005); the creation of the Foyle Fisheries Commission (1952); and the subsequent establishment of the Great Northern Railway Board (Kennedy 1999, 84).

In response to the dawn of contemporary globalisation in the 1960s and the corresponding need for economic modernisation, the then unionist Northern Ireland Prime Minister Terence O'Neill, in concert with the Irish Taoiseach Seán Lemass, attempted to transform the border from a barrier into a bridge. However, the Lemass/O'Neill rapprochement foundered because traditionalist unionist forces led by the fundamentalist preacher, the Reverend Ian Paisley, campaigned successfully to stop the initiative by appealing to the unionist political culture of threat and insecurity. Paisley lambasted O'Neill with his populist invective: 'he is a bridge builder he tells us. A traitor and a bridge are very much alike for they both go over to the other side' (quoted in Mulholland 2000, 84).

Another attempt to transform the Irish border was made in 1974 through the proposed resuscitation of the Council of Ireland model which was first mooted in the Government of Ireland Act (1920) to serve as an institutional bridge between the two devolved parliaments in Ireland. The 1974 Council of Ireland was to comprise a Council of Ministers with seven members drawn from each of the two governments. The Council was to be invested with an executive and harmonising function, as well as a consultative role (Hennessey 1997, 221). Fearing this Council to be a nascent Trojan Horse to an All-Ireland state, Ulster unionists and loyalists mobilised on the streets and brought down the fledgling Northern Ireland power-sharing executive that involved unionists and nationalists.

In the 1970s and 1980s regular meetings between British and Irish governments in the 'neutral' European economic and political space enabled them to transform their relationship, which had been forged in imbalance, antagonism and mutual suspicion, into one characterised by cooperation, especially in the context of Northern Ireland (McCall 2001, Hayward 2005). The 1985 Anglo-Irish Agreement (AIA) may be regarded as a product of that transformed governmental relationship. The AIA gave the Irish government a say in the public affairs of Northern Ireland.

As it was an international agreement between the British and Irish governments, unionist leaders were not able to veto its implementation. Their political impotence induced a period of Ulster unionist and loyalist street protest followed by one of political reflection. Consequently, during the 1990s, Ulster unionist leaders became involved in a protracted series of 'three-strand' negotiations on power-sharing governance for Northern Ireland, as well as the institutionalisation of North/South and Britain/Ireland relationships. Implicit in this involvement was an acknowledgement that cross-border cooperation would be a necessary pillar of any future agreement.

Building a bridge across the border

In the three-strand negotiations leading to the signing of the 1998 Belfast Agreement, the Ulster Unionist Party (UUP) under the leadership of David Trimble challenged traditionalist unionist ideological orthodoxy based on exclusion and the Irish border as a barrier. Though not without eventually inducing a de facto split, the party accepted the principle of inclusion regarding the participation of Irish nationalists and republicans in the governance of Northern Ireland. Furthermore, they acquiesced to the establishment of cross-border institutions aimed at political, economic and cultural cooperation and coordination between Northern Ireland and the Republic of Ireland.

These developments in unionism were undertaken in an attempt to secure the constitutional position of Northern Ireland in the UK, as well as the political position of the unionist community in Northern Ireland in the face of a growing northern nationalist community[7] and a perfidious British government which had developed an intimate relationship with the Irish government regarding Northern Ireland affairs. Crucially, reciprocity was required in the form of an end to the real and perceived constitutional and violent threats posed by Irish nationalists and republicans.

Institutions provided by the 1998 Agreement reflected the three strands of the negotiations that preceded it. They included a Northern Ireland Executive, Assembly and Civic Forum (strand 1), a North/South Ministerial Council and its Implementation Bodies (strand 2), and a British–Irish Council and British–Irish Intergovernmental Conference (strand 3). The importance of the North/South arrangements was highlighted by the mandatory nature of the Implementation Bodies. They concentrated on the specifics of cross-border cooperation in the areas of food safety, minority languages, trade and business development, aquaculture, waterways, and EU Programmes. The provision of the Special EU Programmes Body (SEUPB) was of particular significance, not least because it was given responsibility for managing the EU Peace II and Interreg III programmes. Meanwhile, the North/South Ministerial Council met regularly to discuss wide-ranging cross-border cooperation. These meetings involved ministers with sectoral responsibility for education, health, transport, agriculture, the environment and tourism.

Henry Patterson's verdict on the outcome of the negotiations embodied in the 1998 Belfast Agreement was that it represented a 'constitutional triumph for unionism, combined with a certain political and ideological retreat' (Patterson 2001, 182). However, the implementation of the 1998 Agreement strengthened unionist opposition to it because the narrative of unionist political retreat appealed to a political culture underscored by threat and insecurity. Political retreat became embodied in: the early release of paramilitary prisoners; the actuality of Irish republican Sinn Féin leaders occupying ministerial positions; police reform; the slowness and secrecy of IRA 'decommissioning'; and the perceived challenge to the British symbolic representation of Northern Ireland (McCall 2005).

The unionist perception of retreat and loss was not alleviated by four secret acts of IRA arms decommissioning.[8] Indeed, these acts combined with subsequent charges of IRA intelligence-gathering activity in Northern Ireland, IRA guerrilla training activity in Colombia, and IRA involvement in the £26.5m Northern Bank robbery, to maintain and even intensify the unionist perception of a continuing IRA threat. Consequently, the Belfast Agreement's main institutions faced prolonged suspension and the UUP suffered electoral annihilation in the 2005 UK General Election at the hands of Ian Paisley's rhetorically anti-Agreement Democratic Unionist Party (DUP).

Despite these setbacks there is some evidence of declining Ulster Protestant unionist antipathy to what is termed 'non-political' cross-border activity (MacCarthaigh and Totten 2001, 287–352; Anderson 2005). The North/South aspect of the 1998 Belfast Agreement continued under the auspices of the North/South Implementation Bodies, even though the two key institutions provided by the Agreement – the Northern Ireland Assembly and the North/South Ministerial Council – entered into a prolonged period of suspension after 15 October 2002 and 19 November 2002 respectively.[9] Although Peter Robinson (DUP, Deputy Leader) claimed that the North/South Implementation Bodies posed the 'greatest long-term threat' to the Union,[10] DUP leaders began to engage with politicians and community and business leaders in consultation on North/South cooperation and appeared to be amenable to some form of institutionalised cross-border cooperation during negotiations on the implementation of the Belfast Agreement at Leeds Castle in Kent, England, during September 2004. In 1974 unionist leaders appeared to be willing to acquiesce to power-sharing in Northern Ireland but baulked at North/South cooperation. Thirty years later, cross-border cooperation appeared to be relatively unproblematic for them but power-sharing, especially after the experience of Irish republican Sinn Féin ministers in the Northern Ireland Executive between 1999 and 2002, appeared increasingly to be an anathema.

Dissolving Ulster unionist hostility to cross-border cooperation is closely linked to that community's perception of political and cultural threat emanating from the Republic of Ireland. Articles 2 and 3 of the 1937 Bunreacht na hÉireann (Irish Constitution) were presented as primary evidence of the political threat emanating from the South because they claimed de jure jurisdiction over the whole island territory, though qualified by de facto jurisdiction over the twenty-six counties of the Republic 'pending the reintegration of the national territory' (Lee 1989, 202). The 1998 amendment of Articles 2 and 3 had the effect of neutralising the territorial threat for the unionist community through the introduction of a consent clause: 'It is the firm will of the Irish Nation . . . to unite all the people who share the territory of the island of Ireland, [but] a united Ireland shall be brought about only by peaceful means with the consent of a majority of the people, democratically expressed, in both jurisdictions in the island'.[11] Moreover, the revised article did not necessarily imply a unitary state, should consent for a 'united Ireland' be forthcoming in the North and in the South (O'Leary 2001, 67). As far as the cultural threat from Catholicism is concerned, the diminishing grip of the Catholic Church on the Irish state and society has been a well-publicised development over the past two decades.

Consequently, some unionist politicians have expressed a willingness to entertain the possibility of institutionalised cross-border cooperation. For example, Jeffery Donaldson (DUP) has said:

> You will find today, more so than in 1974 with Sunningdale and the Council of Ireland, that there is less resistance to North/South institutionalised cooperation. That is heavily influenced by changes that have taken place in the Irish Republic. It is seen today as being much less dominated by the Roman Catholic Church, with changes to the constitution that reflect this. It has become a more open society; a more modern society; economically, it is doing very well: all of those things have had an impact here in Northern Ireland and amongst unionists. [We], therefore, feel that perhaps we can do business with the Irish Republic in a manner that will be mutually beneficial. If the North/South Ministerial Council and the Implementation Bodies are about cooperation between both parts of this island then I think unionists rest easy.[12]

The long-term success of changing unionist attitudes to the border depends on a number of factors, not least the absence of political, cultural and violent threat from Irish nationalism and republicanism, and unionist recognition of a rapidly changing Irish state and society. In the broader context of the EU, the 1986 Single European Act signalled the transformation of its borders with the removal of non-tariff barriers.[13] With EU regional funds benefiting the Irish border region and some unionist councillors supporting dual currency towns along the border and improved cross-border transportation links (Morrison 2004), these broader 'European' economic factors have also impacted upon some unionist attitudes to the border. However, other factors in Northern Ireland, not least the strength of 'internal' inter-communal borders, have the potential to compromise the role of cross-border cooperation and the development of a transnational Irish border space in helping to ameliorate the conflict.

Despite the territorial compromise at state level which is embodied in the 1998 Belfast Agreement, as well as the subsequent amendments of the Irish constitution, territorial polarisation within Northern Ireland has remained steadfast. The 1991 census revealed a sharp east–west demographic divide in Northern Ireland between Ulster Protestant unionists and Irish Catholic nationalists, a divide shown by the 2001 census to have been maintained in the intervening years. The 2001 UK General Election resulted in Irish republican Sinn Féin candidates claiming the two remaining unionist seats west of the river Bann,[14] heightening the river's significance as a symbolic border.

The 2005 local election revealed a quite startling decimation of the unionist vote west of the Bann with nine out of twelve councils returning a decisive nationalist majority.[15] The upturn in the territorial significance of the 'Bann border' may also have helped to intensify the symbolic significance of borders between the Catholic nationalist-dominated west and Protestant unionist-dominated east territories that exist in towns and cities across Northern Ireland including Armagh, Portadown, Omagh, Enniskillen, Dungannon, Magherafelt, Derry and Belfast.

Borders within Northern Ireland are particularly explicit in the working-class and under-class areas of Belfast. The 2001 Holy Cross Primary School protest was undertaken by Protestant loyalists because they objected to the route taken by pupils and parents to a Catholic primary school in a 'loyalist area'. A widely cited reason for the action of the loyalist protesters was that the Catholic population of the surrounding area was on the increase while Protestant numbers were dwindling, leaving them insecure territorially. Territorial insecurity may also help to explain the upsurge in racially motivated attacks in Belfast and elsewhere across Northern Ireland.

For example, racist attacks in the loyalist 'Village' area of Belfast have been explained in the media in terms of a working-class community that once felt under threat from the IRA, now feels itself squeezed by property speculators from the South, Filipino nurses and the local Chinese community. However, in this specific context, as in the wider Northern Ireland context, there has also been evidence of the infiltration of some loyalist paramilitary groups by British far right elements, which suggests that many of these racist attacks have had an organised dimension (Chrisafis 2004).

Perhaps the most potent markers of internal urban bordering are the 'peace walls' in Belfast which were erected to separate Catholic and Protestant working-class communities at the cutting edge of the conflict in the city. The number of peace walls in Belfast multiplied in the decade following the 1994 Irish republican and Ulster loyalist ceasefires.[16] Some academic commentators have held the 1998 Belfast Agreement directly responsible for this upsurge in urban bordering, regardless of the fact that the Northern Ireland conflict itself has been, first and foremost, a zero-sum territorial one.[17]

In that zero-sum paradigm, attempts at territorial compromise invite a territorial response from those who believe that they are losing. Parades Commission[18] rulings against some contentious Protestant Orange Order parades through predominantly Catholic areas have precipitated violent reaction on the streets. Another response has been to attempt to work the transnational thrust of the Belfast Agreement and supporting EU Peace programmes in order to help address the dominant narratives of threat and insecurity, as well as the associated narratives of alienation, victimhood, betrayal, loss and defeat.

Creating a transnational border space

In his stimulating and provocative book, *The Politics of Northern Ireland: Beyond the Belfast Agreement* (2005), Arthur Aughey suggested that the 1998 Belfast Agreement was the latest in a line of 'errors of intelligence' that 'repeat themselves by abstracting idealism from earthy circumstance' (p. 13). However, the EU, through its Peace programmes for Northern Ireland,[19] has endeavoured to address 'earthy circumstance' by supporting local grass-roots projects engaged in, among other things, North/South community dialogue and understanding. These programmes represented a sustained, sophisticated and significant attempt at inculcating communal reflexivity at the local grass-roots level and have provided an important precedent for the development of a strategic approach to ethno-national conflict regulation and amelioration in the widening EU.

Peace I (1994–99) was conceived as a conflict-resolution support programme for Northern Ireland and the border counties of the Republic of Ireland in response to the 1994 Irish republican and Ulster loyalist paramilitary ceasefires. The strategic objectives of the programme were: to promote the social inclusion of those who are at the margins of social and economic life; and to exploit the opportunities and address the needs arising from the peace process in order to boost economic growth and advance social and economic regeneration. The objectives of Peace II (2000–06), namely, to address the legacy of conflict and take opportunities arising from peace, followed on from the initial programme's objectives.[20] In essence, Peace II was intended to underpin, at the 'earthy' local community level, functioning institutions delivered by the 1998 Belfast Agreement at the political elite level. However, the key institutions have endured a protracted crisis from their inception, and since 2002 have been subjected to a prolonged period of suspension. Stalemate at this elite level has undermined the sustainability of local and regional cross-border partnerships and the building of a holistic strategy for peacebuilding because political elites and their institutions are intrinsic to such a strategy. Nevertheless, the cross-border partnerships created and developed by the EU Peace programmes have continued to provide a necessary element in this strategy.

In the context of the Peace programmes, the EU has acted as a transnational 'third-party' facilitator for the amelioration of ethno-national border conflict. Third-party facilitators need to engage local agents, who have grass-roots knowledge of ethno-national division, and help develop their expertise in addressing those divisions (Byrne and Keashly 2000, 111). The social partnership structure for the implementation of the Peace programmes, involving the public, private and voluntary sectors, embodied this approach. These partnerships provided for the application of local knowledge, skill and effort at the level of Intermediary Funding Bodies and local community project organisers. With 15 per cent of both programmes specifically designated for cross-border cooperation, such cooperation was judged to play a significant role in helping to ameliorate this ethno-national conflict at the local grass-roots level.

The fundamental focus of cultural and educational projects funded in the cross-border priority of the Peace programmes was on the acceptance of difference and diversity rather than on attempting to narrow political and cultural differences. According to Anton Blok (1998), where the cultural differences between groups are relatively small then the potential exists for a more intense conflagration in the event of an attempt being made to further narrow those cultural differences. In 1993, Ignatieff found cultural difference between Serb and Croat explained to him in terms of the nationality of the cigarettes smoked (1994, 1–2). In comparative terms, cultural conflict in Northern Ireland rests on relatively small cultural differences that have been reinforced by decades of violent conflict.

'Telling the difference' (Burton 1977) and defending social (including territorial) boundaries have been integral to this conflict. For example, in April 2001, the placing of a vase of Easter lilies in the great hall of the Parliament Buildings at Stormont had the seemingly disproportionate effect of forcing an emergency debate and the recall of the Northern Ireland Assembly from the holiday recess. Easter lilies had become a symbol of Irish republican political culture after the Easter Rising of 1916 and the subsequent execution of fifteen republican revolutionaries by the British state. Sinn Féin leaders had wanted to commemorate the Rising with this floral display, keenly aware that it challenged symbolically the territorial and cultural boundaries of Britishness in Northern Ireland (McCall 2005). Jim Wells, the DUP Assembly member who forced the emergency debate proclaimed: 'For the first time in the history of the United Kingdom a government building will be used to display symbols which honour IRA terrorists' (quoted in Sharrock 2001).

By way of contrast, after the 1998 Agreement and the diminished political and violent threats from Irish nationalism and republicanism, the Irish border appeared to offer a less contentious transnational space in which unionist and nationalist culture differences could be explored. Research on the cross-border priority of the Peace II programme found that Ulster Protestant unionist groups involved tended to embrace the cross-border dimension with many seeing it as providing a useful 'detour' on the way to better cross-community relations in the North because it entailed engagement with groups from the South perceived to be nationalist but at one step removed from the post-1969 conflict (McCall and O'Dowd 2005).

It is possible to interpret cross-border cooperation as a 'scenic route' for such unionist groups since it may have provided a convenient means of avoiding or postponing cross-community interaction with the northern nationalist 'Other' experienced at the coalface of the conflict. More damningly, cross-border cooperation may actively promote the intensification of malign social practices across the border, especially those of racism and sectarianism. Hann found that the Carpathian Euroregion across the Polish–Ukranian border actually exacerbated anti-Ukranian prejudices (cited in O'Dowd 2001). Similarly, Hayward (2005) encountered perceptions of an increase in sectarianism in Donegal that was attributed to Derry youths crossing a more open Irish border.

However, there is also evidence to suggest that cross-border cooperation can develop a non-contentious transnational border space for small group encounters and interaction which helps to address the political culture of threat and insecurity, downgrade communal antagonism towards 'the Significant Other' and lead to the articulation of cultural difference in a more constructive way (see Hayward 2004, 22; McCall and O'Dowd 2005; Pollack 2005). Such an articulation is embedded in an approach which challenges the reified and homogeneous conceptions of culture associated with nationalist and unionist communities, conceptions forged in a long history of political and violent conflict. It embraces Kevin Avruch's maxim that 'culture is to some extent always situational, flexible and responsive to the exigencies of the worlds that individuals confront' and applies it in a cross-border, cross-cultural dialogue (1998, 20).

Conclusion

If state borders remain synonymous with the exercise of social and political power, and consequently continue to represent the physical parameters of possession, protection and exclusion, then the deterritorialisation and reterritorialisation intrinsic to the processes of contemporary globalisation and Europeanisation feed narratives and perceptions of threat and insecurity because they undermine territorial borders as physical parameters. If political bargains brokered by elites in remote centres like Brussels, Dublin and London have the capacity to reinforce feelings of threat, insecurity and alienation in local communities and even 'bring out the worst in a country', then border towns and regions offer connective sites for the EU to facilitate practical grass-roots cross-border cooperation that can help address these issues. While this case may be made in the general context of the widening system of EU governance, it has even more resonance in the particular context of European ethno-national border conflict.

The EU has paid increasing attention to developing strategies for tackling real and potential ethno-national conflict. As well as engaging in political elite level diplomatic initiatives in order to off-set or ameliorate such conflict, the EU has also developed a 'peacebuilding from below' strategy in its Peace programmes for Ireland. Cross-border cooperation and the inclusion of intermediary agents and local grass-roots groups in cross-border partnerships have been integral elements in the strategy. Such cooperation enables these groups to address perceptions of threat emanating from 'the other side' and help transform the border from being a primary site of conflict to an important transnational space for its amelioration.

The Irish border as a barrier was the major ideological and practical focus for ethno-national conflict in Northern Ireland. However, the transformation of the border has the potential to help further diffuse that conflict through the creation of a transnational border space in which ethno-national groups can address narratives of threat, insecurity, victimhood, loss, betrayal and defeat, and begin to explore and accommodate their differences in the absence of threat. While there is the possibility of some cross-border activity actually fuelling the malign social practices of racism and sectarianism, there is also evidence to suggest that a transnational border space can help to diffuse ethno-national tensions and engender a climate of respect for diversity and the accommodation of difference. Such a pursuit is one that Adenauer, Schuman and Monnet would recognise as being embedded in the EU's founding principle of peacebuilding.

In the widening EU of the twenty-first century, the onus for sustaining the development of such transnational border spaces falls increasingly on member state and regional governments as EU structural funds and community initiatives become increasingly stretched. Consequently, pressure is being applied on member state governments to 'mainstream' the cross-border work of social partners and support the transnational endeavours of meso-level transnational bodies like the SEUPB, as well as the voluntary and community groups that are helping to develop transnational border space. Whether they succumb to such transnational pressure will doubtless be the subject of future research.

Notes

1 Consequently, the Estonian government came under particular pressure by the EU to provide equal citizenship for Estonia's ethnic Russian-speaking minority (Kronenberger and Wouters 2004, xix). This experience has been maturing into strategies for ameliorating ethno-national conflict and inter-communal divisions in the widening EU. One such strategy came in the form of the Conference/Pact on stability in Europe, which was an exercise in 'preventative diplomacy' undertaken by the EU aimed at Central and Eastern European accession states. The conference in May 1994 and subsequent regional roundtables focused on borders, minorities and economic cooperation. A final conference in May 1995 delivered a Stability Pact detailing over one hundred agreements (Wouters and Naert 2004, 40–41).

2 An EU official in DG Regio with responsibility for the EU Peace II programme has commented that the EU is well placed to engage in such an approach because it does not place a higher priority on 'quick results' (during the Ireland/Northern Ireland roundtable organised by the EUBorderConf project in Brussels on 24 November 2005).

3 The European economic and political space also extends beyond the EU, not least because its economic and political principles are adhered to by other West European states and have been adopted by Central and Eastern European states that aspire to EU membership (Axtmann 2003, 123).

4 Moreover, some evidence suggests that territorial and cultural borders between indigenous ethnic-national communities and migrants are being reconstituted within European states (O'Dowd 2003).

5 In the United Kingdom, much of this fear is stoked by alarmist headlines in the tabloid media. In 2005, Douglas Alexander, then Minister of State for Europe, maintained that after EU enlargement the influx of migrant workers from Central and Eastern European accession states into the UK was relatively modest (Alexander 2005).

6 In an ICM opinion poll published in the *Guardian* newspaper on 21 August 2001, the question posed to a sample of British people in Britain was: 'Do you think Northern Ireland should be part of the UK? 26 per cent responded that it should remain part of the UK, 41 per cent that it should be joined with the Republic of Ireland, and 33 per cent responded 'don't know'. In an article in the same newspaper the following day the leading unionist politician Jeffery Donaldson argued that such findings were not cause for unionist concern because, 'the constitutional and political reality [is that] under the principle of consent [unionists'] future will be determined by the people of Northern Ireland themselves' (*Guardian*, 22 August 2001).

7 In 2005, the Irish nationalist community represented approximately 42 per cent of the electorate of Northern Ireland and the Ulster unionist community accounted for approximately 50 per cent.

8 In June 2000, October 2001, October 2003, and finally in September 2005 when the Independent International Commission on Decommissioning announced that the IRA had decommissioned the totality of its arsenal (http://news.bbc.co.uk/1/shared/bsp/hi/pdfs/26_09_05_decommissioning.pdf). However, a subsequent report by the Independent Monitoring Commission (IMC), published in February 2006, concluded that 'not all PIRA's weapons and ammunition were handed over for decommissioning in September' (http://news.bbc.co.uk/1/hi/northern_ireland/4670398.stm). Unionist leaders were easily persuaded by the IMC's conclusions.

9 http://www.northsouthministerialcouncil.org/

10 In remarks to the 2002 annual conference of the Young Democrats, the DUP's youth wing (*Irish Times*, 18 February 2002).

11 From the new Article 3.1, Constitution of Ireland, 1998.

12 Interview with author, 3 December 2001.

13 Including the different standards or regulations regarding goods and services between

states, and the national preferences of state-related purchasing agencies (Pinder 2001, 65).

14 The Bann follows a course that runs down through the middle of Northern Ireland from north to south.

15 In 2005, councils west of the Bann with a nationalist majority included Limivaday, Derry, Strabane, Fermanagh, Omagh, Cookstown, Dungannon, Newry and Mourne, and Down. Councils with a unionist majority included Banbridge and Craigavon. Armagh City and District Council had eleven unionist and eleven nationalist councillors.

16 There were fifteen 'peace walls' in Belfast prior to the 1994 paramilitary ceasefires; by 2003 their number had increased to thirty-seven (Wilson 2003).

17 Wilson and Wilford maintained that 'despite and even *because of* the Belfast agreement, sectarian divisions in the region are as wide as ever' (emphasis in original) (www.devolution.ac.uk/Wilson_&_Wilford_Paper).

18 Established by the 1998 Agreement to adjudicate on contentious political and sectarian parades.

19 Peace I (1994–99) had funds of €503m. Peace II (2000–06) was worth approximately €707m (www.seupb.org).

20 Peace II had five priority areas including:

- Economic Renewal;
- Social Integration, Inclusion and Reconciliation;
- Locally Based Regeneration and Development Strategies;
- Outward and Forward Looking Region;
- Cross-border Co-operation

The measures of the Cross-border Co-operation priority include:

5.1 Increasing Cross-border Economic Development Opportunities (ERDF);
5.2 Improving Cross-border Public Sector Co-operation (ERDF);
5.3 Developing Cross-border Reconciliation and Cultural Understanding (ERDF);
5.4 Promoting Joint Approaches to Social, Education, Training and Human Resource Development (ESF);
5.5 Cross-border School and Youth Co-operation (ERDF);
5.6 Rural Development Co-operation (EAGGF);
5.7 Cross-border Fishing and Aquacultural Co-operation (FIFG)

(http://www.seupbsuccessfulprojects.org/).

References

Alexander, Douglas (2005) *Europe in a Global Age*, London: Foreign Policy Centre, www.fpc.org.uk/fsblob/626.pdf.

Anderson, James (2005) 'Living on the border: spatial behaviour and political attitudes in Irish border communities, North and South, Catholic and Protestant', *Mapping Frontiers Discussion Paper (D15)*, www.mappingfrontiers.ie.

Arthur, Paul (2000) *Special Relationships: Britain, Ireland and the Northern Ireland Problem*, Belfast: Blackstaff.

Aughey, Arthur (2005) *The Politics of Northern Ireland: Beyond the Belfast Agreement*, London: Routledge.

Avruch, Kevin (1998) *Culture and Conflict Resolution*, Washington, DC: United States Institute of Peace.

Axtmann, Roland (2003) 'State formation and supranationalism in Europe: the case of the Holy Roman Empire of the German Nation', in Mabel Berezin and Martin Schain (eds) *Europe Without Borders: Remapping Territory, Citizenship, and Identity in a Transnational Age*, Baltimore: The Johns Hopkins University Press, 118–139.

Bauman, Zygmunt (1998) *Globalisation: The Human Consequences*, Cambridge: Polity.

Berezin, Mabel (2003) 'Territory, emotion and identity: spatial recalibration in a new Europe', in Mabel Berezin and Martin Schain (eds) *Europe Without Borders: Remapping Territory, Citizenship, and Identity in a Transnational Age*, Baltimore: The Johns Hopkins University Press, 1–30.

Blok, Anton (1998) 'The narcissism of minor differences', *European Journal of Social Theory* 1: 33–56.

Brunn, Stanley D. (1999) 'A treaty of silicon for the Treaty of Westphalia? New territorial dimensions of modern statehood', in David Newman (ed), *Boundaries, Territory and Postmodernity*, London: Frank Cass, 106–131.

Burton, F. (1977) *The Politics of Legitimacy*, London: Routledge.

Byrne, S. and L. Keashly (2000) 'Working with ethno-political conflict: a multi-modal approach', *International Peacekeeping* 7: 97–120.

Chrisafis, Angelique (2004) 'Racist war of the Loyalist street gangs: orchestrated attacks on minorities raise fears of ethnic cleansing', in the *Guardian*, January 10.

Cockell, J. (2000) 'Conceptualising peacebuilding: human security and sustainable peace', in M. Pugh (ed.), *Regeneration of War-torn Societies*, New York: St Martin's Press, 15–34.

Diez, Thomas, Stephen Stetter and Matthias Albert (2004) 'The European Union and the transformation of border conflicts', *Working Papers in EU Border Conflicts Series*, No. 1. www.euborderconf.bham.ac.uk/publications/workingpapers.htm.

Giddens, Anthony (1990) *The Consequences of Modernity*, Cambridge: Cambridge University Press.

Hann, C. (1998) 'Nationalism and civil society in Central Europe: from Ruritania to the Carpathian Euroregion', in J. Hall (ed.), *The State of the Nation: Ernest Gellner and the Theory of Nationalism*, Cambridge: Cambridge University Press.

Hayward, Katy (2004) 'Mediating the European ideal: cross-border programmes and conflict transformation in Ireland', *Working Papers in EU Border Conflicts Series*, No. 11. www.euborderconf.bham.ac.uk/publications/workingpapers.htm.

Hayward, Katy (2005) 'Ireland/Northern Ireland: Final Report', *EUBorderConf.* Unpublished report.

Hennessey, Thomas (1997) *A History of Northern Ireland, 1920–1996*, Dublin: Gill and Macmillan.

Ignatieff, Michael (1994) *Nationalism and the Narcissism of Minor Differences*, Milton Keynes: Pavis Centre for Sociological and Social Anthropological Studies, Open University.

Kennedy, Dennis (1988) *The Widening Gulf: Northern Attitudes to the Independent Irish State*, Belfast: Blackstaff.

Kennedy, Dennis (1999) 'Politics of North–South relations in post-partition Ireland', in Patrick J. Roche and Brian Barton (eds), *The Northern Ireland Question: Nationalism, Unionism and Partition*, Aldershot: Ashgate, 71–96.

Kennedy, Michael (2005) 'The realms of practical politics: North–South cooperation on the Erne hydro-electric scheme', Discussion Paper for the research project, *Mapping Frontiers, Plotting Pathways: Routes to North–South Co-operation in a Divided Island* at www.mappingfrontiers.ie.

Kronenberger, Vincent and Jan Wouters (2004) 'Introduction', in Vincent Kronenberger and Jan Wourters (eds) *The European Union and Conflict Prevention: Policy and Legal Aspects*, The Hague: TMC.

Lederach, J.P. (1995) *Preparing for Peace: Conflict Transformation across Cultures*. Syracuse: Syracuse University Press.

Lederach, J.P. (1997) *Building Peace: Sustainable Reconciliation in Divided Societies*, Washington, DC: United States Institute of Peace.

Lee. J.J. (1989) *Ireland 1912–1985: Politics and Society*, Cambridge: Cambridge University Press.

McCall, Cathall (2001) 'The production of space and the realignment of identity in Northern Ireland', in *Regional and Federal Studies* vol. 11, no. 2, 1–24.

McCall, Cathal (2005) 'From long war to war of the lilies: "post-conflict" territorial compromise and the return of cultural politics', in Michael Cox, Adrian Guelke and Fiona Stephen (eds) *A Farewell to Arms? From 'Long War' to Long Peace in Northern Ireland* (Second Edition), Manchester: Manchester University Press.

McCall, Cathal and Liam O'Dowd (2005) 'The significance of the "cross-border dimension" for promoting peace and reconciliation', *Mapping Frontiers Discussion Papers*. www.mappingfrontiers.ie.

MacCarthaigh, M. and Totten, K. (2001) 'Irish political data 2001', *Irish Political Studies*, 287–352.

Morrison, Catherine (2004) 'Unionist calls for motorway to the border' in the *Irish News*, 29 November.

Mulholland, Marc (2000) *Northern Ireland at the Crossroads: Ulster Unionism in the O'Neill Years, 1960–9*. Basingstoke: Macmillan.

O'Dowd, Liam (2001) 'State borders, border regions and the construction of European identity', in M. Kohli and N. Novak (eds) *Will Europe Work?* London: Routledge.

O'Dowd, Liam (2003), 'The changing significance of European borders', in James Anderson, Liam O'Dowd and Thomas M. Wilson (eds) *New Borders for a Changing Europe: Cross-Border Co-operation and Governance*, London: Frank Cass, 13–36.

O'Leary, Brendan (2001) 'The character of the 1998 Agreement: results and prospects', in Rick Wilford (ed) *Aspects of the Belfast Agreement*, Oxford: OUP, 47–83.

Pace, Michelle (2005) 'Images of border conflicts within EU policy-making circles and their impact on policy', *Working Papers Series in EU Border Conflicts Series*, No. 16. www.euborderconf.bham.ac.uk/publications/workingpapers.htm.

Patterson, Henry (2001) 'From insulation to appeasement: the Major and Blair governments reconsidered', in Rick Wilford (ed.) *Aspects of the Belfast Agreement*, Oxford: Oxford University Press, 166–83.

Pinder, John, (2001) *The European Union: A Very Short Introduction*, Oxford: OUP.

Pollak, Andy (2005) 'Educational cooperation on the island of Ireland: a thousand flowers and a hundred heartaches', *Mapping Frontiers Discussion Papers*, www.mapping frontiers.ie.

Ramsbotham, Oliver, Tom Woodhouse and Hugh Miall (2005) (Second Edition). *Contemporary Conflict Resolution: The Prevention, Management and Transformation of Deadly Conflicts*, Oxford: Polity.

Rosamond, Ben (1999) 'Discourses of globalisation and the social construction of European identities', *Journal of European Public Policy* vol. 6, no. 4, 652–68.

Rumford, Chris (2002) *The European Union: A Political Sociology*, London: Blackwell.

Sharrock, David (2001) 'Unionists fail to block Assembly's Easter lilies', *Daily Telegraph*, 11 April.

Shaw, Jo (1999) 'Postnational constitutionalism in the European Union', *Journal of European Public Policy* vol. 6, no. 4, 579–97.

Smyth, Jamie (2005) 'A tough challenge ahead at a time of escalating tension in the Balkans', *Irish Times*, 7 November.

Stiglitz, Joseph E. (2002) *Globalisation and Its Discontents*, New York: Norton.

Tilly, Charles (1990) *Coercion, Capital and European States AD 900–1990*, Oxford: Basil Blackwell.

Wallace, William (1999) 'The sharing of sovereignty: the European paradox', *Political Studies* vol. 47, no. 3, 503–21.

Wouters, Jan and Frederik Naert (2004) 'The EU and conflict prevention: a brief historic overview', in Vincent Kronenberger and Jan Wourters (eds), *The European Union and Conflict Prevention: Policy and Legal Aspects*, The Hague: TMC, 33–66.

Wilson, Robin (2003) *A City for all our Citizens: Reflections on 'Shared Cities'*. Brussels: Directorate General IV (Education, Culture and Heritage, Youth and Sport/Directorate of Culture and Cultural and Natural Heritage Cultural policy and Action Department (DGIV/CULT/PREV/shared-cities (2003)2E).

5 Coping with 'Fortress Europe'

Views from four seaports on the Spanish–Moroccan border

Henk Driessen

Introduction

This chapter considers some outcomes of the recent transformation of the Spanish–Moroccan frontier from an international border between two states into an external border of the European Union with Africa. Rather than taking a top-down perspective from the political centres of Madrid, Rabat or Brussels, I will look at the Spanish–Moroccan frontier from below in four port towns: Algeciras and Tarifa on the northern shore, Ceuta and Tangier on the southern shore. My main focus will be the impact of clandestine cross-Mediterranean migration on these port societies. As a result of European Union integration, the Schengen Agreement and the subsequent policy of tightening external border control, clandestine immigration has increased dramatically since 1990. I begin with an outline of the larger picture of the Mediterranean divide and then present an ethnographic perspective on the port towns.[1]

The geopolitics of the Mediterranean frontier

It is a truism that borders both unite and separate people and their activities. This dual quality has in fact often been claimed by historians, geographers, social scientists, politicians and poets for the wet frontier between Europe and Africa. But the reality of this usually calm sea, its shores, and its high concentration of ports has, in the course of its long history of human occupation, shown highly variable and complex balances between passage and blockade, connection and disjunction, convergence and divergence, inclusion and exclusion. The Inner Sea has more often than not been a contested space – and continues to be – for its natural resources, among which connectivity stands out as the most vital one. The measures of its unitary and dividing qualities have often been decided upon in political centres far removed from the sea itself. Governments of empires and states have for instance been keen to keep a tight control on ports through the direct appointment of port authorities. But people who dwell on the Mediterranean shores have always found ways to ignore or subvert the state's policy to impose borders and customs or have adopted them as a local resource. The history of the Mediterranean is thus also a history of piracy and smuggling, of defiance and opposition.

Since the Second World War, the coastal lands have seen an ever-increasing flow of people, traders, migrants and tourists, goods and ideas across their borders and an intensified urbanisation which is predicated on passage and connectivity. The consolidation and enlargement of the European Union has had the effect of dividing the Mediterranean states into members and non-members. A decisive and, for that matter, identifying event was the abolition in 1991 of most of the internal borders within the European Union so that the Mediterranean borders of Greece, Spain, and Italy became external borders of the European Union.

The main intra-Mediterranean migration over the past two decades has been from south to north and east to west, the southern European states being transformed from countries of emigration into countries of immigration. The Schengen agreement brought the legal migration across the Mediterranean almost to a standstill. In 1991 the Spanish government introduced visa obligations for North Africans. Until then Moroccans could visit Spain without any restrictions. Many of them worked as agricultural workers at harvest times. The redefinition of the wet borders of southern Europe as external boundaries of the European Union has had the effect of remarking the Mediterranean as a divide, separating democratic, developed and Christian Europe from politically unstable, economically underdeveloped and demographically 'overflowing' Islamic North Africa (King 1997; Driessen 1996, 1998).

As soon as the Schengen agreement became operative Spain, Italy, Greece and Portugal found themselves faced with a rush of refugees, some of them political but the vast majority economic migrants. This phenomenon of the 'new immigration' was increasingly perceived as a 'threat' and became a hot issue of domestic politics in the European Union countries throughout the 1990s and into the third millennium. It was defined as 'new' because of its mostly clandestine nature. In contrast to the earlier generations of Spanish, Italian, Turkish, and North-African legal migrants who were overwhelmingly unemployed young men from the countryside finding work in the industrial sector of Western Europe, the new migrants entering Southern Europe through the backdoors work overwhelmingly in the informal economy. They are much more heterogeneous than the earlier Gastarbeiter. They take the heavy, dirty and underpaid jobs which have become unacceptable for local workers even as these remain unemployed. The new migrants have to accept wages far below the official minimum rate (which are nevertheless several times higher than the wages on the southern Mediterranean shores) because they are illegal and lack the tactical bargaining power to demand higher earnings and better working conditions. Men mostly work in agriculture, construction, the tourist industry, fishing and street peddling; women typically work as domestic servants and an increasing number of them end up in prostitution.

By the mid-1990s Spain, Portugal, Greece and Italy were strongly pressed by their northern neighbours to intensify control of their permeable wet borders. Such pressures increased in the wake of terrorist attacks in the USA, Morocco, Turkey and Spain. In spite of increased investment in border guards, equipment and checks to tighten border control, the long sea-coasts are impossible to fence off to non-EU migrants. The arrival of boatloads of refugees from Turkey and Albania on the coast of Italy, from Tunisia in Sicilian ports and from Africa on the beaches of southern Spain and the Canary Islands has become a daily routine. But French public opinion was shocked when in February 2001 a rusty and rickety ship with 900 Kurdish refugees struck the rocks at Fréjus on the Côte d'Azur. Never before had a boat of the people-smuggling racket penetrated unnoticed so deeply into the heart of the European Union.

Spain, Italy and Greece tacitly accept that clandestine immigration is taking place. In spite of the political rhetoric to fight it through intensified policing at the entry points, and monitoring of people through identity cards and residence-permit controls, authorities also tend, or are forced, to turn a blind eye to illegal immigration; so, from time to time, they legalise the presence of tens of thousand of clandestine immigrants, increasingly from Eastern European countries. This ambivalent policy partly reflects differences between political and economic interests. Many entrepreneurs, patrons and other agents of neo-liberal globalisation welcome a cheap and submissive labour force. Indeed, several sectors of the national economies of Southern and Western Europe would barely survive without the input of undocumented labour. In other words, applying fewer formalities to meet the demand for unskilled labour has increased rapidly at the borders of the European Union.

In spite of all attempts by the European Union and its member states to control the movement of 'undesired' people by means of visa, passports, identity cards, residence and work permits, clandestine cross-Mediterranean migration has become an integral feature of border reality over the past decade.

Unofficial border-crossing is often represented as an individual survival strategy of young men and women who try to escape from their desperate situations in their homelands. However, in many cases the 'new migrants' move through transnational networks in which kinship, marriage and ethnicity are the main organising principles. Their passage into Europe is frequently paid for by their families, whereas complex organisations, often with experience in drugs trafficking, are in charge of the border-crossing. The smuggling of human beings requires a high degree of planning and logistics, sophisticated technology, and access to strategic local and global information on routes, transport, laws, labour demands, financial arrangements, and the involvement of corrupt civil servants, guards and policemen on both sides of the frontier (Juntunen 2002). Such practices, which, by definition, are beyond and against the state, are embedded in a border culture with deep roots in Mediterranean history.

Perspectives from four ports

Tarifa is a booming Spanish tourist resort of about 16,000 inhabitants and is Europe's southernmost port at only 13 kilometres from Morocco. Its long and wide beaches offer favourite entry points for clandestine immigrants who are taken across the Strait of Gibraltar in so-called *pateras*, small fishing caiques between four and six metres long and two metres wide, carrying between twenty and thirty people or, more recently, in the faster Zodiac rubber speedboats. Spanish border officials and members of the Red Cross estimate that each year between 15,000 and 20,000 clandestine migrants cross the Strait of Gibraltar to Europe. Between 1995 and 1999 approximately 3,000 migrants drowned in attempting to cross the wet border between Morocco and Spain. Thousands were arrested by the border guards and sent to refugee detention centres in nearby Algeciras.[2]

In December 1998, another bilateral agreement between Spain and Morocco was signed to strengthen police cooperation in the fight against clandestine migration. Moroccans are deported to their home country (often re-entering Spain within the year). The number of migrants who manage to slip through the mazes of the border control is several times higher than the number caught. Together with those who cannot be returned to their home countries, they disappear as faceless 'undocumented ones' in Spain's expanding black economy. If they are lucky, they are included in the periodic legalisation programme.

Until the mid-1980s Tarifa was a more or less dormant town with hardly any cross-border traffic. Over the past fifteen years, however, the unremitting strong winds hitting the town and its vast agro-pastoral hinterland have become the main source of Tarifa's new prosperity. It was discovered as Europe's main windsurfing venue and became the seat of the World Championship of Windsurfing. Its largely unspoiled beaches also attracted foreign investment companies in search of new tourist zones beyond the overdeveloped and overcrowded Costa del Sol. Fifteen years ago one of Spain's largest wind energy parks was developed in the hills of Tarifa.

A fast daily ferry has been established for day trips to Tangier. Depending on the weather, the passage takes about half an hour. The exploitation of this ferry line is a joint venture of a German shipping company and Spanish and Moroccan tourist agencies. It is illustrative of how cross-border cooperation may subvert state rules. A visa is required for most tourists who enter Morocco. However, since this would make day-tripping to Tangier less attractive and more expensive for tourists, an informal arrangement has been worked out with Moroccan customs officers. On their arrival tourists simply hand in their passports or identity cards to the Moroccan guides. The identity papers then disappear into a plastic bag during the tour of Tangier and reappear at the tourists' departure. Profits are shared among all parties involved – at the expense of the Moroccan Treasury. Although Tarifa is a Schengen border post, customs control was lenient for tourists who returned to Spain, packed with Moroccan souvenirs and duty-free cigarettes and liquor bought on board. Recently, the port has been incorporated into the administrative structure of the nearby port of Algeciras. The port area has been fenced in and border control reinforced.

Tarifa is a town of striking contrasts. That the small physical distance from Tangier is, in fact, a wide cultural and socio-economic gap was brought home to me in March 1992. While Tarifa was celebrating the bacchanalia of Carnival, Tangier was fasting through the month of Ramadan. A beach which during the day was a site for the world windsurfing competition, was at night an entry-point for Africans coming to Europe in search of a better life. In the daytime, tourists in pursuit of pleasure and the exotic were ferried from Tarifa to Tangier ('a travel into the Middle Ages' as one brochure put it), while at night Africans made their sometimes dangerous crossings in crowded boats in the opposite direction. Local authorities do their utmost to keep these contrasting worlds on Tarifa's beaches strictly separate.

The town was completely taken by surprise when the first corpses of 'new migrants' washed ashore and increasing numbers of surviving border-crossers were arrested in the winter of 1991. The situation grew so critical that an improvised centre for clandestine immigrants had to be opened in part of an old building on the outer quay of the port, typically the most outlying location available. Here 'new migrants' were being detained under appalling conditions for forty days, the maximum time according to the Aliens Act. At the end of this period they were released, receiving an edict of expulsion signed by the Governor and then abandoned to their fate. In subsequent years, when the numbers of 'new migrants' continued to increase, other facilities were arranged in the sports hall, also located near the port. Immigrants were held there until their transfer to larger centres in neighbouring Algeciras.

Local people reacted in various ways to the 'new immigration'. All had to face the fact, previously largely taken for granted, that they are living in a porous border town at the edge of Europe, or rather the European Union. Small networks of inhabitants began to support the work of the local Red Cross and Catholic Caritas. Several of these early volunteers became members of ACOGE, Spain's first NGO devoted to refugee and immigrant aid, which was founded in 1991. There were also inhabitants who feared that the immigrants posed a threat to the safety of their families and standard of living. They think that if immigrants are 'illegal', they must have come into conflict with the law. This perception is reinforced by the fact that connections have been established between the cannabis trade and clandestine immigration.

Anti-alien slogans have appeared on the walls of public buildings and monuments in Tarifa and Algeciras. But the large majority of Tarifeños tried to ignore what was called 'the problem of illegality', although the border situation imperceptibly slipped into their daily discourse, in spite of the fact that almost all 'new migrants' moved on to the larger towns and cities along the Mediterranean coast. The professed self-image of Tarifeños is one of a non-racist hospitable community. A member of the Red Cross told me that local fishermen do indeed help boats crowded with immigrants in case of emergencies, that most inhabitants are aware of the immigrants' predicament but also realise that these people will not stay in Tarifa.

Twenty kilometres east of Tarifa, Algeciras is one of the towns where an increasing number of migrants try to settle down. A city of more than 100,000 inhabitants, it is the last port of the Spanish Mediterranean and the key to the Spanish enclave of Ceuta in Morocco. In 1999, the municipal office registered 1,400 immigrants, mostly Moroccans, but hundreds more remain unregistered. Five years later the population has increased to 120.000 of whom about 5 per cent are Muslim immigrants from Morocco (Servicio de Estadística de Andalucía 2000, 2005).

The main commercial activity is connected with the port, an important stopping place for transatlantic shipping. Over the past two decades Algeciras has become Spain's largest commercial port in terms of total traffic and the leading pan-Mediterranean centre for the management of containers in transit, having been chosen as a base port by the multinational shipping companies of Sealand and Maersk (Castejón Arqued 1996). Algeciras is also Spain's largest passenger port with eight daily crossings to Tangier and six to Ceuta during the summer months. It is the main port for Moroccan migrants in transit to their native country where they spend their holidays. In the eight weeks from mid-June to mid-August close to one-and-a-half million people pass through the port of Algeciras, including Spanish and foreign tourists who cross the Strait to Ceuta and Tangier on shopping and sight-seeing tours. In the early 1990s, Spanish and Moroccan authorities began to coordinate the massive passage across the Mediterranean in order to avoid the chaos and abuses of the previous years. Between 1994 and 2002 the annual number of passengers moving through the port increased from 3.7 to 4.4 million a year and the number of vehicles from 707,000 to more than one million (Puerto Bahia de Algeciras 2002).

Algeciras is thus very much a place of transit with a strong port atmosphere. In the bars there is a lot of talk among Algecireños about what is called the 'silent invasion of *moros*' (a pejorative term for Moroccans). It is true indeed that in the course of the past decade Moroccan immigrants have become more visible in the townscape. There is a process of appropriation of the destitute residential and commercial areas near the old port by often clandestine immigrants and the emergence of a new ethnic infrastructure, consisting of mosques, cheap boarding houses, cafés and eating places, halal butchers, groceries, recycling and repair workshops, bathhouses, brothels, and contracting offices – niches that are the result of self-help and self-employment on the part of immigrant entrepreneurs.

In other words, part of the rather dense, dynamic and interstitial space at the waterfront seems to be in the process of becoming an informal Moroccan enclave, connected to a cross-border network of people and activities. On the other hand, there is a high turnover with regard to ethnic economic activities. And it may be the writing on the wall that a large mosque almost finished in the autumn of 2000, still remains in the same condition three years later, construction being abandoned and the building already beginning to decay. The terrorist attacks in Madrid in March 2004 have increased the tension between the established Spanish-Catholic inhabitants and the Muslim newcomers. The latter become more and more concerned with their security while Spanish secret agents keep an eye on the local mosques.

Across the bay beyond Gibraltar sits Ceuta or Sebta, an enclaved Spanish town with a territory of 20 square kilometres. The two competing free ports are highly contested territories, their fates intimately tied to one another. Due to its politically anomalous status, Ceuta serves as a node within larger transnational trading networks. The enclave has a hyper-consumptive and parasitical economy based on commerce, transport, tourism and the garrison. There are small fishing, brewing, and metallurgic industries. As Spain's – and by implication the European

Union's – southern external frontier *in* Morocco, this border society is marked by contradictions and paradoxes. Like its sister enclave of Melilla to the east, it is cosmopolitan yet parochial, affluent and poor, African and European, economically liberal yet culturally conservative. Behind its multi-ethnic facade of *convivencia*, discrimination and intolerance prevail.

The approximately 70,000 legal inhabitants are divided along ethno-religious lines. The statistically, politically and culturally dominant group are the Spanish Christians who make up more than 60 per cent of the local population. A further third are Muslims of Moroccan descent, many of whom hold Spanish nationality. Small minorities of Gypsies, Jews and Hindu traders make up the rest.[3] Thousands of soldiers are conspicuously present in the enclave. Spanish-Christian domination is contested both from within and without.

More than other border towns, Ceuta depends on open borders to survive. Smuggling has become a way of life in which both Spanish and Moroccan citizens (and state representatives) are involved in one way or another, ranging from occasional petty consumerist contraband and large-scale subsistence smuggling to professional smuggler networks specialising in luxury goods, drugs, and recently in people. The degree of permeability of the enclave's border is a daily topic in local discourse and the frontier forms an integral part of local identity, much more so than in Tarifa and Algeciras (Driessen 1999). In 1995 the Spanish government approved a status of autonomy for Ceuta, replacing the town council with an assembly similar to those of Spain's other autonomous communities.

Approximately 20,000 Moroccans pass through the border into Ceuta on a daily basis. Some of them are cross-border workers, but the vast majority come to buy. Many gather at the warehouses near the border post where trade is carried on in cheap blankets and quilts made in South Korea, clothes from India and China, and foodstuffs. Women and men, weighed down by heavy loads on their backs, return to Morocco and frequently have to bribe Moroccan border guards to let them pass with their overload of wares. Others have brought cars, bikes and mopeds to the enclave. Moroccans who have gone downtown to buy large luxury goods, such as television sets and refrigerators, hire small pickup trucks that take the goods to the border crossing. An unknown but substantial part of the export from Ceuta to Morocco takes place through smuggling: day and night, small speedboats loaded with contraband shuttle between the enclave and its hinterland. Spanish border guards turn a blind eye to this black export, whereas their Moroccan colleagues either lack the means to stop it or are themselves involved in the smuggling racket.

One of the consequences of intensified border control on the Spanish side of the Mediterranean divide in general and of the barbed-wire fences of Ceuta in particular, has been the filling-up of the enclave with clandestine immigrants from Africa who cannot cross over to the European side. Only a few of them manage to hide in and underneath trucks ferried to Algeciras. Until recently, they were stuck under appalling conditions in an improvised and overpopulated encampment which numbered 2,700 inhabitants in 1999. Several times over the past ten years there have been racial clashes in the enclave. From time to time the 'new immigrants' have to be redistributed to refugee centres across the Mediterranean in order to reduce tensions. In 1996 migrants were still entering Ceuta by walking in from Morocco through the hills at night. Since 2000 a wall of high double fences with a patrol corridor in between, monitored by armed civil guards and sophisticated detection electronics and financed by the EU, has been constructed to halt the influx. Nonetheless, migrants still manage to enter the enclave by sea. At the time of my visit there were about 400 of them living under greatly improved conditions in pre-fabricated buildings with sleeping quarters and dining halls, equipped with TV sets and a broad view across the Strait to the promised lands of Europe.

Recently, thousands of young African men have been gathering under appalling conditions on the Moroccan side of Ceuta's barbed-wire fences waiting for a chance to climb them with help of home-made ladders. They are trying out new strategies, for instance the mass storming of the border fences in the late hours of the night. In one of these assaults, on 29 September 2005, more than 600 migrants from Black Africa stormed the three-and-a-half metre fence. Five of them were killed by bullets fired by the Spanish and Moroccan border guards, 108 were wounded and at least 163 managed to reach 'paradise' on the other side of the frontier. The Spanish government immediately sent extra troops to the enclaves (in Melilla there were several mass assaults on the border as well) to reinforce border patrols. Moreover, the decision was taken to double the height of the fences.

Hyper consumption and lack of regular employment create an uncontrolled profusion of itinerant trades and services in Ceuta: peddling of cigarettes, newspapers, cannabis, fruits, chewing gum, trinkets, and second-hand clothes; parking guards, guides, car washers, carriers, cleaners, beggars and prostitutes. There is a clear hierarchy in this informal economy, which is based on race, nationality, gender, age, experience, cunning and sometimes sheer force.

Black Africans are mostly at the bottom of this fluid underclass pecking order. But they are strikingly entrepreneurial and inventive compared to Moroccans, who dominate the local hashish traffic and Algerians who have a monopoly on car guarding. Men from West Africa had improvised several car-washing places along the coastal road, sold newspapers in the streets, and helped to load and unload cars at supermarkets. The Spanish inhabitants make frequent use of such cheap services. All people living in Ceuta are border people but the illegal immigrants are much more so than the established citizens. They are included in the informal economic sphere yet excluded from the socio-political and formal economic domains.

On a clear night one can see from upper Tangier (Tanjah) the lights of Tarifa. The main point of orientation for the 'guides' who smuggle 'new migrants' to the other side are the bright lights of a petrol station two kilometres out of Tarifa town. During my visit to Tangier in March 1992, a young local took me to a street in the old town which was known as the 'street of the blacks' with cheap boarding houses and tea-houses where smugglers (called 'wolves') and their clients (called 'sheep') met to haggle over the price of the nocturnal passage. This was done quite openly, Moroccan authorities turning a blind eye to these practices. Later that year, after mounting pressure by Spain and the EU and with promises of development aid, King Hassan II declared war on illegal emigration, corruption and drugs. A new police chief was appointed in Tangier, some 'big heads' were arrested, black

Africans were deported, and thousands of soldiers were deployed to guard the beaches. When I returned to Tangier in June 1993, there were indeed few black people in the streets but the number of soldiers patrolling the beaches had also been reduced. The smuggling rackets lay low for a while and moved their centres of operation to the nearby Moroccan towns of Tetuan and Larache. In the mid-1990s, however, they were back in business. The northern promontory of Morocco became known as the *bled harraga*, the land of people-smuggling (Juntunen 2002). On a normal day one can see hundreds of young Moroccan men hanging around in the squares of Tangier, Larache and Tetuan, waiting for an opportunity to make the passage to Spain. They often depart in a group of four or five boats with twenty-five to thirty immigrants per boat. In 2000 the average price per passenger was US$1,500. Part of this money is used for bribing coastal guards and policemen.

There are more than 500,000 people living in Tangier, its suburbs and *bidon-villes*. The pulse and focus of city life is predicated on cross-border traffic. Regular ferry services to and from Algeciras bring and take tourists, migrants, and trucks. The port also handles imports of cereals, sugar, and building materials. Tourism, transport, construction, fishing and textile (carpet) industries are the main sectors of the local economy, together with hundreds of small artisan workshops (the so-called *ensembles artisanaux*) and the overcrowded informal street economy (water sellers, hawkers, musicians, tourist guides, beggars, petty thieves, cleaners and day labourers).

The location of the city at the crossroads of Europe and Africa, the Mediterranean and the Atlantic, made it a bone of contention among the European powers. Given its strategic position, Tangier was destined to become an international city in the era of colonialism, a symbol of foreign domination, a node of communication, a place of transit for money and gold, goods and people, ideas and meanings, and a screen for the projection of fantasies (Driessen 1995).

Among members of the Moroccan political and religious elite, Tangier is often referred to as the 'whore of the nation', a place infected by European influences and the evils of smuggling, corruption, prostitution, drugs, and violence. It is perceived as a constant threat to the integrity of the Moroccan state and its Muslim identity. Seen from the political and cultural centre of the kingdom, Tangier is indeed located on the edge of Moroccan society, and has never been an integral part of the Moroccan sultanate nor of the modern nation-state. From a local perspective, a considerable number of inhabitants live with their backs turned to Rabat and with their faces towards Europe. Many of them are Rifian Berbers, second-rate citizens in the eyes of Arabs. Their homelands are in the peripheral Mediterranean part of Morocco with a tradition of emigration going back to the 1860s. As border people they are betwixt and between Europe and Africa, their networks of kinship and marriage often straddling the Mediterranean divide. They try to manipulate the border situation to their own advantage and have learnt to deal with the imbroglio of conflicting loyalties and identifications.

The Moroccan–Spanish border figures prominently in daily discourse in the streets, squares, and households of Tangier.[4] In the exclusively male domain of outdoor cafés, the quality of life in various places in Morocco, Ceuta, Spain and other EU countries is frequently discussed. Recurrent themes are job opportunities, prices and wages, degrees of freedom and repression, the level of social services, the desire to cross over to Spain, differences between Moroccan and European women. Young men often complain about the fastidiousness of Moroccan women as to jewellery, clothes, presents, the high level of marriage payments, and high costs of weddings as opposed to European women who are supposed to be less materialistic and more interested in love and sex. Border talk is an interesting cocktail of collective fantasies (often fed by television programmes) and personal experiences as well as those related by others, and ambivalences towards Spain and Morocco. Border talk flows through the networks of kinship which constitute the backbone of border culture. These networks provide access to smugglers, real or false documents and information about routes and contacts between Morocco and the European Union.

The passage between Morocco and Spain has for more than six generations been a common practice, a way of making a living, for thousands of families living in the Tangier area and beyond. Now that legal border crossing into Spain has become a scarce resource, families have to resort to clandestine practices. Most of them are determined to defy both the Moroccan and the Spanish states.

Comparative remarks

Tarifa, Algeciras, Ceuta and Tangier not only share their port condition, a maritime identity and their strategic position in the contested frontier zone between two continents and on one of the busiest sea lanes in the world, but also deep historical interconnections as border places. From these fundamental commonalities several other shared characteristics result. All depend to a high degree on connectivity as a basic resource for survival. All have somewhat troubled relationships with the Spanish and Moroccan states which by means of their agents – port authorities, customs officers and border guards – have vested interests in controlling cross-border traffic and securing the integrity of their territories and national identities which are most vulnerable at the borders. In all four ports the border situation plays an important role in shaping repertoires of behaviour and meaning in daily life. For instance, smuggling is unequivocally illegal from the state perspective, yet morally acceptable as a way of making a living for many people in this border zone.

To be sure, there are also differences among the four ports relating to demographic size, volume of traffic, openness, types and substance of power resources, local ideology, permeability, inclusion and exclusion of newcomers, and the nature of links with higher levels of integration, the European Union included. For instance, Tarifa and Algeciras have been thoroughly 'Europeanised' whereas Ceuta is a more complex case given its liminal position and ethnic composition. Tangier is the least Moroccan and, together with Nador, probably the most European city of Morocco. Many of its inhabitants live with their face turned to the North. This diversity of seaports is one of the reasons why the European Union is still far removed from a united, integrated and coordinated approach to the border problems. Some of the member states, i.e. Spain and Italy, have tried to counter the social and economic problems resulting from the new immigration and the official policy of excluding uncontrolled newcomers by periodic regularisation measures; through these, tens of thousands of immigrants are legalised and turned into taxpayers. One of the drawbacks of this policy is that it immediately attracts new streams of refugees and other migrants.

A final issue to be discussed is the nature of this Spanish–Moroccan borderland. It is obvious that the four cases considered here are part of one economic and geopolitical field, albeit a field with some major demographic, economic, political and ideological divisions, which seem deeper as seen from the political centres than as experienced on the ground. According to the great French historian Fernand Braudel (1975), the Mediterranean 'Channel' never acted as a barrier between Europe and Africa, but rather as a river that united more than it divided, making a single world of North and South. Although this may have been true during some periods in the long history of this part of the Mediterranean world, the 'river' has certainly deepened and widened over the past few decades. The fact that increasing numbers of African people are willing to risk their lives crossing it indicates the degree of division and divergence.

Notes

1 See also Ribas-Mateos (2005) on border towns around the Mediterranean. This book appeared after this chapter was finished.
2 Personal communication, October 2000. I carried out short-term fieldwork in Tarifa, Algeciras, Tangier and Ceuta in the spring of 1992, the summers of 1993 and 1997, in the autumn of 2000, and in the spring of 2003. ATIME, an organisation of Moroccan immigrants in Spain, puts the number of drowned immigrants at 3,920. The 'present' in this chapter refers to the 1990s, unless indicated otherwise.
3 See for an excellent study of Muslims in Ceuta Evers Rosander (1991).
4 Even in the city of Tetuan, more than 50 kilometres south-east of Tangier, café talk is often border talk (Nyberg Sorensen 2000).

References

Braudel, F. (1975) *The Mediterranean and the Mediterranean World in the Age of Philip II*, Vol. I, London: Fontana/Collins.

Castejón Arqued, R. (1996) 'Commercial ports in Spain', *Tijdschrift voor Economische en Sociale Geografie* 87: 357–363.

Driessen, H. (1995) 'Transitional Tangier. Some notes on passage and representation', *Kea. Zeitschrift für Kulturwissenschaften*, 8: 149–62.

Driessen, H. (1996) 'At the edge of Europe: crossing and marking the Mediterranean divide', in L. O'Dowd and T.M. Wilson (eds) *Borders, Nations and States. Frontiers of Sovereignty in the New Europe*, Aldershot: Avebury.

Driessen, H. (1998) 'The "new immigration" and the transformation of the European–African frontier', in T.M. Wilson and H. Donnan (eds) *Border Identities. Nation and State at International Frontiers*, Cambridge: Cambridge University Press.

Driessen, H. (1999) 'Smuggling as a border way of life: A Mediterranean case', in

M. Rösler and T. Wendl (eds) *Frontiers and Borderlands. Anthropological Perspectives*, Frankfurt am Main: Peter Lang.

Evers Rosander, E. (1991) *Women in a Borderland. Managing Muslim Identity Where Morocco Meets Spain*, Stockholm: Stockholm Studies in Social Anthropology.

Juntunen, M. (2002) 'Between Morocco and Spain. Men, migrant smuggling and a dispersed Moroccan community', unpublished Ph.D. thesis, University of Helsinki.

King, R. (1997) 'Population growth: an unavoidable crisis?', in R. King, L. Proudfoot and B. Smith (eds) *The Mediterranean. Environment and Society*, London: Arnold.

Nyberg Sorensen, N. (2000) 'Crossing the Spanish–Moroccan border with migrants, new Islamists, and riff raff', *Ethnologia Europaea* 30: 87–100.

Ribas-Mateos, N. (2005) *The Mediterranean in the Age of Globalisation. Migration, Welfare and Borders*, New Brunswick and London: Transaction Publishers.

Puerto Bahia de Algeciras (2002) *Annual Report*.

Servicio de Estadistica de Andalucia (2000) *Annual Report*.

6 Europe and Islam

Partnership or peripheral dependence?

George Joffé

In November 2005, the European Union, together with its partners in the South Mediterranean basin, reviewed the progress of its major policy initiative there, the Euro-Mediterranean Partnership, ten years after it was initiated. At the founding conference of the Partnership in the city of Barcelona in November 1995, the new policy had been lauded, through the Barcelona Declaration, as an attempt to create a region of shared peace, prosperity and stability in the Mediterranean basin. The normative objective, of course, which incidentally implied a removal of barriers and divisions between states, concealed the real purpose of the policy, which was to apply the principles of soft security to enhancing European security along its southern periphery – in other words, to reassert the importance of boundaries and division. The soft security objectives were to be achieved primarily by stimulating economic development in South Mediterranean countries in order to minimise labour migration into Europe, seen at the time as a major source of internal social, political and economic tension in both Europe and the countries concerned, given the demographic pressures they faced.

Europe's Mediterranean policies

The detailed policy anticipated the organisation of a series of bilateral free trade arrangements between individual South Mediterranean states and the European Union in industrial goods, thus exposing their industrial sectors – seen as the primary potential generators of growth and employment – to unfettered competition with European industry. This, it was anticipated, would force an optimal use of resources in the countries concerned, attract foreign investment and ensure appropriate economic reforms to meet the European challenge by modernising their economies. It was an approach to the issue that recalled the principles behind the European Union's own construction, culminating in the Single European Market. It was also paralleled by a series of multilateral partnership measures based on the confidence-building approach established by the Conference on Cooperation and Security in Europe, held in Helsinki in 1975 to initiate the process of détente. And it repeated the ideas of the Italian–Spanish non-paper of 1990 which proposed a similar Conference on Cooperation and Security in the Mediterranean. These were to construct the shared zone of peace and stability whilst the integration of Southern markets would provide a shared prosperity.

The new policy was based on the principles of economic integration with the implied assumption of free movement of capital and goods. But it remained faithful to its underlying purpose and did not include the essential third freedom, that of labour. Borders and divisions, in short, were to be preserved for economic and political reasons. Indeed, to this extent, it faithfully replicated the underlying principles of détente which had sought to create confidence-building measures designed to reassure the Soviet Union against its fears of military threat but not to assimilate it, with its alien political system, into Western Europe or the wider Western sphere. That would have to await internal change and the spontaneous disintegration of the Socialist bloc in 1989 with the end of the Cold War. In the same way, the Barcelona Process was designed to promote economic, social and political change within established boundaries and indirectly reinforce their effectiveness, thus primarily serving the objective of European security through Europe's preferred diplomatic instruments.

Thus the basket of economic measures designed to set up the bilateral free trade areas with the Union – which were eventually intended to be integrated into a single South Mediterranean market to match the Single European Market – was matched by two other baskets of measures. One basket dealt with common security concerns in the Mediterranean, aiming to construct a cooperative security regime, an objective that, given the ongoing crisis in relations between Israel and the Palestinians, has remained stillborn. It also advanced the prospect of democratic governance and institutional respect for human rights as an essential part of the modernisation package. The other basket addressed measures directed at creating mutual public appreciation of cultures and societies, alongside others designed to stimulate the development of civil society in the South Mediterranean.[1] It has to be said that there has not been much progress on either objective, both because of the timidity of European politicians and because of Southern resentment of European xenophobia at home and interference abroad, not to speak of the wider implications of Western policy after the events of 11 September 2001 in the United States.

What the new Euro-Mediterranean Partnership, better known as the 'Barcelona Process', did not do was to resolve the inherent contradiction between closer economic cooperation and the persistence of political division. This focused around the issues of migration and visas. Migration had originally been treated by the Union on the basis of a zero-inward migration policy and seen as part of the Justice and Home Affairs pillar of the Maastricht Treaty. By the end of the 1990s, however, Europe recognised that it had become an immigration area and that a policy of managed migration would be necessary – a concern of the Common Foreign and Security Policy because it would involve state-to-state negotiation (Aubarell and Aragall 2005, 8–9). Even though this implied that migration and thus labour flows would be permitted, it was still based on the idea that this would take place between states and thus across borders normatively defined as impermeable.

European visa policy maintained this, whether inside the Schengen area or outside it, so that the difficulties in obtaining a visa came to be a major theme of complaint from the South to the North of the Mediterranean. Similarly, the rapidly increasing flows of illegal migration and asylum-seekers from the South highlighted the reality of the European external border and the growing tensions that it caused – as President Jacques Chirac learned on his famous official visit to Algeria in August 2003, when he was greeted by the mass chanting of 'visas, visas!' by the crowds who welcomed him. Their cries were also a salutary warning to European politicians of the potential failure of the Barcelona Process to achieve its declared objectives, as illegal migration into Europe rose inexorably towards 400,000–500,000 a year (Jandl 2004, 150).

Challenges

The reality of this potential failure has been to prioritise the significance of the boundary around the European periphery and has been highlighted by two other developments that reinforce this tendency, despite the innate contradiction with the normative values of the Euro-Mediterranean Partnership. The first of these has been the European reaction to both the implicit failure of the Barcelona Process and the challenge to it offered by similar American policy proposals such as the US–Middle East Partnership Initiative (USMEPI) or the Broader Middle East–North Africa Initiative (BMENA). The second is the increasing securitisation of Europe's Common Foreign and Security Policy in response to the perceived threat of global terrorism in the wake of the Madrid train bombings in March 2004 and the London bombings of July 2005. This tendency had begun long before, after the events of September 2001, but has accelerated dramatically in recent years and is now conditioning all other external policies.

This highlights the inherent irrelevance of the external European frontier because its primary target is actually an internalised enemy, Europe's poorly integrated migrant communities, and because it is increasingly being seen at the demotic and instinctive level as a cultural confrontation. Indeed, it could be argued that this struggle goes even further back, into the heart of the European project itself with its own normative values of political secularism and intellectual tolerance. In many respects, these are being inverted into statements of cultural intolerance in that, unless they are accepted in their entirety by alien non-European groups within the Union – whether or not they are in the process of being Europeanised through assimilation or integration – such groups are to be excluded from the European project despite their residence in Europe in a deliberate process of migrant cultural and social 'ghettoisation'.

This was, after all, the inherent significance of the message issued by Pim Fortuyn, the charismatic Dutch politician who was assassinated in 2002. His political party, the Lijst Pim Fortuyn, was predicated on the assumption of a cultural clash between European principle and Islamic values which he saw as an inherent threat (Fortuyn 1997) – multiculturalism as a threat to Dutch traditional tolerance (Cherry 2002). Although he was roundly criticised in Europe for his attitudes towards immigrants, he articulated very well a widespread European prejudice, against those who did not accept European principles of democratic governance and human rights observance and who, for that reason alone, should be excluded from the European cultural space. It is an argument that has resurfaced violently in the wake of the murder of the Dutch film and television director, Theo Van Gogh, by a Moroccan Islamist resident in Holland in 2004, and in the Danish cartoon row in early 2006.

In this respect, if not in others, Fortuyn did mirror widely felt views in Europe about the supremacy of European values, views which acted as a respectable counterpart to the even more widespread xenophobia that has, to official embarrassment, often emerged in recent years. Such approaches, of course, as with the securitisation of foreign policy in the face of an alleged terrorist threat, inevitably provoke a response from those perceived to be responsible. The response is often complex but, at one level it involves alienation, either overt or covert, and thus the institution of another parallel cultural boundary to mirror the one created around the European project. This boundary, however, derives its legitimacy from a cultural element seen as the identifier which enables both the migrant community and the multicultural project to be targeted – Islam. Thus the task before us in determining how Europe and the Islamic world will interact is to define the origins and justifications for the cultural boundaries that divide them, as well as to investigate the specific policies that produce them. Part of this process is to appreciate the degree to which, despite tensions over neoconservatism and the invasion of Iraq, current European and American agendas share common values and approaches.

American soft security alternatives

In essence Europe and the United States have a common interest in shaping the Mediterranean environment to enhance their security interests, although those interests differ. For Europe, as described above, the dominant concern relates to the Southern European periphery and seeks to ensure border security within an environment of controlled migration. That concern has now been complicated by the growing security threats within Europe itself which are linked, in part to the external political environment and also to the European reaction to it. The result has been an increasing tendency to internalise these political concerns and to redefine them in terms of a cultural confrontation within and outside Europe that manifests itself as globalised terrorism.

For the United States, the security concern is quite different in that threats in the Mediterranean remain geographically external to the United States itself and relate to its wider strategic concerns. These reflect the security of strategic lines of communication[2] through the Mediterranean itself, given that they are dominated by a series of choke-points, and the situation in the Eastern Mediterranean with respect to Israel and the Persian Gulf. Of course, in the wake of the events of 11 September 2001, the United States has, in effect, adopted Samuel Huntington's concept of the clash of civilisations (Huntington 1993) – an essentially culturalist interpretation of security threat. This has not, however, been internalised as is the case with the European Union but it has emphasised a coincident geographic and cultural boundary, particularly with respect to Israel. Here, the United States, in addition, to its hard security response in the 'war on terror', has now adopted soft security responses in a similar fashion to the European Union. This, in essence, argues – as does Europe – that the adoption of certain specific cultural and political values and practices could eliminate the security threat, provided that innate and indigenous parallel values are discarded. Despite superficial differences between the two projects – European and American – at root, they are surprisingly similar, even if articulated in different ways.

Thus, on 12 December 2002, the then secretary-of-state, Colin Powell, in an address to the Heritage Foundation in Washington introduced a new soft security policy for the Mediterranean.[3] This, the US–Middle East Partnership Initiative, was designed to compensate for deficiencies in governance, economic development, educational approaches and the empowerment of women, to which Congress had committed $302.9 million over a four-year period for the multilateral initiatives, in addition to the $1 billion-worth of bilateral aid that the United States supplies to the region every year.[4] In 2004, the United States opened two regional offices to manage this initiative and has negotiated bilateral free trade areas with Jordan, Tunisia and Morocco. The initiative is also the vehicle through which the individual programmes of the Broader Middle East and North Africa Initiative, proposed by the United States and adopted by the G8 group of states at the Sea Island meeting in 2004, are put into operation.

The interesting feature of this new American policy is that, even though its security justification is quite different, it is in direct competition with the Barcelona Process, at least as far as governance and economic development are concerned. At best, such duplication causes confusion and at worst it provides a mechanism by which Southern governments can avoid commitments they do not wish to undertake by playing off the European Union against the United States. It is not clear why cooperation between both major regional powers was not encouraged when the United States decided to adopt a soft security approach and, although Commission officials today claim that there is no conflict, the Commission presidency in 2002 had no doubt at all that the American initiative was designed, in part at least, to challenge Europe.[5] After all, the United States had been sidelined when the Barcelona Process had been introduced in 1995!

It is also clear that the American initiative also emphasises the existence of a cultural barrier between a realm of assumed secular democratic tolerance and an external arena of cultural otherness characterised by violence and threat. This is to be corrected by the introduction of cultural and political change in a rather more intrusive fashion, particularly with respect to education and the status of women, than that practised by the European Union, although the underlying assumptions are the same in both cases. Both arise from shared perceptions of a new international order, created by the hegemony of a single hyperpower, to use Hubert Védriné's term. Here, Europe must find its place, despite the contradiction this may create with its underlying interests, given the presence of domestic migrant communities and a turbulent periphery in which the turbulence is, in part, a consequence of the attitudes and policies of its dominant partner, the United States.

A new international order

Most analyses of international relations today start with an assumption that a new world order was essentially established upon the ashes of the Cold War. With the destruction of the prolonged stability of the Cold War, a new kind of stability emerged, predicated on the predominance of the United States in security and economic terms – a kind of uni-polar hegemonic stability – and on the universalisation of the liberal democratic model and the market economy – the modern version of globalisation.[6] The first airing of this new world occurred in the aftermath of the expulsion of Iraq from Kuwait by the Multinational Coalition under the leadership of the first Bush presidency and the aegis of a revived United Nations, now set, apparently, to operate as its founders had intended. Intellectually, the spirit of the new age was captured by Francis Fukuyama's concept of the 'End of History' (Fukuyama 1989) and Adam Robert's vision of a developed world as a 'Grotian one, observing norms of cooperation, and perhaps even has its Kantian element: a civil society of civil societies' (Roberts 1991).

There were, of course, competing visions, hinted at by Adam Roberts when he went on to remark that, outside this normatively ideal focus, 'parts of the world beyond are still Hobbesian, with force still a very active final arbiter within and between countries, and sovereignty loudly proclaimed'. It was a vision that was to be given sinews by Samuel Huntington in his famous article, later amplified by an influential book, entitled 'The clash of civilisations,' in which civilisational conflict would replace war based on national interest. At the time, this view was swamped by the confident belief that the Westphalian system was coming to an end, that a world community based on idealistic concepts of an international society ordered through international law and the United Nations would replace it, and that geo-economics[7] would sweep away the neo-realist concept of geopolitics as a definition of the new world order.

During the 1990s, furthermore, a series of new ideas began to emerge, building in part on new, postmodernist concepts of sovereignty. These allowed for intervention in the internal affairs of a state, indeed encouraged it, if it in some way abused universal principles of human rights; or, because it repressed its own population, it could be considered to have forfeited its right to rule, since sovereignty was an expression of general will or collective legitimacy, not solely of the power of the state (Weber 1995). By the end of the decade, this had blossomed into a full-blown ideology of intervention, particularly in the Anglo-Saxon world, as typified by Tony Blair's Chicago speech on 22 April 1999.[8] These ideas were given intellectual substance by Robert Cooper, a British diplomat, who first argued that the postmodern state would be a construct of a state within an ordered international community where sovereignty was voluntarily derogated. He subsequently proposed a reification of interventionism under the rubric of 'reluctant imperialism', which turned out to be suspiciously similar to concepts of liberalism imperialism as developed at the height of the Victorian era (Cooper 1998, 2003).

Such ideas meshed well with those that were to emerge when the Bush administration came to power in 2001 and the neoconservative agenda came to dominate the foreign policy process. The new concepts not only involved the long-standing American conservative vision of the projection of national interest at a global level – first proposed and justified by President Reagan in the 1980s, as a kind of inversion of the moral status of American democracy into the international area as a justification of the practice of diplomatic neo-realism – but also added its own unique assumptions. These involved the practice of unilateral force, on a pre-emptive basis if need be, to establish an international democratic environment sympathetic to, and supportive of, the United States and its allies. The neoconservatives rejected the restraining influence of international organisations or an international, law-based community (Halper and Clarke 2003, 254–257). They also distanced themselves from the European Community's endorsement of such an approach and its innate preference for soft security and the preferred European diplomatic technique of constructive engagement (Kagan 2003).

The neoconservatives were a product of the frustrations felt by the United States during the 1990s and of the underlying American distaste for any kind of restraint on its diplomatic activities. As such, they were well within an American tradition reaching back, ironically enough, to Woodrow Wilson as well as to his Congressional critics at the time who had refused to endorse the international institutions created by the Treaty of Versailles. They also reflected many of the assumptions behind the geo-economics of the Clinton era, much though they decried Clintonian foreign policy. In a sense, they combined the universalism of Francis Fukuyama's vision and the scepticism of Samuel Huntington. Even more surprisingly, they echoed many of the assumptions behind the New Right in Europe, even though they rejected the European project.

Indeed, in many respects, their arrival in power, as articulated through the Bush administration and, subsequently, in the new national security doctrine enunciated by the new administration (White House 2002), marks the end of a long period of transition from the Cold War to a genuine new world order. This has little to do with a rule-based international society and much more to do with the revival of a neo-realist approach to the international arena, albeit now against a globalised economic background. And, of course, it is this conundrum that Europe is now struggling either to digest or reject because of the contradiction between innate, if rarely voiced, European sympathy for such a project and overt European preference for international law as the leaven for international relations. It is a crucial contradiction for it provides the intellectual counterpart to the internalised cultural boundary that has emerged in recent years as a result of terrorist violence.

It is against this intellectual environment that the implications of the events of 11 September 2001 should be seen. Ironically enough, they acted as a catalyst for the application of the neoconservative agenda to the Middle East and for the development of the associated 'war on terror' which now applies to the whole region, together with South East Asia, Afghanistan and Pakistan. They have resulted in profound changes in regional politics and geopolitics, as well as in the underlying assumptions behind American and, to a lesser extent, European regional diplomacy. They have also generated a competition over soft security, as opposed to hard security responses in the Mediterranean region and in the Gulf. Most strikingly of all, they have nourished the development of a major, dispersed and fragmented terrorist threat, exploiting modern means of communication and benefiting from access to a coherent intellectual background that has profoundly affected the internal politics and security assumptions of states throughout Europe, as well as in the United States. And, most importantly, both sides in this conflict are increasingly interlinked through a dialectic of antiphonal, mutually reinforcing violence – a reification, as it were, of the 'clash of civilisations'.

The European response

In the past three years, Europe has had to respond to these new challenges, as well as to some old ones. It has had to face the fact that the Barcelona Process has failed to realise its early promise; it must confront the challenge of American soft security policies in the Mediterranean; and it has had to confront the issue of terrorism within its external frontier. It has also had to face the implications of Enlargement, especially in the East where new states now share its common external frontier, many of them also seeking membership of the Union itself. The issue began to be faced in 2002, at the Copenhagen summit of the Council of the European Union. A fully developed policy was produced by the European Commission in May 2004[9] – the month of Eastwards Enlargement – directed towards the new frontier states of the Ukraine, Belarus and Moldova – Russia was excluded at its own request – as well as the ten remaining partner-states in the Barcelona Process. Turkey was excluded because of its imminent accession negotiations, but Libya was included because of its expressed desire to join the Euro-Mediterranean Partnership. Finally, in June 2004, the states of the Caucasus also joined the new frontier policy (Smith 2005, 760) as a result of a decision taken by the European Union's Council on 17 June 2004.

The policy is designed to create a 'ring of friends' around the European Union and to respond to the problem that Enlargement cannot be indefinitely extended, although European security depends on political and economic change in neighbouring states, something which, therefore – as in the Barcelona Process – the Union would wish to encourage. As such, although much of the policy is copied from the Enlargement experience (Kelley 2005), its roots lie in the European Security Strategy, developed in 2003 (Aliboni 2005, 1). In other words, in security terms, the new policy is primarily concerned with trafficking of drugs and people, organised crime, terrorism and similar trans-border issues including the environment. This is, of course, inevitable, once the decision was taken in Brussels to limit future Enlargement, although the fact that boundaries between the neighbour states concerned and the European Union are to be maintained is to be mitigated by encouraging cross-border cooperation.

The logic behind the policy is, however, unchanged from that behind the Barcelona Process or, indeed, behind the parallel American initiatives; namely that neighbourhood states must accept European values in terms of governance and economic policy to enable them to become 'friends' and 'neighbours' but that doing so only provides proximity to the European Union, not access. Thus the policy proposes that a series of individual bilateral relations be established between the Union and each state. In this, the non-European partner is encouraged to adapt its political and economic policies towards the norms of the European Union. As this occurs, greater and greater access is provided to the instruments of the Union itself, except that participation in the actual governance of the Union will not be part of the agreement. In other words, through a process of positive conditionality, neighbourhood states are encouraged to apply the European *acquis communautaire* (Tocci 2005, 30),[10] on the assumption that this will reduce potential security threats as, in effect, such states adopt the Copenhagen criteria which lie at the root of the Enlargement process.[11]

The policy itself is articulated through a series of Action Plans. These consist of bilateral agreements between the Union and individual states in which a programme of action, over three to five years, is laid out to achieve the overall objective. The state concerned determines the content of the Action Plan, thus establishing what it considers a reasonable programme, whilst the Union monitors progress through a process of benchmarking and provides political, administrative and financial support. From 2007, the old Barcelona MEDA programme, together with the programmes for funding political and economic change in the East, such as the TACIS programme, will be absorbed into a new financial instrument designed specifically for the European Neighbourhood Policy.[12]

Unlike the Barcelona Process, of course, the old principle of horizontal integration has disappeared and the new policy is resolutely bilateral in its conception. It rejects the multilateralism inherent in the Barcelona Process as a complicating factor which led in part to the failure of the Euro-Mediterranean Partnership. Thus it entrenches the 'hub-and-spoke' concept which the Barcelona Process considered to be a temporary stage to be overcome by horizontal integration in the political, security and social spheres once economic integration had been achieved in the South. In security terms, it seeks to build what Attina regards as an amalgamated security community, as defined by Karl Deutsch (Attina 2004, 16–17).[13] As William Wallace has said, 'Western Europe faces the uncomfortable choice of importing insecurity from its neighbours, or of exporting to them security – which necessarily involves prosperity and stability' (Balfour and Rotta 2005, 9).The policy is thus overtly Eurocentric, avoiding any of the linguistic moderation of the Euro-Mediterranean Partnership, even if its underlying purpose was little different. It thus does little to alter or moderate the cultural boundaries within the European Union which replicate its external and political boundary – a situation which is worsened by the growing securitisation of inter-communal relations within the European continent.

Bounded conflict

This has been a direct consequence of the attacks on the United States on 11 September 2001. To a very large extent, European governments adopted the American position that global terrorism represented a substantial existential threat.

To this the appropriate response, after the initial hot war against Afghanistan and the al-Qa'ida and Taliban infrastructure there, was indeed a war of unlimited duration. This war, to be fought by sanctions, proscription and elimination, was directed against the alleged manifestations of terrorism, not against its causes. Terrorism itself was an abominable manifestation of violence, to be countered and crushed on those grounds alone with no allowance made for the fact that it was often driven by perceived injustice in terms of Western policy towards the Islamic world. Nor was there any awareness that such terrorist actions derived their own moral status from perceptions of the immorality of Western policy inside the Islamic world.

To be fair, European statesmen inside the Union, particularly within the European Commission, were well aware of the danger of allowing Muslims, whether inside or outside the Union itself, to believe that Europeans identified Islam as identical to a political ideology associated with political violence. Thus considerable efforts were expended on expanding inter-faith dialogue to counter such sentiments and in trying to separate political violence from Islam. Similarly, the American Manichean discourse, inherent in the 'war on terror' of absolute good and absolute evil, was challenged by the European preference for dialogue between cultures and societies (Silvestre 2005). At the same time, the practical measures taken by European states and the European Union increasingly accepted the innate thesis behind the American view of global terrorism – the unicity and cohesiveness of the global terrorist movement. Thus measures targeting groups and individuals aligned with political Islamic extremism were adopted, irrespective of whether such ideas automatically led to the violent organisations associated with the al-Qa'ida movement. There was no awareness that, within the activist political Islamic movements, there was considerable differentiation between those with global and national agendas and that the globalists were an extremely small minority (Gerges 2005, 43–79).

More serious, perhaps, in the European context was the fact that European states and the Union began to strengthen their links in the field of justice and home affairs with Mediterranean states which had had major problems with domestic political violence; these, since the advent of the 1990s, had usually been couched within an Islamist rhetoric. European statesmen increasingly accepted that the national Islamist violence experienced in countries such as Egypt, Libya, Tunisia, Algeria and, in 2003, Morocco was a manifestation of the integrated globalist network operated by al-Qa'ida and that North African violence had its replicates inside Europe itself. The result of this was to belie the virtues of dialogue evinced by European statesmen and to emphasise the cultural boundaries that existed both within Europe and between populations, whether migrant or indigenous, and the governments that rule over them. Such governments were, in any case, often perceived as illegitimate, particularly by Islamists. Since they were now seen to be in collaboration with the European Union and European states, despite their discourse of democratic governance and respect for human rights, the result was to alienate political activists at home and migrant communities within Europe from the European ideal.

European states, therefore, began to root out alleged networks of potential terrorists on their own territories. Some of those arrested undoubtedly did have terrorist projects in mind, others did not but all were forced into a common security mould reflecting the globalised assumptions of the 'war on terror'. But there was little awareness that the causes might also have to do with social problems, arising from the double alienation and the imposition of cultural boundaries within Europe itself that are described above. The result was merely to entrench within migrant communities a sense of isolation and alienation that encouraged the further adoption of Islamist paradigms of violent action. Thus the gulf between migrant and host community deepened.

In fact, the involvement of migrant communities in terrorism and violence long predates al-Qa'ida, as the example of France shows. It has been the target of concerted terrorist actions carried out by migrants in both the 1980s and the 1990s. In the 1980s, the actions were connected with the Middle East and France's perceived role there, particularly in Lebanon, Iraq and Iran. There was a series of attacks on the French transport network in 1985 and 1986, mainly by sympathisers with two groups of Lebanese militants, some of whom had been imprisoned in France. Two prisoners, in particular, were important, Georges Abdullah, a Marxist, and Anis Naccache, a Shi'a activist with links to Iran. It is difficult to argue an Islamist paradigm behind such actions in such disparate cases, even though the activists concerned were largely North African residents of France and Belgium, some of whom had been sympathisers with the Iranian revolution. In large measure, these incidents revealed another, more important consideration that is extremely important today. North African residents of France were involved, not because of their global concerns but because of their sense of alienation within France itself. It is a phenomenon now widely recognised as the 'banlieusard' (suburbanite) problem because of the conditions and isolation in the ghetto-like suburbs occupied by North African migrants and French citizens of North African origin around most major French cities; this is demonstrated by the cycle of violent demonstrations there in late 2005.

The pattern was to be initiated in the 1990s, only then the catalyst through which this sense of alienation was voiced was the crisis in Algeria, essentially concerned with a crisis over political legitimacy, albeit couched in Islamic terms. All clandestine Algerian Islamist groups involved in confrontation with the Algerian government had developed logistic networks in Europe, mainly in France, based on migrant communities and on French nationals of Algerian and wider North African origin. There was also a spate of terrorism in the mid-1990s, centred, with one exception, on the domestic French migrant community, typified by the Chasse-sur-Rhône and Chalabi networks which were implicated in the bombings on the Paris underground system in 1995.

The profound alienation was revealed by a famous and very lengthy interview published by the highly respected French daily newspaper, *Le Monde*, in mid-1995 with Khalid Kelkal, a leading member of the Chasse-sur-Rhône group who was killed shortly afterwards by French police in a notorious incident which came close to extra-judicial execution. Before this, however, there had been a series of explosions on the RER system in Paris and the spate of terrorism came to an end after a shoot-out in Lille. The one incident that did not involve French citizens of North African migrants was the attempt to crash an airliner on Paris in December 1994; that was organised from within Algeria itself, with heavy suspicions now that the Algerian security services may have been implicated in the event (Keenan 2005, 625).

The intellectual background

The interesting consideration has been the form that this alienation has taken, for it is this that highlights the cultural boundaries that have formed. It also underlines the failure of the European Union's preferred option of dialogue, in the face of the policy options adopted by its member-states, particularly towards the situation in the Middle East and the wider world. In essence, the Islamist ideal now prevalent inside the European migrant communities and amongst opposition groups in North Africa seeks an ideal Islamic community.

Were this to be achieved, adherents of these views believe, then it would be possible for every Muslim to live a life to ensure salvation, and Muslim society would achieve its own perfection. Associated with this is the view that the Islamic revelation contains the intellectual corpus to emulate European – 'Western' – success, the essence of the nineteenth-century *Salafi* movement. There is also a long tradition in the Muslim world of seeing contemporary circumstance as the consequence of the loss of the original ideal; there is, therefore, an equally long tradition of seeking to purify the Islamic corpus of accretions on this core-body of doctrine, practice and belief; an essential aspect of *jihad* – the struggle for self-improvement and, by extension, the externalised struggle for the defence of the Muslim world.

In a sense, this intellectual background to political violence linked to Islamic paradigms in Europe is not directly relevant, for it is not itself directly linked to the question of alienation or the internal cultural boundaries that migrant communities face. Yet, insofar as these communities reject European paradigms because they are excluded from them – by xenophobia, intellectual Euro-centrism, or state security practices – they will seek alternative structures of belief that elucidate their situations and give meaning to individual and collective life. The *salafi-jihadi* belief system is immediately available, via the internet and by word of mouth; it is satisfying, as well, as it offers identity and collective meaning. Violence is not a necessary outcome but for those who seek action, it also offers a ready justification.

The striking aspect of the phenomenon is its diametric opposition to the European ideal. In this respect, it forms the parallel and mirror-image cultural boundary wending its way through the migrant communities of Europe, alienated and isolated as a result of the growing gap between European demotic culture and the European ideal. It is a response available to deracinated and alienated youth and, given its unicity – after all, the Islamic ideal reflects a single Islamic community, the *umma*, not a multiplicity of states – it becomes a meaningful counter to the European project itself. As it contains principles of governance and administration, it offers an intellectual challenge as well. Since, finally, it highlights the discordance between European principle and European practice in terms of foreign policy objectives of both European states and the European Union itself, it provides a justification for alienation and confrontation.

Its power, however, is not only based on intellectual and moral persuasiveness; it also offers a powerful inducement to deracinated communities, particularly as far as incorporation into violent action is concerned. An interesting approach to the issue of choices of violence in the context of activism is provided by Marc Sageman (Sageman 2004). He demonstrated that persons involved in apparently extreme ideologically motivated violence, were – superficially at least – normal individuals who had not suffered significant personal deprivation or victimisation. Nor were they necessarily rootless, disoriented individuals seeking a sense of identity after this had been deconstructed through personal experience of, say, globalisation, for they were in part intrinsic to such phenomena.

The one arena in which this was not true was the fact that those directly involved in violence had generally experienced the traumas of migration into Western society and often felt the alienation implicit in such an event. This has been particularly the case with those who were second or subsequent generation migrants, thus being, in effect, European but often still suffering the discrimination and alienation that had faced their parents. It has given rise to the 'banlieusard' phenomenon, which has been linked to political violence and the rise of political Islam there. Similar developments have been noted in other European countries, particularly in Holland and, now, Britain.

One important conclusion that can be drawn from Sageman's study, apart from the fact that it does provide an explanation as to why European immigrants or Europeans of immigrant origin are so heavily involved in political extremism, is that such extremism is not necessarily – initially at least – ideologically linked. Instead, it has a lot to do with isolation, both physical and psychological, and alienation, which is countered by group membership and emulation. In other words, there is no inherent reason why the ideological motivator should be a variant of Islamic doctrine. Indeed, Wiktorowicz, in his study of Islamic activism, does make the important incidental point, in that the means used to express Islamic activism are not unique to the phenomenon itself and he goes on to remark that

> This indicates that the *dynamics, process, and organisation* of Islamic activism can be understood as important elements of contention that transcend the specificity of 'Islam' as a system of meaning, identity, and basis of collective action. Though the ideational components and inspiration of Islam as an ideological worldview differentiate Islamic activism from other examples of contention, the collective action itself and concomitant mechanisms demonstrate consistency across movement-types. In other words, Islamic activism is not sui generic.
>
> (Wiktorowicz 2004, 3)

The importance of this statement is that it immediately undermines a significant body of scholarship that argues that there is a unique quality about the reactions and violence that have emerged in the Middle East and elsewhere in recent years. It is a view that is shared by Olivier Roy, a highly respected commentator on Islamic affairs, who has argued that Islamic activism has colonised the space occupied in the past by other ideologies of protest. However, he adds that it also counters a sense of lost cultural identity, as much as responding to specific political provocation. The same underlying explanation generally permeates purely sociological analyses of such oppositional movements worldwide, thus distancing them from the specific political events that might have acted as catalysts for resistance (Roy 2004).

In other words, the current violence faced by the European Union has little to do with globalised terrorism as an ideological movement or a movement of existential political challenge. It relates, instead, to the consequences arising from the construction of an internal cultural boundary to parallel the social reality of its external frontier; all this against a rhetoric of inclusion that is betrayed by an alienation created by the host community which sees a threat in difference. Immigrants are isolated from their host community inside Europe, just as the Union's external borders isolate the Middle East and North Africa, despite the constant theme of inclusion within Europe and partnership across the Mediterranean.

Notes

1 There is now an extensive literature on the Euro-Mediterranean Partnership, the correct title for the Barcelona Process. Two short introductions to it and to its main activities over the past ten years are provided by the European Commission and the Euro-Mediterranean Human Rights Network. See: http://europa.eu.int/comm./external_relations/euromed www.euromedrights.net/english/barcelona-process/main/html

2 Strategic lines of communication, as defined by the Pentagon, carry 99 per cent of global maritime trade by volume. Four of the nine critical choke-points for global trade exist in the Mediterranean system – the Bosporus and the Dardanelles for access to the Black Sea, the Bab al-Mandab and the Suez Canal which control access to the Red Sea, and the Straits of Gibraltar which controls access to the Atlantic. To these could be added the Straits of Hormuz which control access to the Persian Gulf and 70 per cent of the world's oil reserves. The Mediterranean itself, of course, is a major pathway for the transfer of oil to both Europe and the United States. A choke-point is defined as a waterway narrow enough to be closed by simple military action involving artillery, air or naval power. These issues are studied in detail in Nincic D.J. (2002), 'Sea lane security and US maritime trade: chokepoints as scarce resources', in Tancredi S.J. (2002) (ed.) *Globalisation and Maritime Power*, Institute for National Strategic Studies, National Defense University (Washington DC).

3 http://www.state.gov/secretary/former/powell/remarks/2002/15920.htm

4 The detailed commitments ($ million) are as follows:

	2002	*2003*	*2004*	*2005*
Economic development	6	38	32	23
Political development	10	25	20	22
Educational development	8	25	22	14.4
Women's empowerment	5	12	15.5	15
Totals	29	100	89.5	84.4

Source: http://mepi.state.gov/mepi

These can be compared with funding levels (€ million) under the MEDA programmes for the Euro-Mediterranean Partnership:

	MEDA-1 (1995–1999)	*MEDA-2 (2000–2003)*	*MEDA 1 & 2 (1995–2003)*
Bilateral funding			
Algeria	164.0	181.8	345.8
Palestine	111.0	277.8	388.8
Egypt	254.0	194.5	880.5
Jordan	254.0	169.4	423.4
Lebanon	182.0	55.7	237.7
Morocco	656.0	525.3	1,181.3
Syria	99.0	82.7	181.7
Tunisia	428.0	306.6	734.6
Total bilateral	2,580.0	1,793.8	4,373.8
Regional funding	480.0	560.1	1,070.1
Total funding	3,060.0	2,383.9	5,443.9

Source: Europe Aid

5 Personal communication.

6 Globalisation, of course, is no new phenomenon but, in its contemporary guise, based on deregulated global financial markets powered by information technology, together with free trade dominated by the triad of the United States, Europe and Japan, it has some quite unique characteristics. See Barber, B.R. (1995, 2001), *Jihad vs. McWorld: Terrorism's Challenge to Democracy*, Ballantine Books (New York).

7 Geo-economics, the concept that factors related to economic globalisation would determine international relations, with the United States seeking to dominate the globalised world-economy.

8 A useful and sympathetic review of the speech and its subsequent implications is provided by Bentley T. (2003), 'Countdown to war: Tony Blair, issue by issue', *Le Monde Diplomatique* (English version) (February 2003).

9 See Commission of the European Communities, *European Neighbourhood Policy: Strategy Paper*, COM (2004) 373 final, Brussels 12.05.2004.

10 The body of European regulation that goes to make up the shared legal system of the European Union and makes access to the Single European Market possible, as well as, in the case of members, access to the Union's policy-making and administrative activities. The implications of this could be very costly! See Tocci N. (2005), 'Does the ENP respond to the EU's post-Enlargement challenges?', *The International Spectator*, XL, 1: 30.

11 These were laid down at the Copenhagen summit in June 1993 as the basis upon which Enlargement could proceed as they determined the conditions that an accession state would have to fulfil to actually join the Union. They are:

- political: stable institutions guaranteeing democracy, the rule of law, human rights and respect for minorities;
- economic: a functioning market economy;
- incorporation of the Community *acquis*: adherence to the various political, economic and monetary aims of the European Union.

http://europa.eu.int/scadplus/glossary/accession_criteria_copenhague_en.htm

12 The figures for the new financial instrument, known as the European Neighbourhood and Partnership Instrument (ENPI), in constant 2004 prices, are taken from Smith (2005) and given below:

Year	*2007*	*2008*	*2009*	*2010*	*2011*	*2012*	*2013*	*Total 2007–2013*
€ million	1,433	1,569	1,877	2,083	2,322	2,642	3,003	14,929

This can be compared with the budget for the East and the Mediterranean in 2004 (€1,420 million, with €953 million for the Mediterranean) but the figures are not fully comparable.

13 Deutsch's concept of an amalgamated security community is one in which the community considers war as an obsolete instrument of conflict resolution. Deutsch K. *et al.* (1957), *Political Community in the North Atlantic Area*, Princeton University Press (Princeton).

References

Aliboni, R. (2005) 'The geopolitical implications of the European Neighbourhood Policy', *European Foreign Affairs Review* 10, 1.

Attina, F. (2004) 'European Neighbourhood Policy and the building of security around Europe', in Attina, F. and Rossi, R. (eds) *European Neighbourhood Policy: Political, Economic and Social Aspects*, Jean Monnet Centre, University of Catania (Catania), 16–17.

Aubarell, G. and Aragall, X. (2005) *Immigration and the Euro-Mediterranean Area: Keys to Policy and Trends*, EuroMeSCo Paper No. 47 IEEI (Lisbon), 8–9.

Balfour, R. and Rotta, A. (2005) 'The European Neighbourhood Policy and its tools', *The International Spectator* XL, 1, 9.

Cherry, M. (2002) 'Have the lovely liberal Dutch finally lost the plot?', *New Humanist* 117, 2.

Cooper, R. (1998) *The Post-modern State*, Demos (London).

Coope, R. (2003) *The breaking of Nations: Order and Chaos in the 21st Century*, Atlantic Books (London).

Fortuyn, P. (1997) *Against the Islamisation of our Culture: Dutch Identity as a Fundamental*, Bruna (Utrecht).

Fukuyama, F. (1989) 'The end of history?', *The National Interest*.

Gerges, F.A. (2005) *The Far Enemy: Why Jihad Went Global*, Cambridge University Press (Cambridge), 43–79.

Halper, S. and Clarke, J. (2003) *America Alone: The Neo-Conservatives and the Global Order*, Cambridge University Press (Cambridge), 76–81, 254–257.

Ibrahim, S.E. (1988) 'Egypt's Islamic activism in the 1980s', *Third World Quarterly* 10 (2), 632–657.

Jandl, M. (2004) The estimation of illegal migration in Europe', *Studi Emigrazione/ Migration Studies* XLI, 153, 150.

Kagan, R. (2003) *Paradise and Power: America and Europe in the New World Order*, Atlantic Books (London).

Keenan, J. (2005) 'Waging war on terror: the implications of America's "New Imperialism" for Saharan peoples', *Journal of North African Studies* 10, 3–4, Special issue: Keenan, J. (ed.) 'The Sahara, past, present and future', 625.

Kelley, J. (2006) 'New wine in old wineskins: policy adaptation in the European Neighbourhood Policy', *Journal of Common Market Studies* 44, 1.

Roberts, A. (1991) 'A new age in International Relations?', *International Affairs* 67, 3.

Roy, O. (2004) 'Radical Islam appeals to the rootless', *Financial Times*, 12.10.2004.

Sageman, M. (2004) *Understanding Terrorist Networks*, University of Pennsylvania Press (Philadelphia).

Silvestre, S. (2005) 'EU relations with Islam in the context of the EMP's cultural dialogue' in *Mediterranean Politics*, 10, 3, Special issue edited by Pace, M. and Schumacher, T. 'Conceptualising cultural and social dialogue in the Euro-Mediterranean area: a European perspective'.

Smith, K. (2005) 'The outsiders: the European Neighbourhood Policy', *International Affairs* 81, 4, 760.

Tocci, N. (2005) 'Does the ENP respond to the EU's post-Enlargement challenges?', *The International Spectator* XL, 1, 30.

Weber, C. (1995) *Simulating Sovereignty: Intervention, the State and Symbolic Exchange*, Cambridge University Press (Cambridge).

White House (2002) *National Security Strategy of the United States of America*, White House.

Wiktorowicz, Q. (ed.) (2004) *Islamic Activism: a Social Movement Theory Approach*, Indiana University Press (Bloomington and Indianapolis), 3.

7 Inside/outside the European Union

Enlargement, migration policy and the search for Europe's identity

Brigitta Busch and Michał Krzyżanowski

This chapter discusses the close links between EU migration controls, border regimes and conceptions of European identity, in the context of EU enlargement. It examines how the question of delineating 'Europe' from its 'other' has become a central concern in political and media discourse since 1989. The first parts of the chapter focus on the EU's shifting external borders and how the structure of border regimes form concentric circles of more peripheral zones around the EU's core regions. Then it discusses how these macro level policies create different 'degrees' of EU citizenship, how they define and exclude non-citizens, and how the de-territorialisation of inner borders means in practice that controls can be implemented anywhere throughout society. Faced with this new complexity, the EU and member states fall back on traditional discursive strategies based on nation-state repertoires in their search for Europe's identity. We see how these new delineations of 'insiders' and 'outsiders' are reflected in the thinking of the European Convention, the EU's most recent attempt to create a constitutional basis for enlargement and are also, in effect, a search for 'Europe's soul'. We draw on a sample of interviews with members of the Convention from both 'old' and 'new' member states, concentrating on their ideas about Europe as a geographical and/or political entity, and its self-image in terms of European heritage and European values.[1]

Shifting borders, reconstructing 'Europe'

Europe has long been in search of its identity, its definition of itself, its 'soul' (Weiss 2002, Wodak and Weiss 2004). As an *imagined* construct, Europe needs some common characteristics in cultural and political terms; and since the 1970s what is now the European Union has made numerous attempts to create a European identity and build an image of itself as a legitimate polity and a coherent actor on the international stage. Since the 1973 Declaration of European Identity,[2] the EU has been attempting to create a self-definition which links the defence of 'Western' values with the delineation of borders against non-European 'others' (Stråth 2000). This entailed attempting to define some strictly 'European' values, a distinctive foundation of 'European culture' or some 'pan-European public sphere' (B. Busch

2004). These have been seen as indispensable for creating a new identity for Europe in the new millennium.

It should be noted that for much of the post-Second World War period up to 1989, the public discourse of 'Europe' did not require any special effort for Western Europeans: for them the 'other' was clearly provided by the countries of the Communist bloc, while the south was unambiguously 'Third World' Africa. Thus, the eastern border and limits of 'Europe' converged with the ideological and economic border dividing the continent into Western-capitalist and Eastern-Communist zones. The EEC, and its later descendant the EU, were thus provided with a clear definition of its own limits. But already in the 1980s this border paradigm had begun to shift with the weakening of the once very clear-cut bloc system. There followed the changing political situation in Central and Eastern Europe, and the further integration of the EU space in the form of the Single European Market.[3]

With 1989 – the (abstract) fall of the Iron Curtain and the (concrete) fall of the Berlin Wall – Europe's border paradigm not only shifted, it became much more problematical and its east–west meaning was inverted. Up to 1989 it was the Communist bloc to the east which was the hermetically sealed zone, its border with the West a 'protection from imperialist capitalism' and a means of preventing its own population from moving to the West. In contrast after 1989, it was the EU which gradually became the more closed space, using its external border as a line of protection against unwanted immigration from the east. Although the border stayed in the same place, its meaning was transformed.

With the collapse of the Communist bloc from 1989, its border regime dissolved: borders which had been set in stone by the Yalta and Potsdam Treaties after the Second World War suddenly became changeable. The geopolitical world-order based on bloc logic was ended, and the multinational states in which ideological orientation had served as a basis for cohesion (the USSR, Yugoslavia, and CSSR) disintegrated. In this process of disintegration, and as new national states inscribed themselves on the European map, the question of nearness/distance from Western Europe played a crucial role. Discursively, in the nationalist stories told by each state or nation, each sees itself as an integral part of Europe, its western borders with the rest of Europe being quasi-nonexistent while in contrast its eastern borders are constructed as culturally determined (B. Busch 2001, 152).

Simultaneously, the discursive constructs of 'tides' of 'illegal' migrants from the east and south 'threatening' the EU's external borders, and subsequently of crime being imported along with migration, could all be easily linked up with the nationalist discourses of the period of disintegration. But in practice, new visa requirements and the tightening of borders intersected and disrupted areas of deep-rooted transborder contact: cross-border family ties, established cultural relationships, and access to education for instance, were suddenly hampered. This became particularly visible in border regions with linguistic and ethnic minorities (e.g. among the Hungarian-speaking minorities along the Slovakian, Romanian and Ukrainian borders with Hungary). For example, the Schengen requirements necessitated the imposition of a visa regime between the Ukraine and Hungary, and there were several months of debate about whether the Hungarian-speaking population in western Ukraine should be granted exemptions or special conditions for visas on the grounds of ethnic affiliation. This debate accentuated already latent processes of ethnicising in the Ukraine.

Concurrently, the reconstruction of the EU's external border continued when one of the former 'eastern countries', the German Democratic Republic, was incorporated into EU territory with German reunification in 1989. By the same token, the EU made ever stronger attempts at incorporating two countries which had clearly been missing from its pre-1989 'border structure', and when Austria and Finland finally joined the EU in 1995 the former border of the Communist bloc was reproduced as an external border of the EU. But, surprisingly enough, this process of consolidating the EU's external borders coincided with contradictory tendencies often subsumed under the term 'globalisation', including the growing internationalisation of capital and labour markets, and an increasing demand for cheap labour within the world's core economies, and not least within the EU. Hence, in a situation when increased mobility and freedom of migration might have seemed especially desirable, the EU actually started closing and tightening its borders and classifying 'others' as 'third-country nationals' or 'aliens', quite contrary both to its own expressed liberal goals and its actual economic needs.

It is in this context that the long-debated eastern enlargement of the European Union of May 2004 posed yet another challenge to Europe's borders as imagined social and political constructs and added to their long-standing ambivalence. With the 2004 enlargement, many of those traditionally defined as non-EU or third-country nationals (e.g. from the Central and Eastern European countries such as Poland, the Czech Republic or Hungary) who were traditionally recruited as 'unskilled labour', were indeed given the right to reside in all the countries of the former fifteen-member EU, but were subsequently refused active and equal labour rights in these countries (Ireland and the UK were exceptions). It is likely that further EU enlargements – Bulgaria and Romania in 2007, and Croatia and other possibles including Bosnia and Turkey in more distant perspective – will see similarly ambivalent positions adopted towards EU-newcomers. Since further enlargements mean incorporating people who were traditionally defined as Europe's 'others' (e.g. in religious terms Muslims in the Balkans and in Turkey), there are already pressures to attempt to again define Europe's borders as 'quasi-natural', implying a culturally determined divide.

Schengen and a Europe of concentric circles

The EU's external borders, rather than being a simple line on the map, more closely resemble a system of concentric circles and buffer zones. The Schengen Treaty signed in 1985 by Germany, France, Belgium, the Netherlands and Luxemburg marked the first major step towards an official common European border regime and migration policy. It was initially determined by this sub-group of five EU states which saw themselves as the core of Europe, and it was implemented by bodies which, up until the Amsterdam Treaty of 1999, were located outside the standard EU administrative and political structures. The abolition of internal border controls between the five contracting states was from the beginning coupled with so-called compensatory measures to counteract resulting 'security deficits'. Whereas the Treaty itself was more a political declaration foregrounding the abolition of inner borders, the migration and security policies were designed by a multitude of different expert bodies and committees (such as the TREVI group, the Ad-Hoc Committee on Immigration, the Vienna Club) mainly comprising civil servants, which – as the European Parliament critically commented – largely escaped democratic control.[4]

With the Schengen Implementation Treaty, signed in 1990 (by Germany, France, the Benelux states, Portugal and Spain), and, entering into force in March 1995, internal border controls were abolished and external border controls were increased. The Implementation Treaty focused mainly on compensatory measures with three themes: (a) border regimes (common polices on visas, non-EU citizens and rights to asylum); (b) enhanced cooperation between different police forces and increased judicial support (especially in crime prevention, terrorism and drugs); and, (c) the Schengen Information System. The Schengen group proclaimed itself a 'laboratory' and a 'motor' for the integration of European policies concerning border regimes, internal security and migration (N. Busch 2001, 9).

Formally, the current, legally binding, common EU migration policy began only with the Amsterdam Treaty of 1999, previous Schengen cooperation having taken place outside the normal community decision-making structures. The Amsterdam Treaty originally aimed, among other things, at harmonising European border regimes, asylum and migration policies up to 2004. Its foundations and the proposals and provisions of the Treaty were firmly rooted in the spirit of the 1951 Geneva Convention, primarily with respect to guaranteeing the right to asylum. Thus, the European proposals, which were far less restrictive than some of the existing national laws (especially in Germany and Austria), were originally welcomed by the Office of the UN High Commissioner for Refugees. However, following the terrorist attacks of 11 September 2001, there was a change of paradigms, with combating illegal migration becoming the EU's top priority at the 2002 EU Summit in Seville (Holzberger 2003, 118).

Thus, with ever tighter cooperation with respect to borders and immigration controls, the construction of 'fortress Europe' as a set of concentric circles began to take shape. Schematically, there is an inner core formed by the EU member states which fully conform to the Schengen agreements; and immediately beyond this inner core there is an outer core comprising the rest of the pre-2004 member states which are not full partners in the Schengen scheme (and some of which are not in the Euro-zone) (see Figure 7.1).

Outside the inner and outer core there are the more peripheral circles. The first of these encompasses the states which joined the EU in 2004 and 2007 and which have to align to the 'core' standards of Schengen within a given period in order to fulfil the criteria for EU accession. Beyond these are states which are to (perhaps) join the EU at successive dates in the future, subject to meeting similar criteria, and finally there are those states which are not expected to join but which have

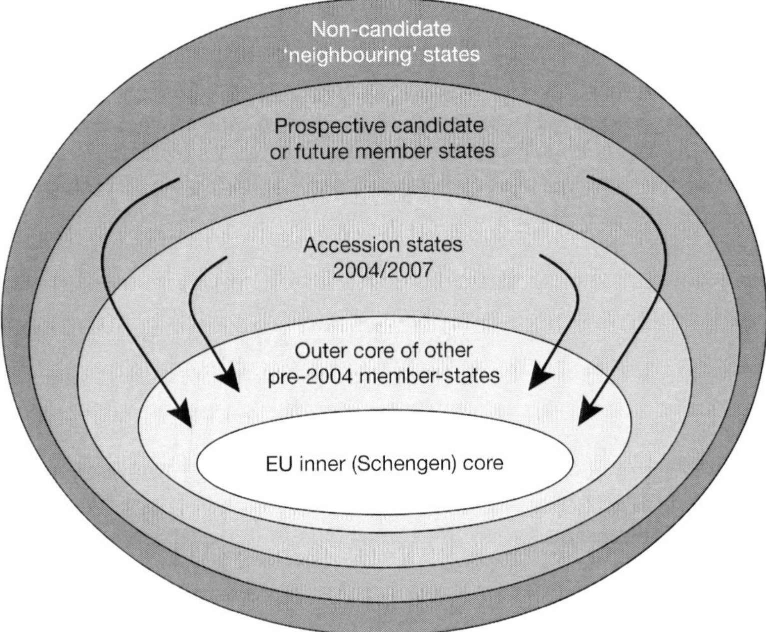

Figure 7.1 Schengen and a Europe of concentric circles

formal 'neighbour' relationships with the EU, including joint agreements on border controls, and policies to limit migration and combat illegal cross-border movements. In the case of the inner peripheries these policies are enforced by the promise and conditions of enhanced economic cooperation and eventual EU membership; and in the case of the outer periphery by development aid and other economic inducements (the Contonou Treaty, the ASEM Treaty).

The overall aim is to intercept movements and routes of migration outside the actual borders of the EU, as far as possible implementing border controls within so-called transit and emigration countries and combating illegal networks along their whole route, if possible right from their point of origin rather than at their point of destination (Holzberger 2003, 119). A crucial role in this regime of concentric circles is played by Readmission Agreements which oblige a country not only to take back 'its own' citizens who have entered the Schengen space illegally, but also to take back citizens from third countries who used the country concerned as a route into the Schengen area.

The concentric circles which constitute the outer defences of 'fortress Europe' have an internal counterpart in a structure of differentiated social exclusion inside the EU. European citizens (in the sense of the French *citoyens*, now functioning in EU terminology as *civic citizens*) are categorised into different classes with more and less rights. Those with most rights are citizens who hold an EU passport from a pre-2004 member state. No matter in which of the EU countries they live they have full access to social and cultural rights (e.g. social security, choice of professional affiliation, freedom of settlement) and to some extent also to political rights (e.g. right to vote in local elections). However, since 2004, and up to 2014 – and probably beyond – there are two broad classes of EU citizen: first, those from the fifteen pre-2004 member states, plus Malta, and, secondly, those from the other 2004 and 2007-accession states. The latter 'second-class citizens' do not immediately enjoy full freedoms to live and to work anywhere within the EU (and similar restrictions will probably apply to people from other states which join in the future).

Thirdly, there are people who constitute a mobile elite from mainly 'rich' so-called 'third countries', including, most notably, highly skilled and highly valued professionals (often allowed entry according to quotas based on labour market demand, and usually not called 'migrant workers'): they generally have almost the same social rights as EU passport holders. Fourthly, and in sharp distinction, there are the large contingents of migrant workers also from so-called 'third countries' but in this case low paid and often classed as 'low-' or 'un-skilled' (and deemed not to be 'in demand' despite their usually greater numbers).

Workers from (generally poorer) 'countries of emigration' have different legal statuses ranging from a permission for permanent residence to the precarious status of seasonal workers where basic social rights, such as the right to family life and reunion, are not guaranteed; and even further down the scale of social inclusion/exclusion are 'illegal migrants', the pariahs of contemporary society, deprived of rights and protection and especially vulnerable to suffering 'super exploitation' in employment. The *jus sanguinis* rule (where one's citizenship is granted according to one's *parents*' country of origin/citizenship rather than according to the territory in which one is born) is applied in several of the pre-2004 member states of the EU; and there are further obstacles to EU citizenship in the denial of dual nationality and in the generally high thresholds in naturalisation procedures and in access to them (e.g. in language and cultural knowledge tests, in the high fees demanded, or in the long duration of stay before admission to naturalisation), all of which serves to draw a sharp line dividing EU and non-EU citizens.

This line is very hard to cross, but there is a large group of people living in the EU, a group perhaps as numerous as the population of one of the middle-sized member states, which is excluded from basic rights. The status of these internal 'others' is precarious as they have no guaranteed rights and their residence or work permits have more the character of a temporarily granted favour which can be withdrawn. In connection with this 'new class division', Balibar (2003, 15) speaks of a 'European apartheid' which not only accentuates exclusion but also actively fuels racist sentiment.

For the new member states of 2004 and 2007, the requirement to align their immigration and asylum laws to the Schengen/EU standard[5] has also meant that previous, historically developed relationships were disrupted, and a similar stratification process has taken place within their societies. In several of these countries the notions of '*sans-papiers*' and 'illegal migrants' did not previously exist (Nauditt 2000, 4). But now most of the migrants in these countries are in a kind of 'waiting-room' position: very few intend to stay in the country (Nauditt 2000, 7) but they are stopped on their way to one of the Western European countries and either cannot continue on their way or are expelled to Eastern European countries. On the other hand, visa regimes imposed by the Schengen logic interrupt social ties and push people into situations of illegality. For example, in 2000 the Czech Republic imposed visa requirements for citizens from Ukraine, Russia and Belorussia, and thousands of citizens from these countries working on temporary contracts or studying in the Czech Republic were rendered 'illegal' overnight. Visas could only be issued at Czech consulates outside the country (where the average time to get a long-term permit is about five months), and visa applicants had to have the necessary documents for the Schengen area (including an invitation from a citizen, or a guarantee of work). Not surprisingly, the tourist industry also complains about these visa requirements.

In parallel with the consolidation and expansion of the Schengen area, migration, and, in particular, 'illegal immigration' became the key topics in the political and media discourse around borders. Discursive strategies include the explicit designation of in-groups and out-groups (us and them), dominated by an overall strategy of positive *self*-presentation and negative *other*-presentation (cf. Reisigl and Wodak 2001). Immigrants are stereotypically represented as being different, deviant and a threat to 'us'; and such discourses employ a specific rhetoric in which the hyperbolic use of metaphors borrowed from the military register (e.g. invasion, army of illegals) and from the semantic field of threatening water (e.g. flood, tide) is characteristic. Such metaphors imply that immigrants are numerous, violent and a threat (van Dijk 2000, 43); and this serves to justify a corresponding rhetoric and practice of fortifying and securing the border.

As some studies on 'racism and cultural diversity in the mass media'[6] in EU states have shown, there are close links between political agendas and media discourses, especially in connection with restrictive policy proposals linked to 'a very generalised trend . . . the over-emphasis on ethnic and immigrant crime' (Ter Wal 2002, 38–42). The negative images of migrants in the media are only rarely compensated by positive images or by in-depth reporting of their living conditions. In some of the EU's new and candidate states migration had not been a topic in the early 1990s, yet towards the end of the decade migration and asylum had become major media topics all over Central and Eastern Europe, in general taking their cue from the Western European media and Schengen concerns. The discourses of exclusion seem to 'travel' from the inner to the outer circles. In Austria, for example, such discourses were massively prominent in 1989–90 when Austria imposed visa requirements for Bulgarian, Turkish and Romanian citizens as it prepared to sign the Schengen Implementation Treaty by concluding the Readmission Agreement with Schengen countries (Busch 1990). These migration and border discourses, with their distinct patterns, then moved to Slovenia towards the middle of the 1990s when Slovenia started to prepare for EU membership and had to prove its capability of fulfilling the Schengen criteria. The Slovenian Open Society Fund (Media Watch) published a series of studies on media discourses which indicate a serious shift of discourse between 1992 and the end of the decade. Similar to what had earlier happened in Austria, the term 'refugee' was increasingly replaced in public discourse by other terms such as 'asylum seeker', 'alien', and 'illegal immigrant', while migration was frequently associated with cultural difference and with crime (Doupona *et al.* 2001, 7).

Deterritorialisation and the ubiquity of borders

The tightening of border regimes on the EU's outer frontiers is frequently paired in political discourse with the promise of a 'Europe without frontiers'. However, the abolition of controls at the inner territorial borders of the EU has not in fact led to an abolition of controls as such within the EU, but rather to their displacement throughout the whole territory and society at the social 'borders' between 'indigenous people' and 'alien others'. Furthermore, the former controls at the inner borders can be reintroduced temporarily and the Schengen provisions can be suspended for particular 'security' reasons. This occurred, for example, when during the G8 summit in Genoa in 2001 the Italian authorities withdrew from the EU's open borders treaty in order to be able to exclude what they termed 'potential rioters' from Italian territory.

Similar measures have been regularly taken with respect to 'crowd control' at large international sporting events. Thus the tightened border regimes at the EU's external borders is not the only form of displacement. Different kinds of control are imposed at different places within the Schengen space, including the use of identity inspections, hygiene checks and security controls. Balibar (1997, 397) speaks in this context of 'the ubiquity of borders'. Zones of particularly dense controls include major transit axes (trains, motorways, airports), zones which Marc Augé (1995) has called 'non-places'. Augé derives his definition of non-places from the conception of anthropological places as 'formed by individual identities, through complicities of language, local references, the unformulated rules of living know-how' (Augé 1995, 101). Non-places, in contrast, do not show these characteristics: they are 'a world surrendered to solitary individuality, to the fleeting, the temporary and ephemeral' while they 'create solitary contractuality' (Augé 1995, 78, 94).

This establishes conditions of space in which 'individuals are supposed to interact only with texts, whose proponents are not individuals but 'moral entities' or institutions (airports, airlines, Ministry of Transport, commercial companies, traffic police, municipal councils)'. Non-places 'fabricate the "average man", defined as the user of the road, retail or banking system. They fabricate him, and sometimes individualise him' e.g. when he breaks the traffic rules, when they do not suit the pattern of the average. Non-places are spaces of anonymity, but the space of anonymity is only accessible to those who have given proof of their identity, in a way the users of non-places are always required to prove their innocence (Augé 1995, 96, 100, 102). What Augé did not stress is that it is precisely the non-places which are also places of increased surveillance: video cameras, police patrols, uniforms of different kinds are also part of the inventory of non-places, and it is also in non-places that no rights are guaranteed (e.g. transit spaces in airports).

Non-places function as a kind of sorting mechanism where those who do not correspond to the 'average' are filtered out using criteria of visible or audible markers of identity (physical appearance, 'foreign' language), or of 'deviant behaviour'. Increasingly, biometric data are being used to effectuate this sorting process. In several European airports (Frankfurt am Main, Munich, Amsterdam Schiphol, Zurich Kloten), so-called 'systems of dissuasive surveillance' have been implemented on a trial basis for some years (*Neue Zürcher Zeitung*, 6–7 July 2002, 69). In contrast to 'observational surveillance' (e.g. of objects and streets) and to 'invasive surveillance' (observing particular 'suspect' individuals), 'dissuasive surveillance' aims at 'crime prevention in the preparatory phase' and allows for comprehensive screening of entire categories of people. In the above-mentioned airports, cameras monitor all passengers arriving from 'destinations of suspected illegal immigration' (*NZZ*, 9 July 2002, 25), while computer software ('FACESNAP') is used to analyse selected parts of people's faces and compare them automatically with pictures stored in a database containing pictures of asylum seekers previously refused residence.

Another software system registers 'patterns of relevant forms of behaviour characterising willingness to escape or to panic' (*NZZ* 6–7 July 2002, 69). The system installed in Zurich Kloten airport is designed to cope with approximately half a million face screenings a year, while there are only about 200 'illegal' migrants attempting to enter Switzerland via this airport. The creation of another biometric system database, decided by the DG Justice and Home Affairs of the European Commission in 2000, the so-called: 'EURODAC' system, will contain fingerprints of all who asked for asylum in any of the member states (N. Busch 2001, 29). Moreover, the controls are no longer simply a prerogative of public authorities as the responsibility for passenger controls has been partly delegated to the airlines and other private carrying companies which are held responsible for the entry of 'illegal' migrants (N. Busch 2001, 12) under so-called 'carrier sanctions'. As the costs of returning passengers who do not possess the required documents or visas for the Schengen space have to be covered by the private airlines or boat companies, their controls tend to be very strict. It seems that where the EU's inner borders are concerned, the Schengen regime has not resulted in a 'Europe without frontiers' but rather in a partial deterritorialisation of borders and an increased ubiquity and unpredictability of potential controls.

Europe: imagined and constructed

It seems that the construction of Europe pursued in the EU in recent years is very much an extension of the national process of community construction (also Malmborg and Stråth 2002). Yet it is not identical to that process, according to our interpretation of Benedict Anderson's (1991) conception of '*imagined* communities'. As Anderson suggested, each nation is: (a) 'imagined because the members of even the smallest nation will never know most of their fellow-members, meet them, or even hear of them, yet in the minds of each lives the image of their communion'; (b) '*limited* because even the largest of them . . . has finite, if elastic, boundaries, beyond which lie other nations'; and (c) 'imagined as a *community*, because, regardless of the actual inequality and exploitation that may prevail in each, the nation is always conceived as a deep, horizontal comradeship' (Anderson 1991, 6, 7, our emphasis).

However, the process of 'defining' and 'imagining' Europe, as undertaken by political elites within the EU, centrally entails defining Europe against a 'non-European other' and hence is a process of shaping Europe as a more *limited* construct. The definition and delimitation of Europe has not entailed the construction of a horizontal (and thus equal) European *community* which Anderson suggests is central to imagining the nation. Instead, the process of constructing Europe has involved an element disregarded by Anderson, namely the construction and reproduction of inequality between various social, cultural, religious, national and other groups living in Europe.

This diversity and the lack of uniformity of rights is in fact more reminiscent of empires than of national states. The inequality between the various groups does not stem from a bottom-up process of people choosing to identify or not identify with Europe, nor is it rooted in the fact that no one would 'die for Europe' (Haltern 2003), a criterion in Anderson's outline of nation construction. Rather the diversity is highlighted by a top-down process of classifying the various nations, cultures and other social entities which make up the putative European *demos*, some of which are classified as 'the other', as 'non-European', rather than all being included in a polity whose standard-bearers emphasise a singular European identity. Furthermore, the imagined construction of 'new borders' and secure frontiers for the EU creates a conception of the EU as an elite entity within Europe, recreating Europe in the sense of EUrope and projecting a self-legitimising EU-ropean identity (Edwards 2003).

This self-definition and limitation of (politically) imagined Europe must be seen as a dual process, one taking place with reference to the 'outside' and to the 'inside'. On the one hand Europe, in the sense of EUrope, constructs itself with reference to the outside, to the external, to the 'non-European', to those not seen as a part of 'core Europe' (a conception which is challenged by the current process of EU enlargement – see below). Selective incorporation into 'fortress Europe', defining who is more or less European, or who actually deserves (by conformity to imagined constructs) to become 'part of Europe' (or, as it is often suggested with regard to the enlargement countries, 'come back to Europe' – Hagen 2003), these are the primary ideological objectives in this 'new' definition of Europe in relation to its outside. On the other hand, in this process of 'definition by self-limitation', in relation to its inside the EU also creates various mechanisms of exclusion, most notably of those discriminated against as 'the enemy within', whether covertly in the institutional structures of EU immigration policy or in the direct exploitation and oppression of migrant and minority groups in civil society.

Further light on the processes of self-defining Europe was cast by our interviews with members of the European Convention, by their various competing visions of Europe, and how these conceptions are located between Europe's past 'scope of experience' and its future 'horizon of expectations' (Koselleck 1989).

The interviews also point to different nationally specific visions of Europe, and particularly to differences between the pre-2004 member states and the 2004 accession states and some candidates for membership. In general our analysis shows that discourses are constitutive of social and political realms, and thus the meanings of discourse 'reproduce society and culture as well as being reproduced by them' (Wodak 1996: 18).

The members of the European Convention had the responsibility of drawing up a constitutional reform plan for the EU and sketching its future. A 'quasi-institution', the Convention constituted a breakthrough by the EU where representatives of governments and national parliaments of the accession and candidate states participated fully for the first time in drafting and constructing the future of Europe, on (almost) equal terms with representatives from the pre-2004 member states and the EU's central institutions. It can therefore be treated as an arena where various discursive constructions and definitions of Europe were displayed, confronted and negotiated (see Krzyżanowski and Oberhuber 2007 for further details). From a discourse-analysis of the various definitions of Europe proposed by members of the Convention we can see how Europe was often seen in the 'exclusive' and limited way already discussed,[7] and this applied to interviewees from the new as well as the old member states. The former outsiders have very rapidly become part of the EU's inside, directly involved in reproducing the vision of Europe which originated in the core member states, a vision involving clear borders and limits to Europe.

The following sample of extracts from interviews (labelled by country of origin) illustrates how this core vision was articulated.

> UK1: There are very strict criteria for the membership of the EU and they are becoming stricter, and the threshold is becoming much higher all the time and that's what we're up to in Convention, we are raising the threshold of membership.
>
> UK2: I think we've got to draw the conclusions from our attempt to create a single area of people, freedom, security and justice, so individuals can move around freely or within the territory of the EU. If that is the case, we've got to control our frontiers and we've got to share the pressure of refugees and asylum seekers.

As suggested in some recent studies (Krzyżanowski 2005, Oberhuber 2005, Krzyżanowski and Oberhuber 2007) the fact that Convention members from accession states were 'speaking the core EU voice' (unexpectedly representing visions identical to those from countries long involved in shaping Europe according to the EU's political and economic interests) is rooted in the process of the discursive creation of the so-called 'mainstream voice' and its implicit acceptance, whether by insiders or former outsiders. Thus our analysis suggests that the incorporation of new member states will continue the further reproduction of exclusive visions of Europe. All that the previously excluded are allowed to do is reproduce the existing core vision (though this often fits their own traditional view that they constitute 'Europe's last outpost' and that 'non-Europe' starts the other side of their own eastern borders).

Most interviewees from accession states when asked how they would define Europe (in geographical, cultural, political, religious or other terms) immediately looked for some abstract 'spirit of Europe' (Weiss 2002, 62) in defining its identity and sameness. However their visions of sameness and identity seemed to be highly exclusive, inasmuch as they immediately entailed demarcating the borders of Europe and looking for the non-European 'other'. As some of the interviewees, like the ones from Hungary and Romania below, even suggested explicitly, Europe should be defined in geographical terms, and that included the idea that future enlargements were only possible within the 'geographical dimensions of Europe' (cf. Wodak and Weiss 2004).

> HU1: I think the most important problem for the European Union is that it wouldn't define itself geographically. The only message which the European Union was sending to the outside world was that at a certain point you can become a member and if you are a member everything is okay.

> RO1: We have in the constitution a provision saying that all European countries sharing the same values in the constitution have the right to follow the EU . . .
>
> INT: Yeah but it does not say any European country but any country which means that- they do not have to be geographically [European] . . .
>
> RO1: No no no no no no, they have to be geographical. This is the understanding of this.

Europe's sameness was usually constructed by the interviewees by referring to a shared European culture, and the notion of a common culture generally entailed reference to European history, often to a common Christian history:

> HU1: I think it's a cultural or rather cultural and common historical phenomenon which obviously has a very strong [basis] in history. . . . You have all this Roman and Christian tradition which is coming, bringing it together.

In Central Europe this 'Christian Europe' is generally limited to western Christianity: the borders of Europe are limited to Roman Catholic and Protestant Europe and often exclude the European territories of the eastern Orthodox Church as well as Europe's Islamic areas.

> HU1: If you see a railway station in East Hungary . . . you can find more in common than if you go a little more further to the east. So it has something to do with religion as well. So in that sense Christianity as a root and the unifying force is a very important point. . . . The orthodox Christianity is already

> somewhat out in these cultures. . . . I wouldn't mean that I would exclude them but . . . I mean that's already a kind of different culture, the Greeks, the Russians and the Romanians or the orthodox is a different kind of Christian tradition already, so I would define by that.

Since 'every search for identity includes differentiating from what one is not' (Benhabib 1996, 3), 'others' are not only defined in general, religious terms, but also by specific examples of who are different, and, by the same token, not worthy of actually being or becoming 'European'. Here Turkey, because of its bid for EU membership, it's predominantly Islamic culture and its geographical location, is usually the defining case.

> SI1: A part of that of course is in Europe, geographically historically part of Europe. But the bigger part is part of Asia.

The perception of Turkey as non-European is often juxtaposed with references to other regions/countries (which might be seen as problematical in other contexts), so that the Balkan and former Soviet countries, and even, surprisingly Mongolia, can be seen as definitely European, or at least 'Eurasian' which implies an extension of 'European'.

> SI1: I mean they if or Russia would be part of it then, then this is Eurasia, what is it called?
>
> INT: Eurasia.
>
> SI1: Europa–Asian yeah and for me, Byelorussia and Ukraine and Mongolia could be part of the political Ural of the European Union, you know, of course Balkans I don't see problems in that, I think this definitely belongs to Europe. I'm not so sure for Turkey.

For some, admitting Turkey would open the door to the whole Middle East (which is not even seen as 'Eurasian').

> SI1: We say yes for Turkey, then why not for Lebanon, why not for Israel . . . ?

In line with our discussion of 'a Europe of concentric circles', our interviewees also see Europe in terms of 'core' and 'periphery'.[8] On the one hand, the core and periphery are seen 'inside' the EU in terms of economically more and less developed countries, between bigger and smaller states, or between old and new EU members:

> INT: The Union will be a unity but there will be the core and the periphery?
>
> PL1: Unfortunately I do have an impression that it will be so and I have an impression, and I will be saying about it today, and we have to get ready for

> that, and not just because the big countries want to do it to the smaller ones, or those more advanced ones.

On the other hand, the core and periphery idea is also used in connection with the cultural sameness and degrees of 'Europeanness' already discussed, demarcated by an outer non-European periphery.

> PL2: As far as heritage is concerned, the heritage of let's say the ancient culture of Rome which can be measured in thousands of years, this is Europe, this is the root, the nucleus, in which others, it's hard for others to be proud of something similar. But there is also the problem which will come because Europe, with its opening, well it turns out that the peripheries are getting different and the east, the south, and if for example Turkey will become a member of the Union.

The Convention focused mostly on external as distinct from internal 'others', putting the latter and their problems aside as perhaps complicating or being in contradiction with the issue of which new potential members qualified as European. Thus issues of migration and asylum policy (unlike issues of autochthonous national minorities) were not debated in the Convention.[9]

> INT: The issue of immigration, asylum and all that has not been at all discussed.
>
> PL2: Well it is marked and written somewhere, it is being talked about together with competencies, but in the Convention the future challenges are not spoken about in an explicit way, the future challenges and one of those elements is actually demography.

Many in the Convention preferred to see the issue of immigration in mainly economic terms and in relation to an ageing European population, though its relevance to conceptions of who is 'European' could hardly be denied.

> PL1: The issue of immigration and asylum, generally speaking the relation to others and human flows, Europe is afraid of that and is closing. But it is also aware of its needs due to reasons of labour market and demography. But it will be a challenge in which we will have to pass the test in Europe.

Conclusions

In political discourse the topic of European identity gained central importance with the first steps towards eastern enlargement. As the interviews with members of the European Convention show, representatives from old and new member states in their visions of Europe rely heavily on discursive strategies stemming from a nation-state repertoire: the confabulation of a common history and heritage, the reference to common values, the perspective of a common fate and future, and the territorial definition given through 'natural borders' which separate Europe from its 'other'. In political and media discourse the 'other' is not defined on the basis of ideological differences, as was the case throughout the phase of the Cold War East–West divide, but rather remains vague, the main characteristic of the 'other' being that it is always located somewhere further to the east or south.

In contrast to these discursive constructs, political practices around EU borders suggest that inside/outside is not conceived as a clear-cut binary opposition but rather as a complex system of concentric circles encompassing traditional member states, new member states, prospective candidate states and neighbouring states for which membership is not an option. The political architecture of the border regime simultaneously has features of premodern feudal hierarchy and of postmodern ambiguity. The core zone is protected by concentric rings in a fortress-like, empire-like manner (see Chapter 1). At the same time, the internal borders become more ambiguous in their physical location (as controls have shifted from the state borders to axes of transport and places of transit); more uncertain in their temporal validity (as the treaty abolishing EU internal borders can be suspended unilaterally at any moment); and more equivocal in their meaning (as they take on different implications for different groups of citizens).

The necessity for such a complex and tight border regime is justified in political and media discourse by evoking an external threat. It is not a military threat to the territorial integrity of the EU, but military vocabulary (e.g. an 'invasion' of immigrants) is widely employed, as are metaphors of threatening water (e.g. a 'tide' of refugees). The discursive construct of an external threat finds its internal equivalent in the theme of 'the enemy within'. Not by chance do we find that across Europe this lumps together such problems as criminality, drug abuse, human trafficking and terrorism with the presence of migrant communities. The system of more or less peripheral member states and complex border regimes (re)produces inequality across European space: it threatens to fragment society into groups of people with more or fewer rights and to exclude millions of Europe's inhabitants from basic rights.

Notes

1 The interviews used in the third part of our contribution come from the research project 'The Discursive Re-/Construction of European Identities', financed by the Jubilee-Foundation of the Austrian National Bank (ÖNB Jubiläumsfonds), and carried out at the Department of Linguistics, University of Vienna between August 2003 and March 2005. Michał Krzyżanowski was a member of this research project along with Florian Oberhuber (Vienna) and Ruth Wodak (Lancaster). An extensive analysis of those interviews can be found in Krzyżanowski and Oberhuber (2006).

2 The declaration stemmed from an Ad Hoc Committee debating the World Oil Crisis (Stråth 2000, Delanty 1995 and 2003). As the declaration states, 'The nine member countries of the European Communities have decided that the time has come to draw up a document on European identity. This will enable them to achieve a better definition of the relations with other countries and of their responsibilities and the place which they occupy in world affairs' (*Bulletin of the European Communities*, 1973, No. 12, Section 5, Clause 2501, 118–122, quoted in Delanty 2003)

3 The crucial moment for increasing EU integration was the 1986 Single European Act.
4 Cf. the decision of the European Parliament of 14 June 1990 concerning the Schengen Agreement and the results of the works of the Ad Hoc Committee on Immigration.
5 New immigration laws were decided in Poland and Lithuania in 1997, in Hungary in 1998, in Bulgaria in 1999 and in the Czech Republic in 2000 – mainly with the assistance of one of the EU member states (Nauditt 2000, 4).
6 Cf. The European Monitoring Centre on Racism and Xenophobia (EUMC) commissioned comparative a study published in 2002 (Ter Wal 2002).
7 Because of space restrictions, we use only a small sample of the (altogether forty) interviews with Convention members. They included members from: Hungary (1, labelled HU), Slovakia (1, SK), Slovenia (1, SI), Poland (3, PL), Romania (1, RO), and the UK (2, UK).
8 The idea of Europe as comprising a 'core' and 'periphery' has become very visible in recent years, and has been made explicit in, for example, the famous Joschka Fischer speech at Humboldt University in May 2000 or, most recently, in Jürgen Habermas and Jacques Derrida's vision of the 'Rebirth of Europe' (Habermas and Derrida 2003).
9 National (autochthonous) minorities are usually seen as being part of Europe and its heritage of diversity. In contrast, immigrants and asylum seekers are usually seen as not part of Europe, and are often defined as a 'threat' to it.

References

Anderson, Benedict (1991) *Imagined Communities: Reflections on the Origin and Spread of Nationalism*, London: Verso.

Augé, Marc (1995) *Non*-places. *Introduction to an Anthropology of Supermodernity*, London, New York: Verso.

Balibar, Etienne (1997) *La crainte des masses. Politique et philosophie avant et après Marx*, Paris: Galilée.

Balibar, Etienne (2003) *Sind wir Bürger Europas? Politische Integration, soziale Ausgrenzung und die Zukunft des Nationalen*, Hamburg: Hamburger Edition. (Original title: *Nous, Citoyens d'Europe? Les frontieres, l'Etat, le peuple*, Paris: La Decouverte, 2001.)

Bauman, Zygmunt (1998) *Globalisation. The Human Consequences*, Cambridge: Polity Press.

Benhabib, Seyla (1996) *Democracy and Difference*, Princeton: Princeton University Press.

Busch, Brigitta (1990) 'Mauerbau und Rassismus rund um die "Festung Europa": Österreichs Fremdenpolitik im ausländerfeindlichen Harmonisierungstrend', in: Gero Fischer; Peter Gstettner (Hg.) *Am Kärntner Wesen könnte diese Republik genesen*, Klagenfurt/Celovec: Drava, 50–67.

Busch, Brigitta (2001) 'Grenzvermessungen: Sprachen und Medien in Zentral-, Südost- und Osteuropa', in: Brigitta Busch, Brigitte Hipfl, Kevin Robins (Hg.) *Bewegte Identitäten. Medien in transkulturellen Kontexten*, Klagenfurt/Celovec: Drava, 145–173.

Busch, Brigitta (2004) *Sprachen im Disput*, Klagenfurt/Celovec: Drava.

Busch, Nicholas (2001) *Ein "Raum der Freiheit, der Sicherhait und des Rechts"? Polizeiliche und justitielle Zusammenarbeit, Migrations- und Asylpolitik in der EU.* Reihe Materialien Nr. 1, Fraktion der Vereinten Europäischen Linken/ Nordische Grüne Linke im Europäischen Parlament.

Delanty, Gerard (1995) *Inventing Europe: Idea, Identity, Reality*, London: Macmillan.

Delanty, Gerard (2003) 'Is there a European identity?' Paper presented at the Conference 'Institutional Dynamics and Democracy in the EU', ARENA, Oslo, 3 October.

Doupona, Marjeta, Jef Verschueren and Igor Zagar (2001) *The Pragmatics of Legitimisation. The Rhetoric of Refugee Policies in Slovenia*, Ljubljana: Mirovni Institut.

Edwards, Sobrina (2003) 'Creating a European identity: prospects and implications', Paper presented at the BMW Centre for German and European Studies (CGES Conference, Georgetown, March 21–22).

Forschungsgemeinschaft Flucht und Migration (2000) 'Anpassung an die festung Europa', in Ost-West Gegeninformation Nr. 4/2000 12. Jg. Graz: Center for the Study of Balkan Societies and Cultures, 9–14.

Habermas, Jürgen, and Jacques Derrida (2003) 'Nach dem Krieg: die Wiedergeburt Europas', *Frankfurter Allgemeine Zeitung*, May 31.

Hagen, James (2003) 'Redrawing the map of Europe: the rise and fall of the "Center"', *Political Geography* 22: 489–517.

Haltern, Ulrich (2001) 'Europe goes camper: The EU Charter of Fundamental Rights from the consumerist perspective', Con-WEB: Constitutionalism Web Papers, no. 6/2002.

Haltern, Ulrich (2003) 'Pathos and patina: the failure and promise of constitutionalism in the European imagination', *European Law Journal* 9(1): 14–44.

Holzberger, Mark (2003) 'Die Harmonisierung der europäischen Flüchtlingspolitik', in Christoph Butterwegge; Gudrun Hentges (ed.) *Zuwanderung im Zeichen der Globalisierung. Migrations-, Integrations- und Minderheitenpolitik*, Opladen: Leske & Budrich, 111–123.

Koselleck, Reinhart (1989) *Vergangene Zukunft*, Frankfurt am Main: Suhrkamp.

Krzyżanowski, Michał (2005) 'European identity wanted! on discursive and communicative dimensions of the European Convention', in Ruth Wodak and Paul Chilton (eds) *A New Research Agenda in CDA: Theory and Multidiscilpinarity*, Amsterdam/Philadelphia: John Benjamins, 137–164.

Krzyżanowski, Michał, and Florian Oberhuber (2007) *Un-Doing Europe. Discourses and Practices of Negotiating the EU Constitution*, Brussels: PIE – Peter Lang (in press).

Malmborg, Mikael af, and Bo Stråth (eds) (2002) *The Meaning of Europe*, Oxford: Berg.

Nauditt, Kristina (2000) 'Vor den Toren der Europäischen Union. Der Versuch einer Bestandaufnahme', in *Ost-West Gegeninformation*, Nr. 4/2000 12. Jg. Graz: Center for the Study of Balkan Societies and Cultures, 3–8.

Oberhuber, Florian (2005) 'Deliberation or "mainstreaming"? Empirically researching the European Convention', in Ruth Wodak and Paul Chilton (eds) *A New Research Agenda in CDA: Theory and Multidisciplinarity*, Amsterdam/Philadelphia: John Benjamins, 165–195.

Reisigl, Martin and Ruth Wodak (2001) *Discourse and Discrimination*, London: Routledge.

Stråth, Bo (2000) 'Introduction: Europe as a discourse', in Bo Stråth (ed.) *Europe and the Other and Europe as the Other*, Brussels: PIE-Peter Lang, 13–44.

Ter Wal, Jessika (ed.) (2002) *Racism and Cultural Diversity in the Mass Media. An Overview of Research and Examples of Good Practice in the EU Member States, 1995–2000*, Vienna: European Research Centre on Migration and Ethnic Relations.

Van Dijk, Teun A. (2000) 'New(s) racism: a discourse analytical approach', in Simon Cottle (ed.) *Ethnic Minorities and the Media*, Buckingham, Philadelphia: Open University Press, 33–50.

Weiss, Gilbert (2002) 'Searching for Europe: the problem of legitimisation and representation in recent political speeches on Europe', *Journal of Language and Politics* 1(1): 59–83.

Wodak, Ruth (1996) *Disorders of Discourse*, London: Longmans.

Wodak, Ruth, Rudolf de Cilia, Martin Reisigl and Karin Liebhart (1999) *The Discursive Construction of National Identity*, Edinburgh: Edinburgh University Press.

Wodak, Ruth and Gilbert Weiss (2004) 'Visions, ideologies and utopias in the discursive construction of European identities: organising, representing and legitimising Europe', in Martin Pütz, Jo-Anne Neff-van Aerstselaer and Teun A. van Dijk (eds) *Communicating ideologies: Language, Discourse and Social Practice*, Frankfurt am Main: Peter Lang, 225–52.

8 Fixing capitalism and Europe's peripheries

West European imperialism

James Anderson and Ian Shuttleworth

Exporting capital to economically 'peripheral' areas of cheaper labour has long been seen as the major spatial solution or 'spatial fix' for the economic problems and crisis tendencies of 'core' economies. Ever since Hegel argued that Adam Smith's 'hidden hand of the market' could not provide prosperity and social harmony, there has been an emphasis on 'external' solutions, on the economic importance of colonies and the movement of investment, industry and jobs to lower-wage countries. This was the emphasis of liberal and Marxist theories of imperialism from the end of the nineteenth century.

A century later, however, there is an emphasis on the importing of cheap labour from the world's economic peripheries to its core economies. Recently this has increased dramatically, though it has been partly hidden and underrated empirically and theoretically.

It is now estimated, for instance, that during the 1990s more than 13.5 million workers entered the United States; they arrived at an even greater rate than during the 'Great Wave' of immigration around the end of the nineteenth century; and they came from a much wider range of mostly, though not exclusively, 'Third World' and former 'Second World ' countries (Sum *et al.* 2002). The 1990s boom in the USA – and by extension in the global economy as a whole – was reportedly 'created on the back of foreign workers' (*Guardian* 3.12.02), though this was hardly reflected in theories of 'globalisation'. Countries of the European Union core also benefited, perhaps most dramatically the Republic of Ireland's 'Celtic Tiger', itself largely an extension of US capital in Europe. It seemed that almost overnight, and certainly within a decade, Ireland went from being a country of emigration to one of immigration; and as with Western Europe in general, large numbers of the migrant workers came from Eastern Europe, from what became the EU's accession states of 2004, and ones further to the east. Furthermore, it seemed that unprecedented proportions of these workers were transitory rather than permanent settlers (at least initially), and disproportionately they constituted cheap and often very cheap labour. State territoriality and border controls operated in paradoxical and contradictory ways which served to further cheapen this labour, in the most extreme cases through the withholding of political and social rights where cross-border migrants were 'illegal' or 'undocumented'. Of the estimated (perhaps underestimated) 13.5 million workers who entered the USA in the 1990s, an astonishing 9 million were said to be undocumented or illegal immigrants working in mostly low-paid jobs (Sum *et al.* 2002).

On such evidence we hypothesised that these periphery-to-core flows of (mostly cheap) labour constitute 'a new spatial fix for capitalist crisis' (Anderson and Shuttleworth 2004 and 2004a). We argued that the traditional spatial fix of exporting capital *to* peripheral areas of cheap labour – which we called 'Fix 1' – had been partly replaced by a new, unacknowledged reverse spatial fix of importing the cheap labour *from* such areas – 'Fix 2'. However, there was also evidence that the traditional capital-exporting Fix 1 not only continued to operate but might indeed be making a comeback. So both spatial fixes may now be operating simultaneously or in tandem, as is suggested by the flows of labour and capital in Europe.[1]

Eastern Europe provides Western Europe with cheap migrant labour, and Eastern Europe has also been sharing in what appears to be a more general resurgence of investment and jobs moving to economic peripheries. Countries such as Poland, the Czech Republic, Slovakia, Hungary, Slovenia and the Baltic Republics have been recipients of increasing Western investment, particularly since the mid-1990s when they began preparing for EU membership. Now with accession might they perhaps switch from being predominantly the senders of cheap migrant labour to Western Europe, as in Fix 2, to being more the Fix 1 receivers of surplus capital from Western European and other core economies? And might countries remaining beyond the EU's external borders, such as Belarus and Ukraine, continue to function primarily as sources of cheap migrant labour – and not only for Western Europe but also for the new accession countries as 'peripheries of the periphery'?

In this chapter we schematically outline the main characteristics of the traditional Fix 1 and our hypothesised Fix 2. We discuss the structural and circumstantial evidence for Fix 2's recent emergence, and how borders exert extra-economic pressures on supposedly 'free' labour. This model of two alternative or complementary spatial fixes is then linked to ideas of imperialism and 'formal' and 'informal empire' in Europe. Since the fall of the Berlin Wall, Europe provides the clearest evidence of the fixes working together; and illustrative data on labour flows from Eastern to Western Europe and on capital flows from West to East put some flesh on the bones of the theoretical model. The political economy of spatial fixes gives substance to the idea of 'Europe as empire' (see Chapter 1). It provides structural insights into the underlying imperialistic relations between Europe's core and periphery.

The old Fix 1: countering crisis tendencies by exporting capital

Fix 1 in its traditional guise has been clearly outlined by David Harvey (2001) who traced it back to Hegel and von Thünen in the 1820s, before it was developed by Marx in his theory of capitalist over-accumulation, falling profit rates and a shortage of profitable investment outlets. Their theorising about the export of capital was borne out in the empirical reality of the 'high noon' of empire and inter-imperialist rivalry before the First World War. It was further theorised by Hobson, Lenin, Luxemburg, Bukharin and others after it had emerged in practice with exports of capital and labour to formal and informal colonies. However, in the inter-war period the export of capital (and labour) was reduced in the general 'autarky' of closed economies, and Harvey (2001) suggests that the fix of capital exports may alternate historically with autarky.

Hegel and von Thünen did not believe that the 'internal solution' of Adam Smith's 'hidden hand of the market' was capable of delivering social harmony and a 'just wage' in the core economies. Setting up colonies to take surplus capital and population was Hegel's answer, while for von Thünen (who objected to imperialism on ethical grounds) 'colonies' were only a theoretical device which he thought enabled him to calculate a just minimum wage for workers which could be ensured by the state (the minimum being that required to retain workers from leaving to set their own businesses in his hypothetical 'colony') (Harvey 2001, 286–293). Marx, in contrast, rubbished this internal solution as 'childish'. He saw the poverty of a 'reserve army' of unemployed workers as part and parcel of capital accumulation, and an internal solution as impossible given capitalism's inherent tendency to generate economic crisis.

The whole weight of theoretical argument was thus on the export of capital and on capitalism as a geographically *expanding* system (as distinct from the recently contracting or imploding one – as we shall see). Imperialism created new markets beyond the existing core of capitalism, though according to Lenin and others it also fuelled the interstate, imperialist rivalries which led to the First World War. But despite theoretical and political disagreements, it was generally agreed that capital export was a key short-term counter to capitalism's crisis tendencies (though there were also disagreements about how short or long the 'short-term' might be); and there was a corresponding underemphasis on the potential of labour imports (despite the Marxist stress on the 'reserve army of labour').

Stated (over-)simply, crises are inherent in capitalism because its 'overproduction/underconsumption' tendencies are tied up with an inbuilt tendency for the rate of profit to fall: over time capitalists have to invest more and more capital to get the same return in profit. The overaccumulation of capital and the relative underconsumption of its products is manifested in a shortage of further outlets for profitable investment – in short, capitalism is the victim of its own success. These however are tendencies, not absolutes, because there is a variety of *other* tendencies which can offset or counter them, at least in the short-term. It is not just an abstract theory but an historical process which also has a geography. The counter-tendencies include our two spatial fixes, and technological innovations to improve production efficiency. But they also include more malign processes such as the devaluation of capital in a crisis, with bankruptcies leaving increased profit-making possibilities for surviving capitals; the large-scale physical destruction of capital in wars; and its peacetime equivalent of a 'permanent arms economy' where huge expenditures on stockpiled weaponry are in effect also a massive destruction of capital (Kidron 1970).

The new Fix 2: countering crisis by importing cheap labour

The possibility of a switch from exporting capital to importing peripheral labour was foreseen by Lenin and by the Austrian Marxist, Otto Bauer, though it was scoffed at by Rosa Luxemburg who underestimated the huge untapped reserves of labour power in the colonies 'once self-sustaining rural producers could be detached from the land' (Cohen 1987, 252–253). Now, of course, to a considerable extent they have become detached by proletarianisation in the periphery, a necessary though not sufficient, precondition for importing peripheral labour.

It may be that Fix 2 has more limited effects on profitability than Fix 1 and lacks the latter's historic importance in spatially expanding new markets. Nevertheless, it is systematically underrated for several reasons. They include the traditional and continuing emphasis on Fix 1 and global expansion, and a corresponding lack of awareness of spatial contraction tendencies; an overemphasis on the mobility of capital and on the relative *immobility* of labour; and the sheer complexity of labour flows and often hidden nature of migrant labour. Thus critics of capitalism stress the contradictions between the relatively free transnational movement of capital, goods and information across borders and the lack of such freedom for people in general and labour in particular (see e.g. Amin 1996). Across different political perspectives (see also e.g. Stiglitz 2002) labour migration is often ignored in accounts of contemporary globalisation, and where mentioned it is usually simply as an effect rather than a formative influence.

The very nature and complexity of labour flows make them difficult to track. In contrast to the often directly state-regulated labour recruitment of the postwar boom, the recent Fix 2 immigration is largely organised in and by the private sector in a neo-liberal context, in some cases evading state controls and enumeration. Because of the often transitory character of jobs at the level of individual migrants, they may 'escape' official censuses even where they are fully documented in a legal sense. In general they are low-paid, socially marginalised, unassimilated and often largely 'unseen' by the host society, as is reflected in the labels attached to them: the 'new helots' (Cohen 1987), the 'new untouchables' (Harris 1995). And while the flows are less transitory at a collective level, they are very diverse in their origins and destinations. For simplicity we talk of core and periphery in the singular, but the reality is a very complex geography of cores and peripheries in the plural and different hierarchies of relative wage-cost advantage. The migration flows are more like cascades spilling between a series of peripheries and cores – one country's periphery being another's core. The same country is often both origin and destination – we shall see, for instance, that Poland sends migrant workers to Western Europe and itself receives cheap(er) labour from areas to its east.

Partly in consequence, much of our evidence for Fix 2 is structural and circumstantial. Indeed the importance of historical context is underlined by the contrast with the labour immigration of the postwar boom which was *not* a response to a crisis of overproduction, *nor* part of a neo-liberal, cost-cutting 'race to the bottom' (neither of which then existed). So our evidence for Fix 2 includes the rise of neo-liberalism; the highly uneven and restricted nature of contemporary globalisation; the relative immobility of some capital and the mobility of some labour (reversing the normal stereotypes); and the contradictory nature of state borders and border controls as filters which further cheapen already cheap labour, allowing it in under duress (rather than actually stopping entry), and thus also rendering it in neo-liberal terms more 'flexible'.

Neo-liberalism and 'imploding globalisation'

We can situate Fix 2 in terms of the neo-liberal deregulation of core labour markets in the 1980s and 1990s (see Peck 2001, Jessop 2003), especially in the more neo-liberal countries such as the USA, Ireland and Britain; and in terms of neo-liberalism's destabilising effects in peripheral economies which in many cases became more risky for, and hence got an even smaller share of, foreign investment. There has been a relative retreat of core capital from large areas of the world – what Michael Mann (2001) calls 'ostracising imperialism', and what for Ankie Hoogvelt (1997) is 'imploding globalisation'. This ostracisation/implosion has created huge reserve supplies of unemployed or underused labour in the periphery, and it has simultaneously concentrated increased demand for labour within the core in order to absorb its surplus capital. These are the basic preconditions for Fix 2, and its association with global contraction tendencies can be seen as the reverse side of constraints on Fix 1.

The core's relative share of investment has been rising since the 1950s (Mann 2001). With some exceptions, peripheral countries have received relatively less 'Fix 1 investment' as profitability and risks outside the core increased (including ironically because of the de-stabilising effects neo-liberal policies foisted on some 'Third' and 'former Second World' countries to make them 'safer' for capital). So most foreign investment stayed within the core. The scene was set for Fix 2 and the exploitation through immigration of the un- or under-employed labour in the periphery which was becoming less accessible *in situ*. About 90 per cent of all investment and trade now takes place within the core of the world economy. China has increased its share of investment from the core, accounting for well over half of it (Mann 2001, 54, 55, 72) – and is indeed in the process of becoming part of the core, as are parts of Eastern Europe – but much of the world periphery will continue to have little to offer the core economically except its 'helots and untouchables' as Fix 2 migrant labour.

Fix 2 has also been boosted by the changing structure of industries and employment in the core: by an increasing 'tail' of menial jobs, a relative and absolute expansion at the low-paid end of the labour market (Peck and Theodore 2001); and more particularly by the relative growth of immobile capital and production processes which cannot (or cannot easily) be relocated to cheap-labour peripheries. Much of the core's construction industry, its low-paid and labour-intensive service sectors which sell directly to the general public in the core, and its highly productive (highly subsidised) agriculture and agri-industrial sectors which depend on cheap and/or seasonal labour, simply do not have the option of relocating to the periphery. And these are just the sectors where the majority of low-paid immigrant workers find demand for their labour.

State borders and labour's 'third freedom'

Thus both ends of the migratory chain from periphery to core are shaped by essentially the same core-inspired neo-liberalism, and it seems that neo-liberal orthodoxy disappears only at borders where state regulation appears to be rigorously enforced. At first glance this seems to run completely counter to all the circumstantial evidence for Fix 2. But appearances are often misleading, and sometimes intentionally so (see e.g. Heyman 1999). There is often more – and less – to border controls than meets the eye. The critics see a major contradiction between hypermobile capital and immobile labour caged by borders, but the full story is more complex and even more contradictory. Some capital is immobile, some labour highly mobile; cheap immigrant labour is both attracted to and excluded from the core, and is seen simultaneously as essential and as undesirable. Employers want the cheap labour of immigrants, economic success often depends on them, and hence state authorities may 'turn a blind eye' or avoid dealing effectively with illegal entry by immigrants or illegal employment by their employers. But others in the host community may see, or be encouraged to see, immigrants as a threat to their own jobs and/or levels of state welfare, and/or to national identity and cohesion (themes which are the meat and drink of right-wing racists and scapegoaters). State authorities (who may include some of the latter) therefore try to maintain the appearance of strict control while in reality national borders generally function as flexible filters or partial or variably ineffective barriers which weaken and cheapen labour rather than blocking the supply. This works to capital's advantage (and is not quite so contradictory in the sense that critics of capitalism often imagine).

It adds a 'third freedom' to what Marx ironically dubbed labour's 'double freedom'. In capitalism, labour is legally free to work for any employer but has to work for some employer, because of the *economic* compulsion of also being 'free' of ownership of means of production. This double freedom applies at the abstract level of Marx's aspatial mode of production (and in a single 'closed' national economy if treated in isolation). But in the concrete reality of transnational labour markets operating in the highly territorialised space of national states in the plural, it is more accurately a 'triple freedom'. In addition to the economic compulsion to work for some employer, migrant workers are generally subjected to additional *extra*-economic compulsions stemming from state territoriality and borders and capitalism's contradictory unity of economics *and* politics which is most in evidence at borders (Wood 1995; Anderson 2001). The contradictory nature of borders as 'bridges', 'barriers' and 'symbols' (O'Dowd 2003), as hurdles to be jumped rather than as insurmountable obstacles, allows migrants entry while denying them various legal and democratic rights, or national and cultural 'belonging', and hence reducing their economic bargaining power (see also Chapter 7). In general, capital benefits, but only to the extent that indigenous workers allow migrant workers to be (mis)treated differently, allowing the working class as a whole to be divided on nationalistic lines, rather than making common cause with them.

The model: fixes in tandem in a 'new imperialism'

Both spatial fixes bring together surplus capital and surplus (usually cheap) labour in a new round of production. Fix 1 gets rid of the core's surplus capital by exporting it; Fix 2 absorbs the core's surplus capital *in situ* by importing labour and making further investment within the core more profitable than would otherwise be the case. However this simple model needs several qualifications or refinements. Both fixes involve additional economic flows (see Table 8.1) but both in different ways become self-defeating in later rounds of production. They are complementary, and in self-defeat feed off each other. Particularly in the case of Europe, both have to be seen in terms of the political territoriality of 'formal' and 'informal empire' rather than as simply economic flows.

Additional flows and the self-defeating character of the fixes

In the nineteenth century, labour as well as capital was exported from the core to the colonies, but with surpluses of cheap proletarianised labour now available in the periphery it is no longer generally necessary (apart from some technical or managerial staff) – indeed, the main basis of Fix 1 is now the cheaper labour already available in the periphery. In Fix 1 there are also reverse flows of capital or profits back to the core. In the case of Fix 2 there are reverse flows of immigrants' remittances back to the periphery, and also knowledge transfers from the more technically advanced core – both benefits to the periphery, unlike its debt repayments to the core.

The effectiveness of each fix and the benefits for core capital in general are, however, time-limited. While each can be highly beneficial for the individual

Table 8.1 Two spatial fixes for crises of overaccumulation in core economies

	Fix 1	*Fix 2*
Main flow	Capital moves from core to periphery	Labour moves from periphery to core
Reverse flow	Profit remittances sent back to the core	Wage remittances sent back to the periphery, plus knowledge transfers
Subsidiary flow	In nineteenth century, core labour 'colonisation' of periphery	Since 1980s, debt repayments from periphery to core

capitals directly involved, each fix in the longer term is self-defeating overall and actually worsens the very problem it is meant to solve, exacerbating overaccumulation and crisis tendencies. Fix 1 can be very profitable for core investors who harness new resources and labour in the periphery, create new markets for core products, and effectively turn periphery into core – Fix 1's positive expansionary element. But this ultimately develops rival centres of production, increases the overaccumulation in the whole system, and creates further pressures on the original core (as nineteenth-century Europe found with the rise of the USA; and the USA found with the economic resurgence of Germany and Japan in the late 1960s – see Brenner 2002).

Likewise, Fix 2: while it provides additional cheap labour to absorb surplus core capital, facilitates further profitable activity in the core, and obviously benefits the individual employers of cheap labour, it directly stokes up the problems of overaccumulation within the core. And it may become self-defeating more quickly than Fix 1, with a more limited timespan. Its malign features are associated with global contraction or implosion, rather than expansion. The new markets created by Fix 2 are within the core (rather than the needier periphery); they are largely created by generating new demands from the same set of consumers through advertising and the extension of loans and personal debts, which have grown enormously in recent decades and bring their own problems. Fix 2 also has political limits: its basis in cheap immigrant labour and 'super-exploitation' can be undermined both malignly by chauvinistic attempts to exclude immigrants, and benignly by solidarity with them and their self-unionisation to improve their wages and conditions. Yet Fix 2 is likely to persist, given the large reserves of cheap migratory labour to which immobile capitals want access, while its transient, hidden and criminalised dimensions can militate against effective solidarity. But it is likely to persist in tandem with Fix 1.

Complementarity and combinations

'Capital moving to labour' or 'labour to capital' echoes the traditional industrial policy choice of moving 'work to the workers' or 'workers to the work'. Clearly there are various alternating and combinatory possibilities here, as both fixes contain the seeds of their own destruction and feed off each other, and this leads to a range of different geographical strategies and effects. For example, capital flows from the USA to Ireland had the Fix 1 effect of reducing the pressures of overaccumulation in the USA, but simultaneously they strengthened Ireland's position in the core and made it a major destination for Fix 2 peripheral labour in order to absorb the incoming capital. Similar effects can be expected in Eastern Europe, with Fix 1 investment, in for example Poland, turning it into part of the core and it sucking in cheap(er) labour from more peripheral countries further east in cascading flows. Additionally, by fostering peripheral development, Fix 1 investment can release further reserves of labour, as for example in modernising Polish agriculture and proletarianising much of its rural population, making it available for exploitation by Western capital, either in Poland (Fix 1) or as migrant labour (Fix 2). Indeed some individual Western capitals may have a direct choice. And in so far as Fix 2 encourages the 'reverse flows' of remittances and knowledge back to the periphery, it may be seen as preparing the ground for another round of Fix 1 core investment in the periphery.

But, it is the self-defeating element in the main flow of each fix and hence its short-term effectiveness which most actively encourages the alternative spatial fix; and it also promotes a cyclical element in their interrelationships. Thus, in producing ever greater accumulations of capital in the core, Fix 2 increases the pressures for a Fix 1 export of surplus capital. Indeed the recent prominence of Fix 2 may well have contributed to a Fix 1 comeback. With it comes the need for a selective reincorporation or recolonisation of parts of the 'ostracised periphery', including parts of the 'Third World' and Eastern Europe – a different way of accessing their underused supplies of labour and other resources if only they could be made safe(r) for Western investors. The formal political enlargement of the EU is one way of doing this – albeit one which runs counter to the dominant pattern established in the twentieth century.

The territoriality of 'informal' and 'formal empire'

This is the last piece of our theoretical jigsaw before fleshing out the model with some illustrative data. As we have seen, Fix 1 has a history steeped in imperialism, first, in 'formal' empires where investments from the core country could be protected and risks minimised by the direct territorial control of colonies; and then later through more 'informal' empire where control from the centre was much less direct and relied heavily on local elites, and increasingly on separate, politically (if not economically) independent states. Thus the British Empire in the nineteenth century combined both formal and informal empire, with the latter increasingly important in economic terms (e.g. in the politically independent countries of South America); while since the twentieth century the empire of the USA has been very largely 'informal', the overseas operations of its multinational corporations being secured and protected not by direct territorial control from the US but by the states in which they are located. This decreasing need for direct control has been greatly facilitated by the partial separation (or contradictory unity) of politics and economics which is unique to the capitalist mode of production. It makes plausible the claims of states to independent political sovereignty within their borders (by separating off economic realities); and it simultaneously facilitates the cross-border or transnational spread of economic influence and control (shorn of, or masking, its overtly political aspects which would clearly contravene the sovereignty claims of other states and invite nationalistic reactions) (see Anderson 2001). This 'empire of capital' (Wood 2003) is the dominant geopolitical/geo-economics context within which both spatial fixes now operate: most capital exports go to politically independent countries, most immigrant labour comes from them. The clear historical tendency has been for less reliance on the territorial extension of political control.

However (as we saw in Chapter 1), this picture has to be qualified and in particular there are several counter-tendencies which help explain EU developments. First, independent states cannot always be relied on to secure conditions in which foreign investments will prosper; the worldwide empire of capital is largely controlled by US hegemony (along with allies including the EU); and the US has a global archipelago of military bases for the enforcement of 'indirect control' where needed. As the British sent the occasional gunboat to secure their informal empire in South America, so today the US can threaten recalcitrant or rogue states with warplanes and aerial bombing, or in the last resort military occupation and direct control (though its disastrous occupation of Iraq shows why it generally prefers not to have to actually carry out this ultimate threat).

Secondly, it is possible – and generally much more effective – to extend formal territorial control by peaceful means (e.g. by economic and other 'carrots and sticks') where independent states cannot be relied on to provide a secure economic environment. And EU enlargement in Eastern Europe is the prime example of this. After 1989 the economies of the former Soviet bloc were destabilised by a privatising nomenclatura, Western-prescribed neo-liberalism and other factors; they were characterised by Elmer Altvater (1998) as 'arbitrage economies' where production came a poor second to short-term, opportunistic and more questionable activities, including trading on tax and price differences, smuggling, and financial fraud. In this context, EU enlargement, including especially the imposition of prior conditions for membership, have already gone a long way towards resecuring much of what was a high-risk periphery, making it safe for Fix 1 investment from the West.

Thirdly, while historically the leading powers have relied less and less on the territorial extension of political control, with territoriality apparently becoming progressively less important as capitalism and the politics/economics separation developed worldwide, their home territories, the base for their transnational operations, have generally become progressively larger. In the case of the hegemonic USA the home territory is continental in scale, in comparison to which the home territories of the previous world hegemons, Britain and the United Dutch Provinces, were tiny. Likewise, the territories of the USA's major rivals, China and Russia, are of continental scale; and for the EU to 'live in this company' there are strong pressures to enlarge and consolidate a larger territorial base. It too is a rival (as well as sometime ally) of the USA (see Anderson 2003) and a competitor with the other world powers, in economic if not military terms, and this global competition is now the main driving force behind EU enlargement and integration.

Thus while the bulk of Fix 2 migration worldwide and most Fix 1 export of capital take place in the 'informal empire of capital', in the case of Europe they now operate in a directly controlled political setting more like formal empire. Initially the newly established independent states to the east provided cheap migrant labour for Western Europe, but taking fuller advantage of their massive reserve army of un- and under-employed has also required Fix 1 and political incorporation.

Fix 2: Eastern labour moves west

East European labour has traditionally moved west (Grecic 1993), as in the mass emigration in the nineteenth and early twentieth centuries from the Polish and Czech lands to the industrial cores of Germany and the Austro-Hungarian Empire, and to North America. Between the two World Wars migration decreased but the turbulent aftermath of the Second World War and the westward relocation of state borders unleashed large-scale population redistributions (Okolski 1998). In this historical context, the Cold War period, with its relatively low levels of movement, was the anomaly.

All that changed, and changed quite suddenly, with the fall of the Berlin Wall and the collapse of the Soviet empire. Political barriers to migration were removed and it was again possible to imagine the integration of Eastern Europe into a pan-European labour market. Initially, in the early 1990s, the shock of the transition from centrally planned to market economies, combined with the transformation of state borders, prompted West European fears of mass migration from the East, one alarmist estimate predicting 20 million migrants (Grecic 1993). However these exaggerated fears proved completely unfounded and consequently abated, though they were to resurface in the run-up to the accession of the ten new member states in 2004, again saying more about West European chauvinism than about the reality of migration processes. The fears were to some extent allayed by official estimates that migration to the West would have minimal impact (European Commission 2001), with total labour flows of between 70,000 and 150,000 workers per annum decreasing over time, and with many returning to their countries of origin. The UK government made similarly low-key estimates of the likely levels and impact, and it is noteworthy that it, along with the Republic of Ireland, was one of the existing EU member states that did not place transitional restrictions on immigration from the new members.

The truth about immigration from Eastern Europe probably lies somewhere between the intentionally alarmist chauvinist fears whipped up by unscrupulous politicians and the low ('reassuring') estimates made by governments and the EU. Immigration from some accession states such as Poland is clearly substantial and has had major impacts in some labour market sectors in both the UK and Ireland. Polish communities have arisen in cities such as Dublin and Belfast, for example, as well as in parts of England; and in some sectors, such as agribusiness, construction and the hospitality industry, east European labour appears to be gaining in importance. It is difficult, however, to gauge with authority the extent and numerical significance of migration because of the data inadequacies and the sometimes short-term or transitory nature of individual migration paths. There are problems in agreeing common definitions of international migration (Kupiszewski 1996) and not all migrants who cross international borders are recorded by either the sending or the receiving countries. The true extent of migration is therefore unknown, but it is probable that official figures underestimate it because of data deficiencies, and there is growing acceptance of its economic significance. For example, in a speech in Edinburgh on 12 June 2006, Mervyn King, Governor of the Bank of England, stated that net inward migration to the UK between 1995 and 2004 was estimated at 1.3 million, compared to a total increase in the labour force of 1.7 million. This is not quite in the same league as the USA with its estimated 13.5 million immigrant workers in the 1990s, but in both cases there have been major impacts on the labour market.

Despite the difficulties of accurately estimating migration flows between the EU accession states, places further east, and the 'old EU', the data that are available indicate some clear trends. First, the direction of migration flows has changed, as continued restrictions in the more traditional destinations such as Germany and France have led to greater migration to Britain and Ireland. Likewise, Southern Europe has recently become a more important destination for short-term and informal migration, with for example East European immigrants in Spain showing a ten-fold increase in the four years between 1998 and 2002 and rising from under 2.5 per cent to over 9 per cent of Spain's foreign-born population (I.N.E. 2003). Indeed the greater geographical spread of migrant labour may indicate the increased structural importance of Fix 2.

Secondly (and further complicating the picture) it seems that the phenomenon of migration 'cascades' is increasing, and here the case of Poland is interesting. The shock of its rapid neo-liberal transition from a planned economy forced many people out of their jobs and created a dual labour market. Large numbers had to rely for employment on Poland's rapidly expanding informal sector, but increasingly they also came to rely on the formal and informal sectors in Western Europe (Iglicka 2001). Some who had to emigrate for work could sell their skills, but many were 'overqualified' for the menial and low-paid jobs they were forced to take. But furthermore, Poland, according to Iglicka (2001), is now making the transition from a country of emigration to a country of immigration, and becoming a destination in its own right rather than simply a transit point to the West. Polish emigration will probably continue, but paradoxically the same neo-liberal creation of a dual labour market which encouraged emigration to the West has also facilitated immigration from more peripheral areas east of Poland – the cascading effect. The need for low-cost labour in Poland's informal sector – as in other accession states like Hungary and the Czech Republic – draws in migrant workers from countries such as Ukraine, Belarus, Romania and Russia, and it was estimated that in 1995 there were already some 500,000 Ukrainians working illegally in Poland (Iglicka 2001). With accession and as Fix 1 continues to take effect, the demand for labour in countries such as Poland will grow, and its attractiveness for more peripheral immigrant labour is likely to increase further, and possibly in further contradiction with the immigration controls of 'Fortress Europe'. Return migration by Poles will probably increase as well (as happened when Ireland joined the EU and received large inflows of capital).

Estimating the economic impacts of migrant labour on receiving and sending countries is difficult and contentious, and 'proving' that it is a spatial fix – and a fix for what – is inherently problematical. There is a wide literature which ranges from microlevel studies of the impacts of remittances to macrolevel analyses of the effects of migration on the world system, but generally the conclusions are mixed and sometimes contradictory. However, there is increasing evidence that policymakers and business leaders in the UK acknowledge that immigration is having positive economic effects. The Bank of England Governor, in the speech previously cited, stated that 'Migration on this scale raised the potential growth rate of the UK economy and probably dampened the response of costs and prices to changes in demand'. And he was echoing the February 2006 UK economy forecast of the National Institute of Economic and Social Research which argued that migration boosted GDP and kept the brakes on inflation. As well as benefiting particular sectors and regions, labour immigration brings macroeconomic benefits for the whole economy.

Fix 1: Western capital moves east

Foreign direct investment (FDI) is a 'key element of the neo-liberal transition' in Eastern Europe (Williams *et al.* 1998, 139) and it is central to Fix 1. Here the data are less inadequate than the migration statistics, and a preliminary analysis of UNCTAD figures quickly establishes the broad pattern of capital flows to Eastern Europe. The UNCTAD category of 'Central and Eastern Europe' does not quite match the new accession states, and the data cover all capital flows without discriminating between direct investment in productive capacity and other forms of capital. However with these caveats, the data are indicative of the relationships that the accession and other East European states are developing with Western Europe and other parts of the global core. They support our contention of a reasserted Fix 1 and its differentiated development across Eastern Europe.

Data on investment flows between 1976 and 2002 clearly illustrate the opening up of 'Central and Eastern Europe' (in this case including Russia) to Western capital. There were virtually zero flows to the region up to 1989 and then a rapid and almost continuous increase in levels of investment, reaching around $30,000 million worth by 2002. But this investment is geographically differentiated. Taking the four states with the largest flows of inward investment in 2000 (Poland, Hungary, the Czech Republic, and the Russian Federation), the great bulk of this investment came from the EU, in the case of Poland (94 per cent), Hungary (77 per cent), and the Czech Republic (80 per cent). In contrast, the EU accounted for only about a third of inward investment in the Russian Federation, where North American involvement was greater.

Taking account of the relative size of the countries, there is a clear preference for what became accession countries as against those remaining on the edge or beyond EU influence. It is however unclear how far prospective membership of the EU shaped these uneven investment patterns, how far they would have happened anyway because of other factors, and also the extent to which the stabilising effects of EU enlargement spilled over to non-candidate countries which are now subject to the EU's European Neighbourhood Policy (see Chapter 9). Lower wages – some four to six or seven times lower than in some EU states – are significant in driving manufacturing investment to the East, but non-cost factors such as labour quality, state incentives, and access to markets are also important. Poland, Hungary and the Czech Republic have received much more investment than either the much larger Russian Federation or Ukraine, while ('unreformed') Belarus has consistently had the lowest capital inflows. Russia may possibly receive more investment in the future, given its huge market potential and resource and manufacturing base, and this could partly be at the expense of further investment in the accession states such as Poland, but the latter are likely to remain important destinations for the foreseeable future.

Investment in Eastern Europe has to be seen in wider perspective. In terms of total EU investments it might in fact seem relatively unimportant. For example, only around 3–4 per cent of the investment flows from the UK, Sweden and the Netherlands go to Central and Eastern Europe. Likewise, all investment inflows to Central and Eastern Europe (regardless of origin) were equivalent in value to less than 10 per cent of total investment outflows from the EU (to all destinations) in the 1990s. At first glance this suggests that 'Central and Eastern Europe' is not a major investment partner from the perspective of the EU, whatever the EU's importance from an East European viewpoint. But first glances can be deceptive. If instead of considering total investment, we focus on capital moving to the periphery of the world economy, then Eastern Europe assumes much greater significance, though it is only one among many possible destinations for Fix 1 capital exports from the core. First, we must remember that most new investment by capital based in core countries takes place *within* its country of origin; secondly most of the smaller proportion which crosses borders still, despite globalisation, stays *within* the core (increasing the pressure for Fix 2, as we have seen). So, thirdly, when we talk of Fix 1 capital exports from the core we are nearly always talking of a relatively small residual of total investment. However its qualitative significance for offsetting the overaccumulation of capital in the core is much greater than the bald percentage figures might imply. In this context Eastern Europe may become a very important destination for West European capital – it is already a more important destination than all the rest of the developing world for Swedish and Dutch capital. And here Fix 1 is building up the EU's territorial base, in the longer term converting periphery to core, as in the shorter term it siphons off surplus core capital.

Conclusions

The expanding EU and its empire-like gradation of peripheries provide a good 'laboratory' for the necessarily imprecise study of the two spatial fixes. Conversely, our two fixes model of capital and labour flows provides a stimulating and open-ended political economy framework for studying the EU's enlargement and its asymmetrical and imperialistic power relations with new member states, candidate states and other neighbours.

We saw that the traditional Fix 1 spatial solution – exporting surplus capital to the periphery in order to relieve the problem of overaccumulation in the core – was at least partly replaced in the 1980s and 1990s by a new Fix 2 – using cheap labour imported from peripheries to absorb surplus core capital *in situ*. We also saw that in Fix 2, state borders operate in contradictory ways but generally have the effect of weakening and cheapening labour; and here capitalism's contradictory unity of politics and economics is clearly in evidence. There are political pressures to reduce immigration but economic imperatives to obtain cheap labour no matter where it comes from – a situation not amenable to straightforward positivistic or functionalist analysis.

There is also clear evidence of a reassertion of Fix 1 and it fits with the EU's rolling programme of territorial expansion. Furthermore, the EU evidence supports our conclusion that both fixes are now working in tandem. Instead of Fix 1 alternating historically with autarky (as Harvey seemed to suggest), it may oscillate in relative importance with Fix 2, both operating simultaneously in a dialectical manner. As we have seen, the limits of one may stimulate the other. They may be in competition with each other, or operate selectively for different parts of the periphery – Fix 1 perhaps predominating in the case of the EU's new member states, Fix 2 in the case of less secure countries further east. The combination of Fixes 1 and 2 may indeed be capitalism's spatial fix for the foreseeable future. If so, the EU 'empire' will be a major beneficiary.

Note

1 Our hypothesis of a new spatial fix was first presented in a paper on 'International borders as regulators in transnational labour markets' at a conference on *Global Regulation*, University of Sussex, May 2003 (see Anderson and Shuttleworth 2004 and 2004a). The application of the two fixes model to EU enlargement was first presented at conferences of the European Consortium for Political Research in Bologna, June 2004, and European Urban and Regional Studies, Pultusk, Poland, September 2004. Our thanks for comments and suggestions at those conferences, and for the support of the Centre for International Borders Research at Queen's University Belfast – www.qub.ac.uk/cibr.

References

Altvater, E. (1998) 'Theoretical deliberations on time and space in post-socialist transformation', *Regional Studies* 32: 7, 591–605.

Amin, S. (1996) 'The challenge of globalisation', *Review of International Political Economy* 3:2, 216–59.

Anderson, J. (2001) *Theorizing State Borders: 'Politics/Economics' and Democracy in Capitalism*, Centre for International Borders Research, Electronic Working Paper Series, CIBR/WP 01-1, Queen's University Belfast (*www.qub.ac.uk/cibr*).

Anderson, J. (2003) 'American hegemony after September 11: Allies, rivals and contradictions', *Geopolitics* 8:3, 35–60.

Anderson, J., O'Dowd, L. and Wilson, T.M. (eds) (2003) *New Borders for a Changing Europe: Cross-Border Cooperation and Governance*, London: Frank Cass. Also published as *Regional and Federal Studies* vol. 12, no. 4.

Anderson, J. and Shuttleworth, I. (2004) 'A new spatial fix for Capitalist crisis? Immigrant labour, state borders and the new ostracising imperialism', in L. Assassi, K. van der Pijl and D. Wigan (eds) *Contextualising Global Regulation: Managing Crisis after the Imperial Turn*, Basingstoke: Palgrave, 145–61.

Anderson, J. and Shuttleworth, I. (2004a) 'Theorising state borders: spatial fixes old and new', Centre for International Borders Research, *Electronic Working Paper Series*, CIBR/WP04-2, Queen's University Belfast (*www.qub.ac.uk/cibr*).

Brenner, R. (2002) *The Boom and the Bubble*, London: Verso.

Cohen, R. (1987) *The New Helots: Migrants in the International Division of Labour*, Aldershot: Avebury.

European Commission (2001) *Information Note: The Free Movement of Workers in the Context of Enlargement*, Brussels: European Commission.

Grecic, V. (1993) 'Mass migration from Eastern Europe: a challenge to the West', in King, R. (ed.) *The New Geography of European Migrations*, London: Belhaven, 135–51.

Harris, N. (1995) *The New Untouchables: Immigration and the New World Worker*, Harmondsworth: Penguin.

Harvey, D. (2001) 'The spatial fix: Hegel, Von Thünen and Marx', in *Spaces of Capital: Towards a Critical Geography*, Edinburgh: Edinburgh University Press, 284–311. (Originally published in *Antipode*, 1981.)

Heyman, J. (1999) 'Why interdiction? Immigration control at the United States–Mexico border', *Regional Studies* 33:7, 619–30.

Hoogvelt, A. (1997) *Globalisation and the Postcolonial World: The New Political Economy of Development*, Basingstoke: Macmillan.

Iglicka, K. (2001) *Poland's Post-War Dynamic of Migration*, Aldershot: Ashgate.

I.N.E. (2003) *Los Extranjeros Residentes en España 1998–2002*, 24, Madrid: Instituto Nacional de Estadística.

Jessop, B. (2003) *From Thatcherism to New Labour: Neo-Liberalism, Workfareism and Labour Market Regulation*, Department of Sociology, University of Lancaster.

Kidron, M. (1970) *Western Capitalism since the War*, Harmondsworth: Penguin.

Kupiszewski, M., (1996) 'Extra-union migration: the east-west perspective', in Rees, P., Stillwell, J., Convey, A. and Kupiszewski, M. (eds) *Population Migration in the European Union*, Chichester: John Wiley.

Mann, M. (2001) 'Globalisation and September 11', *New Left Review* 12, Nov–Dec, 51–72.

O'Dowd L. (2003) 'The changing significance of European borders', in Anderson *et al.* (2003) above, and *Regional and Federal Studies* 12:4, 13–36.

Okolski, M. (1998) 'Recent migration in Poland: trends and causes', in Iglicka, K. and Sword, K. (eds) *The Challenge of East–West Migration for Poland*, Basingstoke: Macmillan, 15–44.

Peck, J. (2001) *Workfare States*, Guildford: Guildford Press.

Peck, J. and Theodore, N. (2001) 'Contingent Chicago: restructuring the spaces of temporary labor', *International Journal of Urban and Regional Research* 25: 3, 471–96.

Stiglitz, J.E. (2002) *Globalisation and its Discontents*, London: Allen Lane.

Sum, A., Fogg, N., Harrington, P. with Khatiwada, I., Trub'skyy, M. and Palma, S. (2002) *Immigrant Workers and the Great American Job Machine: The Contribution of New Foreign Immigration to National and Regional Labor Force Growth in the 1990s*, Washington, DC: National Business Roundtable.

Williams, A., Balaz, V. and Zajac, S. (1998) 'The EU and Central Europe: the remaking of economic relationships', *Tijdschrift voor Economische en Sociale Geografie* 89:2, 131–49.

Wood, E.M. (1995) 'The separation of the "economic" and the "political" in capitalism', in E.M. Wood, *Democracy against Capitalism: Renewing Historical Materialism*, Cambridge: Cambridge University Press.
Wood, E.M. (2003) *Empire of Capital*, London: Verso.

9 Carving out a 'ring of friends'

The impact of the ENP on the shape of Europe

Pertti Joenniemi

Introduction

The onset of the 'Big Bang' of May 2004 compelled the EU to address questions concerning Europe's East. It then quickly turned out that the various issues, originating with the narrowing of the distance between the new neighbours and the enlarged EU, could not be settled on their own merits. Nor could they be addressed in isolation from broader questions and so a comprehensive European Neighbourhood Policy (ENP) saw the light of day.

This kind of down-to-earth reasoning constitutes the usual way to account for the emergence of an explicit and comprehensive neighbourhood policy. It was coined, the argument goes, because changes in the EU's external environment and the background consist, in essence, of an altered outer sphere posing challenges that the EU is obliged to address and deal with. In this view, the ENP has been developed for rather pragmatic reasons and it is a relatively natural outcome. Moreover, rather than representing anything qualitatively new, it is seen as consisting – in terms of its contents – of policies which have been there already for a considerable period of time, although they are now to cover, in the context of post-enlargement, a far broader sphere.

The accounts on offer appear to be rather linear in essence, but there might also be reasons to approach the ENP as representing a politics of emergence. In that vein, a broader and more critical examination is called for both as to the background and the contents of the recently devised neighbourhood policy. In the first place, there seem to be grounds to argue that the ENP stands for something qualitatively new rather than reflecting a mere updating of entrenched policies. I also argue here that many of the processes in the new policy are far from pragmatic in content, and that they entail, in many instances, quite contentious departures.

I further argue that the ENP has not only grown out of an encounter with a broader and different neighbourhood, i.e. the gist of the matter does not just consist of an unaltered EU reacting to challenges posed by a changing neighbourhood in the context of the 'Big Bang'. Some of the origins of the new neighbourhood policy are actually to be located within the EU itself. They become visible by focusing on the changes in the character of the EU itself, with an altered Union then also pursuing different policies vis-à-vis its external domain. The ENP is, in this perspective, to be probed as the Union's constitutive outside which serves as a crucial inroad in exploring the unfolding of the EU in the post-Cold War and post-9/11 period, i.e. a period of radical destabilisation.

There is an underlying geopolitical logic, particularly as the ENP's goal of streamlining the various approaches represented by the East, South and the North into a *single* neighbourhood policy is targeted. The North and South have experiences different from each other and the East has until recently remained largely without any particular policy of its own. So, the effort of devising a single model suiting all of them with this policy then taken to be generally applicable in all EU's 'near abroads' is bound to be problematic. Hence, the aim here is to tap into the process and probe some of the issues relating to this effort of generalising and streamlining, part of the new EU.

More generally, this chapter investigates the background, the notions behind the ENP and its evolution. This is done to track some of the main voices in the devising of the ENP and to explore in greater detail the various ways in which the initiative has been schematised in terms of its constitutive logic. The chapter concludes with an effort to spell out the broader consequences of the ENP as a framework imbued with holistic and yet diversified aspirations. It is a structure that aims to define what the EU is and where it ends, and, in this light, to comment on relationships between the ENP and the unfolding of Europe as a whole.

Initiating the ENP

In 2002 the UK sent a letter to the Commission pointing out that the political significance of the post-enlargement neighbourhood was bound to increase.[1] The question had to be addressed, it was stated, whether a shrinking of the spatial distance to a set of new neighbours implied that there was also a narrowing down of the temporal cleavage with the neighbours to be included in the EU, i.e. seen as future members. It was claimed that the challenges ahead could this time not be settled by further enlargement, and that the effects of such exclusion had to be mitigated in some manner. This bordering called, it was held, for a more substantial strategy vis-à-vis the EU's prospective neighbours.

Clearly, the prime British concern was that of security, in the sense that the negative aspects of the new neighbourhood might potentially spill over into the Union. Such a danger would mandate, it was thought, the creation of a 'special neighbourhood status' to be established for the new Eastern European neighbours, i.e. Ukraine, Moldova and Belarus.

The letter seems to have been formative in impact precisely in the sense of security being used as an inroad into neighbourhood issues. Importantly, the approach staked out in the letter was then applied in the EU's new security doctrine (ESS), a document endorsed by the European Council in December 2003.[2] Enlargement continues to be viewed positively in the ESS, but it is also noted that it 'brings the EU closer to troubled areas'. The conclusion is drawn that,

'Neighbours who are engaged in violent conflicts, weak states where organised crime flourishes, dysfunctional societies or exploding population growth on its borders all pose problems for Europe' (ESS, 7). A central aim of a neighbourhood policy is then set by stating that 'it is in the European interest that countries on our border are well governed' (ESS, 1).

The Commission took a similar approach in devising the European neighbourhood policy in March 2005. Notably, the ENP is described as 'a response to a new situation'.[3] It is being offered as a framework for developing a closer relationship with the new post-enlargement neighbours. The aim of closer relations would, however, not include membership or a role in the Union's institutions, at least in the medium term. This is to say that the increased spatial closeness stemming from enlargement is not to augur, for reasons of security, improved prospects for membership. In fact, practical issues posed by proximity and neighbourhood should be seen, the Commission states, as separate from the question of accession. A line is thereby drawn between the political aspects of integration and the more 'practical', economic ones on offer to the neighbours.

Structuring the sphere of chaos

One might argue, along the lines of Sharon Pardo, that the ENP is – as to the underlying narrative – about drawing a line between chaos and cosmos. Security looms large as a constitutive departure, although no longer in the form of endeavouring to prevent a relapse to a classical realpolitik as to the EU internally nor in terms of applying the concept of common security to the external environment (if allotting the EU any external security-related role at all). The new division, as reflected in the ENP, appears to be premised on the EU itself representing an ordered and de-securitised cosmos whereas the rest of Europe is taken to stand for a threat-infested chaos.[4]

EU enlargement, in this context, moves a number of countries from one sphere to another, while the ENP is there to deal with some of the residual cases still part of the zone of 'troubles'. They are invited, as 'neighbours', to form a 'ring of friends' in order to mitigate the effects of chaos encroaching on cosmos. Overall, an order is established which leans on a strict dividing line between the two spheres opposite each other (with EU-membership as a key dividing line). The ENP aims, in this perspective, at differentiating the sphere of chaos through the establishment of the category of neighbours, with these positioned as not too close and not too far. The best option in view of the East consists of keeping it separate but friendly, Pardo concludes.

Thus, while partnership is upgraded into a particularly close relationship in relation to the EU, with something like inclusion into the European Economic Area (EEA) as a long-term goal, it nonetheless stays severed from membership.[5] Closeness in the practical and economic sphere remains different from genuine political integration. With security weighing heavily as a formative argument and a way of framing the concept of neighbourhood, a rather traditional view of borders and bordering is also replicated. The bordering element of creating the ring of friends implies that they are seen as belonging to the realm of 'foreign' relations rather than as part of further enlargement.

It further appears that there is a shift from the concept of *common* security towards *liberal* security to be traced in the discourse. Whereas common security invites the parties to regard each other as equals (due to a joint interest in survival and an aversion of serious threats), calls for a rather de-bordered Europe ('Europe free and whole') and allows for flexibility as to the aspired outcome, liberal security builds on a hierarchy, invites bordering and is premised on quite categorical conceptions in regard to the desired goals.

As to these two departures, the plot structure underpinning the ENP seems to be predominantly grounded in a liberal security discourse; importantly, the EU itself gets increasingly depicted in terms of *finalité*. The previous openness – with the otherness to be kept at bay – consisting of a possible return of Europe's political past is no longer there. In essence, the master discourse in the EU appears to have changed drastically, this then also being reflected in the way the neighbourhood is being devised.

As indicated by the new strategic doctrine: 'Europe has never been so prosperous, so secure and free'. The document adds: 'Large-scale aggression against any member state is now improbable' (EES, 1). It then follows from this fulfilment and move of closure as to the overall size of the EU, that in order for outsiders to be eligible for inclusion, they must accept a rather strict set of conditions. The most probable case is that they have to remain outside, but even so they are induced to abide by the criteria set by the EU, i.e. those embedded in the liberal discourse. They have to do so in order to qualify for inclusion in the category of 'friends'. In other words, the EU is not merely using its magnetism to impact potential members; it now also feels obliged and entitled to reach further out. And the legitimacy for this activist stance originates in the EU being seen as a beacon of generally valid and rightful departures.

A shift of gears

In essence, the inducement offered by the ENP consists of closer integration along the lines of the *acquis communautaire* in the sphere of the 'four freedoms'. Some of the neighbouring countries are allowed closer access in exchange for reforms that bring about domestic structural stability, international economic integration and peaceful interstate relations. As concluded by Roberto Aliboni (2005, 1), 'the ENP updates and upgrades the conflict-prevention endeavours already embedded in the EU's overall policy agenda'. It implies 'a shift of gears'[6] and signals a shift from passive to active engagement.[7]

It may be noted that the ENP has, during its short history, undergone quite volatile change. Among other things, it began as 'Wider Europe', with that title soon to be discarded in favour of European Neighbourhood Policy (the latter allowing, among other things, going beyond 'Europe'). Likewise, the eastern-specific emphasis put there to soften the exclusion effects of the Big Bang was short-lived.

The initiative was soon expanded to include a number of southern countries so that these would not be relatively disadvantaged by the new initiative. Therefore, countries from both the southern and eastern shores of the Mediterranean (Morocco, Tunisia, Jordan, Israel and the Palestinian territories) were included.

Once Georgia, Armenia and Azerbaijan – countries from the Southern Caucasus – had been added to the list, the remainder of the Mediterranean Arab states of the Barcelona Process also had to be let in. Russia – although in many regards a clear 'neighbour' – has assumed the position of being half in and half out. It was included for a start but then soon excluded itself by opting instead for the position of a 'special partner' in trying to maintain its appearance of a *primus inter pares*. However, through a back door, Russia is nonetheless – in having joined the financial instrument (ENPI) related to the ENP – part of the same policies, albeit in a somewhat detached manner.

No doubt, the recalibration, clarifying and further development of the ENP will continue in the future. Some crucial decisions are still to be taken and one of these pertains to financing. Given that the mega-incentive of EU-accession remains excluded, financial support remains of crucial importance. Initially, the Commission proposed a doubling of the grant funds available over the period 2007–2013 for the entire ENP region, but as member countries seem, in general, to want a tighter EU budget, one may assume that there will be less money available for the ENP to 'buy reform'.

Money is tight and therefore conquering space, ensuring political attention and securing access to sufficient means for a new initiative is a daunting task. It is to be noted, however, that in one aspect, the goal has been substantiated by the prospect of a single financial instrument which draws together the separate funds for the ENP into a unified budgetary framework. Initially the new tool replacing and not only supplementing the previous ones was called the New Neighbourhood Instrument (NNI), but then later altered into the European Neighbourhood and Partnership Instrument (ENPI). 'Partnership' was added so that Russia could join the process of creating a single fund.

The challenge of the East

As outlined above, the EU's prime concern in the case of the new eastern neighbours relates to various security-related challenges (with security being understood in broad social rather than classical military terms). These could, in principle, be addressed by applying a set of tools for negative prioritisation, such as requiring the establishment of demanding visa regimes, insisting on the signing of readmission treaties and calling for stricter border controls.

Yet, although deemed to be important, the remedies offered by this approach have seemed insufficient and are in any case to be applied cautiously. Shielding and containment have, in reality, been out of the question as overall strategies because pursuing such a policy would have been taken for an abandonment of the aim of creating a Europe 'whole and free' (along the lines of common security). It would have been seen as inhibiting a uniting of the continent and preventing a bridging of the old Cold War divide. Above all, the new immediate neighbourhood created in the East by enlargement has been taken as calling for positive engagement. This conclusion was further strengthened by the fact that, with enlargement, there existed a group of new members (consisting primarily of the Balts and Poland) pushing for more active involvement. In sum: the need was there primarily to tap into the potential offered by positive prioritisation.

Out of the relevant countries, Bulgaria and Romania had already been singled out as candidates to be drawn into the sphere of European integration by furnishing them with the perspective of full accession. Croatia is also well on its way towards starting membership talks in due time. The question then consists of how to approach countries like Belarus, Moldova and Ukraine. A system of Partnership and Cooperation Agreements was already in place, although it had proven less than wholly satisfactory as the agreement with Belarus (PCA signed in 1995) was still to be ratified and problems of implementation had been chronic in the cases of Moldova and Ukraine (both in force since 1998).

In general, the available carrots and sticks seemed insufficient for *conditionality* really to work. The new neighbours were clearly difficult to integrate to start with, and yet some of them – Ukraine in particular – were pushing for a much closer relationship premised on accession. The issues at stake were further complicated by the decision of the EU Council in 2004 to include the Caucasian republics among the ENP partners. This extension of the list of partners took place after considerable lobbying and the peaceful 'rose revolution' in Georgia.

Opting for region-building as a general solution seemed to be out of the question for a variety of reasons. In the first place, the eastern arc is plagued by a considerable number of different frictions. Secondly, the new eastern neighbours aspire for solutions tailor-made to settle their own demands and, thirdly, it would be difficult to think of region-building without granting Russia a prominent role in that context. That move would raise fears of Russian dominance among many other parties in the area because Russia's position in the region has been, and tends to remain, stronger than that of the EU.

Moreover, Russia itself has turned out to be 'a reluctant regionaliser'.[8] As indicated by the fate of the Eastern Dimension, the options for progress in the sphere of region-building remain generally rather slim. The Polish proposal has been carefully devised to meet the EU's various requirements, but the initiative has nonetheless encountered difficulties in making it from a mere proposal to a distinct policy.[9] Similarly, the modest progress that has been there in the case of the Black Sea Regional Cooperation – with the EU remaining lukewarm about its participation – further confirms that there is not much room available for region-building in the case of Europe's East.

A shared neighbourhood with Russia

Clearly, the ENP is bound to stretch over a very large geographical area, one encompassing already in the East a considerable variety of countries with aspirations and problems that differ widely from each other. There are 'frozen' conflicts particularly in the cases of Moldova (Transdnistria), Georgia and South Caucasus (Abkhazia, South Ossetia). The question is then whether there exists a 'natural' headline goal common to all the partner countries and if it is really possible to condense the ENP into a single neighbourhood policy. Hiski Haukkala and Arkady Moshes conclude, on the basis of their survey stretching across Europe's East, that this is hardly possible.[10] Differentiation is required, they argue, and that has, in fact, also been the approach adopted by the EU.

The effort of the EU in trying to engage itself more actively in its eastern neighbourhood compels the Union to develop a more explicit and nuanced policy vis-á-vis Russia, and the emergence of a vast common neighbourhood also calls for Russia to become more specific about the EU. The challenges are formidable and both parties appear to be somewhat confused about their encounter in the context of an increased sharing of joint 'near abroads'. Being drawn closer to each other in areas containing a number of unsettled issues might well lead to strains and perhaps even bring about explicit clashes. Yet, it may be noted that the two actors largely seem to share the understanding that they should not drift into any old-style competition for influence in their common neighbourhood.

In general one might argue that whilst the ENP has so far failed to become central for the EU–Russia relationship – be it as a bone of contention or a key channel for friendly cooperation – the unfolding of their relations is in any case quite decisive for the future of the ENP. There are slim prospects for the new neighbourhood programme to flourish if the neighbourhood to the East is heavily plagued by clashes between the EU and Russia.

Initially, in this regard the launching of the ENP was less than promising. The approach chosen by the EU was inclusive for a start, and yet Russia decided to turn down the offer of becoming a partner (although later that decision was to some extent reversed by Russia's signing of the ENPI). Russia's reasons for deciding, in the end, to stay aloof from the ENP have been numerous. In the first place, it has no intention of joining the EU or even searching for association, and secondly, the new programme has been regarded by Russia as both intrusive and competitive in relation to the country's own interests. Moreover, due to its strict conditionality and an allegedly hegemonic purpose, the ENP has been taken to be too condescending for Russia to support. Overall, Russia has decided to remain a member of the 'outer ring' despite being influential in the sphere of the 'inner ring' devised through the launching of the ENP. The ENP has thus failed to turn into a route of joint EU–Russia relations. The alternative framing then available has consisted of aspiring to 'strategic partnership' in the context of the four 'common spaces' – that relation being less binding and intrusive as well as more equal in appearance.

There has also been the option of discussing various issues pertaining to the joint neighbourhood opened up by the Union's enlargement in the context of the general talks between EU and Russia; importantly, that option was for the first time employed in the context of the EU–Russia May 2005 summit.[11] In general, it is agreed that it is in the interest of both actors that their joint neighbourhood remains stable and becomes prosperous, but beyond this general stance there seems to be little meeting of minds. In any case, the paradox appears to be that despite Russia remaining outside the ENP proper, a fundamental requirement for the success of the new neighbourhood policy consists of stronger EU–Russia cooperation.[12]

It appears more generally that the ENP has become inadequate, at least in the case of Russia, and there are also problems in regard to many eastern neighbours who are part of the ENP. The breadth of the issues encountered calls for a more differentiated approach – so differentiated that questions emerge as to the cohesion that is allegedly an ingredient of the ENP. In its aspiration for long-term stability, the EU is bound to be drawn closer to a number of instabilities through the effort to establish an inner ring of friends. This is also to say that the ENP is not just about closer integration in the economic sphere. There is also a need for expanded political involvement as well as an endeavour to keep the political and economic aspects of integration apart.

Obviously, fostering reform through the initiation of the ENP remains an uphill struggle, taking into account the various challenges of the region. Being drawn into the ring of friends is rather demanding for those included, and enthusiasm has also been modest because the ENP has often been perceived as a kind of consolation prize and a substitute for accession. At the same time, the EU itself has had to be cautious about not being too deeply entangled with tensions internal to the parties or part of their external relations. One of the problems consists of a certain ambiguity about which the ENP is being challenged, particularly in the case of Ukraine.

The EU is under pressure (also internally) either to dispel ambiguity by clearly saying 'no' to further enlargement, or saying 'yes', thereby breaking one of the essential borderlines underpinning the ENP. It would turn, in the case of a promise concerning eventual accession, from a system constituting privileged-partner status on a more permanent basis to yet another station to be passed on the way to membership. The question then reads: what remains of the ENP if the departure premised on 'anything but institutions' being available to the neighbours' falters?[13]

. . . And the South joins in

The ENP aims at covering the areas adjacent to the EU at large. It is to be noted, however, that the initial endeavour was more modest in scope as the aspiration was merely one of coining a policy in view of the challenges posed by the new eastern neighbours. Thus, the concerns raised were quite specific as to their spatiality and did not cover adjacent areas as a whole.[14]

The broadening which took place originated very much with the South becoming worried that a distinct focusing on the East might lead to its own marginalisation. Less political attention might be devoted, it was feared, to the problems of the South and for this then to be followed by a diminished flow of resources from the core to the periphery. Therefore, the South insisted on being brought into the same policy framework with the East. The ENP was subsequently perceived as a single geopolitical arc surrounding the EU as a whole and as one imposing subject-specific borders throughout the Union's edges. Thus, the extensive scope element of the ENP came into being by default rather than by design.

Moreover, the new policy is neither based on an evaluation of the previous policies pursued vis-á-vis the South, nor does it stand for a conscious and well thought out effort to complement or remedy some of the previous shortcomings. It merely represents an extension of a policy initially designed for the challenges encountered in the East and then broadened spatially to meet the pressures emanating with the South. The EU accepted the extension, but did not push for it. This is so, in some of its aspects, because there were worries that the Union might be overextending its ambitions, given the limited financial and other resources available for proximity policies. Moreover, it was thought from the very start that extending the promises underlying the ENP of 'joint ownership', i.e. the entire *acquis* to the southern partners (democracy and the freedom of movement in particular) might turn out to be quite problematic.[15]

A further reason for concern consists of the great differences between Europe's East and South. In the case of the East, a policy had to be designed because of enlargement whereas in the South the EU already had an explicit and region-specific neighbourhood policy in place. Questions thus arose in the latter region regarding the relationship between the old and new policies. Does the ENP represent an application of the enlargement logic with its strong emphasis on conditionality that tends towards bilateralism between the EU and the partner countries? Is this to replace the previous policies based largely on regionalism and efforts to contribute to social and economic stability by interconnecting the countries of the South? Is the aim one of subordinating the Euro-Mediterranean Partnership (EMP) to the ENP or are the two framings seen as complementary in nature?

The EU Commission itself addressed this last issue by claiming that the relationship is basically non-competitive. It has argued that the ENP is not there as a re-evaluation and it does not imply a move away from the EMP, an approach implemented since 1995. The new policies are merely designed to 'complement' and 'consolidate' the previous approaches, it is argued.[16]

Yet it appears that the ENP suggests that the EU wishes to engage itself more actively and far more directly in the adjacent areas. Consequently, and as the ENP is premised on an increased emphasis on European-level decision-making, the new EU policy is bound to have precedence over the previous one which prioritised the regional and local levels. In other words, the ENP does not complement and build on previous policies; it rather comes into being at their expense.

The EMP was from its inception devised in a rather vertical and top-down manner, although space has also been provided for horizontal endeavours and views that allow for a non-traditional understanding of borders. Thus, the countries of the region have not merely been encouraged to 'go to Europe' individually, with each of them devising their own relationship directly with the EU. They have also been invited to come together as a caucus in the context of a broader and horizontal configuration so as to be better able to tackle the root causes of instability and insecurity in their region. Clearly, this spurring of a collective form of togetherness is different from keeping the partners aloof from each other by the establishment of vertical structures and country-specific deals. In practice, the collectiveness has been backed up by MEDA, a special fund that aims to support regional cooperation around the Mediterranean (now to become part of the ENPI).

The ENP's aim of encouraging the partners to be active themselves and to coalesce as a regional grouping has allowed the EU itself to become somewhat more passive and less engaged. Shouldering considerable responsibility by the partners has enabled the EU to keep at a certain distance from the South instead of opting, as is now called for by the ENP, for a more direct 'case-by-case' relationship that invites certain partners to get closer to the EU than others. The vertical aspects of organising political space in the South – adding, more generally, to a rather concentric European configuration – will undoubtedly grow with the ENP-related bilateralism being combined with an emphasis on the need to pursue 'joint', 'coherent' and 'consolidated' policies.

Complementary or competitive?

It could, thus be claimed that the ENP genuinely stands for a 'consolidation' of previous policies while the EMP entails a significant bilateral element in the form of similar association agreements signed between the individual EMP partners and the EU. Arguably, the ENP merely refines an already existing bilateralism and takes it further. It seems, however, that instead of 'consolidation' one should speak about a shift in the underlying priorities and a downgrading of the regionalist element of the EMP.[17] This is so as the internally non-bordered 'ring' of the EMP is quite different from the 'ring' aimed at in the context of the ENP. In fact, the EMP has to change if it is not to contradict and compete with but to complement the new neighbourhood policies.

However, now the process of bringing about such a kind of complementarity may well be underway. As noted by del Sarto and Schumacher, the previous principle of regionality inherent in the EMP is no longer there and has, in their view, been replaced by an emphasis on differentiated bilateralism. They argue that, owing to the new neighbourhood thinking, the idea of an encompassing Euro-Mediterranean region as an intermediate space between the inside and the outside of the Union is no longer in place. They further observe that, whereas the EU claimed in 2000 that in its Mediterranean policy 'multilateralism is now as common as, and even prevails over, traditional bilateral approaches', the Commission now acknowledges that the regional dimension of the Barcelona Process is only a complementary element, limited to intra-regional trade and sub-regional cooperation at best.[18]

Crucially, the key argument facilitating the encounter between the two frames – with the EMP assuming a 'complementary' relationship to the ENP – revolves around security. It is predominantly the added weight of security, in 'soft' as well as 'hard' forms, that seems to account for the altered priorities. As to time, the perception was there during the mid-1990s, with the Middle East being characterised by peace talks, that multilateralism could be enhanced. The temporal expectations then spoke of a narrowing down of distance, above all among the partners in the region, for this then to increase proximity between them and the EU in the longer run.

However, in hindsight this reading was far too optimistic, and security is again high on the agenda for a broad variety of reasons. It can thus be argued that whilst the achievements of the EMP have remained modest, other avenues – less burdened by the conflicts of the region – have to be explored. Priorities have to be reversed. Once the countries of the South have proved themselves unwilling and unable to exploit the option of region-building, why not settle for a bilateralism based on conditionality and the benchmarking component of the ENP? In other words, with security as a core constitutive argument being as strongly present in the South as it is in the East, why not turn the ENP into a common frame? In this reading it is the failure to activate and capitalise on the regionalist aspect of the EMP that calls for altered thinking and a prioritising of bilateralism over regionalism.

Thus, despite being applied to the South almost by default, the discourses currently underpinning the ENP in the East and the South do not seem to be very different from each other. In the end the pre-eminence of security implies that a good case can also be made for the ENP in the South. But the area-specific consequences are different in the sense that in the South the ENP is introduced at the expense of a previous policy inviting a horizontal rather than the core–periphery-related and vertical structuring of European space.

The exclusion of the North

Of the various neighbourhoods, the North displays distinct features of its own and may suffer rather than benefit from being exposed to the ENP. If seen from the perspective of the North, there is little need to introduce any brand of new neighbourhood policy as the one already in place works quite well. Moreover, the effort to remedy the situation (if there is a need in the first place) should definitely not consist of Europe's core trying to impose a framework like the ENP that clearly contrasts with, and possibly even undermines, the one already developed within the North itself and applied successfully for quite some time.

Hence there is much in favour of the North receiving special treatment. It is in a category of its own already in the sense that the enlargement of 2004 does not bring about new neighbours nor cause security-related problems in the same way as it does for the East. In other words, the region is less explicitly tied to the integration–security issue than other parts of Europe, and the East in particular. Seen from the North's perspective, Russia is not a new but an old neighbour which has, in any case, decided to stay aloof from the ENP. The others are either EU members or are able to join the EU if they so decide (i.e. part of the EEA).

Moreover, in contrast to the East, there are local and regional endeavours at present creating stability and fostering economic well-being. Unlike the South, these efforts have been rather successful. The formula for mobilising local and regional resources through a lowering and an erasing of borders at the fringes of the Union seems to work, with the North thus able to challenge centralised understandings about the location of power. The northern actors have been able to propose and device various co-operative policies among themselves without explicitly clashing with those promoted by the EU's core.

This is to say, that prior to the coining of the ENP, there existed – in the sphere of European spatial development – considerable room for diversity within the unity provided by the EU, and this is something that the North has been able to capitalise on. As Tassinari notes, regionalism in the North has been far more inclusive than seems possible in the context of the ENP.[19] Issues pertaining to accession have been off the agenda and the various regional formations, Baltic, Barents and Nordic cooperation in addition to some Euregions and various cross-border arrangements, have been provided with their own structures and separate secretariats.

So, there exists a clear northern model premised, in one of its aspects, on how questions of otherness and security are to be approached. Although somewhat similar in character to those now plaguing the East, the various security-relevant issues in the North were downplayed and sidelined rather than provided with constitutive impact during the 1990s. They have not been tackled head-on, but approached indirectly, with the North developing into something of a 'laboratory' promoting various socio-economic and co-operative endeavours; the objective is that the off-shoot will promote security and stability over the longer run.[20] Importantly, there has been willingness to think of security as something held in common with others instead of remaining focused – as has largely been the case in the context of the ENP – on an 'us and them' conceptualisation of security that results in the negative 'other'-creating of outsiders; it also promotes an emphasis on viewing the external borders as a line of exclusion and control.[21] Allowing this 'laboratory' to unfold has given credence to the Union's often professed preference for proactive and innovative policies in the form of spurring multilateralism and efforts to do away with divisive borders.

As this strategy has largely worked in the case of the North, why should the EU now ride in and try to fix something that seems neither to be in need of repair by a new set of policies or, if really a problematic region, has been rather successfully handled and coped with by the policies that are already in place?

There are thus good reasons for why the North, in contrast to Europe's East and South, has remained largely outside the sphere of the ENP. One may, for example, note that the official commentary on the new neighbourhood policy tends to emphasise its impact on the East and the South, with little – if any – mention being made of the North. This is easy to understand as the North remains institutionally detached in the sense that no country in Europe's North (with Russia being the only candidate) has been eligible for the status of an ENP partner.

However, at the same time, the North is institutionally included in the sense that, with the all-encompassing aspirations of the ENP, it is brought in through the ENPI. With the previous proliferation of financial instruments – including those relevant for the North – being terminated through their amalgamation into a single financial instrument, conditionality will also apply in the case of the North. With Russia joining the ENPI and the single financial instrument also relevant for the region as a whole, the North assumes the position of being half in and half out of the ENP.

Concluding remarks

In essence, the ENP constitutes a regime of meaning and power. It is very much trying to furnish the EU with a singular figure that invites the elimination (and not just mediation) of otherness and heterogeneity by ousting them from the inner core of an EU depicted as a sphere of 'cosmos'. The comprehension of a concentric singularity grows largely out of security being reconfigured and provided with a different formative meaning. Constructing a ring of friends within such a pattern gives the impression that the EU proper, once the ENP is fully in place, will be encircled by an in-between space occupied by countries elevated to the category of special partners.

Michael Emerson asserts that the new neighbourhood programme is there, in part, 'to define the EU's new outer edges'[22] or to state it differently, to form the Union's constitutive outside. It delimits the cosmos and borders it vis-à-vis the encircling chaos. Furthermore, it is performative in aiming at a hierarchisation of otherness. The ENP does this by bringing about, on the one hand, special partners regarded less than foreign and, on the other hand, leaving out those seen as foreign. For the EU – seen in terms of a sphere of cosmos – to be kept apart from the external chaos, the ENP partners also remain externalised in the context of an EU which, in principle, used to be open to indefinite expansion without pre-established limits. With the EU now standing for closure rather than openness, the 'camp' established on the outside through the ENP, also gains an increasingly permanent character.[23] In being there in order to articulate what the EU is not and where it ends, the appearance of the category of 'neighbours' tends to signal that a considerable change has taken place in the Union's self-understanding.

So, in this context, the partners are induced to position themselves around the EU – and also to be treated individually pending their preparedness to abide by the benchmarks of the ENP-related Action Plans – thereby providing an all-encompassing buffer against those not interested in abiding by the norms set by the EU and actors located elsewhere in Europe and beyond. The ENP thus stands for an inversion between efforts of drawing a group of 'friends' closer to the EU and at the same time making them 'foreign'. Consequently, a variable geometry (Tassinari speaks of 'diversified "hub-and-spoke" geometry')[24] comes into being with the ENP not only devising a category of adjacent friends, but also leaving a number of countries in the position of non-friends and geographical others. The latter are already taken to be far too heterogeneous from the outset to warrant an effort to render them more homogeneous by exposing them to ENP-related disciplining. They are then positioned by the establishment of an additional border beyond the one separating members from non-members.

Yet, it turns out on closer inspection that the ring of friends does not just stand for a graded and an evenly spread-out configuration. Rather, it takes a twisted shape in the sense that the ring actually covers the EU's near-abroads in a quite uneven manner.[25] Although it aims to apply to the EU's vicinity at large, it nonetheless stands for differentiation, and does so both as to individual friends as well as to Europe's main regions. The aim of establishing a single framework based on the reinforcement of bilateral ties between the neighbours and the EU and stretching across the various neighbourhoods appears to be relatively unproblematic in the case of the East.

There, the effort of streamlining the different neighbourhoods and dealing with them within a singular framework premised on a spatial, centre–periphery-related configuration seems applicable (Russia is a notable exception, indicating that, in the end, the measurement of distance is not purely spatial but political in essence). This is so as the approach chosen does not have to compete with, or try to oust and replace, some previous strategy which, instead of eliminating otherness, aims to mediate it. The South is already a different story, although now included in the sphere of the ENP largely on its own initiative. The South may cave in without much resistance as the EMP has been as much top-down and hierarchic in design as the new ENP. Moreover, there is a considerable dose of bilateralism present already in the EMP, and it may further be noted that the multilateral and mediating aspects of the Mediterranean process have not brought about any noticeable success.

All this implies that the ENP can be incorporated into, and harmonised with, the EMP without much resistance. In fact, achieving complementarity between the ENP and the rather regionalised North seems much more challenging. This is because the logic of the two frameworks – and the regionalist constructs present in the North more generally – is so different that even aspiring to a rather loose cohabitation between them appears problematic. The underlying departures are, indeed, constitutive of quite different Europes.

Thus, the rhetoric of the ENP concerning the option of bridging and ameliorating the cleavage between the two logics most apparent in the North is contentious indeed. There is, actually, little room for mediation of otherness by the use of multilateral and decentred approaches to allow heterogeneity to be encountered on its own terms. Instead, the aim is to deal with it in a bordered fashion within a ring of friends and to buffer the gates of the EU by adding to the distance between the EU and supposedly untreatable heterogeneity. The question also becomes one of either/or in a regional context once the ENP confers a strict and 'general' meaning on differences previously not merely tolerated but also seen as a resource in some local and regional contexts. Against this background it is obvious that clashes will unavoidably arise with the increased and assertive emphasis within the EU on a centre–periphery framing (at the expense of more decentred options) and the aspiration to cast Europe unambiguously into a radial and concentric configuration.

Being new, the ENP is often purported to be a policy designed to deal with the challenges that emerged with enlargement and is seen as being innovative and visionary in essence. Undoubtedly, being premised on a radial centre–periphery model is far more progressive than being modelled along the lines of a 'clash of civilizations' paradigm with the latter calling for quite categorical borders and bolstering the security argument to the extreme. The latter would not allow for the concept of friends and neighbours to be applied outside the internal sphere of order.

Yet the claim can be made that the ENP represents regress rather than progress. It hardly stands for a step forward if it is seen as representing a selling-out of the 'global village' or 'global network' models. These two are sometimes associated with the EU and comprehended as spatio-temporal endeavours. Both aim, in general, to mediate heterogeneity and allow for further strolling along the path to what has sometimes been called a 'multiperspectival' Europe,[26] i.e. a Europe that allows for considerable flexibility – among other reasons because security does not stand out as the key constitutive argument. There is regress in the sense that, in addition to de-bordering performed at the edges to sort out those who are foreign, the ENP aims – as an aspect of a concentric configuration, with the EU as a closed and ready-made configuration – above all at bordering and keeping out.

The ENP, in aiming simultaneously at attracting and repelling potential partners, is not about overcoming and crossing the hedge between the insiders and the neighbours. Instead, it aspires to rejection and elimination in the name of an EU-Europe. As with the EMP, there appear to be increasingly limited prospects for non-members (not yet in the sphere of accession) to make their own choice as to whether they want to join the EU or not. The choice is, to some extent, made for them with the optimal posture on offer that of becoming an 'enhanced partner'.

The metaphor of a 'Fortress Europe' seems to be gaining added weight. It does so in temporal terms by pushing the prospects of membership into an uncertain future, but also in terms of carving out a new spatial borderline between members and the ENP-related special partners. In this latter regard, the ENP functions, at the borderline between the special partners and the rest, not as an insurmountable wall but rather as a 'European sieve'. Simultaneously it makes use of two rather different discourses with one being exclusive and the other inclusive. This implies that the ENP not only defines the outer edges but also impacts on the EU more generally. The Union is now being more strongly defined than has been the case so far, by a clear inside/outside architecture.

Notes

1 For an analysis of the British, Polish and Swedish letters, all dealing with the issue of neighbourhood, see Haukkala (2003).

2 See, Council of the European Union, *A Secure Europe in a Better World. Security Strategy* (Brussels, 12 December 2003), at http://ue.eu.int/pressData/en/reports/78367.pdf.

3 See in particular, *Wider Europe – Neighbourhood: A New Framework for Relations with our Eastern and Southern Neighbours*, Brussels (1 March 2003) COM(2003)104 final, 3–4, and Commission of the European Communities, Communication from the Commission, *Paving the Way for the New Neighbourhood Instrument*, Brussels, 1 July 2003, COM(2003)393final, 2.
4 See Pardo (2004, 735).
5 It may be noted, however, that the member countries of the EEA have the option of membership if they decide to apply and join whereas the same does not apply to the new neighbours. For them the ENP, as an EEA-type of arrangement, is more of an end-station rather than a stepping stone for eventual membership. It entails, according to Aliboni (2005, 3), a 'status that excludes political integration but provides for full economic integration'. It may also be noted, in comparing the ENP and the EEA, that there exists within the EEA, among other bodies, a joint biannual ministerial level EEA Council, a committee of senior officials and a joint parliamentary committee, whereas the ENP has at least so far been void of any joint structures and is administered by the EU secretariat itself.
6 For this characterisation, see Del Sarto and Schumacher, (2005, 22).
7 This latter characterisation comes from Emerson, (2004a, 69–75).
8 This characterisation comes from Haukkala, (2001).
9 On the Eastern Dimension, see Browning and Joenniemi (2003.)
10 See Hiski Haukkala and Arkady Moshes (2004). A similar conclusion has been drawn by Gromadzki, Lopata and Raik (2005, 14).
11 For an account along these lines, see Trenin (2005) (www.cer.org.uk).
12 This conclusion has been drawn by Aliboni (2005, 14).
13 This characterisation has been used by Romano Prodi (2000).
14 This argument comes from Del Sarto and Schumacher (2005, 28).
15 On this, see Malmvig (2004, 18–21).
16 In particular, see COM(2003)final, 15 and COM(2004)final, 6.
17 It should be noted, however, that the 'second window' to follow in the future of the prospective ENPI opts, in particular, for financing cross-border projects and it may thus offer some space for multilateralism.
18 See Del Sarto and Schumacher (2005, 22). They refer to the statement of the European Commission, *The Barcelona Process, Five Years On – 1995–2000* (Office for Official Publications of the European Commission). Luxemburg, (2000, 15).
19 Tassinari (2005, 16–17).
20 Clive Archer (2001) and see also Holger Moroff (2002).
21 The theme is developed more in detail in Browning and Joenniemi (2004).
22 See Emerson (2003, 1).
23 The 'less than foreign' category consisting of the ENP-related neighbours comes close, as an in-between category, to Bauman's liminal category of 'strangers'. See Bauman (1996).
24 See, Tassinari (2005, 9).
25 This observation is made by Ulla Holm (2005).
26 The term has been coined by Ruggie (1993) in arguing that the EU stands out as the first truly postmodern configuration.

References

Aliboni, Roberto (2005) 'The geopolitical implications of the European Neighbourhood Policy', *European Foreign Affairs Review* Vol. 10 (1), 1–16.

Archer, Clive (2001) 'The Northern dimension as a soft-soft option for the Baltic States' security', in Hanna Ojanen (ed.) *The Northern Dimension: Fuel for the EU?*,

Helsinki and Berlin. Ulkopoliittinen instituutti and Institut für Europäische Politik, 188–208.

Bauman, Zygmunt (1996) *Postmodernity and its Discontents*, New York University Press: New York.

Browning, Christopher and Joenniemi, Pertti (2003) 'The European Union's two dimensions: the Eastern and the Northern', *Security Dialogue* Vol. 34(4), 463–78.

Browning, Christopher and Joenniemi, Pertti (2004) 'Regionality beyond security? The Baltic Sea region after enlargement', *Co-operation and Conflict* Vol. 39(3), 233–53.

Del Sarto, Rafaella and Schumacher, Tobias (2005) 'From the EMP to the ENP: what's at stake with the European Neighbourhood Policy towards the Southern Mediterranean?', *European Foreign Affairs Review* Vol. 10(1), 17–38.

Emerson, Michael (2003) 'The shaping of a policy framework for the wider Europe', *CEPS Policy Brief* No. 39. September, Brussels.

Emerson, Michael (2004a) *The Wider Europe Matrix*, CEPS Paperback: Brussels.

Emerson, Michael (2004b) 'European Neighbourhood Policy: strategy or placebo?', CEPS Working Document, No. 215/November.

ESS: European Security Strategy. *A Secure Europe in a Better World*. Brussels, 12 December 2003 (http://ue.eu.int/pressData/en/reports/78367.pdf)

Gromadzki, Gregorz, Lopata, Raimundas and Raik, Krista (2005) 'Friends or family? Finnish, Lithuanian and Polish perspectives on the EU's policy towards Ukraine, Belarus and Moldova', FIIA Report No.12. Finnish Institute for International Affairs: Helsinki.

Haukkala, Hiski (2001) 'Two reluctant regionalisers? The European Union and Russia in Europe's North', Programme on the Northern Dimension of the CFSP. UPI Working Paper No. 32. Finnish Institute for International Affairs; Helsinki.

Haukkala, Hiski (2003) 'New forms of EU Neighbourhood Policy: the case of the "Eastern Dimension"', *Yearbook of Finnish Foreign Policy 2003*, Finnish Institute of International Affairs: Helsinki.

Haukkala, Hiski and Moshes, Arkady (2004) 'Beyond the "Big Bang": the challenges of EU's Neighbourhood Policy in the East', Report Commissioned by the Foreign Affairs Committee of the Finnish Parliament. The Finnish Institute of International Affairs: Helsinki.

Holm, Ulla (2005) 'Space and security: the EU's representation of the Southern Mediterranean', DIIS Working Paper No. 20, Copenhagen.

Malmvig, Helle (2004) 'Cooperation or democratisation? The EU's conflicting Mediterranean security discourses', DIIS Working Paper No. 8, Copenhagen.

Moroff, Holger (2002) *European Soft Security Policies: The Northern Dimension*. Helsinki and Berlin. Ulkopoliittinen instituutti and Institut für Europäische Politik.

Pardo, Sharon (2004) 'Europe of many circles: European Neighbourhood Policy'. *Geopolitics* 9(3), 731–37.

Prodi, Romano (2000) *A Wider Europe – A Proximity Policy as the Key Stability Factor*, speech at the conference: 'Peace, Security and Stability. International Dialogue and the Role of the EU'. Sixth ESCA World Conference. Jean Monnet Project. Brussels. 5–6 December.

Ruggie, John, Gerard (1993) 'Territoriality and beyond: problematising modernity in international relations'. *International Organisation* Vol. 47(1), 139–74.

Tassinari, Fabrizio (2005) 'Security and integration in the EU neighbourhood: the case for regionalism', CEPS Working Document No. 226.

Trenin, Dmitri (2005) 'Russia, the EU and the common neighbourhood', *Essay*, Centre for European Reforms: London.

10 New borders in a new Europe

Eliminating and making borders in Central Europe

Milan Bufon and Anton Gosar

Introduction: the changeable European political map

The 2004 expansion of the European Union and the EU's incorporation of eight former nation-states of East–Central Europe (Estonia, Latvia, Lithuania, Poland, the Czech Republic, Slovakia, Hungary, Slovenia) and two Mediterranean island states (Cyprus, Malta) raise a number of geopolitical issues. Globally, expansion has most likely strengthened the EU's competitive position in relation to other major economic cores (NAFTA, Russia, East Asia, South Asia), as well as in relation to the developing world. Internally, Europe has become weaker as it faces several challenges: (1) the link between the Western European Romance–German and the Central European Slavic socio-cultural space; (2) the shift from a functional integration to creating a melting pot aimed at 'unity in diversity'; and (3) the erection of external borders touching on the Orthodox Christian and Muslim socio-cultural spaces, so generating immigration and multicultural issues.

These processes lead to a reconsideration of the most representative topics of modern political geography in Europe: *territoriality* and *borders*. As Poulantzas pointed out, space–time matrices in the pre-capitalist period were open. There was only a single known space based on common civilization and religion; the rest was perceived as a barbarian-inhabited no man's land (Poulantzas 1978). Capitalist space, on the contrary, differs by the appearance of borders – the territorialisation of space being a precondition for modernity. The previously open space is thus re-formed as a series of territories. Territory not only exists in the sense of belonging, nationally embracing territory, language, and culture (Sack, 1980). It deals with citizenship, alien cultures and minority and majority citizens' cultural iconographies.

A form of geopolitical iconography on a global scale can be found in the division between North and South, and East and West. Galtung, for example, suggests that the border between North and South follows the Rio Grande, crosses the Gulf along the US coast, heads for the Straits of Gibraltar, runs through the Mediterranean south of Malta, Sicily and Cyprus, follows the southern border of Turkey and the former Soviet Union, passing north of the Koreas and crossing the Pacific with Japan south and Hawaii north of the line. The East and West border historically follows the line of the Schism from 1054 between Orthodox and Catholic and later

Protestant Christianity, and picks up another line, the schism produced in 1095 – by the declaration of Crusades – between Christianity and Islam. Euro-Asia is, in Galtung's opinion, divided into three distinct units: the European Union, the Russian Union, and the Turkish Union. These three units found a common point of contact and conflict in Sarajevo (Galtung 1994).

Europe, the homeland of nationalism and the continent where political borders and diverse territorial and cultural identities are interrelated, is now facing the challenge of integrating the many nation-states' interests into one operational system. The post-Second World War European integration process had to follow several stepping stones. The first macro-regional unions, though mainly technical and limited in their binding character, limited countries' competence through the introduction of common interstate coordinating bodies.

With the intensification of integration, states began to devote greater attention to border areas that had to undertake certain functions in the international integration process. In the 1960s, the non-flexible model of industrialisation, characterised by the investment, capital and job concentration, by the depopulation of peripheral areas and by forced introduction of internal social and cultural standardisation, began to disintegrate. The fostering of a more balanced regional development within nation-states resulted in the strengthening of regions, which new European development models could no longer ignore.

A parallel process of ethnic or regional awakening of minorities, local communities and democratic processes accompanied the process. The fundamental cause that determined the 1990s sudden collapse of the Communist regimes in East–Central Europe is probably similar to that which contributed to the western regions' gradual transformation, i. e. the obsolescence of a socio-economic paradigm based on forced industrialisation and social standardisation. In East–Central Europe this model could not be stimulated by the corrective mechanisms that stemmed from Western democratic multi-party systems. The fall of the Iron Curtain has removed the Second World War's geopolitical outcomes: Germany has become reunited; the small nations of East–Central Europe are undergoing the same development phase which the outbreak of war had stopped – namely the phase of national emancipation (Bufon 1996a).

The major geopolitical question facing Europe at present is related to the collapse of the bipolar system and globalisation in general. There are at least two contradictory processes at work. The first is the opening up of Europe to democratic ideals and representative politics. The second is the advancement of the so-called 'social democratic capitalism' eastwards and the creation of new markets, picking up on new resources and restructuring the social organisation of the space. The case of Germany and East–Central Europe is typical. German exports have risen since 1991 yearly by 25 per cent in the case of Poland, and 13 per cent and 10 per cent for the Czech Republic and Hungary. German imports of finished goods from these new EU member states have risen from 1994 to 1997 on average by 25 per cent (Boesler 1997). New inter-regional trade and activity has accelerated since the demise of the centrally planned economies, especially in terms of cross-border cooperation as several previously 'strategic regions', previously depopulated, have been transformed into pivotal nodes in an expanded European network of communication and trade.

Another trend is the conservative reaction which seeks to close, limit and protect the 'national' character of nation-states – in particular from newcomer cultures and non-European racial groups. The latter is posing a threat to the conventional territorial relationships and to the widening of diverse forms of inter-regional and global exchange of information and multi-service networks. Globalisation is seeking to break down this particular problem by opening up the spatial and societal process of deterritorialisation. The key question for contemporary Europe is: How will these processes be summarised under the twin labels of globalisation and deterritorialisation and the persistent maintenance of regional identities and corresponding regional spaces (Williams 1997)? 'Unity in diversity' is a tough question for Europe to solve.

On the other hand, have instability, fragmentation, nation-state and border making within South-eastern Europe become a matter of international concern? Yugoslavia, a multi-ethnic entity since the First World War, in 1991 largely disintegrated into entities of ethnic dominance. The weakening of the idea of Communism and the implementation of democracy, based on nation-state principles, combined with the altered periphery–periphery relationship were major factors for the instability. This has caused violence and wars and resulted in forced migrations, impacting on Europe in a large extent. The international community was able to prevent a major, multinational outbreak of hostilities. But the final resolution of the problem, in particular in Bosnia–Herzegovina and Kosovo, by different international mediators, has yet to be proven. In particular, will spatial disputes hot spots, already registered on or near borders, encourage arbitrators to use their expertise and imagination?

The Bosnia–Herzegovina's entity border is such an innovation, produced at the dawn of the twenty-first century, not to be proven in regard to its earlier success. A similar problem of smaller proportions: could the international community and the nation-states' professionals work out a fair solution for the borders in the Adriatic Sea (Gosar and Klemenčič 2000)? In regard to the latter, many experts argue that disputes will slowly disappear as Croatia (and other countries of the Western Balkans) become part of the EU. Other scholars are less optimistic as they argue that historically based stereotypes, the development gap in market-economy-based 'colonialism', old offences and newborn nationalism will hinder a swift settlement and a permanent solution. In this paper we will focus on the brighter side of Yugoslavia's devolution and will mainly analyse the structures and cross-border impacts of borders in the new established nation-state of Slovenia, now a member of the European Union.

Borders in Central Europe: from conflict to cooperation

Central Europe, including the Upper Adriatic, may be seen as a historical construction of the Habsburg Empire. The Habsburg monarchy developed a multinational state model, which in some respects acted as an alternative to the

West-European nation-state model. The Iron Curtain froze the nation-state building process which had started in this region after the First World War and ended with the (second) spring of nations in the 1990s. Nationalism in Central Europe is characterised by its cultural nature and seeks now to institutionalise it. Thus new states were created with no space left for the 'stateless nations'. More national minorities and contact areas have, therefore, come into existence.

The general border settings are the result of border modifications after the First and Second World Wars, and are therefore quite recent. The national minorities so created, had already participated in the nineteenth-century emancipation of their own cultural group (the first spring of nations) and, after partition, maintained strong cultural and social ties with their mother-nations. For instance, Trieste in the Habsburg Empire was a city with more Slovenian nationals than any other town in the monarchy. It preserved the function of a Slovene cultural centre even after its inclusion into Italy in 1919 and again, in 1954. In the past, this situation produced a potential for conflict because overlapping cultural spaces created difficulties in boundary-making processes, which sought ethnically based political borders. As a consequence, individual states either tried to adapt the existing ethnic structure to the current political situation or continuously expressed irredentist demands.

The new concept of multiculturalism, which is the basis for European integration, is embedded in several declarations and resolutions, most often initiated by the Organisation for Security and Co-operation in Europe (OSCCE) and the European Parliament. It is also part of the European Charter for regional or minority languages, produced by the Council of Europe in 1992 and signed by over twenty European nation-states. All these developments eventually gave national and other minorities the chance to avoid cultural standardisation or assimilation. Modern research on the economic base and social discrimination shows that the costs of maintaining discrimination policies are becoming higher than the costs of their abolition (Castells 2004).

One of the basic rights of national minorities is that of communicating with the mother-nation. This process is no longer seen as a way of changing political borders, but as a contribution in reducing their effects. In this way, the 'natural' cross-border attitudes of national minorities and other regional groups is becoming more and more important in implementing integration processes in Europe. Research in East–Central Europe has shown that the new cross-border role of national minorities is implemented at the level of institutional and social integration, as well as in their structure and level of urbanisation. Cross-border socio-economic integration contributes not only to the strengthening of coexistence practices between neighbouring nations and ethnic groups, but also to the forming or re-establishment of cross-border regional structures (Klemenčič and Genorio 1993; Maier 1986).

In fact, forms of cross-border structure in Central Europe tend to differ from those in Western Europe. There, a typical 'Euro-Region' could be seen as a 'region of regions', an assembly of several basic administrative units and regions, which decides to co-operate on an institutional level to solve common interests and promote cross-border contacts. The best-known examples of this type of cross-border cooperation are to be found in the Euregio on the border between the Netherlands and Germany and in the Regio (Basiliensis) at the three-borders between Switzerland, France and Germany. On a larger scale, the Alpine cross-border associations, such as the COTRAO or the Alps–Adriatic Working Community (Alpen–Adria Arbeitsgemeinschaft), are also examples of this type. The last institution was established in 1978 and has included Bavaria in Germany, regions of northern Italy, Austria, western Hungary, and the former Yugoslav republics of Slovenia and Croatia.

This working community was the only European cross-border cooperating institution, connecting regions from both East and West, across the Iron Curtain. But, in contrast to these institutionalised forms of cross-border cooperation, the East–Central part of the continent has produced other cross-border structures which could be viewed as 'regions within regions'. They consist of parts of administrative units in which there is no cross-border institutional frame provided, but where a spontaneous, grass-roots cross-border relation is maintaining and reproducing formerly existing common social spaces, as in the case of the historical province of Gorizia (see Bufon 1996b).

In a broader sense, the integration process opens up the question of how to combine different territorial identities in a single functional space. In this regard, multicultural habits, past experiences of multinational coexistence in a single state, and the intensity of social and cultural cross-border contacts within shared historical areas, seem to help the integration of East–Central European nations in the so-called 'common European home'. Actually, they are not forced to replace their state-based identity with a new superstate one, as has been suggested for Western European nations, but only to relocate their culturally based identity in a broader functional unit. For this reason, the Central European social and political environment could be of particular interest for the study of multiple identities and their transformation; this also means the study of political and cultural boundaries in a periodically reinterpreted spatial context.

The East–Central European experience of fragmentation of ethnic and spatial identities along with cultural persistence and political transformation, may thus give an answer to those who wish to understand how current processes of modernisation coincide with the 'unity in diversity' concept. This is probably the only way for Europe, the cradle of nationalism and a continuous battlefield of convergence and divergence in the social, cultural, economic and political spheres, to maintain its variety and avoid a new global 'melting pot' experience.

Intense political, economic and other developments from 1989 to 1999 have induced the process of relocation and reorientation of East–Central European countries. Among this group, Slovenia is the smallest, with about two million inhabitants, but with a GDP per capita almost double the size of the Czech Republic's. Its strategic position on the crossroads between North and South, East and West seems to have been sufficient reason to opt for a NATO and EU membership. The geographical relocation of the sovereign nation-state since 1991 is particularly interesting: until 1918 it belonged to the Roman Germanic Empire and the Habsburgs, being thus included in the frame of Central European countries and having strong economic and cultural relations with Vienna and Prague.

In the period of the Yugoslav kingdom (1919 – 1941) and Communist Yugoslavia (1945 – 1991) it turned towards Belgrade and Zagreb. At the earliest in 1991, but definitely since 2004, as Slovenia was granted EU and NATO membership, those centres of power were replaced by Brussels (and Vienna to a certain extent). Slovenia's geographic position remains controversial even in its own textbooks. Most textbooks have placed the new nation-state within the frame of Central Europe, but some have preserved the formerly more common definition and have positioned the country in South-Eastern Europe.

This 'border' situation of Slovenia between West and East, North and South, and currently between the EU and the western Balkans was confirmed by both the former and the current presidents of the US when visiting Slovenia. President Clinton stressed that the US and the Western countries are expecting Slovenia to play a major role in bringing coexistence practices into the region; President Bush (during his first summit with Mr Putin at the Brdo castle, near Ljubljana in June 2001) asserted that Slovenia represents a 'successful story' in terms of democracy and economy which should serve as a good example for other former Yugoslav republics. But the very Bush–Putin summit in Slovenia, which contributed to the country's recognition and visibility, opened the debate as to whether Slovenia would benefit more by remaining 'neutral', as a sort of an Alpine–Dinaric Switzerland, so maintaining its leading position in the region of the western Balkans.

Borders and cross-border interdependence – the Slovenian case study

The political geographical context

As member of the European Union, Slovenia is the most westerly positioned Slavic nation-state in South–Central Europe, bordering Romance, German, Ugric and south Slavic nations. Since the country's natural composition is of equal diversity, as it encompasses the ecosystems of the Alps, the Mediterranean, the Danubian (also Pannonian) plains and the central karstic area of Europe, Slovenia can be viewed as a major transitional area of the continent. Its geopolitical position within Europe is, therefore, of particular importance (Brunn and Cottle 1997). It is supportive of all three development scenarios, being discussed in Brussels: (1) the European Central Axis Model (London–Brussels–Frankfurt–Milan); (2) the Isolated Metropolitan Regions Model (the Milan, Vienna, Munich and Budapest Metropolitan Areas); and (3) the Intra-Regional and Intra-Metropolitan Cooperation Model (the so called Core/Axis Model) which is, in part, a combination of all the above. Understandably, priority is given to the model, which calls for INTERREGional cooperation. Within this model Slovenia could realise its own intentions most easily. Otherwise the young nation-state might be forced to accommodate other states' and regions' development policies. In this case

Slovenia's territory of 20,256 km^2 would be asked to adapt its economy to the interests of Milan, Lombardy and Venice, Veneto in Italy, or to become the outer ring of the Budapest–Bratislava–Vienna, or Munich–Salzburg metropolitan areas (Gosar and Klemenčič 1994).

Because of transportation routes, Slovenia is often on the centre stage of Brussels' political and regional-policy theatre. Agreements to construct a substantial highway net were signed in 1992. Two major traffic corridors (north–south and east–west) are in their final stage of construction and already impact the cultural landscape, while contributing to the improvement of the local economy. The opening of borders towards East–Central Europe has introduced new markets, and other new, non-Balkan-based outer rings of economic exchange have emerged. In this respect, priority was given to plans which anticipate improvement of traffic conditions and construction of highways and railroads along the corridor from Barcelona to Kiev (Milano–Trieste/Koper–Ljubljana–Maribor–Budapest–Bucharest–Kiev) (Ravbar and Klemenčič 1993).

Since 2000, the realisation of a direct, modern railroad artery linking the Danubian and Mediterranean basins (Venice/Trieste–Ljubljana–Murska Sobota–Balaton–Budapest) is under discussion, and by 2010 the modern highway East–West axis, Italy–Hungary and the North–South axis, Austria–Croatia, criss-crossing Slovenia, will be completed. The ports of Koper, Trieste and Venice are becoming major gateways for the southern part of the area of East–Central Europe. The Slovenian port of Koper, the fastest growing port in the Mediterranean with 13 million tons of transhipment in 2005, is particularly fond of being Austrian, Bavarian, Hungarian, Slovak and Czech firms' main partners. (Gosar 1996a).

Four major European cultures groups meet here: the Slavic, German, Romance, and Ugric (Magyar); Slovenia is thus the only European country representing the contact area of four large-scale language/culture groups (Bufon 2002). The neighbouring ethno-linguistic communities, particularly the German, but also the Italian and the Hungarian, were politically and culturally dominant in historical times, and the Slovenian population was constantly subject to assimilation. This was evident in particular at the 'border' of the Slovenian ethnic territory, outside of the present-day nation-state Slovenia. According to Slovenian estimates there are currently more than 80 thousand Slovenes in Italy, more than 40 thousand in Austria, and about five thousand in Hungary (Zupančič 1998), whilst the 1910 census for the same areas showed different data: 130 thousand Slovenes in present-day Italy, 65 thousand in present-day Austria and about 10 thousand in present-day Hungary. Similarly, by 1921, the German community in Slovenia had been heavily reduced and was barely existent after the Second World War (2002 census: 499 German-speaking nationals); the Italian community of Istria decreased in the first two decades after the Second World War, but from 1961 onwards the number has stabilised at around 2,500 citizens (2002 census: 2258); only the Hungarian community in Prekmurje went through a less severe reduction: the 2002 census registered 6,258 Hungarians.

Due to intense immigration of labour from other Yugoslav republics and subsequent wars in the western Balkans, the population structure of Slovenia changed from largely mono-structured, after the Second World War, in the 1970s and the subsequent years, to multi-ethnic again (Gosar 1996b). The share of Slovenes in 1961 was close to 97 per cent, in 1991 around 88 per cent and in 2002 83 per cent. But the immigrant communities outnumber the autochthonous minorities (which counted in 2002 for less than one per cent of the population).

They are especially present in the urban centres – Jesenice, Koper, Celje, Ljubljana, Velenje – where, according to the 2002 census, this group of immigrants represents between 10 and 40 per cent of the urban residential population. In coastal towns of Istria the immigrants from inland Slovenia and Yugoslavia have had in the post-Second World War years a 'revitalising' function as well. They have almost completely replaced the once dominant Italian population, which migrated towards Italy for economic and political reasons (Medica 1987). In consequence Slovenia is, in fact, the only transitional state in East–Central Europe to have experienced such a strong immigration flux, equivalent to that only of Switzerland.

The regional function of Slovenian border areas

The present status of Slovenia as a borderland is clear from the ratio between the surface area of the state and the total length of the political borders (1160 km). On the basis of these two data we can calculate that there are 5.7 km of borders per 100 km^2. A higher proportion of borders to territory is to be experienced only in Luxembourg (nearly 9 km per 100 km^2). Even if we consider as a criterion for defining the border status, a 25 km-wide stretch of border area, and multiply it by the length of the political borders, we realise that in Slovenia border areas include nearly the whole territory of the state. The 'border character' of Slovenia can also be understood by calculating the ratio between the bordering municipalities, i.e. the municipalities that are located within 25 km of the border, and the other municipalities of Slovenia. According to this measurement, 61 per cent of the Slovenian municipalities are bordering municipalities. Even if we limit the border belt to a width of 10 km, the percentage of bordering municipalities still accounts for more than 50 per cent. The border character of Slovenia is furthermore made evident by the fact that the nation-state's capital Ljubljana is by road only 54 km away from the Austrian border, 81 km from the Italian border, and 82 km from the Croatian border. The most distant border is the Hungarian, about 193 km distant.

Cross-border traffic is also consistent with Slovenia's borderland status. The number of people annually crossing the Slovenian border by car increased between 1992 and 2002 from about 140 million to 180 million. On average, half a million people cross the borders daily. If we consider that 30 per cent of these are Slovenian citizens, who make about 50 million border crossings a year, we find that about 140 thousand Slovenian citizens, or 7 per cent of the resident population, transit the border daily. This information is also an important feature in measuring the border character of Slovenia. It enables us to calculate that each Slovenian citizen (including children and elderly people) visits a foreign country on average once a fortnight.

According to the Statistical Office of the Republic of Slovenia, of all foreigners who have crossed the Slovenian border in 2002, 22 percent were residents of Croatia, followed by Italy (21 per cent), Austria (13 per cent), Germany (12 per cent), the Czech Republic (2 per cent), Hungary (2 per cent), Switzerland (1.1 per cent), Slovakia (1.0 per cent) and Netherlands (1.0 per cent). The inhabitants of other former Yugoslav republics made up in total about 2.5 million border crossings. The above shows us that the structure of border crossing is a combination of dominant local or interstate, and international transitional traffic, which is more frequent in summer. The Schengen border arrangements (obligatory visas for non-EU residents – with exceptions) also have to be taken into account. Table 10.1 shows the structure of border crossings between the years 1992 and 2000.

There was a 45 per cent increase in cross-border traffic on the Slovenian–Italian border between 1992 and 1995: from 51 to 74 millions. The flow has stabilised since at about 65 million border crossings. This was the consequence of the introduction of fuel cards in Friuli-Venezia Giulia, which enabled Italian residents of the province to purchase fuel in Italy at the Slovenian price. The traffic across the Austrian–Slovenian border increased between 1992 and 1995 by a quarter, and has stabilised at about 50 million border crossings a year. The biggest increase of cross-border traffic has occurred on the Slovenian–Hungarian border which was virtually closed before the 1990s. The cross-border traffic increased 1992 – 1995 by 150 per cent and has since stabilised at about 4 million border crossings a year. Such an intense increase is the result of the democratisation and liberalisation of the Hungarian society and economy, and by the modification of the Hungarian borderland and its adjustment to the cross-border gateway function.

The border city of Lenti (Hungary) has become an attractive shopping centre for the broader region (Hungary, Austria, Slovenia and Croatia). Changes are noticed on the Slovenian–Croatian border as well. There, the maximum flow was reached in 1994 with 66 millions border crossings, a 33 per cent increase in comparison to the year 1992. The next year, however, the number of cross-border traffic dropped, but it has improved recently and is constantly rising with Croatia's improved position in world tourism. In 2005 about 35 per cent of the total passenger traffic

Table 10.1 Slovenia: structure of border crossings per sectors, 1992–2002

	1992	*1995*	*2002*	*1992*	*1995*	*2002*
	(million passengers)					(%)
SLO/I	51.4	74.5	64.9	36.0	41.3	36.3
SLO/A	39.4	50.7	48.6	27.6	28.1	27.1
SLO/H	1.9	4.8	4.1	1.3	2.7	2.3
SLO/CRO	50.2	50.3	61.0	35.0	27.0	34.0
Total	142.0	180.0	178.0	100.0	100.0	100.0

Source: *Statistični letopis/Statistical Yearbook 1993, 1996, 2002*, Statistical Office of the Republic of Slovenia.

crossed the Italian–Slovenian border, about 34 per cent the Croatian–Slovenian border and about 27 per cent the Austrian–Slovenian border. The traffic on the Hungarian–Slovenian border is growing and is at present close to four per cent.

From Table 10.2 it is evident that the most intense cross-border traffic was, and is, on the Italian–Slovenian border. The borderline is just 17 per cent of the entire nation-state border length, but handles up to 38 per cent of the whole cross-border traffic. The traffic across the Austrian–Slovenian border is more proportional with length, although not on the borders with Croatia and Hungary. The Italian–Slovenian border is also the most permeable, with close to 40 per cent of all border posts. On average, it has seventeen border-posts per 100 km, but in the southern part of the border, in the section Trieste–Gorizia, the density is greater at about twenty-five border-posts per 100 km. The average for the nation-state is eight border posts per 100 km and the Croatian–Slovenian border has the lowest number – just five border-posts per 100 kilometres of the border.

Border area development depends on a number of factors. These include the geopolitical situations and historical experiences in each border section; the nature of political and economic relationships between bordering states; the extent of border permeability; regional conditions; the dynamics of socio-economic development in the border area, and the attitude of the population towards the maintenance and development of cross-border links. Slovenian surveys show that the combination of international factors – the increase of economic exchange, tourist fluxes and transitory traffic – and regional factors that are prevalently linked to the movement of people and goods within the border area stimulate complex development, creating traffic corridors and infrastructure border centres (as in the areas: Trieste–Koper/Capodistria; Opicina/Opcine–Sežana, Gorizia–Nova Gorica, Tarvisio–Arnoldstein–Kranjska Gora, Maribor–Leibnitz–Graz, Lenti–Lendava/Lendva, Krško–Brežice–Samobor–Zagreb).

Table 10.2 Selected characteristics of borders of the Republic of Slovenia, 2002

	1	*2*	*3*	*4*	*5*
SLO/I	17.4	35	38.5	17.3	38.0
SLO/A	27.9	24	26.3	7.4	27.6
SLO/H	7.6	6	6.6	6.8	2.2
SLO/CRO	47.1	26	28.6	4.8	32.2
Total	100.0	91	100.0	7.8	100.0

1 Percentage of the total border length
2 Number of border posts in accordance with the relevant cross-border traffic
3 Percentage of the total border posts
4 Number of border posts per 100 km
5 Percentage of the total cross-border traffic

Source: *Statistični letopis/Statistical Yearbook 1993, 1996, 2001*, Statistical Office of the Republic of Slovenia.

They impact broader border areas in regard to labour, produce and services. Some segments have already developed into stable border regions despite the fact they are not institutionalised. In contrast to the Euroregions, they are based on spontaneous cross-border links, so creating relatively small development territories (Bufon 1996b and 2003). Their common feature is the great influence of the local conditions, which derive from common territorial bonds and history, and much less from international monetary, political and economic resources.

The analysis of cross-border interdependence reveals pronounced differences between border areas. Occasional residential visits to neighbouring countries range on average from 70 to 80 per cent in all borderlands except on the Croatian–Slovenian border sector, (just 40 per cent). Despite being a relatively open border, with no natural hindrances (mountain passes etc.) over half the residents living along the Slovenian–Croatian borderland never visit the neighbouring country. Physical barriers are more pronounced in the Austrian–Slovenian borderland, where a third of the border dwellers never visit the neighbouring country.

The highest interdependence is thus registered in the Hungarian–Slovenian and Italian–Slovenian border sectors, where over 90 per cent of the population takes part in cross-border mobility. Table 10.3 illustrates the local impact in five sectors where cross-border interdependence is high (only 5 per cent never visit the neighbouring country, with the exception of Istria where it exceeds 15 per cent). Daily cross-border mobility is an important factor in the Gorizia border region and in the Austria, Hungary and Slovenia three-border region (10–20 per cent). Work-related migrations dominate in these border regions. Work and supply-related motives generally impact those cross-border sections with dominant weekly visits. This type of cross-border migration is most pronounced in the Gorizia border region (nearly half) and less in the three border regions. Supply is the most cited motive for less frequent cross-border visits – representing about 65 per cent

Table 10.3 Selected cross-border mobility patterns, 2000 (in %)

	A	*B*	*C*	*D*	*E*	*F*
Three-border region (I, A, SLO)	0.0	0.0	11.0	6.0	79.0	4.0
Gorizia border region	20.0	23.2	24.5	18.7	13.5	0.0
Istrian region	2.0	4.6	9.2	15.6	50.3	18.3
Three-border region (A, H, SLO)	10.5	5.0	15.5	20.5	42.3	5.2
Three-border region (H, CRO, SLO)	5.5	10.0	5.0	28.5	34.3	5.5

A Every day   *D 2/3 times a month*
B 2/3 times a week   *E Occasionally*
C Once a week   *F Never*

Source: Fieldwork results (1999–2000).

of cases: this motive is less evident in the Gorizia border region (33 per cent) but is an obvious motive in the three-border region of Slovenia, Italy and Austria (85 per cent).

Eliminating border effects through cross-border cooperation

Support for socio-cultural cross-border links and a cultural affinity of populations on both sides of the border are crucial for a successful and prosperous arrangement in border regions. The Slovenian minority in Italy, for instance, was accustomed to maintain a large part of the 'institutional' cross-border links in regard to sport, culture, economy, information, and municipality cooperation. As the border opened in the 1960s, it represented. Communist Yugoslavia's 'gateway into Europe' as a substantial part of Yugoslavia's transactions with Italy and Europe passed through banks owned by the Slovenian minority in Trieste. In addition to these early 'intra-ethnic' and spontaneous cross-border contacts, others have developed. Since Slovenian independence in 1991, more formal and institutionalised types of cross-border integration between border municipalities and institutions have begun.

Some co-operative forms which had earlier developed in this area now exist in several current 'East–West' European Euroregions; others are innovative and often go beyond limited bilateral interests – in particular, in the Alpen–Adriatic context (incorporating Bavaria-Austria-Italy-Slovenia-Croatia), with cross-border broadcasting, including (minority) radio and TV signal providers. The bid to organise Winter Olympic Games in the three-border area of Slovenia, Austria and Italy in 2006 was another such step. The Slovenian Cultural Centre in Trieste/Trst and the Italian in Koper/Capodistria are also planned in association with respective minorities. Examples of cross-border relations include:

- The formally non-existent Trieste cross-border region (an Istrian Euroregion in the making?) in the southern part of the Italian–Slovenian border incorporates most of the Istrian peninsula (in Slovenia and Croatia), as this region has traditionally gravitated towards what is the actual 'capital' of the Upper Adriatic – Trieste. With the Slovenian inclusion in the EU in 2004, south-western Slovenia, including Istria, is redirecting its interest and potentials towards its own nation-states' Mediterranean Adriatic (Koper/Capodistria) and so Trieste is regaining its former regional function. A very significant development in this regard was the decision made in 2000 by the Luka Koper (Port of Koper) enterprise to manage the Trieste container terminal. The retreat from the agreement in 2005 does not reduce chances for future cooperation between the two major ports and towns of the upper Adriatic, as it could contribute to the development of a new cross-border urban conurbation Trieste–Koper (Gosar 1996a). Moreover, enlarged urban centres, such as Sežana, will also co-operate intensely with Trieste in the future (Minghi 1994). The expected consequence of cross-border urban–rural integration is that Trieste will again become more multicultural. Its autochthonous Slovenian population, restricted for most of the twentieth century, as Trieste was targeted by irredentists and fascists to become the 'most Italian town of Italy', will again obtain an important function in communications between Slovenian and Italian cultural spaces (Kaplan 2000). An increase of socio-economic cross-border relations will, therefore, support the 'Europeanisation' of this border area, together with a pragmatic and peaceful relationship, and thus a 'normalisation' of inter-community and inter-ethnic relations.

- In the central Italian–Slovenian border section, the Gorizia border area was, for several decades after the Second World War, characterised by the separate development of the historically regional centre of Gorizia in Italy and the newly established Nova Gorica, in Slovenia. Since the 1950s, the latter has become a 'substitute' for the lost regional centre Gorizia, across the Iron Curtain in Italy. Recently, Nova Gorica has developed into a gaming and gambling centre for residents and tourists, especially Italians. Towns and communities on both sides of the border are now establishing comprehensive links with each other, which will help in the creation of a single urban area, as existed before the closing of the border. The extraterritorial road across Italian territory, linking Nova Gorica with the hilly hinterland of Goriška Brda (Collio), cooperation between hospitals and institutions of higher education, and the unified intra-urban bus lines are steps in the right direction.
- The three-border region of Italy, Austria and Slovenia already reflects advantages and disadvantages in the social and political transformation and the processes of spatial convergence and divergence. The fact that this has long been a united cultural space with a common way of life, where different ethnic-linguistic communities have coexisted, has to be emphasised. The creation of nation-states divided the region into three parts and hindered normal communication. Social and economic developments have resulted in three regions with different characteristics and goals. But the tourist flows have become consistent, although not equally spread. Plans are underway for the integration of this segment of the economy in several ways. Several steps, which followed the unsuccessful bid for the 2006 Winter Olympics ('Senza Confini'), have already been made: (1) The creation of a cross-border regional information centre in Tarvisio, Valcanale, in Italy; (2) The construction of a cable car connecting skiing areas between Italy and Slovenia and Austria and Italy; (3) The organisation and promotion of the cross-border cycling and walking path, called Europeaus Sine Finibus, linking natural and cultural heritage in the territory of Austria, Italy and Slovenia; (4) Introducing a voucher system aimed at tourist services (skiing, gastronomy) in border areas of the three states (Gosar 2005).

Following the above, we conclude that cultural spaces are much more stable than the political ones, in spite of evident changes caused by the partition of the original social and cultural structures in the twentieth century (Armstrong 1998; Bufon and Minghi 2000). A recent Italian survey of places along the Slovenian–Italian border showed that about 60 per cent of the respondents in the Italian Collio (Goriška Brda) and Valcanale (Kanalska Dolina) areas felt the need for a move from cross-border cooperation towards integration, whereas in urban Trieste the idea of a cross-border integration was supported by just 30 per cent of respondents. Fieldwork results from the Slovenian side showed a similar disposition in border municipalities where most of the respondents were not enthusiastic about integration (Bufon 2002).

So, following the fall of the Iron Curtain, 'normalisation' of the Italian–Slovenian cross-border relationship has neither reached the local level, nor yet found the basis for stronger cross-border integration. This is also due to the lack of proper infrastructure and institutional decision-making to support cross-border communication, such as a forum for cooperation between municipalities of the border area, the creation of other common social, economic, and cultural institutions, a common co-ordination plan, or information centres. Other reasons can be sought in the shortage of improved transportation corridors, the lack of larger urban centres, the low demographic and economic potential of the area, and the lack of active national minorities on different sides of the border.

Conclusion

Europe is in a remarkable state of transformation. Clearly, East–Central Europe is changing rapidly and radically. There are many shocks associated with these processes and more are yet to come. But as well as the traumas, the region in general has experienced positive advances since 1991. All states have made progress politically, and most have experienced economic progress as well. But, East–Central Europe is more heterogeneous than ever before and there is a very clear West–East trend in terms of the rate and success of transformation and transition. It should be noted that these are remarkably dynamic, but also very dangerous times as well. South-eastern Europe is the epicentre of distress in Europe at present. But, one exception is noticeable: the now sovereign nation-state of Slovenia – economically the best-off new member state in the European Union.

Slovenia has developed its political system and economy to the standards of the European Union, surpassing even older members in regard to economic power and has become the powerhouse of the area. Within East–Central Europe, a star of prosperity and stability has arisen. Slovenia's major advantage is in its geopolitical location, based on the multitude of natural and cultural landscapes. Preconditions are there for Slovenia to become a major gateway-state of Europe. Based on Slovenia's experience, cooperation and integration perspectives in today's Europe may be discussed on two different but inter-related levels: (1) The first involves 'regional globalisation', namely the integration of an increasing number of Central European countries into a wider trans-continental dimension; (2) The second concerns regional aspects of cross-border cooperation. A direct consequence of the first process will be to eliminate the (negative) mental legacies in the region. Good cross-border relations are crucial in this regard.

Regarding Slovenia and its borders, has the new pre- and post-2004 situation, namely EU accession and membership, changed the function of borders in the Alpen–Adriatic region completely? The previous international borders with Italy, Austria and Hungary now represent internal borders within the EU space, whilst the border with Croatia, once just an internal, provincial border, has become, at least for some years, the outer border (a Schengen border) of the EU, facing challenges in terms of control of international migration and security.

The case of Slovenia's borders provides an interesting illustration of an apparently paradoxical process within borderlands: the greater the conflicts created by the political partition of a previously homogeneous administrative, cultural and economic region (as on the border towards Italy and Austria), the greater – in the longer run – are the opportunities for such a divided area to develop into an integrated cross-border region. Reflecting on the border landscape concept on the basis of Slovenia's border areas, it becomes clear that a political or economic 'macro' approach in studying cross-border regions has limitations. The true nature and qualities of these regions may only be established when local cultural and social elements of cross-border relations are also taken into account. The great variety of micro-transactions at the local level and supported by the border population mainly results from its spatial mobility in satisfying daily basic needs – work, leisure/recreation, supply, and education. These functions are also the outcome of border population activity in maintaining the many traditional cultural links rooted in the relatively stable period preceding political partition.

So, the study of border regions undoubtedly brings additional aspects to bear on the standard theory of the centre–periphery relations, while opening up new problems. These are becoming increasingly topical in today's world, as we try to enhance mutual understanding in the culturally rich and diverse European space. The geography of border landscapes in its social and cultural dimensions is thus assuming an important role in the 'humanisation' of the traditional geographical approach to borders and border conflict resolution.

Three major factors which contribute towards a positive evaluation of cross-border cooperation were detected while writing this paper: (1) In orchestrating a functional and intense cross-border mobility, existing relations determine a generally positive evaluation of cooperation; (2) By stimulating cultural/ethnic affinity between the resident populations on both sides of the border, cross-border activities become more natural, and more intense in their impact on the relationship in the long run; (3) By stressing how cross-border cooperation is greater in areas where differences in the socio-cultural and socio-economic structure of landscapes on both sides of the border are small and/or compatible.

References

Armstrong, W. (1998) 'Belonging, ethnic diversity and everyday experience: co-existing identities on the Italo-Slovene frontier', Oxford: University of Oxford *Transnational Communities Working Paper Series*.

Boesler, K.-A. (1997) 'Neue ansätze der politischen geographie und geopolitik', *Erdkunde* 51, Bonn: 309–17.

Brunn, S. and Cottle, C. (1997) 'Small states and cyberboosterism', *The Geographical Review* 87 (2), American Geographic Society, New York: 240–59.

Bufon, M. (1996a) 'Some political-geographical problems of transition in Central Europe: the case of Slovenia', in F.W. Carter, P. Jordan and V. Rey (eds) *Central Europe after the Fall of the Iron Curtain*, Peter Lang. Frankfurt: 73–89.

Bufon, M. (1996b) Social integration in the Italo-Slovene border landscape: the Gorizia transborder region, *Tijdschrift voor Economische en Sociale Geografie* 87, 247–58.

Bufon, M. (1998) 'Le regioni transfrontaliere nel processo di unificazione europea', in P. Bonavero and E. Dansero (eds), *L'Europa delle regioni e delle reti*, Torino: Utet, 295–306.

Bufon, M. (2002) 'Slovenia – a European contact and border area', *Annales* 11/2. Koper: 445–72.

Bufon, M. (2003) 'Cross-border cooperation in the Upper Adriatic', in J. Anderson, L. O'Dowd and T.M. Wilson (eds), *New Borders for a Changing Europe – Cross-border Cooperation and Governance*, Frank Cass, London: 177–96.

Bufon, M. and Minghi, J. (2000) 'The Upper Adriatic borderland: from conflict to harmony', *GeoJournal* 52, 119–27.

Castells, M. (2004) *The Power of Identity*, Oxford: Blackwell.

Galtung, J. (1994) 'Coexistence in spite of borders: on the borders in the mind', in Gallusser, W.A., (ed.), *Political Boundaries and Coexistence*, Berne: Peter Lang, 5–14.

Gosar, A. (1996a) 'Slovenia – selected topics in political geography', in Gosar, Anton (ed.). *Slovenia: a Gateway to Central Europe*, published on the occasion of the 28th International Geographical Congress, The Hague, August 5–10. Ljubljana: Association of the Geographical Societies of Slovenia, 7–16.

Gosar, A. (1996b) Die zeit- und raumspezifischen merkmale der volksgruppen in Slowenien, in *Mitt. Österr. Geogr. Ges.* 138, 183–206.

Gosar, A. (2005) 'The cross-border bricklaying concept in the Alpen–Adria region', in *Tour. anal.* vol. 10, no. 1, 65–78.

Gosar A. and Klemenčič V. (1994) 'The European integration from the Slovenian viewpoint', in Z. Hajdu and Gy. Horvath (eds) *European Challenges and Hungarian Responses in Regional Policy*, Pecs: Centre for Regional Studies, 67–78.

Gosar, A. and Klemenčič, M. (2000) 'Les problèmes de la délimitation de la frontière Italie–Slovénie–Croatie en Adriatique septentrionale', *Mare Nostrum. Dynamiques et mutations géopolitiques de la Méditerranée*, Paris: l'Harmattan, 123–34.

Kaplan, D.H. (2000) 'Conflict and compromise among borderland identities in Northern Italy', *Tijdschrift voor Economische en Sociale Geografie* 91, 44–60.

Klemenčič, V. and Genorio, R. (1993) 'The new state Slovenia and its function within the frame of Europe', *GeoJournal* 30/3, 323–35.

Maier, J. (1986) 'Ausländische investitionen und ihre auswirkungen aus der sicht der regionalwissenschaften', *Arbeitsmaterialien zur Raumordnung und Raumplanung* 47, Bayreuth, 1–7.

Medica, K. (1987) 'Socialno demografske značilnosti slovenske Istre po letu 1945', *Revija za narodnostna vprašanja, Razprave in gradivo* 20, 81–92.

Minghi, J.V. (1994) 'The impact of Slovenian independence on the Italo-Slovene borderland: an assessment of the first three years', in W.A. Gallusser (ed.) *Political Boundaries and Coexistence*, Berne: Peter Lang, 88–94.

Poulantzas, N. (1978) *State, Power, Socialism*, London: New Left Books.

Ravbar, M. and Klemenčič V. (1993) 'Actual problems of regional development in Slovenia', in Z. Hajdu and Gy. Horvath (eds) *Development Strategies in the Alpine-Adriatic Region*, Pecs: Centre for Regional Studies, 143–65.

Sack, R.D. (1986) *Human Territoriality*, New York: Cambridge University Press.

Williams, C.H. (1997) 'European regionalism and the search for new representational spaces', *Annales* 10, 265–74.

Zupančič, J. (1998) 'Slovenci v zamejstvu', *Geografski atlas Slovenije*, Ljubljana: Državna založba Slovenije, 174–177.

11 Citizenship beyond the state

On the formation of civil society in the Three-Border Region

Robert Minnich

Borders are useful prisms through which to test theories of social integration and gain insight into the mechanisms of social inclusion and exclusion. These processes are well illustrated by the making and unmaking of states and nations in borderlands (Wilson and Donnan 1998, Sahlins 1989). It is here that institutions upholding the territorial integrity and legitimacy of modern states are firmly anchored. And, it is here that they are challenged. The residents of contested borderlands, such as the Three-Border Region (TBR) at the juncture of the Austrian, Italian and Slovene state borders, often demonstrate allegiances and pursue interests at odds with those of the state holding jurisdiction over them. Yet, we discover across the region's borders patterns of political practice and collective self-understanding that challenge classic concepts of *citizenship* and *civil society* in so far as the latter are seen as epiphenomena of the modern nation-state.

These two concepts arose at a time of profound social transformation in Western Society (cf. Marshall 1964, Hann 1996, Seligman 1995). It is therefore no surprise that they have regained currency over the past decade. The dissolution of the Soviet Empire, the subsequent expansion of the European Union and the growing domination of market liberalism (and global capitalism) in the affairs of Western states are seen to challenge that relatively stable social order enjoyed both within and among European nation-states during the Cold War. The role of the nation-state as the source and guarantor of citizenship rights, as the instrument of social inclusion and integration, is being challenged. Likewise the public sphere has lost its integrity as a domain of communication and action contained by the nation-state, if indeed this was ever the case.

This situation gives new salience to the study of *local level politics*, a classic theme in political anthropology (Swartz 1969). Here locally founded political traditions are viewed *in articulation with* those of greater society, any given individual and the groups to which s/he belongs is observed in relation to that full range of polities that influence his/her life situation; ergo, institutions of the nation-state are not seen to predetermine the framework for investigating political practice and culture.

Citizenship

In the following I adopt an analytical understanding of citizenship that frees it from association with the nation-state. Drawing upon French political philosophy, Catherine Neveu (2000, 120) distinguishes between citizenship and nationality, where the former refers to 'membership in a political community' and the latter refers to 'a legal status, according to which an individual owes allegiance to a state and obtains its passport'. This understanding enables us to investigate the life-worlds of individuals in terms of memberships and political participation in diverse polities reflecting an individual's positioning in society. These can range from local communities to the state and suprastate political and economic institutions such as the EU. As Neveu reiterates in her article on European citizenship and European Citizens (2000, 125) 'it is this very distinction [between citizenship and nationality] which provides for the possibility of thinking in forms of citizenship not linked to the national level'. Furthermore, it allows us to imagine different paths which the development of citizenship has followed in various social formations, without first submitting ourselves to endless argument about the normative ideal of citizenship in connection with a particular nation-state.

The above distinctions open a broad understanding of citizenship. Bryan Turner (1993, 2) suggests 'Citizenship may be defined as that set of practices (juridical, political, economic and cultural) which define a person as a competent member of society, and which as a consequence shape the flow of resources to persons and social groups'. Although I initially identify citizenship in terms of rights and obligations, my ultimate goal is to elucidate the practices enabling competent membership in society in all the domains noted by Turner. Since membership manifests the experience of belonging, that is, self-identification, we must inevitably consider 'national identity' and the fact of one's legal status within a nation-state, that is, nationality.

Citizenship, nationality and national identity, as stipulated above, are thus distinctions especially salient to the study of the life-worlds of borderland residents; they allow us to distinguish differing forms of political participation and collective self-reference which integrate the life-worlds of those we study.

Civil society

Explicitly avoiding digression into the extensive Western discourse on civil society, I wish here to apply the term with regard to the social space and historical period with which this paper deals. Joining Michał Buchovski (1996, 80) I assert that civil society springs from the precondition that 'individuals share some moral values and pursue their internalised goals via freely established institutions. These associations fill in the space between the family and state', and, I would add, 'more extensive polities'. Such an understanding of civil society is fundamental to modern thinking about citizenship; it alludes to the formation and maintenance of a public sphere (based on free association) where, among other things, the rights we associate with citizenship are contested and political practices underlying modern representational government take form.

Civil society can thus be seen to manifest itself in social movements promoting new forms of association in the face of jointly perceived inequities. Jean Cohen and Andrew Arato (1994, 16) call this 'a new terrain of democratisation'. I suggest that regionalism, as I present it later, is representative of such movements; it is a context for institutionalising new forms of association that mediate local life-worlds with the political and economic institutions upon which they are contingent.

However, as foundation for later discussion of the status of civil society within the TBR, it is first necessary to account for the historical formation of polities in the TBR. In this way I work from the ground up by describing a locally founded institutional basis for citizenship practices. At the same time this is a description of circumstances facilitating civil society in local society.

Research background and orientation

An important source of material for this chapter is initial field research in the Three-Border Region conducted over sixteen months between 1981 and1986. At that time I focused attention on Slovene-speaking villagers indigenous to Val Canale (Italy) and Gailtal (Austria). By means of participant observation I investigated local collective self-understandings in terms of the material and cultural arrangements shaping local life-worlds. Because of these borderland residents' status as speakers of Slovene dialect in countries dominated by other language groups I inevitably extended my investigations to the history and institutions of the nation-state as they have manifested themselves in the region. Namely, the politicisation of linguistic difference has been a central feature of the formation of citizenship and civil society in the region.

Until a couple decades ago, scholarly presentations of the TBR were generally based upon an a priori understanding of the region as a multi-ethnic social formation. Throughout the past century the TBR was a zone of ethnic contest and confrontation orchestrated by protagonists of the modern nation-state. Scholarship on the TBR seldom disassociated itself from the assumed primacy of the nation-state and its ethnic constitution in the territory of the former Habsburg Empire.[1] Along with others (e.g. Šumi 2000, Armstrong 2003) I have attempted to convey an understanding of this borderland social order in terms of locally held collective self-understandings.

The collective self-images of TBR villagers cannot be reasonably reduced to ethnic or national affiliations. Rather, they are invariably complex, referring to numerous associations in one's life, ranging from one's membership in a household and local community to his/her legal status as the member of a nation-state, nationality, and eventually sense of membership in the nation, national identity (Minnich 1996, 1998). If we are to realistically account for one's political participation in society (i.e. citizenship), representation of political culture must be equally nuanced, stressing the uniqueness of our informants' positioning in society at large.

The formation of polities in the TBR – the case of Ugovizza/Ukve

Ugovizza, the initial focus of this study, is the best-preserved Slovene-speaking enclave in Val Canale (the Italian segment of the TBR), and, sadly became the focus of European media on August 31, 2003, when a significant portion of the town was obliterated by a flash flood. Called 'Ukve' in local dialect, this village is stereotyped throughout the TBR as one of its most conservative, backward-looking, communities. I concentrated my initial participant observation upon Ugovizza households still engaged in a traditional system of household production involving commercial milk and meat production, herding, forest exploitation and limited subsistence gardening. In 1983, 33 of Ugovizza's 140 households still retained livestock and the number has since declined. But to attribute this statistical evidence to a fundamental transformation of the village is quite misleading (Minnich 1989), as will be clarified below.

From the perspective of cultural ecology I have investigated political institutions in terms of the ecological circumstances and resource base affording a given population possibilities for its subsistence and reproduction. The socio-cultural institutions facilitating these processes are of equal importance to my considerations. In the TBR, as elsewhere in the Alps, this points toward the importance of domestic households both as production systems and as estates.

The organisation of rights

The oldest political organisations in Ugovizza are directly founded upon the rights and interests held in common by local historical households. These include the commons association (Nachbarschaft) and the Servitude Representation (Servitutsvertretung). In 1983, 111 of Ugovizza's 140 households possessed servitude rights empowering them to exploit an annual quota of timber in local forests, as well as rights to the pasture and limited forest of the village commons. These are the historical households of Ugovizza; they are the referent for constructing a prototype of what I have called elsewhere (1998) 'homesteads'.

The above timber quotas are currently administered by Italy's Department of Forestry, and the servitude forests are owned by Fondo per il Culto (the so-called Sacred Fund, held jointly by the Italian state and the Vatican). And although it has been possible for several decades to sell servitude rights to the state, no Ugovizza household had done this up to the time of my fieldwork in the 1980s, while it had occurred elsewhere in Val Canale. Regardless of whether or not Ugovizza's householders were engaged in agrarian activity they were unwilling to sell their right to a steady, though nominal, source of income.

Since Ugovizza's incorporation by Italy, local homesteaders have repeatedly engaged lawyers to defend their servitude rights in the face of the state's several attempts to discontinue this institution. And along with neighbouring Austrian villages, Ugovizza households have attempted to recapture portions of highland commons lost to neighbouring states in 1919 as a result of the region's partition by Austria and Italy (Kándut 1982). Such political mobilisation is a clear demarcation of Ugovizza's, and other TBR villages' territorial integrity against the state of which they are part; it demonstrates loyalty to village polities, which supersedes allegiance to the state. Citizenship practice is formed in terms of the contested interests of the village and the state.

These rights in the commons and servitude land are invested in households and not persons. Thus, despite the apparent de-agrarisation of Ugovizza, local historical homesteads with land holdings and dwellings in both valley and highlands retain an intrinsic value that inhibits estate partition. Furthermore the system of property transmission is relatively closed. I discovered that since incorporation by Italy in 1919 very few of Ugovizza's historical homesteads (those holding rights in the commons and servitude land) had been transferred to non-indigenous residents of the valley. Furthermore, those homesteads that retain agrarian production in Ugovizza, and thereby have the greatest benefit from these rights, continue to dominate village-level politics. And values associated with the traditional agrarian household retain hegemony in moral discourses integrating village affairs. This is readily evident, for example, in the organisation of and participation in village funerals, wakes and patron saint day celebrations as well as in less formal public settings of the village.

The local polity

The above repertoire of homestead rights have historically constituted the core institutions of a local polity, that is, a village-based system of self-governance based upon household representation in a council run by elected officers. This mode of political integration approximates what Robert K. Burns, Jr. (1963) has designated as a trait of the Alpine region, namely, the 'closed corporate community'. This forms the basis for a local political culture that has proven itself highly adaptive to the intrusion of electoral, regulatory and administrative institutions imposed upon the local community by the modern state and more recently, by the European Union. Such a tradition of self-governance is replicated throughout the agrarian settlements of the TBR and attests to a common political heritage antedating the intervention of the modern territorial state in these communities.

In sum, many of the rights and expectations associated with a modern idea of citizenship were institutionalised well in advance of the intervention of the state as the instrument for shaping these practices. Among these we find the civil right to hold land as freeholders, the political right to representation in local councils and the social rights addressed by village mobilisation around matters of social welfare among its residents.

It is now in place to relate this historical foundation for citizenship in Ugovizza to the intervention of the modern state in local society. By altering the focus slightly to the institutionalisation of civil society, that is, the formation of a public sphere in late Habsburg society we must consider extension and universalisation of the right to free association, fundamental to the formalisation of representation in a parliamentary system of governance.

Institutionalising civil society in the periphery of a multi-ethnic empire

The modern idea of civil society presupposes a tension within Western society between the private and public domains, between realisation of individual self-interest and attainment of the collective good (Keane 1988). By citing above Cohen and Arato's belief in the democratic potential of civil society to resolve these tensions I adopted a normative understanding of the term as an 'ethical ideal of the social order' (Seligman 1995, x).

But my immediate concern here is to outline the institutionalisation of civil society around a shared understanding of free association; I focus upon the institutionalisation of modern civil society in the Dual Monarchy, a process which became pervasive and irreversible upon the abolition of feudal bondage in 1848. During the remaining decades of Habsburg rule the Kaiser's subjects were incrementally empowered as legal persons. Under the auspices of an increasingly effective constitutional authority in Vienna it became possible to participate as an autonomous moral agent in a public domain secured by the state, a tenet of the modern liberal variant of civil society (Keane 1988).

Former personal subjects of local nobility became citizens through extension and standardisation of the civil rights to hold property, enter into contracts, establish voluntary organisations and the political rights to vote for public officials and stand for public office – all fundamental to the modern idea of citizenship (Marshall 1964). TBR residents became participants in a public sphere facilitated by the 'Empire of Bureaucrats' (Johnston 1983).

The convergence of civil society from above and below

Premodern forms of civil society are commonly associated with the burgher class and its incorporation through civil code as free citizens of towns and trade centres. Such pockets of nascent civil society were established in the TBR. But the majority of its population resided in villages that are representative of what Burns (1963) has called 'the Circum-Alpine Culture Area'. As I have already shown, one can *also* document here in agrarian villages the early formation of representational forms of political association (self-governing village-based corporations) developed in relative isolation from more direct forms of feudal subjugation confined to the region's very few manorial estates.

Within the TBR we thus detect a historical approximation in village society of what Burns terms 'self-governing republics-in-miniature' (1963, 148) which have managed common lands, regulated inheritance, promoted local welfare and otherwise organised the public sphere of village society. Thus, the post-1848 intervention of central government in local polities accommodated established traditions of democratic association; it standardised existing political cultures within pervasive structures of an imperial state.

Following extension of the right of association in 1867 the pre-existing civic institutions in TBR villages were supplemented by a plethora of voluntary organisations which organised commercial affairs (e.g. savings associations and agricultural cooperatives), promoted social welfare (e.g. poor houses, voluntary fire-brigades), and furthered public enlightenment (e.g. schools, school boards, newspapers, weeklies, libraries, reading circles) (Moritsch and Baumgartner 1992). A pre-existing infrastructure for participation in the civil affairs of local communities was expanded and standardised throughout the TBR.

Civil society and parliamentarianism in local society

These locally based voluntary organisations readily became vehicles for consolidating political factions seeking position in a nascent parliamentary system (Moritsch and Baumgartner 1992). Ideological opposition between liberalism and conservatism propagated by burgeoning secular and clerical elites throughout the Habsburg lands (Kann 1974, 346) increasingly pervaded the public domain of local communities. (The essentially agrarian economy of the TBR confined the advance of Socialism during this formative stage of Austrian parliamentarianism to the region's few industrial and mining centres with a nominal proletariat.) The Catholic Church competed with liberal elites in the promotion of village-level welfare and cultural institutions as a base to build support for their respective political factions. At the beginning of the twentieth century when the franchise was extended to the monarchy's adult male population, village polities became the setting for party politics and factional strife.

In the Slovene- and German-speaking villages and towns of the TBR this extension of the public domain to a statewide political arena was accompanied by the politicisation of ethnic difference based upon linguistic identity. A highly simplified model of a complex local political landscape suggests that the Catholic Church in its quest to conserve the old order elicited support from the region's newly enfranchised Slovene-speaking rural population, while the liberal agenda was promoted by a largely German-speaking bourgeoisie. The aspiration of increasingly influential ethnic elites to promote the self-determination of their respective peoples readily became an important factor in mobilisation around the ideological positions outlined above (Pleterski 1996). Within the three provinces of which the TBR was a part (Carinthia, Carniola and the Coastal Province) liberal and clerical conservative factions enlisted ethnic support in their quest to dominate these provincial governments.

This development manifested itself in Ugovizza in various ways. For example, the local parish church was associated with conservative political factions promoting Slovene national identity while Kanaltal's School Association (Deutscher Schulverein) was associated with liberal factions driven by German nationalism. Taking stock of their own communal interests, Ukljani succeeded in this period in building a school in the highlands so that they could retain the practice of relocating their entire households between April and October and yet accommodate the new demand for compulsory elementary education which spanned over their presence in the highlands. And the school was built with the enthusiastic support of the German School Association even though it conserved the traditional social order.

Disruption of a local social order: co-optation of civil society by totalitarian regimes

Through the state's further institutionalisation and standardisation of the public sphere in the TBR the stage was set for effectively implementing ethnically defined terms of citizenship under the regimes that succeeded the Habsburg Vielvölkerstaat (multi-ethnic state). The TBR was partitioned by Austria, Italy and Yugoslavia following the most devastating war in the region's history. TBR residents became the citizens of three nation-states that proceeded to fortify their common borders and propagate images of 'hostile neighbours', building upon collective memories of the Great War conducted between the Austrian and Italian monarchies along the Soča Front.

With the rise of Italian Fascism in the 1920s the southern and western segments of the TBR with a predominantly Slovene-speaking population (i.e. incorporated by Italy following the First World War) were subjected to state policy that systematically administered citizenship rights on the basis of ethnic ascription. Local traditions of self-government and participation in civic institutions were severely disrupted by the deportation, exile and imprisonment of local elites. Leadership and control of local civic and political institutions were co-opted by a largely monolingual cadre of Italian officials and immigrants recruited to the region by various economic incentives.

Following *Anschluss* with the Third Reich in 1938 the northern segment of the TBR (Carinthia) was subjected to a similar form of administration for which, significantly, a German nationalist elite could be recruited locally. Slovene leaders and intellectuals suffered fates similar to their compatriots in Fascist Italy. And in an effort to ethnically homogenise their respective dominions, Hitler and Mussolini contracted with one another the infamous Berliner Vereinbarung of 1939 that coerced German speakers of Val Canale and Alto Adige to opt for repatriation in the German Reich. (Veiter 1961). The democratic social order of pluri-lingual ('multi-ethnic') communities founded upon local traditions of self-government was destroyed through the imposition of ethnic loyalty as a qualification for participation as an equal in the public sphere. A situation was created in advance of an eminent war that is reminiscent of conditions in Bosnia following the war and imposition of the Dayton Accords during the past decade.

In Bosnia the immediate and pervasive experience of war conducted in the name of ethnic difference has transformed local life-worlds and traumatised individual lives such that reconstitution of the original multi-ethnic social order of Bosnia's villages and towns seems unlikely. To what extent was this also the case in the TBR following the Second World War?

TBR civil society in the wake of war

Much of the territory of the TBR was liberated by a Communist-led partisan army that was recruited locally from the ranks of a resistance movement dedicated to the overthrow of totalitarian regimes noted above. As a result of Fascist and Nazi campaigns to promote ethnic homogeneity in their respective segments of the TBR, the region underwent pervasive demographic changes reminiscent of contemporary Bosnia. The German minority of Val Canale was greatly reduced through the aforementioned option while the Slovene minority remained in place but subordinated to a monolingual Italian-speaking majority (Veiter 1961). And multitudes of Italians fled the Julian Province of Imperial Italy as it was reclaimed by Yugoslavia through the advance of the Partisan Army at the conclusion of the war. Autochthonous Slovene-speaking communities have thus persisted in Carinthia (Austria) and Val Canale (Italy) under the numerically and politically dominant presence of the respective German and Italian majorities while the Italian population of the Yugoslav part of the region was very nearly depleted following the war.

The War of Liberation set the stage for interstate relations and redefining the terms of citizenship in the TBR following the Second World War. And Cold War divisions came to prevail over ethnic difference in the conduct of interstate relations. Reminiscent of the situation in Bosnia today, the Allies initially supervised the borderland marked by the Iron Curtain between Yugoslavia and Italy. However, the final adjustment of TBR borders (especially between Yugoslavia and Italy) and the 1955 reintegration of Austria in the international community were contingent upon treaties that, among other things, formally secured the rights of ethnic minorities on both sides of the Iron Curtain. In contrast to the Dayton Accords these treaties have been subsequently supplemented and implemented without the direct intervention of foreign powers. But, as we shall see, the implementation of minority rights remains a pressing issue in the public sphere and forums of democratic association within each of the neighbouring countries and between them.

Post-war transfer of sovereignty from states to greater polities – the opening of local borders

The post-war period has been marked in the TBR by the increasing transfer of sovereignty from local states to international organisations such as the Common Market, European Union and European Parliament. In the 1960s the Iron Curtain was radically dismantled as an obstacle to intra-regional commerce and freedom of movement when Yugoslavia initiated an economic policy based upon the employment of Yugoslav workers in Western and Northern Europe. The Yugoslav state became increasingly subject to the conditions of bilateral and international agreements promoting its integration in global economic institutions. The terms of citizenship and participation in the public sphere throughout the TBR became increasingly contingent upon common membership in the same interstate organisations and agreements.

The opening of local borders also facilitated the reunion of families dispersed by war and exile; it revitalised informal and formal contacts among village institutions and provincial governments which were significant for the eventual reintegration of the Slovene Republic in the Western European sphere of political and commercial intercourse discussed below.

In comparison with the highly centralised collectivist regimes of Nazi Germany and Fascist Italy, the progressive decentralisation of government in Communist Yugoslavia facilitated the revival of local civic institutions in some areas of public life, particularly in the Socialist Republic of Slovenia. The former dominant role of the Church in the public sphere of village and town life was, however, rigidly constrained and the formation of political factions was prohibited. Nonetheless, nominal local control of cultural, educational, sport and welfare institutions was reinstated. The praxis of voluntary association and free exchange of information in the public sphere of local society was revived under the constraints outlined above.

Political mobilisation across state borders – foundations for citizenship beyond the state?

By turning to the arena of minority politics within Austria, Italy and Yugoslavia during the Cold War it is possible to detect new patterns of political mobilisation and association that exploited suprastate institutions within Europe. The formal guarantee of minority rights obtained in the treaties described above enabled minority elites in the TBR to engage democratic procedures in their quest to implement rights, a quest which local nationalist groups have consistently opposed in the borderlands of both Italy and Austria. And, as we know from the post-war period in the South Tyrol, Carinthia and Friuli–Venezia Giulia, state institutions have relatively effectively inhibited the outbreak of ethnic violence. The potential of the TBR to become another Bosnia–Hercegovina of the mid-1990s has been minimal.

Minority politicians and cultural elites in Austria and Italy have been innovative in forming political alliances with other minorities throughout Europe and with institutions such as the European Parliament. As a result they have effectively countered ethnic nationalist policy tolerated within the framework of nation-states and particularly within borderland provinces which are home to exile communities in north-east Italy (Ballinger 1996, 2003) and unreformed Nazis in Carinthia which, in both cases, comprise a vocal and occasionally violent right-wing fringe.

Already in the 1950s Socialist Slovenia's political leaders, many of whom were optimally positioned in the federal government and diplomatic corps of the Belgrade regime, began to promote contact with, and improve the situation of, the Slovene minorities in Austria and Italy. They were instrumental in initiating a series of laws and institutions within Communist Yugoslavia which provided a model for implementing minority rights which has since been emulated elsewhere in Europe. And this 'enlightened' domestic policy was systematically exploited in the quest to attain within the international arena sanctions against provincially inspired assimilatory policies directed toward indigenous Slovene-speaking communities in Carinthia and Friuli–Venezia Giulia.

These interstate political initiatives have transformed provincial politics and local understandings of one's place and possibilities within greater Europe. On the basis of my contact with Slovene speakers in Austria and Italy, who are not active in minority organisations, it is apparent that the above patterns of interstate mobilisation around minority rights issues have come to shape local understandings of the potential range for democratic association far beyond the confines of the classic nation-state.

Furthermore, one encounters considerable individual versatility in evaluating and exploiting various subsidies and information networks maintained by the EU, available, for example, through local INTERREG and PHARE-CBC projects (Busch 2003). In rural TBR communities local councils are increasingly aware of the potential of association with organisations and counterpart groups located outside their respective nation-state. For example, in recent years the movement for attaining sister-cities in other countries has blossomed. Since tourism is an increasingly important source of income in the TBR local municipal councils have formulated, with EU support, marketing strategies that stress both the diversity and integrity of the region as a cultural region. Local and regional cultural traditions are being objectified and mobilised in pan-European marketing strategies of the region as a tourist attraction under the slogan 'Europaeus sine finibus' (Europe without boundaries).[2]

Regionalism – the germ of transethnic civil society?

Initiatives of provincial and state leaders to promote political and economic cooperation across state-frontiers erode the sovereignty of the state institutions that empower them. And in the TBR it is as much political initiative from elected and appointed leaders as the civil and commercial undertakings of local citizens that have generated a broader public sphere in which to establish new terms of citizenship, new patterns of association.

Although Slovenia's secession from the Socialist Federal Republic of Yugoslavia in 1991 has been attributed to ethnic-nationalism, I find it more useful to view it as the culmination of numerous government sponsored initiatives taken in Belgrade and Ljubljana that sought increased political and economic integration with Western Europe.[3] Following the constitutional decentralisation of Yugoslavia in 1974, Slovenia's socialist leadership readily acknowledged the potential of regional movements as a vehicle to subordinate nation-states (in this case their mother state, the Socialist Federal Republic of Yugoslavia) to a pan-European political and economic order.

In 1978 elected leaders of the Austrian Bundesländer of Carinthia and Styria, the Socialist Republic of Slovenia and the Italian Region of Friuli–Venezia Giulia established a Working Group dedicated to promoting the idea of the Alpe–Adria Region, a replication of the south-west corner of the former Dual Monarchy. The

TBR is the axis around which the Alpe–Adria Region is formed. It is both the historical zone of language contact at the heart of the region and integrates it as an important hub of communication. The Alpe–Adria idea immediately attracted the attention of adjacent regional polities (provincial governments) that are clearly peripheral to their own nation-states. As a result, the Alpe–Adria movement was joined by Bavaria in the north, Istria in the south, the South Tyrol in the west and western parts of Hungary (Gyor) in the east. Various cultural and commercial activities conceived with reference to the region have since taken place. The Alpe–Adria Working Group was attractive not only for European Union initiatives promoting regional integration. It helped define new terms for political association and mobilisation. (Moritsch 1996, Klemenčič 1994).

In the 1980s the mayors of local towns (Arnoldstein, Kranjska Gora and Tarvisio) jointly proposed the TBR as the host for the 2002 Olympic Winter Games. More recently support for this candidacy was revived on a higher rung of the regional political ladder. In June 1996 the heads of the provincial governments of Friuli–Venezia Giulia, Carinthia and the prime minister of Slovenia discussed a renewed joint application for the 2006 Olympic Winter Games that was ultimately submitted. Despite the failed 2006 candidacy, the initiative established the basis for intra-regional initiatives. In recent years such undertakings have successfully elicited financial support from EU programmes created to promote regional integration (INTERREG) and self-determination within the European Union – an explicit strategy for diminishing the prominence of the nation-state as the primary actor in the movement for European unification.

Austria and Slovenia's incorporation in the EU, respectively in 1995 and 2004, trail intra-regional political initiatives. The arrival of the EU in the TBR was not startling news but rather the fulfillment of local expectations and political agendas. Increasingly, the TBR is attaining status in local media as an icon of the EU slogan 'unity in diversity'.

Foundations for intraregional civil society

The above politically guided intraregional agenda has been accompanied during the past decade by increased contact initiated directly between locally based voluntary organisations such as parish churches, local choral societies, sport clubs, alpine tourist associations, volunteer fire brigades, etc. Ironically, many of the same organisations, which during the waning decades of Habsburg society became the instruments of ethnic-nationalist confrontation, are today transcending ethnic parochialism by initiating cooperation conceived to promote mutual commercial, cultural and welfare interests of the 'borderland region'. The massive, immediate and well-coordinated intra-regional relief effort after the August 2003 devastation of Ugovizza (and surrounding villages in north-east Italy) demonstrated how deep-rooted cultural and social understandings shared across the region lay the foundation for a common civil society across the 'ethnic borders'.

A notable grass-roots example of the above change is to be found in the frequent encounters of local voluntary fire brigades across the Austrian–Italian–Slovenian frontier. In the 1980s these encounters were highly formalised and stressed national identification of the participating teams through the use of flags and carefully orchestrated speech protocols during the awards ceremony. While attending one of these events held in 1996 near the recently dismantled Austrian–Italian border in the Carnian highlands the above-mentioned formalities were greatly reduced and national flags were missing, making the encounter resemble that of a domestic gathering of neighbouring villages rather than an international summit. The nation-state was noticeably absent in this assembly of TBR citizens (Minnich 1998).

Slovenia's adoption of parliamentary democracy and a constitution written to conform to democratic standards established in the European Parliament has been significant for the revitalisation of common civil and political institutions in villages and towns throughout the TBR. The classic array of political factions established in late Habsburg society – liberal, conservative, social democratic – have re-entered local-level politics throughout the region. A common politico-ideological landscape has been re-established which embellishes and legitimates a political culture that is now largely uniform throughout the TBR.

While the foregoing superficially suggests no more than reintegration of a former Alpine cross-roads – the reconstitution of a multi-ethnic social order – a closer look at the patterns of association and types of social movements, which today are manifest in the lives of TBR residents, indicate new trends. And it is especially from the perspective of local bilingual members of the Slovene minority that we can anticipate commercial, cultural and social initiatives that seek to network and integrate local communities across old borders. While the lives of older representatives of this group are marked by the trauma of war and separation and a classic understanding of citizenship as the domain of the nation-state (Minnich 2000), younger bilinguals are more open to possibilities and commonalities on the other side of now dismantled borders. And in contrast to their predecessors they actively seek participation in suprastate institutions, such as various EU regional programmes, and global movements for human rights and environmental improvement that connect lives they perceive as rooted in their *Heimat* with these more global concerns. Within the relatively stable social order of the TBR citizenship beyond the state has potential to provide the basis for 'trans-ethnic' civil society.

Notes

1 And this perspective persists. In her recent presentation of 'language and identity in the border region of Austria and Slovenia' (2003) Brigitta Busch continues to assign primacy to ethnic identity and the nation-state in the construction of local collective self-understandings. She fails to acknowledge the possibility of alternative self-identifications where other forms of association are primary (Minnich 1996).

2 A banner entitled 'Eurpaeus sine finibus' with translations in the three local languages was hung over the Austrian–Italian border post between Thörl and Coccau following its dismantling in 1995.

3 In much of the literature on the break-up of Yugoslavia ethnic-nationalism has been emphasised as the primary motive for Slovenia's succession (e.g. Hayden 1993). As

others have noted (Muršič 2000) such an approach reveals very little about the socio-cultural (and de facto political) context in which this process transpired.

References

Armstrong, Warwick (2003) 'Culture, continuity and identity in the Slovene–Italian border region', in James Anderson, Liam O'Dowd and Thomas M. Wilson (eds) *Culture and Cooperation in Europe's Borderlands* (*European Studies* 19): 145–69.

Ballinger, Pamela (1996) 'The Istrian esodo: silences and presences in the construction of exodus', in Renata Jambrešić Kirin and Maja Povrzanović (eds) *War, Exile, Everyday Life: Cultural Perspectives*, Zagreb: Institute of Ethnology and Folklore Research.

Ballinger, Pamela (2003) *History in Exile: Memory and Identity at the Borders of the Balkans*, Princeton: Princeton University Press.

Buchovski, Michał (1996) 'The shifting meaning of civil and civic society in Poland', in Chris Hann and Elisabeth Dunn (eds) *Civil Society: Challenging Western Models*, London: Routledge.

Busch, Brigitta (2003) 'Shifting political and cultural borders: language and identity in the border region of Austria and Slovenia' in James Andersen, Liam O'Dowd and Thomas M. Wilson (eds) *Culture and Cooperation in Europe's Borderlands*, (*European Studies* 19): 125–144.

Burns, Robert K., Jr. (1963) 'The circum-alpine culture area: A preliminary view', *Anthropological Quarterly* 36 (3): 130–155.

Cohen, Jean and Andrew Arato (1994) *Civil Society and Political Theory*, Cambridge, MA: MIT Press.

Habermas, Jürgen (1989) *The Structural Transformation of the Public Sphere: An Inquiry into a Category of Bourgeois Society*, Cambridge: CUP.

Hann, Chris (1996) 'Introduction: political society and civil anthropology', in Chris Hann and Elisabeth Dunn (eds) *Civil Society: Challenging Western Models*, London: Routledge.

Hayden, Robert (1993) 'The triumph of chauvinistic nationalisms in Yugoslavia', in *War Among the Yugoslavs*, in David A. Kideckel and Joel M. Halpern (eds) *Anthropology of East Europe Review* 11 (1–2): 72–78.

Johnston, William M. (1983) *The Austrian Mind: An Intellectual and Social History 1848–1938*, Berkeley: University of California Press.

Kándut, Jakob (1982) 'Ku'adje' (manuscript from programmes presented on: Glas iz kanalske dolina (Radio Televisio Italiana – January 14 and 21).

Kann, Robert A. (1974) *A History of the Habsburg Empire: 1526–1918*, Berkeley: University of California Press.

Keane, John (1988) *Civil Society and the State: New European Perspectives*, London: Verso.

Klemenčič, Vladimir (1994) 'Narodne manjšine kot element politične, prostorske, socialne in ekonomske stvarnosti v alpsko-jadransko-panonskem prostoru', 1–8, in *Manjšine v prostoru Alpe-Jadran – zbornik referatov*, Ljubljana: Delovna skupnost Alpe-Jadran.

Marshall, T.H. (1964) *Class, Citizenship, and Social Development Essays*, New York: Doubleday.

Minnich, Robert Gary (1989) 'Tradition in the face of modernisation: cultural continuity and "deagrarisation" in the village of Ukve/Ugovizza, Kanalska dolina/Val Canale', *Slovene Studies – Toussaint Hočevar Memorial Issue* 11 (1–2): 97–108.

Minnich, Robert Gary (1996) 'The individual as author of collective identities: reconsidering identity formation within a multilingual borderland', in Irena Šumi & Salvatore Venosi (eds) *Večjezičnost na evropskih mejah – primer kanalske doline // Multilingualism on European Borders – The Case of Val Canale*, Val Canale, Italy: SLORI: 159–175.

Minnich, Robert Gary (1998) *Homesteaders and Citizens: Collective Identity Formation on the Austro-Italian Frontier*, Bergen: Norse Publications.

Minnich, Robert Gary (2000) 'Under the linden tree: a Slovenian life on a contested state frontier', in Joel Martin Halpern and David A. Kideckel (eds) *Neighbours at War: Anthropological Perspectives on Yugoslav Ethnicity, Culture and History*, 143–163, University Park, PA: Pennsylvania State University Press.

Moritsch, Andreas (1996) 'Geographische voraussetzungen der geschichte der Alpen-Adria-Region', (Working paper – stencil).

Moritsch, Andreas and G. Baumgartner (1992) 'The process of national differentiation within rural communities in Southern Carinthia and Southern Burgenland 1850–1940', *Comparative Studies on Governments and Non-Dominant Ethnic Groups, 1850–1940* 8: 99–143.

Muršič, Rajko (2000) 'The Yugoslav dark side of humanity: a view from the Slovene blind spot', in Joel Martin Halpern and David A. Kideckel (eds) *Neighbours at War, Anthropological Perspectives on Yugoslav Ethnicity, Culture and History*, University Park, PA: Pennsylvania State University Press: 56–77.

Neveu, Catherine (2000) 'European citizenship, citizens of Europe and European citizens', in Irène Bellier and Thomas M. Wilson (eds) *An Anthropology of the European Union: Building, Imagining and Experiencing the New Europe*, Oxford/New York: Berg: 119–135.

Pleterski, Janko (1996) *Slowenisch oder deutsch? Nationale Differenzierungsprozesse in Kaernten (1848–1914)*. Klagenfurt: Drava/VG.

Sahlins, Peter (1989) *Boundaries: The Making of France and Spain in the Pyrenees*, Berkeley: University of California Press.

Seligman, A. (1995) *The Idea of Civil Society*, New York: The Free Press.

Šumi, Irena (2000) *Kultura, etničnost, mejnost: konstrukcije različnosti v antropološki presoji*, Ljubljana: Založba ZRC.

Swartz, Marc J. (ed.) (1969) *Local-Level Politics: Social and Cultural Perspectives*, London: University of London Press.

Tester, Keith (1992) *Civil Society*, London: Routledge.

Turner, Bryan S. (1993) 'Outline of the theory of human rights', in Bryan S. Turner (ed.) *Citizenship and Social Theory*, London: Sage 162–90.

Veiter, Theodor (1961) 'Die volkspolitische Lage im Kanaltal: rechtsprobleme der Kanaltaler', *Ostdeutsche Wissenschaft VIII*: 437–68.

Wilson, Thomas M. and Hastings Donnan (1998) 'Nation, state and identity at international borders' in Thomas M. Wilson and Hastings Donnan (eds) *Border Identities: Nation, State and Identity at International Borders*, Cambridge: Cambridge University Press: 1–30.

12 Evolution and perspectives on intercultural coexistence at the Slovene–Italian border

Mateja Sedmak, Vesna Mikolič and Marina Furlan

Slovenia as a borderland: historical and geographic overview

Slovenia, once a republic within former Yugoslavia, became independent in 1991 following a plebiscite on 26 December 1990. Whereas former Yugoslavia had been characterised by religious, cultural and linguistic pluralism, Slovenia (with the exception of certain border areas) was far more homogeneous. As a consequence of four Habsburg territorial regions – Styria, Carinthia, Carniola and Gorizia – historically established in the area, the geographic region in which Slovenia lies has been one of cultural intertwining since the 1200s. Over the centuries Slovene territory was (at different times and to varying extents) incorporated into neighbouring states, each of which exerted its influence on the lives of the Slovene population (Bufon 2001).

As a small central European country, Slovenia has always been a border area. Its position is reflected in the fact that it is the only European country in which all major language groups of the continent coexist: Slavic, Romance, Germanic and Finno-Ugric. The influence of other cultures is most visible in those Slovene areas in direct contact with its neighbours. Significant Italian influence is present in western Slovenia; Austria's Germanic influence looms large in northern Slovenia; Hungarian influence is evident in the region of Prekmurje in the east; while Croatian influence is present in that border area from the south-east to the south-west of Slovenia. Although Slovenia is one of the youngest European states, its political borders were established in different periods and some are among the oldest European boundaries. Slovenia as a small country has laid emphasis on the relation between ethnic and political borders, while the specific definition of political boundaries has created tensions with Austria, Italy (Bufon 2001, 2004) and, recently, Croatia.

The following section examines a case study of the south-western area of Slovenia – Slovene Istria. Particular emphasis is laid on its border position and certain geopolitical, social, cultural, and ethnic characteristics there. To the north and south Slovene Istria borders with Italy and Croatia; it also borders the Adriatic Sea and contains three main municipalities – Koper, Piran, and Izola. The area is characterised by relative ethnic diversity, the outcome of a variety of historical, political, economic, and social processes. It is also permeated by national, language and religious pluralism as well as coexisting autochthonous Slovene and Italian populations. There are also immigrant groups from the republics of former Yugoslavia (Croats, Serbs, Macedonians, Bosnians, Albanians) whose mainly economically motivated migrations occurred in the post-war period, especially in the 1970s. This ethnic heterogeneity, with its elements of intercultural activity, occurs within the legal bilingualism of the Slovene and Italian languages and the historical and socio-economic connections between the two societies (Sedmak 2004). The border clearly influences neighbourly interactions and this is reflected in daily cross-border contacts and migration (for work, study, shopping, etc.).

The territorial concentration of diverse ethnic groups in a single geographic territory is also manifest in a relatively high number of ethnically mixed marriages (35 per cent). The region is thus marked by the highest degree of ethnic heterogamy in Slovenia. Life in a former Yugoslavia state with its ideology then (the principles of 'brotherhood and unity', absence of real and symbolic intercultural distance) encouraged the preservation of linguistic and cultural diversity. Combined with Slovene Istria's border status, these factors resulted in a relatively slight assimilation of immigrant groups into the dominant Slovene culture and language.

The Slovene–Italian border has evolved during centuries-long cohabitation. It was initially experienced as a perception that people 'over there' spoke a different language and had different habits, culture and ways of life. However, at the end of the eighteenth century, Europe started a complex and uneven process to evolve sovereign national states, culminating in the revolutions of 1848 – the 'Spring of Nations'. This latent feeling gained momentum and became one of the sources for ensuing ruthless political battles and wars.

In the nineteenth century, Italy (a part of the Austro-Hungarian Empire) began its struggle for independence and finally succeeded in 1861. Just five years later the Italians extended their eastern border by taking Venetian Slovenia from the Habsburgs. Later, between the two World Wars, the Slovenes in Slovene Istria and in present-day Friuli–Venezia Giulia (Italy) were subjected to Fascist rule and virtually excluded from public life. In 1941, eighty years after Italian independence, Fascist Italy, supported by Germany and Hungary, attacked and dismembered the Kingdom of Yugoslavia. Part of Slovenia was annexed and joined Italy, forming the 'Province of Ljubljana'. So the border between Slovenia and Italy ceased to exist for nearly three years (Darovec 1992, 2004).

A new border shift occurred after the Second World War when the Italian–Yugoslav border was moved back toward the Italian territory, and Slovenia became a republic of Yugoslavia. The winners pushed the border back and in so doing provoked the notorious 'Trieste Question' that puzzled the world for a decade; it was an early problem in the Cold War. After the Paris Peace Conference, the London Memorandum (1954), and the Treaty of Osimo (1975), however, the turbulent era seemed to pass, and relations between the two countries stabilised (Gombač 2001). Regionally, the status of the two autochthonous ethnic groups (Slovene and Italian) and related language policies in Slovene Istria and in Friuli–Venezia Giulia (the Italian region stretching along the entire Italian–Slovene border) changed a number of times. As a result of the border shifts the populations of both minorities fluctuated dramatically.

The 1910, Austro-Hungarian census data cited by Bufon (2001) reveal that approximately 30,000 Italians, representing nearly 80 per cent of the local population, lived in the coastal municipalities of Slovene Istria. Later, in the period just prior to the First World War, the Italians formed the majority in the coastal towns while Slovenes occupied the hinterland. On the other hand, identical data indicate the presence of approximately 130,000 Slovenes in the region of present-day Friuli–Venezia Giulia in Italy (Bufon 2001).

After the Second World War, the 1954 Memorandum of London was selected from four proposals for the delineation of the Italian–Slovene border primarily because it would settle similar minority numbers in either state (Bufon 2001). Subsequent events caused geopolitical modifications to the border and changes in the structure of the minority communities. Partially as a consequence of the Memorandum of London, state policy allowed Yugoslav citizens with Italian ethnic backgrounds to emigrate to Italy; this triggered mass emigration primarily (but not only) of Italian nationality citizens to Italy. The result of the emigration was a drastic decrease in the number of Italian community members.[1] The Slovene population became a majority in the coastal area of Slovene Istria while Italians formed the minority and organised themselves within the new social conditions. After 1961, the number of Italians in the Slovene coastal area stabilised at around 3,000. On the other hand, today the number of Slovenes in Italy, mainly living in Friuli–Venezia Giulia, is estimated at approximately 80,000.

Throughout the twentieth century and particularly in the period after the Second World War, intense assimilation pressures, especially in Italy, were exerted upon those of ethnic backgrounds different from that of the majority. At the same time the need to grant at least a certain degree of protection and rights to both minorities (Slovenes in Italy and Italians in Slovenia) became increasingly obvious. By signing the Memorandum of London, the Italian government agreed to afford the same rights to the majority and minority populations, including the right to use their mother tongues in informal and formal situations. In 1975, the Treaty of Osimo, signed by Yugoslavia and Italy, defined the reciprocal protection of minority rights. According to the treaty, contracted obligations included the right to education in the mother tongue. Moreover, according to the treaty confirmed by the Yugoslav constitution, legislation and municipal statutes, the Italian minority was granted the right to bilingualism and political involvement in Slovene Istria. However, the situation was quite different on the other side of the border where the rights of the Slovene minority were systematically violated during the post-war period.

After almost thirty years – in 1991 – the disintegration of Yugoslavia, the independence of Slovenia, and the war in the Balkans resulted in new political and territorial demarcations. One of these was the establishment of a new political border dividing the two newly independent Republics of Slovenia and Croatia. The new situation influenced people's perception of boundaries and their significance as well as issues of ethnicity and identity. The 1990s were characterised by growing nationalism, xenophobic intolerance, a redefinition of Slovene identity, cultural markers and attempts to differentiate Slovenia from other nations of the former Yugoslavia. However, in daily life, border people perceived these changes as intrusions into their intimate and business relations. At the end of the 1990s, normalisation and stabilisation of social life gradually took place. People living at the Italian and Croatian borders in Slovene Istria accepted the new social reality and political boundaries. However, this period did not last long. In May 2004, Slovenia joined the EU, and the minority issue and (cross-border) interethnic relations were confronted with new challenges.

The Slovene–Italian border as seen by its minorities

Minority policies and interethnic relations from 1945 to the 1990s

Although some interstate agreements such as the Treaty of Osimo grant both minorities an equal and reciprocal treatment of their linguistic and ethnic rights, the reality is quite different. Given the distinct social, economic and political post-war experience of the populations on both sides of the border, complete reciprocity of treatment was not possible. Slovene Istria with its Italian minority is officially bilingual, with both Italian and Slovene legalised. To comply with the law, all public notices must be written in both languages, both can be used in public offices and at public events the audience must be addressed in both languages. In order to reach this goal, bilingualism is not only promoted in schools for the minority community but also throughout the educational system.

In accordance with the Yugoslav–Italian agreements, Slovenia 'inherited' the same rights. Schools intended for children of the Italian minority are often referred to as 'education of the nationality' schools following the rationale and aims of a bilingual educational programme known as the 'maintenance' model. In such schools – except in the first year when the minority language is the sole medium of instruction – the majority language and its literature are taught as subjects, all remaining lessons being taught in the minority language. One of the main objectives here is the preservation of the minority language and culture and the parallel improvement in the knowledge of the majority language and culture. These are to be mastered to enable people later to function in the larger national context. The aim is to develop a functionally bilingual population. Schools for the majority population hold all lessons in the majority language (Slovene) while the minority language (Italian) is taught on a compulsory basis. According to the categorisation proposed by Skutnabb-Kangas and Garcia (Furlan 2001) this provides a 'two-way' bilingual educational model, in which pupils belong to both linguistic backgrounds, with the two languages used as media of instruction. Even here functional bilingualism is considered the most desirable outcome, representing a form of personal and social enrichment.

The situation is different in Italy. Only a few municipalities with Slovenes and Italians are regarded as partially bilingual with bilingual public inscriptions and documentation. Yet there is no bilingual schooling for majority population children.

This reveals an unequal situation where the minority language (Slovene) is taught in minority schools only, while the majority language is compulsory in every educational institution in the area. As with Italian minority schools in Slovenia, Slovene minority schools in Italy follow a 'maintenance' model educational programme, in which all lessons are held in the minority language except for majority language and literature tuition from the second grade of elementary school on. Majority schools in Italy not only fail to teach the minority language as a compulsory subject but rarely even offer it as an optional subject. Hence, Italian nationals must enrol in leisure-time courses to learn the language of the minority Slovenes. Along the border between Italy and Slovenia, then, only a few villages are officially considered bilingual and it is only in those villages that public inscriptions and documents are written in both languages; so, only in those few instances is the presence of the Slovene minority recognised by the local and state authorities.

In March 2001, after fifty years of continuous effort, the new protection law for the Slovene minority was enacted, raising hopes among the members of the Slovene community for the public use and protection of the Slovene language. But the new law has not been implemented in practice and the minority situation remains unchanged. One of the main obstacles to the application of the new directives is the power of influential right-wing local and national political groups.

As for interethnic and minority–majority relation, on the one hand, distinct ethnic and linguistic backgrounds exert an influence over minority and majority groups living in the same country. On the other, a different course of history on each side of the shared border has an impact on the evolution of minority and majority groups with the same ethno-linguistic background living in different countries. The result is two groups with the same ethno-linguistic background but with differences related to certain aspects of identity, lifestyle and ways of thinking.

As Pertot (1996) found in a 1996 study, most Slovene minority adolescents from Italy identify neither with Slovenes from Slovenia nor with Italians. They develop a particular identity – that of Slovenes from Italy – which is characterised by specific informal speech in which the Slovene and Italian languages are intermixed. Linguistically, something very similar is happening to Italian minority members in Slovenia who also 'mix' the Slovene and Italian languages, though not identifying so strongly with a 'particular' and 'locally defined' Italianism. Research conducted in 1999–2000 (Sedmak 2002), shows that most members of the Italian minority living in Slovenia can self-identify as Slovene citizens who speak Italian yet do not identify either with Italians from Italy or Slovenes from continental Slovenia. On the other hand, while members of the Italian community in Italy do not understand or speak Slovene unless they follow a leisure-time course, members of the Slovene majority in Slovene Istria learn Italian as a compulsory subject at school and can speak Italian, at least to some extent.

How does the learning of Italian affect the national identity, awareness and communicative competence in the first language of the Slovene majority? A study (Mikolič 2004) examining the correlation between Slovene national awareness and awareness of Italian culture among Slovenes living in Slovene Istria in 2001, indicates that belonging to a certain generational group is a vital factor accounting for differences in attitudes toward one's own and second cultures. The research shows that a positive attitude is most prominent among the youngest generation (aged 15–29) and declines gradually through the middle generations, and is lowest among the oldest generation (aged 75 and above).

Furthermore, communicative competence in the first and second languages – the level of bilingualism – is related to attitudes to one's own and second cultures. Weinreich (1953) and Fishman (1972) emphasise the importance of attitudes to one's own national culture and language at the level of communicative competence – even though the feeling of belonging to a cultural community does not necessarily imply a higher level of competence. A question that has existed for a long time in the bilingual environment of Slovene Istria is how to ensure that a higher level of ethnic awareness of one's own and second cultures as well as supranational cultural values might exert a positive influence on the level of bilingualism – or vice versa, how the mastery of both languages might contribute to a better understanding of both cultures and consequently lead to better relations between the two national communities. In the immediate post-Second World War years the designers of the bilingual system in Slovene Istria asked themselves this question. Even though the realisation of the proposed model of bilingualism considerably deviates from the original, research indicates that, since the 1950s, the institutionalised bilingualism in the ethnically mixed area of Slovene Istria has borne fruit – as will be shown in the next section.

Research by Mikolič (2004) that has examined the ethnic awareness and communicative competence of speakers of the majority community in Slovene Istria confirms the influence of the attitude to one's own and second cultures on communicative competence. Higher national awareness leads to superior communicative competence in Slovene while greater awareness of the Italian culture leads to higher communicative competence in Italian.

It is not surprising, therefore, that a more positive attitude to Italian culture among the young in the Slovene community is also reflected in the highest level of bilingualism of this age group. So, we can conclude that organised bilingual education in Slovene Istria has generated the desired results. However, research also showed that while education enhances communicative competence it does not influence the attitude to one's own and second cultures. This leads to the conclusion that awareness and openness to Italian culture as well as the level of bilingualism of the young are also influenced by other factors; these include a positive attitude to European unification and worldwide globalisation processes as well as international connections, contacts with members of the Italian minority and the appeal of Italian culture as depicted by the Italian media. The last, especially television, has played a vital role here. Until recently, Italian television programmes, particularly those of private television stations, were very popular among the young because of their accessibility and dynamic content.

But after independence, the situation in the Slovene media market changed and only time will provide an answer regarding the significance this has for the knowledge of Italian culture and language among the youth in Slovene Istria. On the other hand, those fearing that excessive openness of the youth to the Italian culture and language might contribute to the weakening of Slovene national awareness and mastery of the Slovene language have welcomed these changes. The research (Mikolič 2004) also shows interdependence between the attitudes to the Slovene and Italian cultures among the young; this indicates that people can develop positive attitudes to both cultures while retaining their own cultural identity. The same is true for other generational groups, with the exception of those born in the years from 1941 to 1955, for whom Slovene national awareness and the awareness of Italian culture proved to be inversely proportional. Undoubtedly, these phenomena can be explained by the fact that these generations grew up in the period immediately after the downfall of the Fascist regime and were taught to hate a system known for its cruelty and totalitarian methods; consequently they tended to equate all Italians with Fascism.

The research also indicated that mastery of the Italian language is no obstacle to communicative competence in Slovene; the results show a proportional relation between communicative competences in both languages. In other words, a higher communicative competence in one language suggests the same in the other. Bilingualism, therefore, only represents a problem for those speakers whose competence in either language is poor anyway. National awareness among the majority population in Slovene Istria therefore does not exclude a positive attitude to the Italian culture and language; instead it fosters a high level of linguistic ability in Italian as a second language, with proportional competence in both.

A specific form of interethnic relations is found in ethnically mixed families. At the micro-level of everyday family life in Italian–Slovene families, diverse elements of both cultures coexist. Slovene Istria is distinguished by the highest level of ethnic heterogamy in Slovenia – up to 35 per cent – while ethnic heterogamy in the smaller Italian community, is as high as 68.5 per cent. Given the intense dynamics of interethnic relations within the ethnically mixed family, the next section examines such dynamics within Slovene–Italian families in Slovene Istria. Research carried out on a sample of Slovene–Italian mixed couples shows a clearly expressed tendency of the Italian minority (compared, say, with the immigrants from former Yugoslavia married to Slovenes) to preserve their mother tongue in intra-family communication, and also to transfer their mother tongue to their children (Sedmak 2002). This can partially be explained by the official bilingualism in the region (the element of the 'self-evident presence' of the Italian language) and partially by intergroup cultural closeness if not uniformity given that both ethnicities emphasise language as the only element of group identification and differentiation.

The prevailing pattern of partner and family communication in these mixed marriages is thus a simultaneous use of both language systems where the Italian and Slovene partners speak to the children in their own language. Consequently, the children are mostly bilingual. It is interesting that, among female members of the Italian minority, we note an explicit wish to speak to their children in their mother tongue 'all the time'. This contrasts with immigrants from former Yugoslavia who speak exclusively in Slovene or a mix of languages. Language appears as the sole means for preserving group identity and Italian ethnicity, and the bilingual environment and the historically 'self-evident' presence of Italians are sufficient to preserve Italian within the family.

As far as language is concerned, a kind of duality with respect to the Italian minority can be seen: on one hand, the perception and consequent use of language as a means of expression where different languages are used to achieve highest information efficiency – spontaneous code-switching depending on conversation content and linguistic situations – was evident. On the other hand, there is a conscious attempt to preserve the Italian language as one of the most important elements of group identification/differentiation 'at any cost'. The general awareness of a complex linguistic situation as well as the tendency to preserve Italian within mixed family communication is more often identified among people with higher levels of education, while the tendency to preserve Italian is often closely associated with the wish to preserve the Italian ethnic community as such (Sedmak 2002).

Additionally, the (otherwise completely unproblematic) linguistic situation in Italian–Slovene marriages has proved to be challenging in those cases in which the Slovene partner is not a local, born in the border area, but is an intrastate migrant from another Slovene region. In these cases, the presence of the Italian language in the family communication can provoke radical conflict situations, to quote the words of one Slovene partner, with 'strangers in their own house'. Finally, to better understand the status of Italian–Slovene ethnically mixed families, let us picture a 'typical' reaction of a broad family network to a family member entering an ethnically mixed marriage. It can be described as neutral or positive if the marriage is with a member of the Italian minority (for Slovene parents born and socialised in the cultural context of Slovene Istria); it is, in fact, marriage to 'a local' or 'one of us' (Sedmak 2002).

Considering the above, the least that can be said is that a milestone in attitudinal development among the population on both sides of the border – valid for Slovene and Italian cultures of all generations – was undoubtedly the independence of the Republic of Slovenia.

Slovenia's independence – an important factor for change in ethnic awareness

Beyond doubt, the birth of a new state and the establishment of new borders are significant in triggering psychological and social shifts in the ethnic identity of both majority and minority communities. Thus, the creation of an independent Slovenia led to changes in national awareness – a higher degree of ethnic awareness among Slovenes individually and at the community level. At the macro level, this signified a big step in stimulating national confidence, while among individuals it marked a growing conviction that everyone could engage in social (also international) interaction with greater confidence.

The consequences of these changes are reflected in the Slovene–Italian border area. Slovenes, both as a minority in Italy and a majority in Slovenia, have developed an increased concern for their own community. The feeling of the Slovene minority on the Italian side of the border that the Slovene motherland is not determined enough in the enforcement of its rights can be understood, given the fact that the minority protection legislation, in many respects a compromise, was passed as late as a decade after the independence of Slovenia (in March 2001). Then, in the 1990s, pressures to reduce acquired rights granted to the Italian community were recorded. One example was the demand to introduce monolingual or bilingual documents (e.g. identity cards) although it is a legal requirement that all official documents issued in this area be bilingual. During this period an attempt was made to restrict Italian as an obligatory subject solely to elementary education and cancel it in majority secondary school curricula. Although these pressures yielded no result and the protection of the Italian community remained unaltered, a paradoxical feeling of confidence and concurrent endangerment can be sensed among the majority in certain areas of Slovene Istria.

As a result of a millennia-long Romance cultural tradition and fear of Slavicism, similar feelings of 'superiority' are noticeable among members of the Italian minority but most of all among right-wing political circles in the Italian region of Friuli–Venezia Giulia. It can be inferred that the independence of Slovenia and all parallel processes in Slovene society have exacerbated these feelings. Thus, the Italian minority has become more distrustful, and Italian state right-wing circles have been making louder criticisms of the Slovene state. If, in Slovene Istria, politicians, experts and the wider public seemed to share a common opinion that the area is a meeting point of autochthonous cultures – Slovene and Italian and, close by in Croatian Istria, Croatian culture – and those of other immigrant groups, such an opinion was scarcely shared by the majority in the Trieste region and the wider area of Friuli–Venezia Giulia.

The establishment of Slovenia as a new nation-state was accompanied by the raising of Slovene national awareness in the 1990s, the reinstatement of Slovene identity, and attempts to differentiate itself from the rest of former Yugoslavia. The processes of identification and differentiation were accompanied by increasing nationalism, xenophobia and tendencies toward cultural and linguistic purity. The war in the Balkans and the general discontent which followed the period of great economic and political changes mostly affected Serbian immigrants, although members of other nationalities also reported increasing intolerance directed especially at 'linguistically unassimilated' immigrants. Serbo-Croatian had been considered the official Yugoslav language of the army and state public administration and Slovene children were taught it at primary school. But the use of Slovene in public as well as in private situations has now replaced it. Ethnically mixed marriages were, however, particularly affected by intolerance against their children. Slovene independence and increased nationalism thus had a significantly heavier impact on interethnic relations between Slovenes and members of nations of former Yugoslavia than on Slovene–Italian relations.

In the early post-war period, Italian initiatives led Slovenes along the

Slovene–Italian border to believe that there would be further claims by Italy on Slovene territory. One action offered Italian citizenship to Slovene citizens from Slovene Istria who could prove evidence of Italian ethnic background or national affiliation. As a result, many Slovene citizens applied for, and were granted, dual citizenship. Some applied for symbolic reasons, others for clearly pragmatic ones – for instance, to increase their employment opportunities in Italy.

However, in the second half of the 1990s, normalisation of interethnic relations began and people gradually began accepting the new political divisions between Slovenia and the former Yugoslav republics as well as new interstate relations. This is particularly true for younger generations, not burdened by history and past interethnic conflicts. In that period public opinion concentrated more on issues related to European integration and the potential accession of Slovenia to the European Community.

Slovenia as a new member of the European Union

Slovene accession to the EU was expected to result in a new period of border-related changes. Rather than the establishment of new borders, old borders (among them the Slovene–Italian border) would be dissolved, allowing a more spontaneous intercultural coexistence, in addition to the lessening of still more persistent mental interethnic boundaries.

On 1 May 2004, Slovenia officially became a member of the European community. But what is happening in reality? Do people living in the Slovene–Italian border area really perceive Slovenia as an equal partner? Can they suddenly cancel years of political and economic differences, ethnic and linguistic prejudice, and negative or indifferent attitudes toward the 'cross-border' neighbouring population and adjust to a partnership based on equality and cooperation principles? The following section examines the impact of Slovene accession to the EU on attitudes towards, and the status of, minority communities on both sides of the Slovene–Italian border.

Although Slovenes and Italians (especially in the border area) from different fields of interest (science, education, trade, technology, etc.) cooperate in many projects financed by the European Union (e.g. INTERREG projects) or local authorities, the 'old' border still exists in the minds of many inhabitants not used to the new social and political reality. Slovenia's accession to the EU and the formal dissolution of the border awakened old memories and resentments, especially among right-wing political parties on both sides of the border. The abolition of the political border, then, provided the opportunity for the revisiting of injustices allegedly suffered in the post-war period by both Slovenia and Italy concerning lost territory, post-war victimisation, collaborationism, and related problems.

The fears present among certain Slovene political circles and individuals that, with the opening of the Slovene market to European capital, Slovenia would soon be sold out to foreigners needs to be seen in the schizophrenic context of mutual cooperation and concomitant ethnic differentiation. The law conditioning

Slovenia's accession to the EU was launched in autumn 2003 and acknowledged European citizens' rights to purchase real estate in Slovenia; this aroused fear and disapproval among those convinced that foreign capital would shape the Slovene real-estate market. Moreover, they feared that entire coastal lands would be sold to Italians, especially to those claiming to be from Slovene Istria and forced to leave during the mass exodus of earlier years. Italian right-wing parties expressed a similar fear – that after becoming citizens of the EU, Slovenes would 'buy Trieste' to compensate for the sense of loss they had experienced when the Trieste area, heavily populated by Slovenes, became part of Italy.

Soon after 2004, Italian right-wing circles expressed dissatisfaction with Slovenia domestically and in interstate relations; they argued that autochthonous Italians who, after the Second World War, had fled from Istria to Italy were forced to do so and had unjustifiably lost their property. Certainly the Memorandum of London stated that before 1956 all inhabitants of Italian ethnic background willing to do so should be allowed to emigrate; yet it must be added that the Memorandum was accompanied by Italian mass propaganda inviting all of Italian background to move back. It is also true that the emigration of numerous Italians was 'facilitated' by Yugoslav policy that was – from past war experience – anything but favourable toward Italians. Ever since the Second World War, exiled individuals and political parties claiming to defend their interests have tried to reclaim property on the grounds that they have been unfairly expropriated and their property should thus be returned to their 'legitimate' owners.

Among Italian right-wing circles Slovenia's accession to the EU raised questions of post-war crimes and attempts to criminalise partisans in their wartime struggle. The policy of criminalisation and inculpation of the Slovene and Croatian states, as well as pressures for moral and material retribution, existed at both national and local levels. Another question that has largely remained unsolved and kept in silence was that of 'foibas': the natural caves in the Kras plateau surrounding the city of Trieste were, at the war's end, converted into mass graves for collaborators executed by the partisans. The Italian right argues that the mere existence of 'foibas' is sufficient reason for not accepting Slovenia as an equal EU partner.

Furthermore, Slovene–Italian national conflicts over their past border and today's formally non-existent border touch upon the question of the sea border. Political relations were upset by Italy's one-sided implementation of the ecological-fishing zone without informing either Slovenia or Croatia. The intensity of the conflict grew after Italian accession to Slovene–Croatian negotiations on the sea border. A key moment emerged when the Italian–Croatian agreement respecting the epicontinental shelf in the Adriatic Sea excluded Slovenia. In a period of lively political and social change these border and interstate events clearly influence local interethnic and cross-border relations, as can be seen in the omnipresent media coverage, initiatives and activities of civil society as well as daily lay discourse.

What is the role assumed by the Slovene and Italian minorities in this situation? Recent research (Sedmak 2005) indicates that members of neither minority expect significant changes after the Slovene accession to the EU, yet they do hope for greater support and intervention by their homelands. The Slovene minority, in particular, has not yet lost hope that its motherland might be more determined to protect and improve its status in Italy. Moreover, the recent closure of the Slovene Bank in Italy, accompanied by a total absence of support from the Slovene state, may also result in disastrous consequences for the (economic) vitality and power of the Slovene minority. On the whole, members of neither minority regard Slovenia's accession to the EU as an opportunity to move to their 'homelands'. EU membership, however, seems to be influencing a growing number of decisions to study or work in their homelands. It appears that the younger generations, less burdened by prejudice and history, are more willing to start life in the spirit of a united Europe and good interethnic and neighbourly relations.

Conclusion

Intercultural coexistence along the Slovene–Italian border has a long and variable history, marked by political decisions that have changed political borders, changed the status of minorities on both sides of the border, and changed rights granted both minorities by the two states.

Throughout the post-war period, the status of the Italian minority in Slovene Istria was generally distinguished by a gradual implementation of minority rights and a wider acceptance of the minority presence and rights among the majority Slovene population. Despite attempts to reduce statutory and actual rights granted to the Italian minority during crucial socio-political changes (Slovene independence and its accession to the EU), the position of the Italian minority in Slovenia can be described as at least favourable. The formal protection of the Italian minority in Slovenia exceeds levels defined by EU directives concerning minority rights. The self-assessed high degree of satisfaction with their own (minority) status and rights is revealed in the results of a comprehensive study of members of the Italian minority (Sedmak 2005) This follows previous research indicating that both the Slovene majority population and various immigrant groups acknowledge that the Italian autochthonous minority has a special status and accept that special rights derive from it. So, compared to immigrant groups, the Italian minority is granted broader rights in the preservation of the mother tongue and its public use, in education, and political participation. These greater rights derive from its autochthonous status *per se* (Sedmak *et al.* 2002).

The status of the Slovene minority in Italy is quite different and is generally marked by a continual struggle to acquire and implement at least some minority rights. Its status is thus characterised by an entirely different reality and social dynamic that profoundly influence the self-concept of the minority as well as interethnic relations in general. The Slovene minority expresses dissatisfaction with Italy and its authorities because of constant violations of essential minority rights concerning the use of the mother tongue and other rights. It is also dissatisfied with the motherland – the Slovene state – and resents the absence of interest in minority issues and the failure in the negotiations on interstate relations and Slovene minority rights.

But everyday levels of social life and Slovene–Italian relations on both sides of the border are less problematic than interethnic relations at the macro political level. The micro level is characterised by a high number of ethnically mixed marriages, widespread kinship networks on both sides of the border, everyday interethnic contacts, and daily migrations for work, shopping, school, or informal socialising.

With Slovenia's accession to the EU, the Slovene–Italian border has lost its formal purpose. But, although the local population may notice the absence of border customs checkpoints, a year later the increased presence of border police cannot be overlooked. The border, therefore, not only remains in evidence because of the long queues of vehicles waiting to cross it or the presence of the police, but also because of historical memory and long experience in the minds of people that cannot simply be forgotten. As might be expected, we will need 'something more' than the formal dissolution of official political boundaries and cross-border cooperation in the form of European INTERREG and other project initiatives to reduce the gap between the Italian and Slovene cultural spaces. A momentous step to make would be that towards knowledge and awareness of common historical coexistence, the possibilities and benefits of cooperation, and respect for both one's own and the other's culture and language.

Note

1 After the end of the Second World War, in 1945, Slovene Istria was, first, part of Zone B of Venezia Giulia and then Zone B of the Free Territory of Trieste, and was finally annexed by the Federal People's Republic of Yugoslavia after the Memorandum of London in 1954. In accordance with that treaty, all citizens of Italian nationality were given the right to emigrate to Italy within a limited period of time (by the beginning of the year 1956). The treaty having made clear that Istria would not be part of Italy, a mass emigration (exodus) was triggered, primarily, but not exclusively, of Italian citizens to Italy. After the emigration of Italians (and Slovenes and Croats), Slovenes from the neighbouring villages and other Slovene regions as well as inhabitants of other nationalities immigrated to the towns of Slovene Istria.

References

Bufon, M. (2001) 'Slovenia: a Central European border country' in International Scientific Conference, 'Borders as barriers and bridges – a comparative look at three borderlands: Slovenia/Italy, Ireland/Northern Ireland, West Mediterranean', Koper 14–16 September, *Abstracts*, Koper: Science and Research Centre of the Republic of Slovenia, 39–40.

Bufon, M. (2004) *Med teritorialnostjo in globalnostjo (Between Territoriality and Globalism)*, Koper: Založba Annales.

Darovec, D. (1992) *Pregled zgodovine Istre (A Brief History of Istria)*, Koper: Zgodovinsko društvo za južno Primorsko in Primorske novice.

Darovec, D. (2004) *Davki nam pijejo kri (The Taxes Are Drinking our Blood)*, Koper: Založba Annales.

Eriksen, H.T. (1993) 'Ethnicity and nationalism', *Anthropological Perspectives*, London, Boulder, CO: Pluto Press.

Fishman, J.A. (1972) *The Sociology of Language*, Rowley, MA: Newbury House.

Furlan, M. (2001) 'Mladostnikova osebnost in njegove socialne vrednote v dvojezičnem okolju' (Personality and social values of adolescents in a bilingual environment), Ph.D. thesis. Filozofska fakulteta, Univerza v Ljubljani, Ljubljana.

Furlan, M. (2004) 'Socialno integracijska vloga šole v območjih kulturnega stika in družbenega povezovanja na primeru slovensko–italijanske meje. Uvod k zaključni študiji istoimenskega projekta', (Social-integrative role of the school in areas of cultural contact and social integration – a case study of the Slovene–Italian border. Introduction to the concluding project study), UP – ZRS, Koper, 2002, unpublished material for internal use.

Furlan-Pahulje, M. (1999) 'Renovation of the educational system of the Italian minority: the analysis of needs and a proposal of novelties', *Annales* 16, serie historia et sociologia, 9, 1, 155–60.

Gombač, B.M. (2001) 'Between conflict and friendship. Solving the problems of the border between Slovenia and Italy', in International Scientific Conference, 'Borders as barriers and bridges – a comparative look at three borderlands: Slovenia/Italy, Ireland/Northern Ireland, West Mediterranean', Koper 14–16 September, *Abstracts*, Koper: Science and Research Centre of the Republic of Slovenia, 18–27.

Kellas, J.G. (1991) *The Politics of Nationalism and Ethnicity*, London: Macmillan.

Kymlicka, W. (1995) *Multicultural Citizenship*, Oxford: Clarendon Press.

Mikolič, V. (2000) 'Vloga narodne pripadnosti in narodne zavesti v sodobnih integracijskih procesih' (The role of national affiliation and national awareness in modern integration processes), *Anthropos* 3/4, 159–79.

Mikolič, V. (2004) 'Jezik v zrcalu kultur' (Language in the mirror of cultures), Koper: Založba *Annales*.

Pertot, S. (1996) *'J1 proti J2: Iskanje referenčnega modela' (L1 versus L2: a quest for a referential model)*, Trst: IRRSAE.

Sedmak, M. (2002) 'Kri in kultura. Etnično mešane zakonske zveze' (Blood and culture. Ethnically-mixed marriages). Koper, Založba *Annales*.

Sedmak, M. (2004) 'Dinamika medetničnih odnosov v slovenski Istri: avtohtoni versus priseljeni' (The dynamics of interethnic relations in Slovene Istra: autochthonous versus immigrants) *Annales, serie historia et sociologia* 14, 2, 291–302.

Sedmak, M. *et al.* (2002) 'Identiteta slovenske Istre, 1. delovni zvezek, predstavitev rezultatov raziskave', (Identity of Slovene Istria, Workbook 1, presentation of research results), Koper: Znanstveno-raziskovalno središče Republike Slovenije Koper.

Sedmak, M. (2005) 'A comparative analysis of the minority groups living on the Slovene–Italian borderline' (A case study of the Slovene minority in Italy and the Italian minority in Slovenia), Second Project Report, Koper: University of Primorska Science and Research Centre.

Weinreich, U. (1953) *Languages in Contact: Findings and Problems*: New York: Linguistic Circle of New York.

13 Ideologies of 'Fortress Europe' in two Slovenian–Croatian borderlands

Case studies from Žumberak and Bela Krajina[1]

Duška Knežević Hočevar

Have international borders mattered in social anthropology since 1989?

Among the many radical political transformations in Europe since 1989, the fall of the Berlin Wall, the dissolution of Yugoslavia, and the establishment of the European Union have attracted particular attention. And the 'new realities' have prompted a more systematic research agenda in many social science disciplines related to political borders. Within social and cultural anthropology, attention has been given to studying the international borders (Donnan and Wilson 1999) with a 'distinct sub-genre of studies enquiring more systematically into aspects of social life in the immediate vicinity of borders and the social organisation of "borderlands"' (Hann 2001, 73). Groundwork for anthropological debates on borders and borderlands was laid by the anthropologist Fredrick Barth in his seminal discussion of social boundaries (1969).[2] Social anthropologists have since significantly contributed to clarifying the processes of social transition and transformation in nations as well as nationalism in Europe during the 1990s.

From an anthropological point of view, this chapter examines the processes of border transformation that were triggered by the dissolution of Socialist Yugoslavia in 1991, and the consequences of the European Union enlargement for two communities along the Slovenian–Croatian border region: the south-western Žumberačka krajina in Croatia, and Bela Krajina in Slovenia. Redefinitions of the border regimes from an administrative Slovenian–Croatian border within the Yugoslav federative state to a non-EU international border after the dissolution of Yugoslavia in 1991 and finally to the present external border of 'Fortress Europe' have made deep impacts: at both national level and among local communities, specific understandings of the past, present and future border regimes, and the role of the people living alongside the border in these processes have occurred. The chapter, then, focuses on the ways in which local practices and attitudes interact with the changing geopolitics.

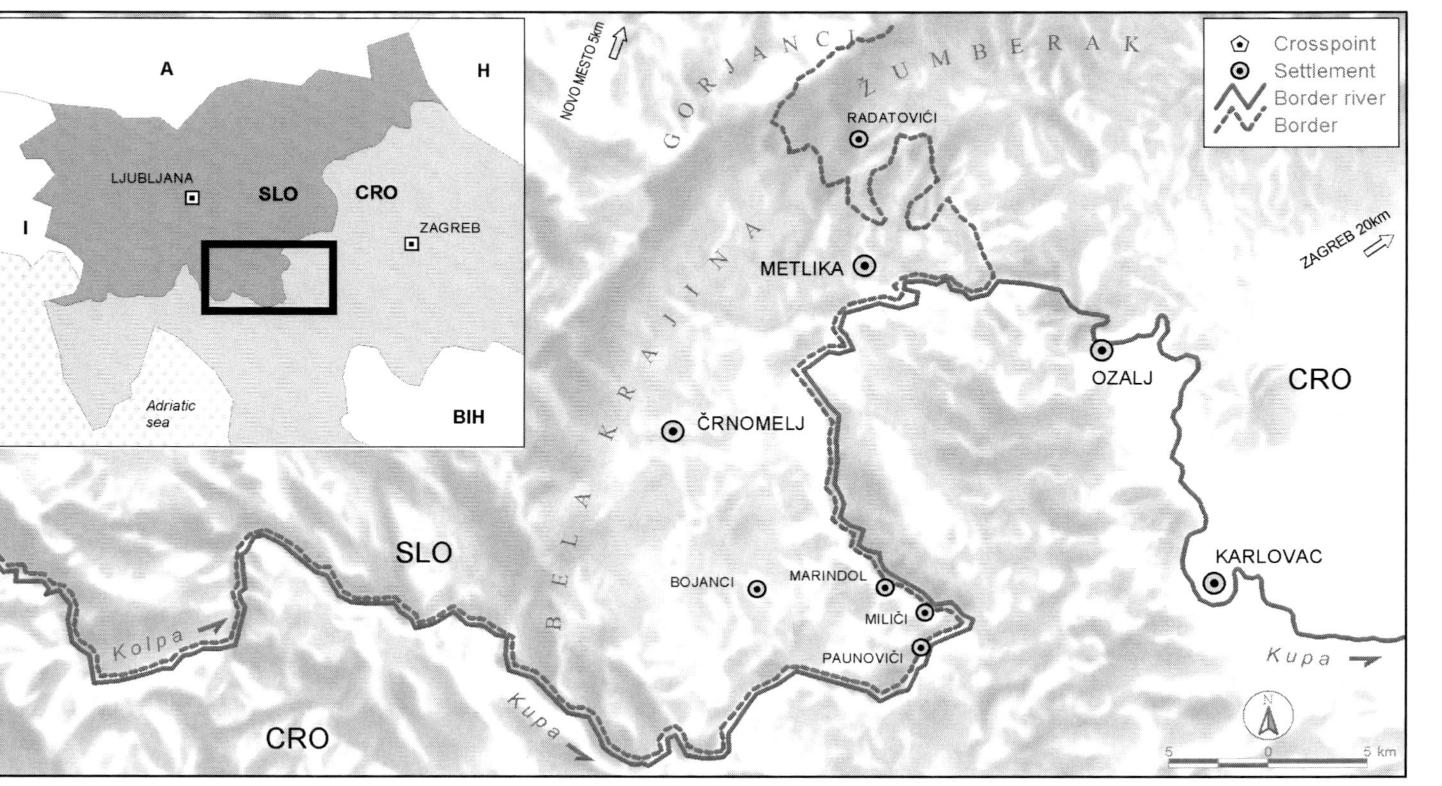

Figure 13.1 The Slovenian–Croatian border[3]

At the Southern frontier

Since Slovenian independence in 1991, the Slovenian media have expressed controversial views about the nature of the new Slovenian–Croatian international border. According to several journalist reports of the time,[4] certain people, a minority, proposed a permeable border, merely an invisible demarcation line. The majority, however, demanded the 'closing of national space' by building a solid 'wall against the dangerous Balkans'. The latter view was shared also by the Slovenian group of territorial experts who, in the period of intense preparations for independence (1989–1991), devised a secret action plan: Kamen (Stone). This plan created provisional security measures at the future border between the two sovereign states; these included the building of improvised customs points, further checkpoints deeper into the border zone and several refugee centres (Čelik 1994, 27). The building of a clearly demarcated and controllable frontier between Slovenia and Croatia at the beginning of the 1990s culminated in the construction of several bunkers in place of the shelters that were built in another Slovenian border county along the border with Croatia. The Slovenian press criticised this measure, asking rhetorically, 'Does this mean the beginning of a bunker democracy?' (Žunec 1992, 11). Believers in a 'Europe without borders' protested against the heavily policed regime along the Slovenian–Croatian border; instead of a policed border on the margins of the European Union, they argued for a politics of 'openness and cooperation' (Žunec 1992, 13).

Yet the voices raised in favour of rigorous measures along the prospective international border prevailed. It was argued that the regime was necessary as a consequence of the wars in former Yugoslavia and the expectations of the European Union for maintaining well-secured gates to keep out illegal migration, smuggling and other crime. A state secretary of the Ministry of Internal Affairs asserted that, by implementing thorough control at the border with Croatia and Hungary, Slovenia was living up to Europe's expectations. Gradually but beyond doubt, Slovenia needed to gain the reputation of a new European state fully capable of controlling waves of illegal immigration into Western Europe (Šimunič 1995, 2).

'Blood is thicker than water'

In the early 1990s, mounting political tensions and conflicts across the former Yugoslavia encouraged the then Slovenian police force, the People's Militia, to pay more attention to the population in the border regions. The inhabitants of four border villages in the lower Kolpa river valley, in the region of Bela krajina, are descendants of Uskoki,[5] largely self-professed ethnic Serbs of the Eastern Orthodox faith; these people were particularly under close observation. According to the ex-head of the Slovenian People's Militia, Pavle Čelik, the police were aware that 'blood is thicker than water', and were gravely concerned about the villagers' potential response to political provocations by Serbs in Croatia whose activities often took place near the Slovenian border (Čelik 1994, 22). Moreover, these

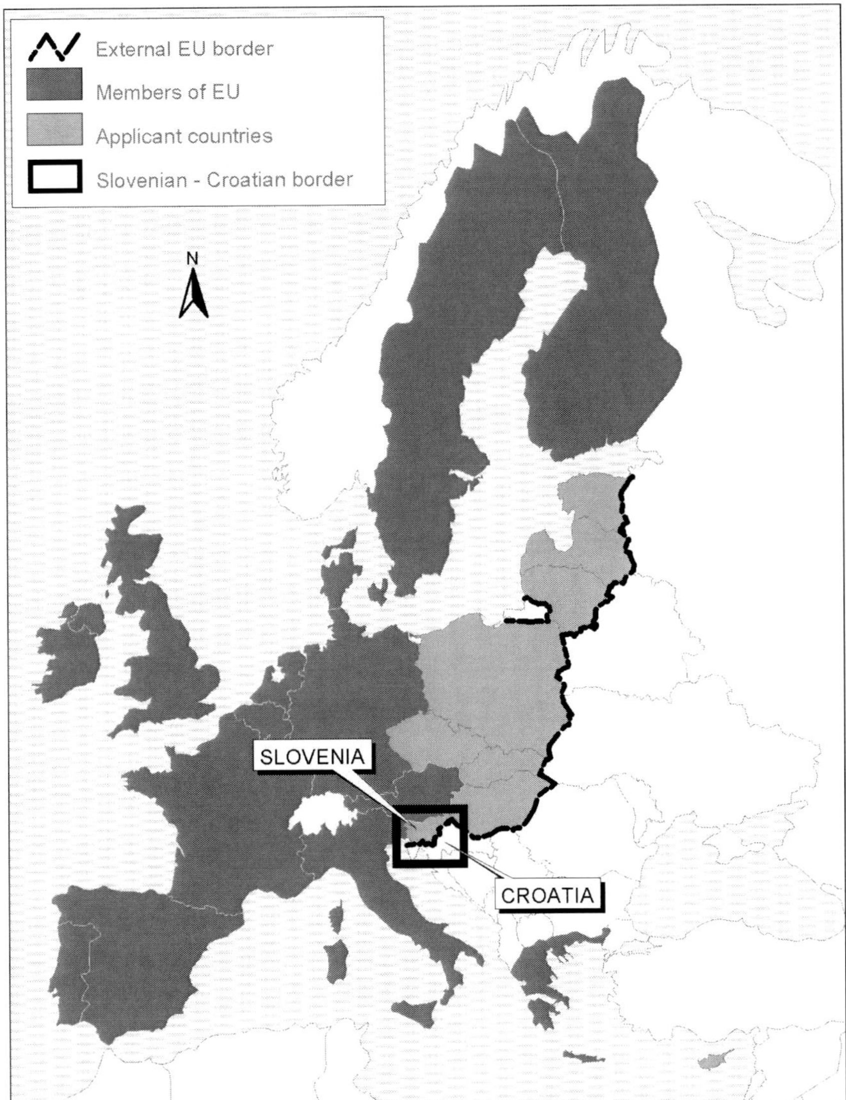

Figure 13.2 The contested frontier as presented in the media

locals were recognised as 'our people' by nationalistic agitators from Belgrade. Overnight, the fewer than three hundred Slovenian citizens of self-proclaimed Serbian origin in the border villages Bojanci, Marindol, Miliči and Paunoviči became a 'hot topic' in the speculations about their 'origin' and loyalties.

In 1989, the Serbian weekly *Politika* (Politics) announced that being an autochthonous Serb in Slovenia is tantamount to severe underdevelopment, a life without basic commodities such as a healthy water supply, and a life deprived of education in one's mother tongue (Laketić 1989). Following this dramatically poetic description of the miserable conditions of the Serbs in the four villages, the journalist praised their autochthonous history as descendants of the Uskoki, ancestors who had settled the area during the sixteenth century. In corroboration of such a miserable image of the Serbs in Slovenia followed a letter from the Committee of Serbs from Marindol and Bojanci, published by the Slovenian media in 1989. In the letter, addressed to the Yugoslav Federal Assembly, the villagers protested at the closing of a school in Serbo-Croatian language, and public neglect of their culture and customs. Upon the publication, however, the locals were quick to deny authorship, insisting that it was in 'someone's interest to impose lies upon them' (Čontala 1989, 26).

In 1990, the residents from the 'problematic' border settlements voted for an 'independent Slovenia' with 90.78 percent of the votes in favour. Their village representative commented on this score in an interview published in the major Slovenian daily *Delo* (Labour):

> This outcome clearly shows how much we are allegedly endangered. It proves that we feel comfortable in the place where we live and where our ancestors lived for centuries. Voting in favour of an independent Slovenia has nothing to do with nationality, but reflects the reality in which we see clearly the position of Slovenia in the present Yugoslavia such as it is. Our decision is quite logical as we are part of our environment and will continue to be in the future. Therefore we feel and think just like all other people in Bela Krajina and Slovenia.
>
> (Dimitrić 1990, 3)[6]

Another group of descendants of the Uskoki – the residents of south-western Žumberak – experienced similar complications. Predominantly Greek Catholics, these people partly live in Bela Krajina in the Slovenian borderland; a larger settlement area is Žumberačka Krajina in the Croatian borderland (see Figure 13.2 above). In 1990, a year before Slovenian independence, the Slovenian press reported on their fears concerning the imposition of an international border that would cut off the vital interactions between Slovenia and Croatia (Kuljaj 1990, 11). As borderlanders of the lower Kolpa valley, they voted in favour of an independent Slovenia. Moreover, the people in South-western Žumberak publicly announced that after the dissolution of Yugoslavia, they would wish their home territory to be annexed to Slovenia because of their vital dependency on the Slovenian hinterlands.

In their claimed role as descendants of Serbs and Montenegrins, the Žumberčani were widely identified as natural 'blood allies' of Serbian nationalism. Both the Slovenian and Croatian press continually reported on Serbian emissaries who conspired in Bela krajina and Žumberak (Kranjc 1991, 27). In response to such allegations, the Mayors of Metlika and Črnomelj, the two border counties where the majority of Žumberčani live in Slovenia, organised a round table discussion on these local 'hot issues'. In the discussion on political provocations in Bela Krajina, and the prospects of everyday life along the Slovenian–Croatian border, a member of the Slovenian presidency stressed that the Slovenian government would insist on an open boundary with Croatia and would refrain from any attempts to annex any Croat territory (Kranjc 1991, 27). Yet in 1992, the Žumberčani from the Croatian local communities of Radatovići and Dragoševci presented the Slovenian and Croatian parliaments, and the political elite in Ozalj and Metlika, with a 'Petition for annexation to the Slovenian Republic' (Čelik 1994, 103). In the petition, they argued that traffic routes in the area are naturally connected to the economic centres in Slovenia, and summarised the short history of the administrative divisions: until 1865, south-western Žumberak belonged to the imperial Province of Carniolia; from then and until 1929 to Croatia; from 1929 to 1941 to Dravska banovina,[7] and finally, after the Second World War, again to Croatia (Čelik 1994, 104).

After Slovenian independence in 1991, the media continued to report on political provocations in the area. In 1993, the public in Slovenia heard an alarming estimate that 20,000 of 26,000 residents in Bela Krajina were Serbs. This 'realistic number' was arrived at by the members of the Party for the Equality of Citizens in Slovenia (Dimitrić 1993, 2). Yet the president of the Party denied the entire claim two days later (Zorič 1993, 2).

In late 1993, another incident stirred the Slovenian public. In a press handout, the members of the Serbian Cultural Centre allegedly informed the Slovenian prime minister, the government and some foreign media that the Centre had established the Serbian autonomous area in Bela Krajina, following the example of their fellow Serbs in Croatia (Bauer 1993, 2). The representative of the Serbian community, however, denied the news, criticising it as political provocation (Zakrajšek 1993, 3). Finally, the members of the Slovenian National Party in Bela krajina insisted that Slovenians in Metlika were a minority endangered by non-Slovenians (Budja 1994, 14).

Media reports on the contested frontier between Slovenia and Croatia were the starting point of my fieldwork in 2002. I wanted to learn, how the 'non-Slovenian' descendants of the Uskoki have experienced and understood the border situation following Slovenian independence, and in the light of a future adoption of the Schengen regime.

From defending Europe to defending the European Union

The history of the Slovenian–Croatian frontier in the Middle Ages is a history of border fortifications (Kos 1987, 219). Until the twelfth century, the region of Bela Krajina and Žumberak belonged to the Hungarian–Croatian Kingdom (Kos 1987, 217). In the 1260s, the German-speaking nobility subjugated the region. In the early sixteenth century, Bela Krajina and Žumberak not only represented the frontier between German and Hungarian states, but increasingly also, in a somewhat categorical historical view, a battlefield between 'Islam and Christianity' – the Islamist and Christian political forces of the day. Totally devastated by the

Ottoman raids, the borderland was convenient for the colonisation by the Uskoki (Zajc 2003, 52).

The Uskoki were Christian refugees from the Balkans who settled in the Austrian Military Border under the Empire's protection. This 'defensive screen' was established in 1522 with a single purpose: to protect the Austrian lands from the devastation of the Ottoman army. It lasted over three hundred and fifty years, until 1881. According to Rothenberg (1960, 13), the need for such protective measures sprang from the constellation of power in Europe in the sixteenth century. When the Hungarian–Croatian kingdom had been overrun, and the Habsburgs and Ottomans were brought face to face, the Hapsburgs established a chain of fortified villages, blockhouses and watchtowers along the border, guarded by a small cadre of mercenary troops, and settled by colonists with permanent military obligations.

The Uskoki populated Bela Krajina and Žumberak in more substantial numbers in the 1530s. The first refugees were mainly from Bosnia, from Serbian parishes in the upper reaches of the river Una, Unac in the middle sector of the river Unac, and Glamoč, north of Livno in Herzegovina (Kaser 1997, 55).[8] The first refugees to Žumberak and its surroundings are thought to have been of Eastern Orthodox faith, yet most, together with their offspring, became Greek Catholics in 1611.[9]

In 1535, a group of more than 3,000 Uskoki asked permission from Archduke Ferdinand to settle in the mountain range around the ruined Žumberak; in 1547, the Uskoki also inhabited Marindol and Bojanci (Zajc 2003, 54). In return for perpetual military service they were granted allotments of land as hereditary fiefs. For the first twenty years they were free of all taxes, and thereafter were obliged to pay a quit-rent to the Archduke. They were free of the usual feudal obligations and subject only to the Austrian military authorities (Rothenberg 1960, 29).

Given the terrain and the climatic characteristics of the region, the Uskoki had to organise their lives in small hamlets. They were predominantly cattle breeders and merchants as the land was barren and the shrubby soil was unfit for agriculture (Hranilović 1990, 596). They bought cattle at low prices in Croatia, selling it at auctions in Carniolia (Kaser 1997, 72) and they lived in formally corporate households, the zadruga,[10] which provided the necessary economic background for the soldiers. It is not by chance that the zadruga was formalised in 1807, when the process of partition of the property among heirs was underway in the Military Zone; it was the cheapest form of economy both for the state and the families providing soldiers (Simič 1990, 10).

In 1881, the Military Border was dissolved and the Uskoki lost all their privileges. Part of the population sought employment in urban centres in Zagreb and Metlika, while the majority migrated to the United States and Canada. During the 1920s and 1930s, when the Immigration Restriction Law was introduced in the United States, people from Žumberak and Bela Krajina reoriented themselves towards European destinations, particularly Germany and France. After the Second World War, migration from the border region all but ceased. During the 1940s and early 1950s, some locals joined the colonists in Slavonia (in Serbia). In the 1960s, with the opening of external Yugoslav state borders, they migrated to West Germany (Hranilović 1990, 605). Nowadays, the descendants of Uskoki still travel daily to work in nearby urban centres in both Slovenia and Croatia.

First fieldwork observations

In July and August 2002, I recorded fifteen interviews with the local people in Bojanci, Marindol, Miliči and Paunoviči (locale 1). Another ten interviews with the residents of Radatovići, Doljani, Pilatovci, Dučići and Dragoševci (locale 2) followed in January and February 2003. I will present those parts of the local narratives pertaining to their understanding of border situations in the past, at present and in the future. In these discussions, I gathered significant information from their narratives about the Uskoki's origins, their national affiliation, and their way of life 'since time immemorial'.

The story of Uskoki origins

The majority of interlocutors from the lower Kolpa villages (locale 1) were proud to be the descendants of the Uskoki. Yet some of them were not interested in the origins and the famous ancestors, or were indifferent to the subject. An elderly woman from Paunoviči told me that it was more important for her to live in the village, till the land and take care of the family. Her neighbour told me that I insulted him merely by asking about his origin because by doing so, I automatically separated him from other people in Bela krajina: 'Who is an Uskok anyway? Who is a Catholic or an Orthodox? Who is a Muslim? Such divisions must stop at once! A person is a person!' He also explained that for the majority of Slovenian-speakers from Bela Krajina, being Uskok means being poor, a 'Vlach', i.e. a backward person from the hills, a shepherd. The interviewees generally held that the descendants of Uskoki in Bela krajina were often called Vlachs, an ascription with pejorative connotations. But, as a young man from Marindol made clear, Vlach was not necessary an insult, and he gave an example: 'If somebody says in an offending tone: 'What are you Vlach doing here?' than it is an offensive word. If a neighbour greets you: 'Hi Vlach, how are you doing?' then it is not.'

Some interviewees were unfamiliar with the Uskoki origin story. Having striven, they explained, for a 'higher standard of living', they did not listen to their parents or grandparents when they 'wanted to burden us with the stories about our descent'. Nearly all interlocutors, however, were well informed on the places that the origin story recounts. They included: Medieval Albania, Kosova, Bosnia and Herzegovina, Dalmatia, Montenegro and Serbia. 'These are rumours and guessing', admit the informants; 'Nobody knows for certain, where our forefathers came from and to which peoples they had belonged'.

Considering the question on national affiliation, most of the locals from Bojanci, Marindol, Miliči and Paunoviči insisted that they were Orthodox, or Slovenian citizens of Serbian origin who have 'nothing in common with the Serbs from Serbia':

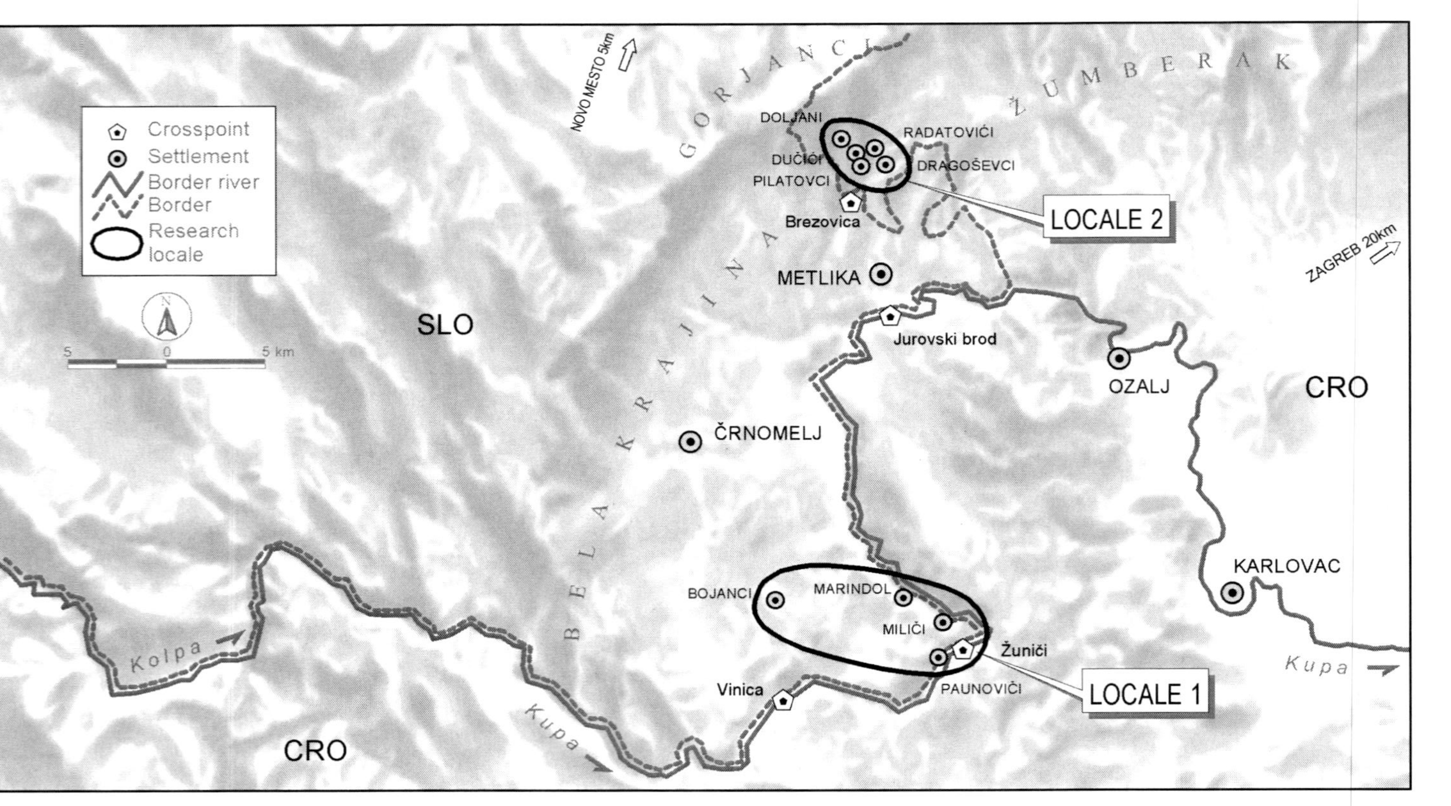

Figure 13.3 The research locales

> We feel we are Serbs. If this is right or wrong, I wouldn't know. Serbs are Orthodox. We have our holidays, customs and our Serbian language. Not quite Serbian, but good enough. For five hundred years we have lived among Slovenians, but we still manage our Serbian quite well. After the last war, people would throw Milošević in our faces. We have nothing to do with Milošević. Or with Serbia. We have been citizens of Slovenia from the beginning.
>
> (Elderly informant from Bojanci)

It seems that nationalistic provocations from the early 1990s strongly affected those among the interviewees who refused to respond to the question on national affiliation. Rather, they emphasised either that they are first of all Belokranjci (people from Bela Krajina), or ethnically and nationally 'non-aligned'. A younger interviewee in Miliči told me that the young people were not interested in national labelling. They regard themselves as Slovenians because it is 'comfortable'. Or, in the words of a middle-aged man from Bojanci:

> The youngsters do not care about these things. They are not motivated as there are no circumstances that would make them want to know. Also, it is not wise to know these things, because of existential issues. So we elders, we let them be and do not force these things upon them.

I heard quite different musings from the Žumberčani (locale 2). The president of the Cultural Artistic Association Žumberak from Novo Mesto told me that nearly all the Association's members, approximately 150, were of Uskok descent because 'even at that time they [the ancestors] had already defended the entire Europe against the Turks'. Now, they – their descendants – would continue the tradition of their forefathers by defending the European Union along the forthcoming external EU border.

The locals in Žumberak do not consider national/ethnic origin important at all. The president told me that they would prefer to call themselves simply 'Žumberčani', and only then 'everything else'. He also stressed that their Cultural Association was established in 1987 in Novo Mesto in order to bring together the Žumberčani who live in Slovenia and Žumberak proper. The only aim of the Association is to maintain the cultural traditions of the people of Žumberak. Therefore, it is written in their statute that no discussions leading to nationalism or religious fanaticism are allowed.

The Greek-Catholic faith is a significant identifier for the Žumberčani, despite the president's observation that the majority of members consider religion more or less a part of the cultural tradition. The locals, however, told me that their Greek-Catholic orientation is a trait that sets them apart from the descendants of the Uskoki in the lower Kolpa river valley. Some of them even emphasised that it is an insult for them that Slovenians and Croats would not distinguish between Greek-Catholics and Orthodox, or when they consider them Serbs.

A similar story to that of the descendants of Uskoki from the border river villages is told by the Žumberčani; it appears that their ancestors had arrived from Montenegro, Serbia, Bosnia and Herzegovina, Dalmatia and Senj. Nobody knew the precise place of origin, so they referred to their family names. An older woman from Doljani told me that she was not certain about the place of origin of her forefathers. But she referred to 'old villagers' who say that those born as Smičiklas, Gajski, Radatović, Rajaković or Sekulić, originate from either Knin or Dalmatia. A person from Radatovići even told me that the origins of Uskoki from Žumberak were so diverse that nowadays, nobody had a 'firm and reliable historical identity'.

Most replied to the question, 'Have you maintained any contacts with the descendants of Uskoki from the lower Kolpa valley?' They told me that the two communities were completely separate, as they had been in the past as well. Moreover, they did not know that the people from Bojanci, Marindol, Miliči and Paunoviči are the descendants of Uskoki. Until now, they have treated them as Serbs from Bela krajina who, compared to themselves, live in even poorer circumstances. They went on to say that the Orthodox used to live in zadruga, were to be economically backward and, like themselves, married only among themselves. However, they were quick to add that the Žumberčani are the 'inventive people', widely known as successful retailers and cattle brokers. The zadruga as a sign of backwardness is deemed a rarity in Žumberak nowadays. As borderlanders, they are compelled to take advantage of 'border life'; as an elderly local from Radatovići put it: 'We have manipulated this border space since time immemorial.'

Past and present ways of life

Informants from the Kolpa river border villages told me that people in Bela krajina in general had lived in poor circumstances for centuries. Before the First World War, they bred cattle and cultivated the land, but rarely engaged in trade. Poverty reigned. The peasants produced just enough to live from 'hand to mouth'. In the main, they grew vegetables, and reared small cattle mostly for resale. The cattle trade took place at cattle markets, which were regularly organised in nearby towns: mostly in Vinica, Črnomelj, Semič, Metlika, and Gradac on the Slovenian side of the border and in Karlovac or Bosiljevo on the Croatian side. According to elderly villagers, the cattle markets were, until the introduction of the tractor in the 1960s, the most frequently visited places where one kept contact with the neighbouring people:

> At the fair, people socialised in the way they do at railway or bus stations. That was a place of communication and trade. There one found out everything about trade, births, deaths, floods, and love affairs. There was plenty of everything.
>
> (A villager from Paunoviči)

It seems that cattle markets were also the places where the descendants of Uskoki from the lower Kolpa valley and Žumberak frequently met and communicated;

however, the Žumberčani more often visited the nearby market in Metlika than in Karlovac.

In contrast to the borderlanders from the lower Kolpa river valley, Žumberčani were engaged in trading throughout Slovenia, Austria, and Germany. A retired retailer from Radatovići still remembers how things were before the First World War:

> A man went after bread, mostly trading fabrics. This was bought in shops. If one went to Slovenia, one would go to Ljubljana or Maribor, to the Jews, because the Jews had all the manufactures there. There one would buy the goods, and then go trading with them.

Yet, the miserable living conditions made migrations a necessity for the borderlanders in Bela Krajina and Žumberak. Some interviewees reminisced about their grandparents, who had, before the First World War, left their homes for America. From there, they would regularly send a part of their earnings to the relatives at home to help them survive. After the Second World War, however, it seems that the living conditions in Bela Krajina would have improved substantially. On the Slovenian side of the border, particularly in Bela Krajina, various factories were built overnight. In accord with the Socialist motto, 'All people into factories', the borderlanders abandoned land cultivation, finding secure employment in the factories in Metlika, Novo Mesto, Črnomelj and Vinica in Slovenia, and in Karlovac and Zagreb in Croatia. According to interviewees from both research locales, the relative vicinity of the workplaces and a completely permeable border regime permitted daily commuting, the schooling of the children either in Slovenia or Croatia, and cross-border marriages. All interviewees maintained that 'ethnically mixed' marriages were rare before the Second World War. After the War they became a normal matter.

The improved economic prospects in Bela Krajina after the Second World War had another important consequence. In 1952, the people from Marindol, Paunoviči and Miliči voted in favour of annexation to Slovenia for 'practical reasons'. Their villages had, until then,[11] formed a Croat territorial pocket on the Slovenian side of the Kolpa river; Bojanci, however, belonged to Slovenia and had done so for at least five centuries. Among practical reasons for their plea for annexation, the informants emphasised the closeness of their places of occupation, health service, postal service, schools, and county offices. Similarly, in 1992, the locals from local communities Radatovići and Dragoševci publicly expressed their desire for annexation to Slovenia for 'economic reasons'. Yet they were, unlike the borderlanders from the lower Kolpa river valley, afraid of the possible consequences of the new border regime between Slovenia and Croatia. On the one hand, they were anxious that the international border regime might obstruct the vital interactions with Slovenia that had been established chiefly after the Second World War. On the other hand, they were afraid of an increased marginalisation by the Croatian authorities, as an elderly villager from Radatovići complained: 'The Croat state behaves towards us as if we do not exist'.

Experiencing the border regime in 1991

From among my interlocutors, no one mentioned any advantages arising from the new international border regime of 1991. They all agreed that they were estranged from their cross-border neighbours. The locals from the lower Kolpa river valley stressed the reduced relations with both Croats and Serbs on the Croat side of the boundary. According to the majority of interviewees, Croats became very patriotic and nationalistic, referring to their previous neighbours as suspicious Serbs. They confessed that they ceased to visit cross-border relatives and friends mostly because of the very annoying police and customs checks. They were particularly dismayed because the local crossing point – the bridge over the Kolpa River in Žuniči – was no longer accessible to them. According to the state border agreement, only those people who live within the regulation distance from the border may use it. Local people from both riverbanks, aided by the then Yugoslav People's Army, built the bridge some twenty years ago by themselves, in order to facilitate communication. The bridge was of great importance to them, especially as they commuted daily to Slovenia from the Croatia. In their view, the bridge in Žuniči was a symbol of cross-border neighbourly relations, a sign of a unified community, and a reminder of a constructive and optimistic period in the local history.

Despite informants' constant complaints that the new border regime cut the people off from cheaper shopping in Karlovac, they all agreed that their cross-border neighbours have found themselves in even worse circumstances. After the dissolution of Yugoslavia, the majority of factories in Bela Krajina went bankrupt, and only a small number of borderlanders from Croatia succeeded in keeping their jobs in Slovenia – provided that they could secure labour visas. Worsening prospects affected the young people as well. Before the 1991 border, most of the youth from Croat border villages attended schools in Slovenia, as it was believed that they would better equip them for competing on the job market. Now, in the locals' view, the prospects for the young people are grim unless a major change occurs shortly in the overall economic situation in Bela Krajina. They are watching the preparations for the Schengen regime with a weary and pessimistic eye. They firmly believe that the regime will have driven the borderlanders still further apart.

The locals from south-western Žumberak avoided the discussions related to the border regime. The memories of the year 1992, when the locals from Radatovići and Dragoševci signed the petition for annexation to Slovenia, and the subsequent arrests of the organisers of the petition by the Croat local authorities, are still vivid. Informants commented that the petition had been motivated by an interest in survival and not by anti-Croat sentiment as the Croat media reported it. An elderly local from Radatovići told me:

> God knows we were not going against the language, as everybody loves their language. I, for one, communicate with greater ease in Croatia than in Slovenia. But it was for economic and geographic reasons. We are surrounded by Slovenia. We only have our highland forest that connects us to Croatia.

The borderlanders from Žumberak, like the people from the Kolpa river valley, felt that the people on the Croat side of the boundary suffered greater disadvantages after 1991 than their neighbours in Slovenia. In the old days, the nearest shopping centre in Suhor (close to Metlika) was only ten kilometres away. After 1991, they had to travel forty kilometres to the distant shopping centre in Ozalj in Croatia. Likewise, the nearest medical centre used to be in Metlika and the elderly Žumberčani often depended on their children who permanently resided in Slovenia. The locals are overwhelmed by the prospect of the Schengen regime, which, in their view, will block their essential connections with family and relatives.

Conclusion

Since the late 1980s and early 1990s, the press in Slovenia has reported exhaustively on the new international border between Slovenia and Croatia in the context of the dissolution of Socialist Yugoslavia. The discussion has shifted from supporting the views in favour of border permeability between two sovereign states, to defending the voices that insist on a solid barrier against the 'dangerous Balkans'. The advocates of the latter also reiterate the so-called EU expectations that applicant countries must provide a well-secured border regime. Since 1995, particularly, the Slovenian press has largely interpreted the emerging Schengen regime at the Slovenian–Croatian border as the making of a fortress to isolate not just Slovenia from the politically unpredictable Balkans, but the entire European Union.

Understandably, the local people along the Slovenian–Croatian boundary are less enthusiastic. This is especially true of those among them who were, immediately before and after Slovenian and Croatian independence, 'discovered' by the media as the descendants of Uskoki, a people of non-Slovenian origin. During the war in the former Yugoslavia, the Slovenian police watched the borderlanders with considerable distrust, as potentially likely to bring the 'ethnic conflict' to Slovenia. The locals are still exasperated at the attitude of the Slovenian authorities who ignored them during the Ten Days' War in Slovenia, despite their proven loyalty at the plebiscite for an independent Slovenia. As one local informant from Bojanci said: 'None of us was called to military duty, although ninety per cent among us voted for an independent Slovenia'.

On top of this bitterly felt stigmatisation of them as of non-Slovenian 'origin', the locals experience the impact of the international border regime in their everyday lives as one of great loss. Unlike the former invisible borderline between two federal republics, they experience the international border as a barrier, significantly interfering with their formerly undisturbed cross-border interactions. After the Second World War, the hitherto mostly endogamous members of the Uskoki descendants in Bela Krajina and south-western Žumberak comprised a homogeneous social space where most of them were employed, attended schools, and made families. Intricately intertwined and diverse social relationships have been seriously damaged by the imposition of the international border regime.

Following these experiences, the people along the border are greatly concerned about the imposition of the Schengen regime at the Slovenian–Croatian border. They are very sceptical when it comes to tourism, the only borderland activity that the Slovenian state *Plan for Regional Development* quotes as realistic and profitable. They believe that the increased presence of police at the frontier cannot contribute to cross-border tourism. And, on the Slovenian side, they also doubt the successful outcome of other prospective cross-border economic activities because, as they say, on the other side of the border their neighbours are impoverished.

Yet, some voices are not entirely pessimistic. Recently,[12] the Slovenian Minister for European Affairs stressed that borderlanders have, in many cases erroneously, ascribed the negative consequences of the independent Slovenian state to the international border or the Schengen regime. He emphasised that it is necessary to take into account the fact that the EU invests into efficient security at its external borders, since the candidate countries will soon have controlled over nearly eighty per cent of the terrestrial EU border. Therefore, it will be in nobody's interest to build a wall against Croatia, or to establish a particularly hampering regime for the borderlanders.

The borderlanders, however, can be persuaded far more by deeds than words.

Notes

1 An earlier version of this essay was published in the Slovenian journal *Razprave in Gradivo* 45 (Treaties and Documents 45) in 2004.

2 Barth's special merit has been in his explicit articulation of boundaries as a specific dynamism of culturally generated differences among members of culturally distinct groups in contact. Barth postulated a beholder's perspective itself, holding that boundaries among ethnic groups could not be taken for granted as a priori static lines but as the very mechanism of inter-group social interaction.

3 I owe many thanks to the geographer Marjan Jarnjak from the Institute of Biology at Scientific Research Centre at the Slovenian Academy of Sciences and Arts for making the maps.

4 The Journalist Documentation *Delo*, Folder – *Border in general*, Ljubljana, is the reference for journalist reports of the time. I reviewed and analysed press-clippings from the Folder *Border in general* in Ljubljana's Journalist Documentation *Delo* (*Labour*).

5 The Uskoki were medieval refugees, mostly of Orthodox creed, who, in the sixteenth century, fled from the Ottoman Empire and were settled in the Military Border Zone. The border officers gave the refugees different titles: 'Valachi Turcorum', 'Valachi', 'Rasciani Voskoky', 'Valachi Uzkoky', 'Pribegi', 'Vsskhokhen' (Kaser 1997, 55).

6 This and all subsequent translations are my own.

7 In 1929, the Kingdom of Yugoslavia was partitioned into nine Provinces – banovinas. The banovina was administered by a Ban who was, upon the nomination of the prime minister, appointed by the King. Dravska banovina was the relatively autonomous administrative unit within the Kingdom of Serbs, Croats and Slovenians roughly on the present Slovenian territory from 1929 to 1941, while Savska banovina comprised most of today's Croatian territory.

8 In the following migration waves to Žumberak in the sixteenth and seventeenth centuries, Uskoki arrived from the river basin of Cetina, continental Dalmatia, western Herzegovina, Lika and Senj (Hranilović 1990, 596).

9 The Christian Orthodox colonists had already built the monastery in Marča at Ivanićgrad in the fifteenth century. In the sixteenth century, when they settled Žumberak and its surroundings in more substantial numbers, the refugee metropolitan Gavrilo and his monks restored the monastery that had been destroyed in battles. Accordingly, Marča became the seat of the Serbian Orthodox diocese. In 1611, however, the monastery united with the Catholic Church, under the influence of the powerful Uniat movement (Janežič 1986, 238; Kaser 1997, 185).

10 A general definition of zadruga says that sons stay together with the parents after they marry, and after the father's death. The property remains common and indivisible (Simič 1990, 5).

11 It was only during a short period during the Second World War that Marindol, Miliči and Paunoviči belonged to Slovenia. During the Italian Fascist regime in 1942, the occupier determined the Kolpa River as the boundary between the Italian Fascist state and the Independent state of Croatia. After the war, the villages were incorporated into Croat territory again.

12 The minister's viewpoint is cited in the video copy of the television broadcast 'Hot: Schengen Regime – who will be the guardian at the southern frontier?'

References

Barth, F. (ed.) (1969) *Ethnic Groups and Boundaries: the Social Organisation of Culture Difference*, London: Allen and Unwin.

Bauer, M. (1993) 'SAO Bela krajina' (The Serbian Autonomous Territory of Bela Krajina), *Slovenske novice*, 3/274, 25 November: 2.

Budja, B. (1994) 'Srbsko avtonomno ozemlje zdaj tudi v Sloveniji?!' (Now, the Serbian Autonomous Territory also in Slovenia), *7D*, 23/1, 5 January: 12–14.

Čelik, P. (1994) *Na južni straži: kronika nastajanja dr_avne meje med Slovenijo in Hrvaško* (At the Southern Frontier: the establishing of the state border between Slovenia and Croatia – a chronicle), Ljubljana: Enotnost.

Čontala, B. (1989) 'Bojanci ali Srbi v Beli krajini' (Bojanci or Serbs in Bela Krajina), *Delo*, 30 September: 26.

Dimitrić, M. (1990) 'Belokransjki Srbi odločno za samostojno Slovenijo' (Serbs from Bela Krajina resolutely for independent Slovenia), *Delo*, 24 December: 3.

Dimitrić, M. (1993) 'Belokranjci izpuhtevajo po vsakem preštevanju' (The people of Bela Krajina are vanishing after each enumeration), *Delo*, 19 February: 2.

Donnan, H. and T.M. Wilson (1999) *Borders: Frontiers of Identity, Nation and State*, Berg: Oxford.

Hann, C. (2001) 'Borders in anthropological perspective', paper published in conference report *Europe 2021: Beyond Visible and Invisible Borders*, Kraków Conference, 26–28 April.

Hranilović, N. (1990) 'Žumberčani – subetnička grupa u Hrvata' (The Žumberčani – subethnic group in Croatia), *Migracijske teme* 6/4: 593–614.

Janežič, S. (1986) *Ekumenski leksikon* (The Ecumenical Lexicon), Celje: Mohorjeva družba.

Kaser, K. (1997) *Slobodan seljak i vojnik. Rana krajiška društva 1545–1754.* (A Free Peasant and Soldier: the Early Border Societies 1545–1754), Povijest i historija, vol. 1, Zagreb: Naprijed.

Kos, D. (1987) 'Bela krajina v poznem srednjem veku' (Bela Krajina in the late Middle Ages), *Zgodovinski časopis* 41/2: 217–55.

Kranjc, J. (1991) 'Naj nas pustijo pri miru' (Let them leave us alone), *Večer*, 47/220, 21 October: 27.

Kuljaj, I. (1990) 'Priključitev k Sloveniji' (Annexation to Slovenia), *Delavska enotnost* 49/53, 27 December: 11.

Laketić, M. (1989) 'Kad he predsednik 'Srb'' (When the President is a Serb), *Politika*, 24 October.

Rothenberg, G.E. (1960) *The Austrian Military Border in Croatia, 1522–1747*, Illinois Studies in the Social Sciences, vol. 48, Urbana: The University of Illinois Press.

Simič, V. (1990) 'Zadružna zakonodaja v 19. stol. na današnjem jugoslovanskem ozemlju' (The Zadruga legislation in the Nineteenth Century in contemporary Yugoslav territory), unpublished thesis, University of Ljubljana.

Šimunič, M. (1995) 'Prilagajamo se evropskim merilom' (We are conforming to the European criteria), *Slovenec*, 22 May: 2.

Zajc, M. (2003) 'Problem slovensko-hrvaške meje v 19. stoletju: žumberško vprašanje' (The Slovenian–Croatian border problem in the nineteenth century: the Žumberak question), unpublished MA thesis, University of Ljubljana.

Zakrajšek, V. (1993) 'SAO Bela krajina, prestolnica Metlike' (The Serbian Autonomous Territory of Bela Krajina, the capital of Metlika), *Slovenske novice* 3/274: 3.

Zorič, B. (1993) 'O Beli krajini nismo govorili' (We did not talk about Bela Krajina), *Delo*, 20 February: 2.

Žunec, B. (1992) 'Policijska meja na evropskem obrobju' (A policed border at the European margin), *7D*, 12 February: 11–13.

Archival sources

Novinarska dokumentacija Delo (The Journalist Documentation of Delo): mapa: 312.1 (497.12) – Nataliteta (folder: Natality).

Video copy

'Aktualno: Schengenski režim – kdo bo varuh južne meje?' (Hot: Schengen Regime – who will be the guardian at the southern frontier?), Slovenian national television, programme: Slovenia 1, 5 August 2003.

14 Fortress frontiers

Global power, global and local justice

Warwick Armstrong

Introduction

That part of Europe lying within the borders of the European Union is in the midst of momentous change. The challenges facing the EU are both domestic and in the Union's relationships with the rest of the world. Internally, the EU is edging unevenly, uncertainly and painfully, almost, towards a more unified status – for some member states at least. The irregularity in its realisation occurs because important members within the Union are ambivalent at best towards the idea of a project that they believe would undermine their own national state sovereignty. The distant authority exercised by EU bureaucrats in Brussels seems even less palatable to populations for whom even the local variety of government power brokers are seen as a necessary evil. Political setbacks in two 2005 referendums on a new constitution for the Union have deepened the uncertainty about the dynamics of the EU's future, at least in the short and, perhaps, the medium term.

The borders within the EU are of uneven status as some states form closer ties, especially on financial matters, while others choose, for political and economic reasons, to remain clear of financial agreements that would limit their control – as they perceive it – over their local currencies. The EU is a patchwork of states at different levels of association and political commitment; as ever in the history of Europe, diversity, disparity and divergence prevail. The will to pursue an outcome that might create a unified European entity is still lacking when faced by the countervailing desire to hang on to deeply-entrenched historical rights and powers at the level of the nation-state.

This has its positives and its negatives. It suggests that the desire for closer political accountability is still pre-eminent among the peoples of the Union. The failure, so far, by the Union to establish itself as a credible democratic institution (as compared to the perception that it is hog-tied by 'faceless bureaucrats') stands as a major obstacle in the way of its further evolution; and this is generally recognised across its territorial space. Change and reform are evidently called for. Yet, because the EU and its members have arrived at an impasse since the rejection in the two constitutional referendums, this can only lessen their ability to play a powerful role on the international stage – and this at a time when other regional powers are thrusting themselves into positions of growing global significance.

Externally, the EU finds itself in a world of tumultuous change. As a still loosely arranged group of largely sovereign nation-states, it has, above all, to deal with the United States of America, an overpowering and often indifferent ally, with which it inconsistently agrees on matters ranging from international trade to environmental issues and global foreign policy. This relationship has often been, and continues to be, a source of friction and division between what Washington – perhaps in the classical ploy of divide and rule – has dismissively labelled 'old Europe' and those who are deemed more acquiescent and receptive to United States' global leadership.

Differences of opinion and of responsive concrete action among the EU's member states concerning the global hegemony of the United States are elements that ensure the persistence of an EU that will remain disunited and deprived of its ability to assume the role that the warmest adherents of a unitary union are pressing for. It seems logical that the centre cannot hold while the constituent parts of the Union are so far in opposition on even the most fundamental question: what sort of European Union is it Europeans wish to see emerge?

The consequences arising from these differences of opinion become increasingly serious. The emergence of other competitive capitalisms – India, Brazil, perhaps, smaller but dynamic Asian tigers and, above all, China – is no longer a distant challenge. Martin Jacques, writing in the *Guardian*,[1] argues that the most momentous change to take place has not been the fall of the Berlin Wall and the collapse of the Soviet system in 1989, but the adoption by China of open-door reforms and its own distinctive model of capitalism in 1978. Yet, he says, the implications of China's rapid rise to world economic power status are being missed by EU politicians:

> As a sign of our parochialism – and almost historically coincident with the rapid rise of China – we have become increasingly obsessed with the 'Islamic problem'. So long a cipher of the US, and now mired in its own travails and sense of decline, Europe has grown myopic and introspective, a poor vantage point from which to see the future.[2]

Europe, once the centre of a radical economic, social, technological and ideological change and once, politically the source of competitive imperial expansions, is now threatened with subordinate status, even beyond its subsidiary role under current United States' supremacy. The Atlantic, argues Jacques, is ceding its position as economic power moves towards the Pacific.

> More dramatically, the transformation of China has decisively moved the global centre of gravity eastwards. The 21st century will be quite unlike the preceding two centuries, in which power was located in Europe and the US and the rest of the world consisted of mere supplicants and bit players.

And, he insists,

> The ramifications are enormous. Power will no longer be located primarily in the west. The assumptions that inform global discourse will cease to be overwhelmingly western. History will no longer be written with a hugely western bias. Chinese interests, history, values, attitudes and prejudices will become familiar to us all.[3]

While this is happening, Europe is caught in yet another of its own regional–global dilemmas concerning its borders and border relationships: what strategy should it adopt towards those on the outside? How far does it intend to expand and what is the corollary of such expansion as far as new states in the Balkans, Eastern Europe and, above all, Turkey, are concerned? The serious differences within the EU as it stands make the formulation of any coherent strategy for future growth extremely difficult to elaborate.

In fact, the only discernibly unified strategy to the outside world lies in the agreement to keep battling the threat of terrorism and to keep terrorists from infiltrating. Foreign workers – illegal immigrants – are also anathema to EU leaders, the media and growing sectors of the population. Yet, the value of proscribing the latter can be questioned on grounds of logic and capitalism's needs. Demographically and economically, many countries of an ageing EU require labour that is cheap and available; it is an essential part of the strategy to ensure the effective and competitive position of European capitalism against outside challenges, especially those coming from Asia.

So, the European Union is caught in a dilemma. It faces the existing power of established global hegemony, that of the United States of America, it is becoming uncomfortably aware of the emergence of a constellation of new powers in Asia – not only the established economic capacity of Japan, but also that of the two demographic superpowers of China and India. And, in the face of these challenges, its own will and practical ability to act is seriously compromised by a succession of differences and disagreements on critical issues among its constituent members.

The narratives

It is in the light of these conundrums that James Anderson raises questions about the options available to the leaders of the EU as they survey the volatile economic and political scene that constitutes global capitalism in the twenty-first century. Anderson considers five competing visions of Europe's possible territorial future, five labels and what lies behind them: a 'Europe of nations'; a 'European super-state'; a 'Europe of regions'; a 'new medieval Europe'; and 'Europe an empire'.

Among the various options, the first reasserts traditional nation-state sovereignty, while the second comprehensively subsumes the nation-state within a large, centralised 'United Sates of Europe' similar to the USA. The third option leads towards a decentralised mosaic of sub-state regions whereas the fourth and fifth suggest radical and multifaceted changes in territorial form so as to capture a concept of association that is specifically European and new. And yet the experiments are fraught with the unpredictable and the unknown. As Anderson argues, the historical road to homogenisation begun by absolutism and nationalism is being followed now as a means to strengthening Europe's global position. Yet, on the way to achieving some form of European singularity, it must face the daily obstacles and delays posed by its own members' nation-state self-interest.

These obstacles operate at a range of levels and not only between the EU authorities and individual nation-states. Within the states themselves, there are examples of roadblocks of a regional, ethnic and border nature to any form of unified European system. Liam O'Dowd takes up the theme of a specific society, Northern Ireland. But he also connects his narrative to wider events and movements, arguing that borders and their regions arise from explicit histories and local/regional interaction as well as broader processes of social transformation caused by changes in the capitalist system.

While the case of Northern Ireland and its border is highly idiosyncratic, the links with the larger world are constantly in evidence. Globalisation has always had a complex relationship with local conflicts; national states, he argues, retain a key role in new and emerging forms of transnational governance. But, even more, his case study confirms that nationalist and ethnic border conflicts will persist and continue to interact with economic, political and cultural globalisation. The Irish border, too, tests whether new forms of democracy might offer a basis both for re-examining the idea of national sovereignty and for the operation of new forms of transnational governance. He concludes on a hopeful note that border change might be more peaceful and democratic than in the past, but the gritty fact is that, so far, such border changes continue to pose a succession of difficulties for state negotiators as well as those seeking greater coherence and stability in the relationships of member states within the EU to each other.

Thomas Wilson takes up a similar theme, linking a specific case study to the question of Europeanisation; he suggests that the very idea of Europeanisation is a confused one and that it is, or should be, a broader concept than political and economic adaptation to European institutions and policies. Little work has been done, for example, through ethnography to relate international and global forces to the everyday lives of local communities in the EU's member states. His own local study on the Ireland–Northern Ireland border is valuable in showing that people perceive Europeanisation largely as international economics and politics and much less as an element of wider cultural globalisation. It is, therefore, removed from their daily lives – and presumably from any sense of deep-seated interest or support.

Certainly, there is a 'culture of European funding', with the EU playing the role of 'milch cow' but with limited involvement in national and regional politics and social relations. Of course, EU initiatives are making an impact on people in their communities but the 'transnational' or 'post-national' aspects of this stay largely on the surface. Unquestionably, in this one small case, he argues, questions of territoriality, sovereignty, citizenship and identity still reside firmly at national level. What this implies is that the resistance (or perhaps indifference) to the idea of European identity runs deep.

Despite the evident practical benefits to be gained from Brussels, local hearts have not been won over to a sense of a shared European identity. Self-identification as Europeans is resisted or ignored; this constitutes a further impediment on the way to the formation of a European Union with collective values and attitudes. It is a replay, rather, of the historical realities of difference and diversity.

In a further study on the complexities of Northern Ireland as a small constituent part of the EU, Cathal McCall investigates the reactions of a small Ulster Protestant 'border British' community to the move towards shared institutions with the mainly Catholic republican state to the south. With a strong sense of their separate identity, it is difficult for the community to accept the British Labour Party's version of Britishness – with its civic values of pluralism, inclusion, multiculturalism and tolerance, all also inscribed in notions of a European identity. This would involve them having to communicate openly with their nationalist adversaries.

Westminster's attempts to break down this opposition led to a grudging acceptance by the Ulster Unionist party of the idea of power-sharing with the Nationalist Sinn Féin party. Since then, however, under the unbending leadership of the Democratic Unionist party, their initial reluctance to make any overtures may now be reinforced.

Northern Ireland is small and on the geographic periphery of the EU, but it looms large as an example of the multilayered difficulties faced by Brussels (or Westminster) as it attempts to create a sense of shared civic values within the one Union. Diversity within Europe spills over into hostile separatism in certain cases and the best efforts from on top meet with little acceptance by those in local areas who have built their sense of identity around distrust and separatism – a sort of apartheid in miniature. All the rational arguments adduced for economic and political union, a larger market for capital and the creation of a springboard from which to launch effective competition on the world stage run headlong into the uncompromising positions of those at the local level who see little benefit for themselves in any of the global arguments.

Henk Driessen also takes a local, 'bottom-up' view of the diametrically different 'wet' Mediterranean external border of the EU between Spain and Morocco. Illegal migration is the centre of his ethnographic study of the port towns on both the northern and southern shores; this is set within the context of larger events occurring in the Mediterranean. While there are pronounced divisions between the two shores, says Driessen, these appear to be less marked when seen from the local viewpoint than from the EU's political centres. But in recent years the Mediterranean has undoubtedly become more of a barrier – the symbol of a mounting divergence between North Africa and the EU – than a bridge between two worlds. This is illustrated by the growing numbers of Africans risking their lives to cross the wet border and the escalating tensions between Madrid and Rabat that have resulted from large-scale persistent migration.

George Joffé's chapter provides an overview of the Mediterranean as a whole in his study of the 1995 Barcelona Agreement This EU–North African partnership, ostensibly aiming to share peace, prosperity and stability in the Mediterranean basin, in fact aims to apply the principles of soft security along the EU's southern periphery and to reassert the importance of boundaries and division. And, once again, it is largely the threat of illegal migration into the EU that lies at the heart of the initiative to strengthen the EU's external border security.

But the border is in fact a side-issue, as Joffé argues, because the key target is Europe's inadequately integrated migrant neighbourhoods which are often little more than ghettoes. Joffé expands his argument from the issue of physical external borders to an examination of the deep-seated problems within European society – the confrontation of mutually exclusive cultures – and the internal segregation that continues on a daily basis. Exclusion, then, is far from just an external phenomenon that seeks to bar outsiders from infringing the EU's borders. So, the construction of an internal cultural boundary as counterpart to a reinforced external border is part of the EU's agenda to deal with difference.

Brigitta Busch and Michal Krzyżanowski pick up elements of Joffé's discussion with their outlining of the EU's migration controls, its border regimes and notions of European identity. Not only are the external borders expanding, but, within the defined territory, concentric circles are established around the EU's core regions. Self-image and the creation of classes of outsiders and insiders are part of the attempt to construct a European entity reflective of Europe's traditional values. The prolix arguments about shared history and common values (among the original members) have heightened since the eastward expansion of the EU's territory and borders. The result is the construction of boundaries within the EU which demonise migrant communities as 'the enemy within'. The corollary is that such attitudes and policies ensure inequality for peripheral groups so that society is split into disparate communities, enjoying varying and unequal levels of human and civil rights protection.

The approach taken by James Anderson and Ian Shuttleworth situates the more empirical discussion of other chapters in a theoretical framework. It argues that capitalism has historically striven to defend itself against the inherent trend for the rate of profit to fall, by exporting capital to peripheral economies. This is capitalism's 'Spatial Fix 1'. But this form of imperialist expansion has ceded ground to a more recent strategy reversing this movement, 'Spatial Fix 2'. The consequence has been – in spite of general and official antipathy to immigration in industrialised societies – a flow of low-cost migrant labour from the world's peripheries to the centre.

But they also acknowledge the evidence that the traditional capital-exporting Fix 1 has continued to operate in the post-Second World War decades and may, in fact, be making a comeback. So, it appears that now both Spatial Fixes are probably operating simultaneously or in tandem, and the authors put forward the idea that their combination is an important (though again largely unnoticed) component of the so-called 'new imperialism'. Europe provides a clear example of this happening, especially as the eastward extension of the EU has opened new economies to western capital export and western economies to flows of labour from the east.

In this way, they link the model of the two complementary capitalisms to ideas of imperialism, territoriality, and 'formal' and 'informal empire'. Europe, since the fall of the Berlin Wall, provides the clearest evidence for the combined operations of the two Fixes. The model also brings empirical support to the theoretical framework as it notes the evidence of the labour flows from Eastern to Western Europe, and of capital flows from west to east.

A matter of additional interest is that this bilateral exchange between Europe's east and west is distinctive because it now operates within the framework of the EU's external borders. Unlike the inflows of external migrant labour from North Africa outlined in Driessen's chapter, these are migrants who have the legal freedom – for the most part – to move from an internal periphery within the EU to meet the capitalism's demands at the core of the Union. At the same time, investment from the centre in the outlying economies now has no borders to negotiate and enjoys a wider and untrammelled domestic market for its products and services.

Pertti Joenniemi looks at another aspect of the new relationship between the EU's original west and its new east with an examination of the European Neighbourhood Policy (ENP). He discusses the fact that the ENP is not just a response to the accession of the new EU members from the east of Europe and the challenges posed by enlargement. Some of the ideas for a neighbourhood policy originated within the EU itself which had to make adjustments for its external domain. It is a response to a situation of change if not instability. And it is an attempt to come to terms with the diversity posed by differences not only in the eastern European societies but also those between member states from the north and the south, by the formulation of a single neighbourhood policy.

His conclusions are that the ENP, despite its apparently amiable title, is more likely to be exclusive than otherwise. In fact, the notion of a 'Fortress Europe' appears increasingly likely with the application of the ENP strategy. It creates deep uncertainty about future possibilities for acceptance of outsiders within the EU's borders. And it also erects another borderline between members and the ENP-related 'special partners'. This ENP wall is not insuperable but acts, rather, as a 'European sieve'. In a sense, what the ENP is doing is to further consolidate the sense of a strongly-defined Union with clear-cut outer borders that act as the filters between those inside and those without. Security lies at the heart of what the ENP is about; encouraging stable communities just outside the borders of the EU and strengthening that external line are both critical to the ENP. The core, or cosmos, is thus reinforced by a ring of space that comprises 'trustworthy' partners. In contrast, those societies perceived as unruly or over-heterogeneous, are placed at a distance beyond the cordon sanitaire[4] created by the ENP of those adjudged worthy to be friends – if not members of the EU cosmos. The EU gives off the strongest of signals that it is turning from the ways of a global reaching out towards those of exclusiveness behind a wall buffered by reliable, if only partially acceptable, cohorts. The fortress architecture, subsuming previous agreements such as the Euro-Mediterranean Partnership, is being further codified and solidified as the EU builds its own regional 'gated community'.

In Anderson and Shuttleworth's terms, the EU can now be seen to be constructing a constitutional framework that will ensure its continued role as a global centre of capitalist profit and progress; it gives the core a large, open market for investment and commerce; and it also puts into place a system of excluded 'friends' who will serve as the cordon sanitaire against perceived or anticipated threats to its security. The irony here is that, as other contributors point out, all the buffering at the gates of the EU borders will almost certainly be of limited value; a considerable part of the perceived threat from terrorists and illegal aliens will already be in place, well within the border fences. The physical and/or constitutional reinforcement of the outer borders may, therefore, amount to a largely futile strategy that steers clear of coming to terms with the deeper global origins of the alleged/perceived menaces to the security of the EU and its population.

Later chapters take on the nature of a series of case studies of a country which is, perhaps, the one characterised most in the EU as a 'border state'. Slovenia's accession to the EU in 2004, along with nine other entrants, has thrown into prominence the impacts of change on a small country that borders four other states and is, in many respects, the meeting point of West and Central Europe and the crossroads between major European linguistic, religious and ethnic groups. Milan Bufon and Anton Gosar make the point firmly that, given their country's 'border landscape', a political or economic 'macro' approach in studying cross-border regions has its limitations. Only by looking at such regions in terms of their local cultural and social dimensions can the observer gain some awareness of their true qualities. It is through the 'humanised' content of studies of the geography of border landscapes, then, that their reality comes to life.

In contrast to the Euroregions, the authors contend, their border zones are marked by spontaneous cross-border links and are relatively small. History and common territorial attachments are more influential than macro issues relating to financial, political or resource issues. In a sense, such zones organically are becoming 'Europeanised'. With the further reduction of official border obstacles, this process will evolve yet further for all communities and ethnic groups. Certainly, the intensity of cross-border movement as well as the wide range of micro-transactions, especially in the erstwhile Italian–Slovenian border zone, suggest that there are almost infinite possibilities for the creation of a European regional entity based on cities such as Koper/Capodistria and Trieste/Trst.

Robert Minnich's study of one of the regions mentioned by Bufon and Gosar intensifies the argument that long-standing personal and cultural connections can and do continue over the borders drawn up by remote political authority. The Three Border Region (Slovenia, Austria and Italy) is the site of historical bonds among people who have been the involuntary heirs of international border decisions that have taken little notice of their local connections and relationships. In the past century, especially, the consequences have been to slice through such social and cultural ligaments in compliance with faraway political priorities and claims.

But now the nation-state as prime rights domain of communication and guarantor of civil rights to the citizenry is under challenge. In fact, he argues that there is and has always been a form of citizenship not linked to the nation-state, but reflecting membership in a political community. This takes place at a series of levels up to and beyond the nation-state. At the sub-state level, civil society also functions on the grounds that individuals share moral values and pursue their goals in the public sphere through freely established institutions. This gives a *raison d'être* to sub-nation entities and a strength to the persistence of collective identities that can endure on occasions when their community space is divided by changes in nation-state boundary lines.

This has been especially true of the Three-Border Region where local inhabitants have suffered from bitter ethnic prejudice, but where there has also been a counter force supporting the communities – that of an existing civil society that transcends the institutional framework of the nation-state. With the 2004 accession of Slovenia to the EU, the formal constraints of nation-state boundary lines have been removed, so allowing the Three-Border Region communities the opportunity to resume a more unified existence; it sees the reconstitution of a multi-ethnic social order unimpeded by artificial nation-state constriction in this reintegrated former Alpine crossroads.

On the other hand, the realignment of Slovenia over the past decade and a half from its status as a constituent republic within the Yugoslav Federation has altered the connections and relationships among communities straddling the border between Slovenia and Croatia. Unimpeded access over an internal border within a federated nation-state up to 1991 gave way to separation by an official border between two distinct nation-states – and between a Europe-leaning Slovenia and the less politically stable Balkan republics to the south.

The curtailing of links has continued still further; with Slovenia's accession to the EU, the country's southern border has also become part of the southern flank of the EU, marking the division between Union's 'insiders' and those outside the pale of the Union – a virtual replay of the centuries-old fortified frontier erected by the Austrian Empire against the encroaching Ottomans. For all the reasons adduced earlier, such a border now stands as Fortress Europe's outer defence shield against unwanted movements/penetrations of drug traffickers, other criminals, illegal migrants and terrorists. As Bufon and Gosar have pointed out, this border is Slovenia's least crossed (and, probably, most carefully surveyed).

How do local border communities, their practices and attitudes interact – or, perhaps, just cope – with such profound and dramatic geopolitical change that so immediately and deeply affects their everyday lives. The twice-reinforced border is seen and felt as a major barrier to their previously connected community lives. Families, work and education have been dislocated; varied and intricate community relationships have been brought to an end. And, despite official reassurances on both sides of the border, a mood of pessimism reigns in many of the divided communities.

Maria Furlan, Vesna Mikolič and Mateja Sedmak unfold another case study on the south-western border of Slovenia with Croatia and Italy. The region has passed through a turbulent post-Second World War history as new border lines were drawn and arrangements made for the migration of people on both sides of the border to those societies in which they felt less threatened by the new regimes. International agreements have been drawn up to ensure just treatment for minorities in the borderlands, but such treaties have been honoured even more in the breach than the observance.

In fact, their account suggests a decided disparity existing between the treatment of the minority Italian population in Slovenian Istria where conditions are seen to be positive and the treatment of the much larger Slovenian minority population on the Italian side of the border where language rights especially are ignored by the Italian authorities. The disappearance of the formal border following Slovenian accession to the EU in May 2004 has been marked by no profound change in nation-state attitudes towards each other – right-wing parties in particular on both sides of the border have hardened their attitudes to each other's minorities – and the disappearance of the old border has not led to the end of queues and frustrating delays or the strong presence of police there.

Most problems, the authors suggest, lie at the macro-political level, for, at the local level, social relations are marked by interethnic marriage, broad kinship networks and daily contact associated with work, school or consumer purchases. A broad-ranging recognition of a common heritage, centuries of convivencia and the positive consequences of cooperation and cultural acceptance would be a vital step forward – and one that needs to be taken by the authorities of each nation-state.

This is reinforced yet again in Duška Knežević Hočevar's chapter on border communities that have undergone the strains, if not traumas, of successive change on the Slovenian–Croatian border. From a situation of unimpeded movement among family and friends across a line internal to one country, the divisions have deepened as the separation has become formalised into a border between two new nation-states; later still, the chasm has widened as the interstate border has come to double as the southern flank of the EU, with all that entails for exclusion from the Schengen regime. The situation is already further fraught because the communities of Bela Krajina and south-western Žumberak comprise people of Serbian descent whose historical role as defenders of Western civilization has been forgotten as they have come to be seen as yet another enemy within.

The newly created EU border then assumes the character of an international barrier with the consequent sense of loss in the everyday lives of people; the homogeneous social space for work, schooling and other personal relationships has been splintered and the reassurances from remote state authorities too often ring hollow in local ears.

Lessons from the narratives

The story that the chapters tell is one of diversity, imbalance and contradiction. It is one in which strong forces within Europe, as Busch and Krzyżanowski describe it, are pushing the European Union towards an objective of 'singularity' (to use Anderson's word). Large corporations, above all, have needed a large, non-bordered single market in which to operate and which will act as a springboard for global expansion. This insistent weight intersects with the ambitions of political classes at the national and Union levels. And, pushing in the same direction, there are the growing challenges emanating from outside the EU that make it clear that success globally means building alliances and engaging in ever closer association. For some, often those politicians at the core of the EU whose states have been edging in this direction for half a century, this is the choice of futures that is not only logical but absolutely essential.

The fact is that global economic and political success now evidently belongs to the big battalions. There is, therefore, the insistent reminder that a diverse Europe, not to say one divided into a series of medium-sized individual nation-states, carries relatively little clout in world affairs – unless harnessed as a camp-follower to the projects of a large ally such as the United States. Yet the situation is far from simply resolved; unity (or singularity) is not just around the corner. There are too many divergent (self) interests as well as mutual worries about the intentions of other members blocking the path to allow for a smooth and direct passage to any great degree of constitutional unity. At the level of relationships between nation-states, as our authors have revealed, even the dismantling of borders within the EU does not always bring a swift realignment of attitudes. Local suspicions and resentments, too, can linger and continue to prejudice communities against each other. On the other hand, local community relationships that have been severely stretched and tested by years of severance across remotely-decided state borders, are now being reinforced as border restrictions dissolve and the borderlands become reintegrated once more.

There are other obstacles that spring from deep-seated divisions within the EU. A growing challenge is that of the emergence of a two-tier EU. Within the EU's borders, an economically and politically powerful core is expanding into and manipulating a weaker and newer periphery. To those with a sense of déjà vu, perhaps this suggests a return to a history of expansion and assimilation redolent of past experience – another *drang nach osten*. It may not be an overreaction to identify this as a latter-day imperial strategy. The situation is at least as controversial when it comes to the EU's dealing with those on its borders. Again, the response of the EU has been to try to enforce 'good neighbour' policies on those contiguous states that it feels that it can trust – or is obliged to – on its eastern, northern and southern borders. The appearance of deep self-interest in this determination to establish a cordon sanitaire around its borders, to protect itself against unstable, weak or threatening states is in no way diminished by its dealing with such neighbours in a bilateral series of agreements – a 'spoke and hub' strategy.

At the risk of sounding simplistic, the European Union appears to be digging itself deeper and deeper into quicksands of complexity and frustration. At the local level, in the new borderlands it creates with each new expansion, the strict regimes it insists upon create profound and prolonged hardships for once closely connected communities. The flinty-eyed refusal of both nation-states and the EU itself to modify the barriers they have erected provides a source of resentment and distress: an imposed local sacrifice and pain to serve larger geopolitical designs.

But neither is it winning many friends with its fortress-like strategies so clearly aimed at keeping out the global 'others'. And, to cap all this, its policies are so often ineffectual and lacking reality. First, in a global order that is so unequal, it is almost inevitable that, where capital goes, labour will follow. And the current state of international financial flows is that of a net movement from the poor to the rich states around the world.[5] If opportunities are lacking at home in the Third World, then workers – and often, their families – have little alternative but to seek out sources of employment in the wealthy economies. And, as the example of the Mexican–US border has shown for decades, no amount of surveillance or numbers of expulsions will drastically alter what is happening. Similarly, the Mediterranean's 'wet border' and the EU's eastern cordon sanitaire will continue to be unquestionably penetrable.

This is further assured by the continued and increasing internal demand in the US and the EU for trafficked workers (including those in the sex trade) – cheap labour – and drugs. The competition that drives capitalism forward is unrelenting on this point. To compete globally, European firms can only use superior technology up to a point: the pressure for low labour costs in a global market is irresistible. A combination of the two Fixes discussed by Anderson and Shuttleworth will doubtless continue to be deployed to suit EU corporate and political interests – and the internal/external tensions inherent in this will also persist.

So, the image of the EU's borders as impregnable barriers is little more than a mirage; they are, and will continue to be, porous. External pressures and domestic needs will ensure this. And the further the expansion of the EU's borders continues the more difficult they will be to patrol and safeguard. Perhaps this is why the ENP may be marking a new strategic departure: the effective closing down of EU border expansion and the shutting out of even those who are being called upon to act as a perimeter shield against global turmoil and instability.

It seems a risky strategy that will probably cause resentment and win little appreciation in a world where the parallel feature of the EU's dealings with others consists, on the one hand, of constant commercial and financial expansion in the search for control over markets and raw materials. But at the same time, commercial protectionism in the EU and its member states – the other major barrier to fair and open trade espoused by the wealthy economies – that keeps out competing products from Third World countries is causing further and greater imbalances between the rich and the poor. The double standards that drive this unashamedly self-centred, dog-in-the-manger approach are only too obvious.

Are there alternatives?

The argument I have been making leads me inexorably to this conclusion: that the EU's borders and those who watch over them are carrying too heavy a burden. Too much is being demanded of them when what is needed are wide and deep social, economic, political and ideological reforms in the societies making up the EU within those external frontiers.[6]

It will not be easy for the EU members and their populations to continue to live an untroubled existence as a privileged tribe in a world of great and growing inequality; there will inescapably be thorny consequences. Nor can the Union maintain itself in splendid isolation as a gated community behind borders erected against the rest while, at the same time, it continues to deploy its global economic and financial clout to impose its own self-interest unilaterally on others in matters of commerce, investment and migration. If, at the same time, it also reserves the right to expand economically into those countries over which it exercises an influence – or intervenes militarily in the rest of the world as the subaltern partner in a unilateral, globally-reaching police force – it will undoubtedly be faced with serious repercussions. There have already been warning backlashes.

With its ageing population, the European Union probably does require people from the outside to work and live within its borders. But these arrangements must be based on principles of justice and equity. The Union also needs, far more, to establish collaborative contacts with other societies across a changing world. It has an obligation, especially, to begin forging relationships of mutual respect in its political and economic connections with other regions; this is an essential first step to ensure a more stable and secure world.

All this will require revamped foreign strategies. Instead of meekly following the lead of the United States (as many EU members do) in its unilateral policing of the world, the EU requires alternative initiatives – those based upon cooperation, dialogue and consultation in which all parties have the opportunity to benefit. Domestically, such change calls for modifications in attitudes and behaviour patterns in the world of wealth and comfort; the necessity to limit consumer appetites that threaten both human welfare and the planet's physical environment is daily becoming more evident.

If this sounds like unrealisable idealism, then I can only suggest that we are now just beginning to live with the consequences of the conventional wisdom: and 'realism' that takes too little notice of the need for strategic change and reform. Rising global tensions and instability, the twin threats of terror and counterterror, the erosion of human rights and the rule of law, billions spent on armaments and military adventures, war-generated petroleum and other price rises, petroleum- (and, soon, water-) generated wars, environmental depredation and species loss and the legacy of deep uncertainty are engendering further suffering over large swathes of the planet. And, self-interestedly for the wealthy, they are depressing rather than enhancing the sense of human well-being in the West in these post-Cold War years.[7] If this is the outcome of embracing strategic 'realism', then perhaps it is time for us to consider other – including apparently more idealistic – alternatives.

It might be worthwhile, too, to remind ourselves that, with the changing global balance of power and the emergence of China, India, possibly Brazil and others onto the world economic and political stage, the presenting of an appearance of restraint – however belated – on the part of the European Union might induce an equivalent response from those about to share the mantle of growth and prosperity. One thing is undoubted: with their appearance, the great game of international competition is becoming even tougher; cooperation rather than competition may well have to be the hallmark of future development on the planet.

It is not just a matter of altruism and a sense of global fair play, then, but also enlightened self-interest and a move beyond the self-centred tribalism of the wealthy which compels me to put the argument in this way. The debate, in fact, needs to be – *must* be – opened a great deal further if Europe's borders are to become bridges to a more justly ordered world rather than protective – and frankly inadequate – barriers encircling a privileged minority in the world. But, this will not happen until there is a major change in the mentalities of the politicians and people who live behind the bastions of Fortress Europe.

Notes

1 Martin Jacques, 'If the 20th Century ended in 1989, the 21st began in 1978', *Guardian* (London), 25 May 2006. http://www.guardian.co.uk/comment/story/0,,1782234,00.html
2 Ibid.
3 Ibid.
4 In *Le Monde Diplomatique* March 1999 (English edition), Jelle van Buuren used the phrase 'cordon sanitaire' in his article, 'Asylum seekers not welcome: fortress Europe raises the barricades', to describe the shrewd stratagem of grooming contiguous foreign states to act as a protective buffer for the EU:

> The Fifteen are in the process of creating a cordon sanitaire around their common borders, with the aim of turning Turkey and the countries of Central and Eastern Europe into buffer states who can receive refugees and process their demands for protection. Europe already has a security-based approach to immigration. Now it is seeking to offload its responsibilities onto third-party countries – with poor track records in human rights.

5 In the L.K. Jha Memorial Lecture, 'Reflections on global account imbalances and emerging markets reserve accumulation' at the Reserve Bank of India, Mumbai, India, 24 March 2006, Lawrence H. Summers (academic, ex-secretary of the US treasury and noted neo-conservative) makes the stark point that net global capital flows are the opposite to what conventional wisdom would suggest. First and foremost, he says:

> the net flow of capital is substantially *from* developing countries and emerging markets *towards* the industrialised world and principally the United States, as the world's greatest power, is the world's greatest borrower.
>
> This broad pattern, which has been going on for several years now and on current projections will continue for quite some time, *runs very much counter to the traditional idea that core countries export capital to an opportunity rich periphery.* (Italics added)
>
> http://www.president.harvard.edu/speeches/2006/0324_rbi.html

A sceptic might see this as the rest of the world saving while the wealthy societies spend – and create job opportunities that draw migrants towards the sources of employment.
6 The following argument was developed at greater length in the opening address entitled 'Fortress Europe's Frontiers and Global Justice' at the Association for Borderlands Studies conference held at the University of Graz in September 2004.
7 Six decades ago, the philosopher Bertrand Russell, in his *History of Western Philosophy* (London: George Allen and Unwin, 1947, 756) had emphasised the importance for modern societies of exercising their undeniable and growing technological power with restraint and moderation:

To formulate any satisfactory modern ethic of human relationships, it will be essential to recognise the necessary limitations of men's power over the non-human environment, and the desirable limitations of their power over each other.

Index

Agnew, J. 14, 21
Algeciras 82–3, 87
Aliboni, R., 145
Alpe-Adria Region 164, 187–8
Altvater, E. 134
Amsterdam Treaty, 1999 110
Anderson, B. 115–16
Anderson, J. 225–6, 228
Anglo-Irish Agreement, 1985 65
Arato, A. 179
Armenia 146
Arrighi, G. 22
asylum 92, 110, 113, 120
Attina, F. 98
Augé, M. 114
Aughey, A. 69
Austria (*see also* Three Border Region) 109, 186; border with Slovenia 168, 169, 170, 174; visa requirements 113
Avruch, K. 71
Azerbaijan 146

Balibar, E. 112, 114
Barcelona Process *see* European Mediterranean Partnership
Barth, F. 206
Bauer, O. 128
Bela Krajina 208–9, 211, 216–17, 232; Uskoki in 208, 212, 213, 219
Belarus 97, 126, 147; migrant workers from 136
Belfast, peace walls 69
Belfast Agreement (Good Friday), 1998 30, 31, 43–6, 53, 64, 66, 69
bilateralism 98, 150, 151, 152
bilingualism 195, 197, 198–9
Blok, A. 70
border controls 111, 114, 130; abolition of, within EU 2, 110; screening 115; at Spanish-Moroccan border 80–1, 84–5, 87
border regimes 110, 114, 121; Slovenian–Croatian border 217–19, 219–20
border towns 61, 80–7, 231–2
borderlands 4, 57; Ireland 30–1, 53–7, 69–71; Slovenia 167–71, 174, 192–5, 230
borders (*see also* cross-border cooperation) 1, 4–5, 108–9, 114–15; as barriers 5–6, 61, 64–5, 130; as bridges 66–9; and exercise of power 63, 72; global 160–1; policing 42; and security 62–4
Borneman, J. 50, 51, 52, 57–8
Bosnia 109, 184; border of 162
Braudel, F. 88
British Empire 133
Broader Middle East and North Africa Initiative 94
Buchovski, M. 178
Bulgaria 109, 147
Bull, H. 16–17
Burns, R.K. 181, 182
Busch, B. 189n
Bush, G.W. 165

capital 21, 22, 134; export of 3, 126–7, 137–8
capitalism 2, 6, 127, 130–1, 139, 228, 229, 234; economic empire and 21–2; social democratic 161–2
Carinthia 184, 185, 186, 187, 192
Carniola 192
Carpathia 71
Central Europe 173–4; borders in 162–5
Ceuta 83–5, 87
Charlemagne 10, 15
China 22, 25, 224–5

Chirac, J. 92
citizenship 178, 182, 230–1; rights of 181
civil society 178–9, 231; co-opted by totalitarian regimes 184–6; institutionalisation of 182; intraregional 188–9; and parliamentarianism 193–4
clash of civilisations 93, 95
Clinton, B. 96, 165
Common Foreign and Security Policy 91, 92, 93
communicative competence 197–8
communism, fall of 108, 135, 161
concentric circles 19, 109–14, 121, 155–6; inequality of 3, 111–12, 233
Conference on Stability in Europe, 1994 73n
core/periphery 3, 19, 119–20, 233; hierarchies 20; relations between 126, 129, 131–2
Council of Ireland, 1974 65
Croatia (*see also* Slovenian–Croatian border) 109, 147, 168
cross-border cooperation 54, 61, 63, 72, 163–4; Ireland 36, 38, 40, 45–6, 54, 65, 67–8, 69–71; Slovenia 171–3, 201
cultural boundaries 93, 94, 98, 101, 228; confrontation 92–3, 99; and political violence 102–3
cultural identity 70, 71, 118 on Slovenian–Italian border 197–8, 200
Czech Republic 109, 113, 136, 137–8

definitions 116, 117–18
del Sarto, R. 151
deliberative democracy 44–5
democracy 12, 13, 16, 17, 18, 161
democratic deficits 12, 18, 25
Democratic Unionist Party (Northern Ireland) 67, 227
détente 90–1
deterritorialisation 63, 114–15, 162
Dimitrovova, B. 20
Donaldson, J. 68, 73n

East, relations with EU 152–4
Eastern Europe 23, 134, 135, 173–4; export of labour 126, 135–6; jobs moving to 126; Western capital exports to 137–8
economics/politics 21
Emerson, M. 154
empire 32, 127, 133; of Europe 10–11, 18–24, 25, 126–7; formal/informal 133–4, 228–9

Estonia 73n
ethnic heterogamy 193, 198, 200–1, 217
ethnic identities 163, 164; in Slovenia 208–11, 215–16
ethno-linguistic communities 166
ethno-national minorities 161, 194, 203–4, 215, 231–2; cross-border attitudes 163–4, 170–1, 186–7, 188–9, 193, 195–9; national awareness 196–7, 198, 199–200; rights of 185, 186, 194, 200, 203–4
ethno-nationalist conflict 61, 63, 67, 69, 72; in borderlands 37, 39, 41–2, 46, 62, 65, 72, 226; EU as facilitator in mediating 63–4, 70, 72
Europe: Christian 79, 118–19; of nations 13; non-EU 10; of regions 14–15
European Commission 17; and Ireland 42–3; neighbourhood policy 144
European Convention 3; members' visions of Europe 117–20
European identity 3, 49–50, 56; in borderlands 57, 227; Europeanisation and 57–8; self-definition 107, 116–19
European Mediterranean Partnership 90, 91–2, 98, 227–8; Neighbourhood Policy and 150–2, 155; potential failure of 92–3; US initiatives and 94
European Neighbourhood Policy 20, 142–6, 154–6, 229, 234; North and 152–4, 155; Russia and 146, 147–9, 152; South and 149–52, 155
European Security Strategy 97, 145; Action Plans 98, 154
European Union 33, 62, 224–5; and Europeanisation 51; frontier policy 97–8; and Northern Ireland 53, 54, 56, 58 (Peace Programmes 61, 64, 66, 69–70, 72); relations with US 24–5, 224; South Mediterranean borders 79, 91, 93
Europeanisation 49, 50–5, 57–8, 226, national identities and 54, 56
exclusion 92, 111–12, 228

Fascism 184, 185, 198
federalism 14
Finland 109
Fishman, J.A. 197
foreign direct investment 137–8
foreign policy 5, 7–8; securitisation of 92, 93
'fortress Europe' 110–14, 156, 229
Fortuyn, P. 92–3

Fouréré, E. 63
Fowler, N. 50, 51, 52, 57–8
France: alienation of migrant communities 100; terrorism in 100–1
free trade 6, 90–1
freedom of movement 2, 91
Friuli-Venezia Giulia 186, 188, 193–4, 200
Fukuyama, F. 95, 96
funding programmes 55–7, 58, 226

Galtung, J. 160
Gellner, E. 11, 15
Georgia 146, 148
globalisation 161–2, 226; borders in 32–3, 39, 40–1, 62, 63, 65; economic and cultural 33, 41–3; impact on ethnic conflicts 46; neo-liberalism and 129–30
Good Friday Agreement *see* Belfast Agreement
Gorizia/Nova Gorica 171, 172, 192
Greece, economic migrants from North Africa 79–80
Gulliver fallacy 12–13

Habsburg empire 162–3, 182, 212
Hann, C. 71, 206
Hardt, M. 22
Harmsen, R. 51
Harvey, D. 126–7
Haukkala, H. 148
Hayward, K. 71
Hegel, G.W.F. 125, 126, 127
hegemony 21–2, 24; US 22, 24–5, 33, 95, 134
Hitler, A. 184
homestead rights 181
homogenisation 225–6
Hoogvelt, A. 129
Human Rights Commissions, Ireland 43–4
Hungary 137, 138; border with Ukraine 108–9; border with Slovenia 168, 170, 174
Huntington, S. 95, 96

identity *see* cultural identity; ethnic identity; European identity; national identity
Ignatieff, M. 70
illegal immigrants 80, 82, 84–5, 92, 110, 112–13; border controls and 130; as cheap labour 125–6, 130; discourse of 108, 113; legalisation of 88
imagined communities 115–16
imperial territoriality 18–24
inequality 6–7, 116; concentric circles of 3, 111–12, 233
insecurity 63, 72; racist attacks and 69, 71
inside/outside 3, 5, 11, 19, 20, 116
integration 5, 15, 57, 62, 161, 163–4, 187; cross-border 171–3; Europeanisation and 50–1; varying rates of 1, 2
intergovernmentalism 16–17
INTERREG 54, 55, 63, 165, 187
interventionism 95, 96
Intra-Regional and Intra-Metropolitan Cooperation Model 165
IRA 42, 53, 64; arms decommissioning 67
Ireland (*see also* Northern Ireland; Republic of Ireland) 30, British control over 30; Home Rule 34; partition 30, 31, 34
Irish border 30, 35–6, 53–4, 72, 226; attempts to transform 65–6, 72; Catholicism/Protestantism 30–1, 36; challenging 39–45; consolidating 34–9; cross-border cooperation 38, 40–1, 42, 45–6, 227; cross-border institutions 43–5, 54, 66, 67; economy and 31, 38; establishment of 33–4, 64; impact of EU membership on 43–5, 54–8, 68, 69–70; phases of 32–3
Irish diaspora 41; as link between US and EU 31
Iron Curtain 163, 185
Islam 93, 101–3; Europe and 99–101; opposition to European ideal 101–2; and terrorism 99, 101, 102
Istria, Slovene 167, 171, 192, 193, 194, 195, 200; bilingualism in 195, 196, 197, 198–9; interethnic relations 196, 198–9, 200–1; Italians in 194, 195, 197, 203, 232
Italy (*see also* Slovenian–Italian border; Three Border Region) 184, 186, 193; attitude to to Slovenes 202–3; economic migrants from North Africa 79–80; Slovene minority in 166, 171, 186, 187, 194, 203–4 (schools for 195–6)

Jacques, M. 224–5
jihad 101

Kelkal, K. 100
King, M. 135, 136, 137
Kohl, M. 49, 57
Koper 166, 167, 171

labour migration *see* migrant labour
Ladrech, R. 51
language 199; preservation of minority 195–6
LEADER 54, 55
Lederach, J.-P. 63–4
Lemass, S. 65
Lenin, V.I. 127, 128
Libya 97, 99
linguistic minorities 108–9, 166, 195–7, 198–9, 203–4
Luxemburg, R. 128

Mann, M. 38, 129
Marx, K. 126, 127, 130
media: discourse on illegal immigrants 113; on Northern Ireland 41–3, 73n
Mediterranean frontier 78–80, 88, 227–8; policies on 90–3
medievalism 23; new medieval territoriality 15–18
Memorandum of London, 1954 194, 202
migrant communities: alienation of 100–1, 102; exclusion of 92, 228
migrant labour 3–4, 6–7, 112, 125–6, 128–31, 132, 228; economic impacts of 136–7
migration 91–2, 110
Mikolič, V. 197
Moldova 97, 147, 148
Morocco (*see also* Spanish–Moroccan frontier) 86–7; Islamist violence in 99
Moshes, A. 148
multi-level governance 16–18
multiculturalism 163, 164, 171–2
Mussolini, B. 184
mutual respect, need for 235

nation-state 12–13, 177, 230–1
national identity, Europeanisation and 54, 56
national territoriality 11–15, 25; 'Europe of nations' 13; 'Europe of regions' 14–15; 'federal Europe' 14
nationalist conflicts *see* ethno-nationalist conflicts
nationality, citizenship and 178
naturalisation procedures 112
Negri, A. 22
neighbours (*see also* European Neighbourhood Policy) 3, 97–8, 111
neo-conservatism 95–6
neo-liberalism 3, 128–9, 129–30, 136
Netherlands, political violence 102
Neveu, C. 178
new world order 95–7
non-places 114–15
North, neighbourhood policies and 152–4, 155
North Africa 99; economic migrants from 79
North/South Ministerial Council 43, 67
Northern Ireland 30, 53, 66, 226, 227; autonomy of 35; British army in 42; Catholics in 36–7, 40, 41, 68–9; civil rights movement 41; democratic institutions 44–5, 66, 70; media images 41–2; Protestant police force 36; sectarian borders in 36, 41, 42, 68, 69
Northern Ireland Assembly 43, 67
Northern Ireland Programme for Peace and Reconciliation 54, 56

O'Neill, T. 65
Orange Order 37, 69
Osimo, Treaty of, 1975 194
other/s 108, 109, 116, 118, 119, 121; hierarchy of 154

Paisley, I. 65
Partnership and Cooperation Agreements 147
Patterson, H. 66
Pertot, S. 196
PHARE-CBC 187
Poland 109; capital/labour in 132–3, 136, 137, 138; emigration from 135
police cooperation 110
Portugal, economic migrants from North Africa 79–80
Poulantzas, N. 160
Powell, C. 94

racism 69, 71, 72, 130
Readmission Agreements 111
refugees 79–80, 84, 92, 113–14
regionalism 12, 14, 16–17, 159, 161, 179; in North 153; Three Border Region 187–9
remittances 131, 136
Republic of Ireland 38, 64, 132; economy 31, 38, 40, 54; independence of 34–5; migration to 136; Roman Catholic Church in 38, 67
Roberts, A. 95
Robinson, P. 67
Roman Catholic Church 38, 67, 153
Roman Empire 10, 15

Romania 109, 147
Rothenberg, G.E. 212
Roy, O. 103
Ruggie, J. 13, 17
Russia: European Neighbourhood Policy and 146, 147–9, 152; foreign direct investment in 137, 138; migrant workers from 136

Sageman, M. 102
salafi movement 101
Schengen Agreement, 1985 1–2, 79, 109–14
Schengen Implementation Treaty, 1990 110
Schengen Information System 110
Schumacher, T. 151
security 2, 92; common/liberal 145; neighbourhood issues and 143–4, 152, 153, 229; soft 90, 93–4, 96; South Mediterranean Partnership and 91, 93
Sedmak, M. 199
self-definition 107, 116–17; and the other 108, 116, 118, 119
self-determination 32–3, 183
self-interest 5, 6, 25, 233, 235
September 11th, response to 96–7, 98–9
Serbs, in Slovenia 209–10, 211, 215
Single European Act, 1986 68
Single European Market 54, 62
singularity 10–11, 18, 24–6, 154
Sinn Féin 42, 68
Slovenes, in Italy 166, 171, 186, 187, 194, 203–4
Slovenia 113, 164–5, 173, 192, 195; accession to EU 201–2, 230; border crossings 167–8, 170; borders 165–6, 167, 174, 192–3, 208; cultures of 166, 192; democracy in 189; independence and changes in ethnic awareness 199–203, 211; Italians in 194, 195, 196, 197, 203, 232; national awareness 196–8, 200–1; secession from Yugoslavia 187; transport links 16
Slovenian–Croatian border 4, 174, 194, 206–8, 232; border regime 218–19; cross-border traffic 168–9, 170; history 211–13, 231; policing 208
Slovenian–Hungarian border 168, 170, 174
Slovenian–Italian border 174, 192–3, 232; changes in national awareness 200–3; cross-border cooperation 171–2, 172–3, 186; cross-border traffic 168, 169, 170, 230; cultural identity on 197–8, 200; interethnic relations 195–9; minority policies 194, 195–9; Slovenian accession to EU and 201–2
Smith, N. 27n
smuggling 80, 84, 85–6, 87
social movements 179, 182–3
South, neighbourhood policies and 149–51, 155
South Armagh 53–4; funding programmes in 55–7; lack of identification with Europe 56
South Caucasus 146, 148
sovereignty 11, 12, 16, 18, 21, 62; EU and 13; multi-level governance and 17; in Northern Ireland 45; postmodern view 95; transfer to international organisations 185–6
Spain, migration from North Africa 79–80, 80–7, 136
Spanish–Moroccan frontier 78, 79; border controls 80–1, 84–5, 87; perspective from four ports 80–7
Special EU Programmes Body 66
Styria 187, 192
sub-state nationalisms 16–17
supranationalism 45, 46, 58
surveillance 114–15

Tangier 81–2, 85–6, 87
Tarifa 80–2, 85, 87
Tassinari, F. 153, 154
territorial control 37, 133–4
territorialism 22–3
territorialities 9–10, 11, 160; imperial 18–24; national 11–15; new medieval 15–18
terrorism 97, 98–9, 100
Three Border Region 170, 172, 177, 179, 185, 187–9, 230–1; civil society 182–4; Olympic bid 171, 172, 188; opening of local borders 185–6; partition of 184; political mobilisation across borders 186–7
tourism 172, 187, 220
trade 6–7
transnational border space 61, 62, 69–71, 72
transnational governance 43–5
Trieste 163, 166, 171–2, 173, 193, 202
Turkey 97, 109; perceived as non-European 119
Turner, B. 178

Ugovizza 180–1, 188
Ukraine 97, 126; European Neighbourhood Policy and 147; Hungarian speakers in 109; migrant workers from 136
Ulster Unionist Party (Northern Ireland) 66, 227
Ulster Unionists 34, 37, 64, 65, 71; and Belfast Agreement 66–7; insecurity of 64, 67; legitimacy of 35; resistance to North/South cooperation 67–8
United Kingdom: migration to 135–6, 137; political violence in 102
United Nations 95; Global Policy Forum 7
United States of America: attitude to 5, 7–8; EU's relations with 24–5, 224; hegemony of 22, 24–5, 33, 95, 134; informal empire of 133, 134; security interests in Mediterranean 93–4; support for Ireland 31
US–Middle East Partnership Initiative 94
Uskoki 208, 210, 212, 219; origins of 213, 215–16

Val Canale 172, 180–1, 184, 185
van Gogh, T. 93
visas 91–2, 108–9, 113
voluntary organisations 182–3; intraregional cooperation 188–9

Waever, O. 19, 20, 24
Wallace, W. 98
war on terror 24, 96, 99, 100
Weinreich, U. 197
welfare state, implementation of in Northern Ireland 39–40
Wells, J. 71
Wiktorowicz, Q. 102
Wilson, W. 96
Winter Olympics, 2006 bid 171, 172, 188

xenophobia 93, 195, 200

Yugoslavia 162, 171, 185, 187, 193, 220n; emigration of Italians from 194, 202; impact of dissolution of on borderlands 206; local civic institutions 186

Zielonka, J. 27n
Žumberak 210, 217, 232; border regime 218–19, 220; and Serbian nationalism 210–11; Uskoki in 212, 215–16, 219
Zurich airport, use of biometric data to screen passengers 115